Alexander Wert

Performance Problem Diagnostics by Systematic Experimentation

The Karlsruhe Series on Software Design and Quality
Volume 20

Chair Software Design and Quality
Faculty of Computer Science
Karlsruhe Institute of Technology

and

Software Engineering Division
Research Center for Information Technology (FZI), Karlsruhe

Editor: Prof. Dr. Ralf Reussner

Performance Problem Diagnostics by Systematic Experimentation

by
Alexander Wert

KIT Scientific Publishing

Dissertation, Karlsruher Institut für Technologie
KIT-Fakultät für Informatik

Tag der mündlichen Prüfung: 15. Juli 2015
Erster Gutachter: Prof. Dr. Ralf H. Reussner
Zweiter Gutachter: Prof. Dr. Wilhelm Hasselbring

Impressum

KIT Scientific Publishing

Karlsruher Institut für Technologie (KIT)
KIT Scientific Publishing
Straße am Forum 2
D-76131 Karlsruhe

KIT Scientific Publishing is a registered trademark
of Karlsruhe Institute of Technology.
Reprint using the book cover is not allowed.

www.ksp.kit.edu

Print on Demand 2018 – Gedruckt auf FSC-zertifiziertem Papier

ISSN 1867-0067
ISBN 978-3-7315-0677-5
DOI: 10.5445/KSP/1000070006

Performance Problem Diagnostics by Systematic Experimentation

zur Erlangung des akademischen Grades eines

Doktors der Ingenieurwissenschaften

der Fakultät für Informatik
des Karlsruher Instituts für Technologie

genehmigte

Dissertation

von

Alexander Wert

aus Kopejsk, Russland

Tag der mündlichen Prüfung: 15. Juli 2015
Erster Gutachter: Prof. Dr. Ralf H. Reussner
Zweiter Gutachter: Prof. Dr. Wilhelm Hasselbring

Abstract

The performance of enterprise software systems has a direct impact on the success of business. Recent studies have shown that software performance affects customer satisfaction as well as operational costs of software. Hence, software performance constitutes an essential competitive and differentiating factor for software vendors and operators. In industrial practice, it is still a challenging task to detect software performance problems before they are faced by end users. Diagnostics of performance problems requires deep expertise in performance engineering and still entails a high manual effort. As a consequence, performance evaluations are postponed to the last minute of the development process, or even are completely omitted. Instead of proactively avoiding performance problems, problems are fixed in a reactive manner when they first emerge in operations. Since reactive, operation-time resolution of performance problems is very expensive and has a negative impact on the reputation of software vendors, performance problems need to be diagnosed and resolved in the process of software development. Existing approaches addressing performance problem diagnostics either assume the existence of a performance model, are limited to problem detection without analyzing root causes, or are applied as reactive approaches during the operations phase and, thus, cannot be effective applied during development for performance problem diagnostics.

In this thesis, we introduce an automatic, experiment-based approach for performance problem diagnostics in enterprise software systems. We describe a method to derive a taxonomy on recurrent types of performance problems and introduce a systematic experimentation concept. Using the taxonomy as a search tree, the proposed approach systematically searches for root causes of detected performance problems by executing series of systematic performance experiments. Based on the measurement data from experiments, detection heuristics decide on the presence of performance problems in the target system. Furthermore, we develop a domain-specific description language to specify the information required for automatic performance problem diagnostics. Finally, we create and evaluate a representative set of detection heuristics. We validate our approach by means of five studies including end-to-end case studies, a controlled experiment and an empirical study. The results of the validation show that our approach is applicable to a wide range of contexts and is able to fully automatically and accurately detect performance problems in medium-size and large-scale applications. External users of the provided approach evaluated it as a useful support for diagnostics of performance problems and exposed their willingness to use the approach for their own software development projects. Explicitly designed for automatic, development-time testing, our approach can be incorporated into continuous integration. In this way, our approach allows regular, automatic diagnostics of performance problems involving minimal manual effort. Furthermore, by encapsulating and automating expert knowledge on performance engineering, our approach enables developers who are non-performance experts to conduct performance problem diagnostics.

Zusammenfassung

In heutigen Unternehmen nehmen betriebliche Informationssysteme eine zentrale Rolle ein. Sie eröffnen neue Vertriebskanäle, ermöglichen effizientere Betriebsprozesse und tragen maßgeblich zur Nutzung von Skaleneffekten bei. Dienstgüteeigenschaften betrieblicher Informationssysteme haben einen direkten Einfluss auf den Geschäftserfolg der Unternehmen. Studien haben gezeigt, dass die Performance solcher Systeme sich maßgeblich auf deren Betriebskosten sowie die Kundenzufriedenheit auswirkt. Somit ist die Performance betrieblicher Software ein entscheidender Wettbewerbsfaktor und ein Differenzierungsmerkmal für Software-Anbieter und Software-Betreiber. Performance-Probleme, die bis zum Betrieb der Software unerkannt bleiben, stellen nicht nur ein finanzielles Risiko dar, sondern können auch einen Schaden in der Reputation verursachen.

In der industriellen Praxis der Software-Entwicklung ist das frühzeitige Erkennen und die Diagnose von Performance-Problemen immer noch eine große Herausforderung. Die Diagnose von Performance-Problemen erfordert nicht nur ein tiefgründiges Expertenwissen in der Disziplin des Performance Engineering, sondern bringt einen großen manuellen Aufwand mit sich. Dies hat zur Folge, dass Performance-Analysen bis in die späten Phasen der Software-Entwicklung aufgeschoben oder gänzlich ausgelassen werden. Performance-Probleme werden meist reaktiv angegangen, wenn sie zum ersten Mal im Betrieb der Software auftauchen, anstatt sie proaktiv während der Software-Entwicklung zu erkennen und zu lösen. Da das reaktive Lösen von Performance-Problemen vergleichsweise sehr aufwändig ist, müssen Performance-Probleme noch während des Software-Entwicklungsprozesses diagnostiziert werden.

Existierende Ansätze zur Erkennung von Performance-Problemen nehmen entweder die Verfügbarkeit eines Systemmodells an, sind auf das Erkennen von Problemen beschränkt, ohne eine Diagnose der Ursachen durchzuführen, oder sind für den reaktiven Einsatz während des Software-Betriebs ausgelegt. Somit bieten existierende Ansätze nicht die notwendigen Mittel, um eine proaktive Erkennung und Diagnose von Performance-Problemen effektiv während der Software-Entwicklung durchzuführen.

In der vorliegenden Arbeit wird ein Ansatz zur automatischen, experimentbasierten Diagnose von Performance-Problemen in betrieblichen Software-Systemen vorgestellt. Basierend auf einer Taxonomie von wiederkehrenden Performance-Problemtypen führt der vorgestellte Ansatz eine Erkennung von Performance-Problemen durch sowie eine systematische Suche nach deren Ursachen. Dabei wird eine Reihe zielgerichteter Performance-Experimente durchgeführt. Die dabei gesammelten Messdaten werden mit Hilfe einer Menge an Regeln und Algorithmen analysiert, um Aussagen über die Existenz entsprechender Performance-Problemtypen in dem Zielsystem zu treffen. Die vorliegende Arbeit umfasst die folgenden wissenschaftlichen Beiträge:

Taxonomie der Performance-Problemtypen Die vorliegende Arbeit führt eine Methode zur expliziten Erfassung von strukturiertem Wissen über Performance-Probleme ein. Dazu wird ein Klassifikationsschema für bestehende, wiederkehrende Typen von Performance-Problemen eingeführt. Die Klassifikation erfasst zum einen verschiedene Charakteristiken von Performance-Problemen sowie die Beziehungen zwischen unterschiedlichen Performance-Problemtypen. Auf Basis der Klassifikation wird eine Taxonomie der wiederkehrenden Performance-Problemtypen abgeleitet. Die statische Taxonomie wird schließlich um die dynamische Information zur experimentbasierten Diagnose von Performance-Problemen erweitert. Im Rahmen der vorliegenden Arbeit wurde die eingeführte Methode auf 27 Performance-Problembeschreibungen angewendet. Das Ergebnis ist ein Evaluationsplan für Performance-Probleme, der zur Koordination der automatischen Performance-Problemdiagnose eingesetzt werden kann und darüber hinaus eine Unterstützung bei der manuellen Diagnose bietet.

Systematisches Experimentier- und Diagnosekonzept Messbasierte Performance-Analyseverfahren haben das inhärente Problem, dass Messdaten auf Grund des Mehraufwands der Messung nicht gleichzeitig genau, umfassend und mit hohem Detailgrad erfasst werden können. Die vorliegende Arbeit beschreibt unter anderem ein systematisches, selektives Experimentierkonzept, dass es erlaubt durch eine systematische Ausführung von Experimenten sowohl genaue als auch detaillierte Messdaten zu erfassen. Dabei wird für jedes einzelne Experiment eine zielgerichtete, selektive Instrumentierung der Zielanwendung durchgeführt, sodass der durch Messung verursachte Mehraufwand in jedem Experiment gering gehalten wird. Die Instrumentierungsanweisungen werden zwischen einzelnen Experimenten dynamisch verändert und erlauben so, detaillierte Daten bei hoher Genauigkeit zu erfassen. Zur automatischen Diagnose von Performance-Problemen wird das systematische Experimentierkonzept mit der beschriebenen Taxonomie kombiniert, um eine systematische Suche nach Ursachen von Performance-Problem zu ermöglichen. Die Taxonomie wird dabei als ein Suchbaum verwendet, während für jeden Knoten in der Taxonomie ein zugeschnittenes Experiment mit selektiver Instrumentierung durchgeführt wird. In der vorliegenden Arbeit werden die Vorteile und die Einschränkungen des systematischen Experimentierkonzepts für die automatische Diagnose von Performance-Problemen untersucht. Des Weiteren wird die Anwendbarkeit des vorgestellten Experimentierkonzepts über die Performance-Problemdiagnose hinaus untersucht.

Beschreibungssprache für Performance-Problemdiagnose Um eine system- und technologieunabhängige und dennoch automatische Diagnose von Performance-Problemen zu ermöglichen, wird in dieser Arbeit ein Metamodell eingeführt, welches eine Sprache zur Beschreibung von Szenarien der Performance-Problemdiagnose definiert. Die Sprache umfasst vier Subsprachen. (i) Eine Experimentbeschreibungssprache erlaubt es, Experimentpläne zur Analyse von Performance-Problemen zu spezifizieren. (ii) Eine Instrumentierungs- und Monitoring-Beschreibungssprache bietet die Möglichkeit, Instrumentierungsanweisungen zielgerichtet und dabei systemunabhängig zu beschreiben. (iii) Ein Datenformatmodell gibt ein gemeinsames, kontextunabhängiges Format für die Messdaten vor. (iv) Schließlich wird eine Sprache zur Beschreibung der Messumgebung eingeführt, welche es erlaubt konkrete Anwendungskontexte des automatisierten Diagnoseansatzes mit geringem Aufwand zu beschreiben. In der Summe schließen die vorgestellten Sprachen die Lücke zwischen dem generischen Kern des Ansatzes zur Performance-Problemdiagnose und den konkreten Anwendungskontexten.

Heuristiken zur Erkennung von Performance-Problemen Während die Taxonomie der Performance-Probleme zusammen mit dem systematischen, selektiven Experimentierkonzept den Gesamtprozess der Performance-Problemdiagnose vorgeben, kapseln dedizierte Heuristiken das spezifische Wissen zur Erkennung einzelner Performance-Problemtypen. Einzelne Heuristiken umfassen dabei jeweils eine Definition einer Experimentserie sowie eine Erkennungsstrategie in Form eines Algorithmus, der die Messdaten aus den Experimenten untersucht. In der vorliegenden Arbeit werden ein Prozess und eine Menge von Regeln zur Erstellung akkurater und generischer Heuristiken für verschiedene Performance-Problemtypen beschrieben. Für eine repräsentative Menge an Performance-Problemtypen werden unterschiedliche Erkennungsstrategien entwickelt und systematisch evaluiert.

Die Beiträge der vorliegenden Arbeit werden mittels fünf Studien evaluiert. Es werden drei Ende-zu-Ende-Fallstudien durchgeführt, ein kontrolliertes Experiment und eine empirische Studie. Die Ergebnisse der Studien zeigen, dass der vorgestellte Ansatz Performance-Probleme in unterschiedlichen, vielfältigen Kontexten mit mittelgroßen bis hinzu sehr großen Zielanwendungen akkurat erkennt, solange die beschriebenen Vorbedingungen erfüllt sind. Teilnehmer des empirischen Experiments bewerteten den Ansatz als eine hilfreiche Unterstützung bei der Diagnose von Performance-Problemen und drückten ihre Bereitschaft aus, den Ansatz auch in eigenen Projekten einzusetzen.

Da der beschriebene Ansatz für eine automatische, testbasierte Diagnose in der Software-Entwicklungsphase konzipiert ist, kann er in den Prozess des Continuous Integration eingebunden werden. Dadurch erlaubt der Ansatz, Zielanwendungen regelmäßig und frühzeitig auf Performance-Probleme zu untersuchen bei einem geringen, manuellen Aufwand. Da der Ansatz Expertenwissen zur Performance-Problemdiagnose kapselt und automatisiert, befähigt er Software-Entwickler, die keine Performance-Experten sind, auch Performance-Problemdiagnosen durchzuführen.

Danksagung

Während der Erstellung dieser Arbeit habe ich Unterstützung von vielen Menschen erhalten, denen ich an dieser Stelle danken möchte. In erster Linie danke ich meinem Doktorvater Prof. Dr. Ralf Reussner für die ausgezeichnete Betreuung und Unterstützung während der gesamten Zeit. Ich danke auch meinem Korreferenten Prof. Dr. Wilhelm Hasselbring für die Hinweise und Ideen zu meiner Arbeit. Des Weiteren möchte ich mich bei Wolfgang Theilmann für die Unterstützung und Rückendenkung bei SAP während meiner Promotion bedanken.

Ich bedanke mich auch herzlich bei Jens Happe, Dennis Westermann und Roozbeh Farahbod für das Wecken meines Interesses an der Forschung sowie die Betreuung und das Mentoring während meiner Promotion. Die konstruktiven und fruchtbaren Diskussionen mit ihnen haben einen großen Teil zur Formung des Dissertations-Themas beigetragen.

Für die ausgezeichnete Zusammenarbeit möchte ich mich bei meinem Kollegen Christoph Heger bedanken, der mich als Sparring-Partner und Freund durch die gesamte Promotion belgeitet hat. Ein Dankeschön gilt auch all meinen Kollegen am SDQ, FZI und der SAP für die gute Zusammenarbeit, die konstruktiven Diskussionen, die zahlreichen Ideen und die nette Atmosphäre. Einen großen Beitrag haben auch meine Studenten geleistet, die mich bei der Durchführung der Forschung und der Ralisierung meiner Ideen tatkräftig unterstützt haben. Hierfür bedanke ich mich bei Yusuf Dogan, Stefan Tran, Marius Oehler, Henning Schulz, Denis Knöpfle und Peter Merkert. Qais Noorshams und Tanja Kohlstedt möchte ich für das Korrekturlesen meiner Arbeit und die hilfreichen Hinweise danken.

Ein besonderer Dank gilt meinen Eltern und meinem Bruder, aber insbesondere meiner Mutter Irina. Alles was ich bislang erreicht habe, inklusive dieser Arbeit, ist auch ein großer Verdienst meiner Mutter, denn ohne ihre

Unterstützung und ihre Aufopferung für ihre Kinder wäre all dies nicht möglich gewesen.

Schließlich möchte ich einen Dank der ganz besonderen Art an meine Frau Oxana sowie meine Töchter richten. Während der Promotion musstet ihr des Öfteren auf den Ehemann und Vater verzichten, habt mir aber durch eure Liebe und den Rückhalt die notwendige Unterstützung geboten, die meine Promotion erst ermöglicht hat.

Contents

List of Figures

List of Tables

List of Acronyms and Abbreviations

AIM	Adaptable Instrumentation and Monitoring
API	Application Programming Interface
APPD	Automatic Performance Problem Diagnostics
AOP	Aspect-oriented Programming
CBMG	Customer Behaviour Model Graph
CVR	Continuously Violated Requirements
EST	Empty Semi Trucks
EDC	Expensive Database Call
GQM	Goal Question Metric
GUI	graphical user interface
IaM	Instrumentation and Monitoring
ILS	Industrial Large-scale System
IIS	Microsoft Internet Information Services
JAX-RS	Java API for RESTful Web Services
JAX-WS	Java API for XML Web Services
JDBC	Java Database Connectivity
JMS	Java Message Service
JPA	Java Persistence API

JTA	Java Transaction API
JVM	Java Virtual Machine
LTM	Lightweight Transaction Manager
LOC	lines of code
LQN	Layered Queueing Network
ME	Measurement Environment
MSMQ	Microsoft Message Queue
MVC	Model-View-Controller
ntu	normalized time units
OCL	Object Constraint Language
OLB	One Lane Bridge
OR	Object-Relational
PCM	Palladio Component Model
PPEP	Performance Problem Evaluation Plan
P^2D^2M	Performance Problem Diagnostics Description Model
QoS	Quality of Service
RBE	Remote Browser Emulator
RMI	Remote Method Invocation
ROC	Receiver Operating Characteristics
RDE	Resource Demand Estimation
RD-SEFF	Resource Demanding Service Effect Specification
SLA	Service Level Agreement
SMM	Structured Metrics Meta-Model
SPA	Software Performance Anti-pattern
SPE	Software Performance Engineering

SUT	System Under Test
SSE	Systematic Selective Experimentation
TPC	Transaction Performance Processing Council
UML	Unified Modeling Language
WCF	Windows Communication Foundation

1. Introduction

The present thesis describes an approach for automatic detection and diagnostics of performance problems in enterprise software systems. The proposed approach supports software development teams during the development of software to ensure a high level of software performance quality. In this chapter, we explain why an approach for automatic performance problem diagnostics is needed. Furthermore, we describe the problem addressed in this thesis as well as corresponding goals and challenges. Finally, we give an outline of existing solutions as well as the contributions of this thesis and explain the structure of the work at hand.

1.1. Motivation

Relevance of Software Performance In contemporary enterprises, software systems are ubiquitous. Enterprise software systems play a central role in most businesses, reaching from enterprises in mechanical engineering to service providers, trading companies and many more since they enable efficient business processes, new channels of sales and effects of scale. The quality of service (QoS) of enterprise software systems has a significant impact on their total cost of ownership, efficiency of supported business processes (Hitt et al., 2002) and the customer satisfaction. Therefore, the performance of software systems plays a crucial role as one of the QoS attributes. A study at *Amazon* has shown that "[...] every 100-ms increase in the page load time decreased sales by 1 percent [...]" (Kohavi et al., 2007). Some investigations at *Google* confirm the impact of performance on the success of enterprises demonstrating that "[...] a 500-ms increase in the search results display time reduced revenue by 20 percent [...]" (Kohavi et al., 2007). Another company *Compuware* providing application performance management solutions conducted an empirical study with 150 IT managers from large companies across Europe (Compuware 2015) to evaluate the importance of application performance management. Their findings show that more than half of the companies have experienced unexpected performance problems in more than 20 per cent of newly-deployed applications. Furthermore, 80 per cent of the IT managers agreed that software performance may affect customer satisfaction as well as total cost of ownership. In sum, for software vendors and operators of software systems, performance is a competitive and differentiating factor affecting the success of business.

Costs of Solving Performance Problems Although a majority of IT managers is aware of the importance of software performance, most performance problems in industry are typically identified and reported by end-users (Compuware 2015). However, the later problems are detected the more expensive their resolution is. According to Boehm, 1981, fixing problems in the operations phase of a software product can be more than a hundred times higher than conducting the resolution in early phases. The magnitudes of cost escalation are illustrated by Stecklein et al., 2004: Errors that have been made during the requirements phase but could be fixed in the design or integration phase entail a cost factor of up to eight and up to 78, respectively. In contrast, fixing the problems during operations is up to 1500 times more expensive. Whilst the named examples refer to software problems in general, the estimates can be similarly applied to software performance problems. Therefore, software performance needs to be addressed from early on in a software development process.

Reluctance to Adopt Performance Evaluation Approaches Software performance engineering (SPE) approaches (Smith, 1993) provide means to systematically evaluate the performance of software systems in early development phases. System and performance models are used to estimate the impacts of design decisions in early development phases when the implementations of systems are not available. In this way, SPE approaches allow early detection and resolution of critical performance problems, thus, reducing the costs for late problem resolution. Nevertheless, SPE approaches are still rarely adopted in industrial software development projects. Applying such systematic approaches requires profound expertise and entails a considerable overhead in creating and managing system models. There are many reasons why SPE approaches are still often omitted in industrial projects (Smith, 2015; Woodside et al., 2007). Most reasons can be reduced to three main obstacles: (i) Due to strong time restrictions in software development projects, IT managers try to avoid the additional overhead of creating system and performance models for SPE. (ii) Since software developers often lack sufficient expertise in performance engineering, they perceive SPE approaches as a burden rather than as help. (iii) Finally, developers do not trust in models and performance predictions (Woodside et al., 2007), which results in a reluctant attitude towards SPE approaches. Moreover, although SPE is suitable to uncover early design problems, performance problems that arise during implementation are not covered by design-time performance evaluation approaches due to their level of abstraction (Woodside et al., 2007). Measurement-based performance evaluation approaches (H. Koziolek, 2010) allow to investigate the performance of implemented software systems either as part of testing during the implementation phase or online, during operations. Since measurements are closer to the actual implementation of the software system, developers typically trust more in performance measurements than in performance predictions. However, analogous to SPE approaches, measurement-based approaches require deep expertise in performance evaluation (Jain, 1991) and entail a significant manual overhead for setting up and managing corresponding performance tests. Therefore, performance considerations are often postponed from the design and implementation phase to the end of the product lifecycle (cf. "fix-it-later" approach (Smith, 1993)). As a consequence, performance problems are revealed by end users which results in reputational damage for the corresponding organization and high costs of problem resolution.

Prevalent Practice in Performance Problem Diagnostics Performance problem diagnostics is the process of detecting and understanding a performance problem as well as localizing its root cause. Based on the considerations in the previous paragraph, in many software development projects, performance problem diagnostics is conducted as a reactive *performance fire-fighting* activity. Performance problems leading to customer complaints put corresponding software development and operation teams under high time pressure when they have to diagnose and resolve the performance problems. Due to insufficient expertise in performance engineering the responsible companies employ performance engineers (e.g. external performance consultants) to quickly identify and resolve performance problems. Performance engineers iteratively plan, set up and conduct performance tests, analyze measurement data, and make decisions on next diagnostics steps until they understand and identify the root causes of performance problems. Depending on the expertise of the performance engineers and severity of the performance problems the diagnostics process may take days, weeks or even month. All in all, the prevalent industrial practice in diagnosing performance problems comprises many manual steps and is often conducted in a reactive manner.

The Need for Automated, Measurement-based Performance Problem Diagnostics While conducting performance tests and subsequent analysis of measurement data requires deep knowledge in performance engineering, conceptually, the corresponding testing and analysis activities are often recurrent among unrelated, yet similar contexts (Heger, 2015). The expertise of highly qualified performance engineers is a result of years of practical experience, encountering similar performance problems in different contexts and learning recurrent activity patterns for detecting and solving performance problems. To be able to diagnose performance problems effectively and efficiently, performance engineers need to go through a long and tedious learning process leading them to profound expertise in their field. However, with regard to performance engineering expertise, we cannot benefit from scaling effects as long as the knowledge remains implicit in the heads of performance engineers and is not explicitly available. Furthermore, in this case diagnostics of performance problems remains a highly manual task requiring performance engineers to manually conduct performance tests and analyze measurement data. This does not scale in the first place, and it is also expensive and time-consuming. The recurrent nature of performance problems (Smith et al., 2000) and corresponding activities for their diagnostics provides a potential for automation through externalization and formalization of knowledge. An automatic approach would provide a means to the scale and cost problems of manual performance problem diagnostics. However, automating performance problem diagnostics poses scientific challenges that are addressed in this thesis. In general, this includes investigation of concepts for the systematization of diagnostics processes, formalization of expert knowledge on performance problems and their diagnostics, as well as concepts to mitigate limitations of measurement-based approaches. The scientific challenges are explained in more detail further below.

1.2. Problem Statement and Goals

The motivation in the previous section exposes multiple problematic aspects of the current practice in diagnosing performance problems during the development of software systems. First, performance evaluation requires deep expertise in performance engineering. Therefore, without proper tool support developers often rely on performance experts with regard to performance testing. Second, a high manual effort for conducting performance tests and analyzing corresponding measurement data is a significant obstacle for performance evaluation during software development. Both aspects lead to the main problem, namely to complete abandonment of performance diagnostics during development.

The field of functional testing yields an entirely different picture. Static code analysis approaches, such as Lint (Johnson, 1977), Findbugs (Ayewah et al., 2008) and Checkstyle (CSL 2015), are widely used in software development projects. Furthermore, developers are often obliged by project guidelines to write unit tests to achieve a certain level of test coverage (Zhu et al., 1997). Finally, integration tests are commonly used to ensure correct functionality across software components. Combining functional testing with the concept of continuous integration (Duvall et al., 2007) allows to keep functional quality of software products on a high level throughout the development.

Hence, while continuous evaluation of functional aspects is a matter of course in software development projects, continuous considerations of performance aspects is rather seldom. The reason for the wide adoption of functional testing lies in the high degree of automation of corresponding approaches, the encapsulated expert knowledge, the adoption of software engineering concepts, as well as the low manual effort to use the approaches. Conversely, performance evaluation is rarely adopted due to insufficient automation, lack of formalized and systematized expert knowledge, and enormous, manual overhead. In an earlier study by Woodside et al., this problem has been identified as a promising potential for future research:

> "There are many weaknesses in current performance processes. *They require heavy effort*, which limits what can be attempted.
>
> [...]
>
> Developers and testers use instrumentation tools to help them find problems with systems. However, *users depend on experience to use the results*, and this *experience needs to be codified* and incorporated into tools. *Better methods and tools for interpreting the results and diagnosing performance problems* are a future goal.
>
> [...]
>
> Promising areas for the future include better visualizations, *deep catalogues of performance-related patterns* of behaviour and structure, and *algorithms for automated search and diagnosis*."
>
> (Woodside et al., 2007)

In the quote of Woodside et al., we emphasized text passages that expose the main research problems addressed by this thesis. By addressing these problems, the present thesis is making a step towards incorporating performance problem diagnostics into continuous, automated testing during software development. In particular, the following high-level goals have guided the research work for this thesis.

Goal 1 — *Reduce manual effort for measurement-based diagnostics of performance problems.*

Reducing the manual effort for applying performance problem diagnostics is a crucial criterion to increase its adoption as a natural part of software development. To this end, manual tasks such as execution of performance tests and consequent analysis of data need to be automated.

Goal 2 — *Enable frequent experiment-based analysis of performance problems.*

Automation of performance problem diagnostics allows developers to conduct regular scans for performance problems and their root causes without additional effort. Diagnostics of performance problems can be, for instance, incorporated into continuous integration (Duvall et al., 2007). In this way, performance problems can be diagnosed as soon as they emerge in the software implementation.

Goal 3 — *Enable non-experts to conduct performance problem diagnostics.*

Automation of performance problem diagnostics takes over many tasks such as configuration of performance tests and analysis of measurement data that, typically, need to be conducted by performance experts. Additionally to the automation, the results of the diagnostics have to be adequately comprehensible for non-experts, in order to increase adoption of performance problem diagnostics.

1.3. Research Questions

The goals described in the previous section entail some challenges regarding the realization of an automatic performance problem diagnostics approach. In the following, we describe the challenges and corresponding, emerging research questions that are addressed in this thesis.

Capturing Knowledge on Performance Problem Diagnostics Due to the inherent complexity and diversity, performance problem diagnostics is a discipline that is strongly based on expert knowledge. Hence, in order to automate performance problem diagnostics, expert knowledge needs to be captured in a certain way, either through acquiring knowledge or through explicit formalization. Performance experts possess profound implicit knowledge of performance problem diagnostics. Furthermore, some knowledge has already been informally written down as typical, recurrent performance problems and performance anti-patterns. However, the available knowledge is loosely coupled, barely structured and insufficiently formalized. In the way the expert knowledge is available up to now, it does not provide sufficient guidance in conducting performance problem diagnostics. Based on this observation, in this thesis, we address the following research questions:

RQ 1 — *Which formalisms are appropriate in order to capture expert knowledge on performance problem diagnostics in a structured way?*

RQ 2 — *Does explicitly structured knowledge provide significant advantages in guiding performance problem diagnostics, as compared to the currently available representations of expert knowledge?*

Achieving High Accuracy and Precision As stated in Goal 2, we aim at providing an experiment-based approach for performance problem diagnostics that can be integrated with continuous testing. Measurement-based approaches share one common problem: Accuracy (i.e. deviation of measurements from reality) and precision (i.e. level of detail) of measurements are contradicting properties due to the monitoring overhead which is inherent to any measurement technique. However, to find a useful performance problem diagnostics approach that allows to identify detailed root causes of performance problems, both high measurement accuracy and a high level of detail (i.e. precision) are required. Hence, further research questions are arising from this consideration:

RQ 3 — *What is a proper solution for overcoming the trade-off between accuracy and precision of measurement data?*

RQ 4 — *If such solution can be found, how significant is the benefit of the solution compared to common measurement-based methods?*

Generalization Automation of processes is often coupled with technology-specific details including tool-specific configurations, automation scripts, etc. Consequently, as mentioned by Woodside et al., 2007 there is "a conflict between automation and adaptability in that systems which are highly automated". Hence, approaches that are highly automated tend to be specific to certain technologies, tools or application contexts. In contrast, to achieve the goals stated in the previous section, a performance problem diagnostics approach must be generic with respect to different application contexts on the one hand and, to technologies and tools used in these contexts on the other hand. In particular, generic diagnostics algorithms must be decoupled from context-specific characteristics without sacrificing the ability to fully automate the diagnostics process. These considerations, in turn, lead us to the subsequent research questions:

RQ 5 — *What are generic diagnostics algorithms for context-independent performance problem identification?*

RQ 6 — *Which abstraction constructs are necessary to decouple generic diagnostics processes from context-specific characteristics?*

RQ 7 — *What is a proper way to bridge the gap between generic diagnostics processes and specific application contexts in order to enable automation of performance problem diagnostics?*

Systematization Experiment-based performance evaluation approaches are inherently time-consuming due to the need of executing multiple, long-running experiments (i.e. in the range of minutes or hours). The practicability of experiment-based approaches highly depends on the number of experiments that need to be executed. Therefore, brute-force diagnostics approaches for performance problems that entail a huge amount of experiments are very time-consuming, expensive and, thus, not practicable. Similar to the manual diagnostics procedure by performance experts, an automatic diagnostics should follow a systematic approach that guides the search for root causes of specific performance problems in a goal-oriented manner. In this context, we address the following research question in this thesis:

RQ 8 — *What is an appropriate means to systematize the diagnostics of performance problems?*

RQ 9 — *How beneficiary is the systematic diagnostics approach regarding efficiency?*

RQ 10 — *Does a systematization of performance problem diagnostics affect the diagnostics accuracy?*

1.4. Existing Solutions

There are various approaches addressing the issue of detecting performance problems. The approaches can be divided into model-based and measurement-based approaches.

Model-based approaches (Cortellessa et al., 2014; Trubiani et al., 2011; Franks et al., 2006; Xu, 2012) allow to detect performance problems in very early phases (e.g. design phase) of a software product lifecycle. Thereby, static analysis of architectural models as well as analytical or simulative solutions of performance models are used to identify performance problems. Beside pure detection of performance problems, anti-pattern-based approaches (Cortellessa et al., 2014; Trubiani et al., 2011) provide deeper insights into the manifestations of detected performance problems. Based on detected performance problems, some approaches (Trubiani et al., 2011; Xu, 2012) make use of models to evaluate different solution alternatives without the need to actually implement the solutions. Though model-based approaches allow an early diagnostics of performance problems, they inherently depend on the availability of corresponding system and performance models. Furthermore, due to the abstraction level of models, model-based approaches detect performance problems at the granularity of software components. In particular, performance problems that are manifested in the implementation details of a system cannot be sufficiently diagnosed by model-based approaches.

Alongside with model-based solutions, there are measurement-based approaches for the detection and diagnostics of performance problems. Measurement-based approaches utilize instrumentation and monitoring of the target system to retrieve measurement data for the analysis of problems.

Online detection approaches (Parsons et al., 2008; Miller et al., 1995; Ehlers et al., 2011) allow to reveal performance problems during the operation of a given software system. However, as discussed before, resolution of problems that are revealed during operation is very expensive and represents a reactive rather than a proactive approach. Frameworks for self-adaptive systems (Kounev et al., 2010; van Hoorn, 2014) comprise performance problem detection and anticipation as part of their control loop for online system adaptation. However, their focus is on detecting performance problems that can be solved through dynamic reconfiguration or redeployment of the target system.

There are several approaches that allow to detect specific performance problem types during development, for instance as part of testing (Nistor et al., 2013; Yan et al., 2012; Chen et al., 2014). However, these approaches focus on some selected types of performance problems and, thus, do not provide a generic diagnostics approach. Approaches that detect performance regressions utilize historical data to identify degradations in performance. Due to their high degree of automation, performance regression detection approaches can be seamlessly incorporated into continuous integration. However, apart from detecting the existence of performance problems, these approaches do not diagnose the root causes of detected performance problems.

Apart from research approaches, commercial application performance management tools, such as Dynatrace 2015 or AppDynamics 2015, provide comprehensive means for monitoring of software systems, as well as management and visualization of measurement data. However, although these tools considerably support performance problem diagnostics, performance experts still have to manually conduct the analysis. In particular, to the best of our knowledge, the are no commercial tools that conduct a fully automatic diagnostics of performance problems.

1.5. Contributions

According to the goals stated before, we introduce an experiment-based approach called Automatic Performance Problem Diagnostics (APPD). The proposed approach combines different concepts that enable a systematic, efficient and context-independent diagnostics of performance problems. The APPD approach is based on a performance problem taxonomy that encapsulates the knowledge about interrelations among different symptoms and causes of performance problems. Using a systematic experimentation approach while traversing the taxonomy, APPD realizes a systematic search for root causes of detected performance problems. A domain-specific language for the description of goal-oriented performance tests and context information decouples the generic diagnostics approach from context-specific characteristics. Detection heuristics for different types of performance problems encapsulate the knowledge about the characteristics of recurrent problems (also known as performance anti-patterns (Smith et al., 2000)).

Three properties are essential for the APPD approach. Firstly, similar to existing operation-time approaches, APPD conducts an in-depth diagnostics of performance problem root causes. Secondly, APPD covers a wide range of performance problem types that can be detected with the approach. Finally, our approach conducts a goal-oriented search for performance problems and their root causes. In this way, APPD is especially suited to be integrated with continuous testing during development of a software product. To the best of our knowledge, APPD is the first approach that fully combines these properties.

The contributions of this thesis cover (i) a systematic process to derive a taxonomy on performance problems, (ii) a goal-oriented experimentation and diagnostics approach, (iii) a domain-specific language for the specification of performance problem diagnostics scenarios, and (iv) a systematic process to design and evaluate detection heuristics for individual performance problem types. In the following, we describe the concrete contributions of this thesis in more detail.

Taxonomy on Performance Problems One way to automate performance problem diagnostics is the imitation of the processes conducted by experienced performance experts through processable algorithms. When performance experts analyse a software system for performance problems, they start by observing its external behaviour. By means of symptoms that the experts observe, they gradually dig deeper into the internals of the target system until they identify the root cause of a performance problem. For the systematic search, performance experts utilize their knowledge on the interrelationships between different symptoms, recurrent performance problems (or performance anti-patterns), and typical root causes. In order to enable an automated diagnostics approach that proceeds in a comparably systematic manner, in this thesis, we introduce a novel method to explicitly capture this knowledge in a taxonomy on recurrent performance problems. Besides, we suggest a process that describes how to derive a generic, taxonomy-based Performance Problem Evaluation Plan (PPEP) from a set of known performance problem types. We first provide a categorization scheme for the classification of recurrent performance problem types. The categorization is used to derive a taxonomy on performance problems. Finally, the static taxonomy is augmented with diagnostics activities that provide guidance in diagnosing performance problems. We apply our classification method on a set of 27 anti-patterns that are described in scientific and industrial literature. The result is a PPEP instance that covers most common performance problems in practice. The PPEP is a core element of the APPD approach. Apart from the automatic diagnostics, a PPEP can be used as a guidance for manual diagnostics of performance problems.

The main scientific insights can be summarized as follows. A causal, hierarchical structure on performance problems (i.e. taxonomy) systematizes a performance problem diagnostics process. A taxonomy-based PPEP explicitly reflects the previously implicit knowledge of performance experts. A PPEP provides guidance in diagnosing performance problems, either manually or as part of an automatic diagnostics approach. A systematic process allows to derive and extend PPEP instances.

Systematic Experimentation and Diagnostics Approach In order to overcome the trade-off between accuracy and precision, in this thesis, we introduce a Systematic Selective Experimentation (SSE) concept. Thereby, several experiments with lightweight, selective monitoring are executed in a systematic way. The collected measurement data is statistically analyzed and correlated across different experiments. In this way, analyses can be conducted on accurate and precise measurement data. The SSE is a generic concept that is applicable not only for automatic performance problem diagnostics. SSE can be applied in all experiment-based performance evaluation scenarios where the trade-off between accuracy and precision of measurement data is a critical issue. Combining the SSE concept with the performance problem taxonomy, we realize a systematic search for the root causes of performance problems following the model of manual performance problem diagnostics by performance experts. Thereby, the performance problem taxonomy serves as a decision tree, while the SSE concept is utilized to conduct tailored experiments for each node in the taxonomy. In contrast to knowledge- and rule-based diagnostics approaches that are typically applied during operation, a systematic search approach, as realized in this thesis, is more appropriate to be incorporated into continuous testing due to its goal-oriented way of evaluating a system.

Scientifically, the main insight of this contribution is that a systematic experimentation concept with selective monitoring allows to overcome the trade-off between accurate and detailed measurement data. However, as the experiments of such an experimentation concept are independent, corresponding analysis methods must rely on statistical measures rather than on correlation on raw data.

Problem Diagnostics Specification Languages In order to enable system-and technology-independent, yet automatic, performance problem diagnostics, we introduce the Performance Problem Diagnostics Description Model (P^2D^2M). P^2D^2M comprises a set of description languages that decouple the generic diagnostics processes from context-specific details. P^2D^2M comprises four interrelated meta-models: (i) An *Experimentation Description* language allows to define experimentation plans for experiment-based analysis of performance problems. (ii) An *Instrumentation and Monitoring (IaM) Description* language provides means to specify instrumentation and monitoring instructions in a context-independent way. (iii) The *Data Representation* model constitutes a counterpart to the IaM Description language capturing the measurement data generated by the instrumentation and monitoring instructions. (iv) Finally, the *Measurement Environment (ME) Description* meta-model provides domain-specific modelling constructs for the specification of concrete application contexts. The former three meta-models constitute the basis for generic, system- and technology-independent diagnostics heuristics that are based on systematic experiments and analysis rules evaluating corresponding measurement data. Thereby, the IaM Description language plays a crucial role allowing to specify goal-oriented instrumentation instructions without explicit relations to context-specific elements. The ME Description instances close the gap between specific application contexts and generic definitions of diagnostics processes and algorithms. By providing a minimalistic domain-specific description language that is tailored for the purpose of performance problem diagnostics the ME Description allows to simply describe the components of an application context that are essential for problem diagnostics. In particular, the ME Description language relieves software engineers from creating comprehensive and complex architecture and performance models.

The scientific novelty of the proposed languages is manifested in the context-independent specification of experimentation plans for performance problem diagnostics as well as a language for a light-weight coupling to specific contexts. In this way, the languages allow a high degree of reuse of diagnostics algorithms that are based on the experiments specified using the proposed languages.

Detection Heuristics for different Types of Performance Problems
While the performance problem taxonomy and the SSE concept jointly constitute the high level diagnostics process, the evaluation of individual performance problem types is encapsulated in *detection heuristics*. For each node in the performance problem taxonomy a detection heuristic exists that is responsible for the investigation of the corresponding performance problem type. A detection heuristic comprises two main parts. First, by using the languages defined by P^2D^2M a heuristic defines an experimentation plan that describes which experiments (e.g. which load, etc.) to execute and which IaM instructions to apply on the target system. Depending on the type of performance problem to be investigated, experiments with selective instrumentation are executed to conduct a goal-oriented evaluation of the system characteristics that may be affected by a corresponding performance problem. The second part of a heuristic is an analysis algorithm that evaluates the measurement data gathered during the experiments. A detection heuristic provides a report on the investigated performance problem, stating whether the performance problem has been detected or not. In the case of a positive detection, a detection heuristic provides further information on the location and severity of a performance problem. A good detection heuristic must exhibit two essential properties. On the one hand, a detection heuristic must

provide accurate detection results. On the other hand, detection heuristics must be generically applicable along different target systems. In this thesis, we introduce a common process for designing accurate and generic detection heuristics. For a selected versatile set of performance problem types, we provide multiple alternative detection heuristics. Investigating their accuracy and general applicability we extract the most appropriate detection heuristics for the APPD approach.

The main scientific insights with respect to designing experiment-based detection heuristics for performance problems can be summarized as follows. Overall, if properly designed, experiment-based heuristics allow to accurately detect performance problems. To achieve a high degree of accuracy and generalization, detection heuristics need to be evaluated on a broad variety of micro-benchmarks before they are applied on real scenarios. This allows to identify weaknesses, improve heuristics and identify better suited alternatives. Furthermore, for the sake of generalization, detection algorithms should not rely on absolute thresholds for performance measures. They rather should utilize relative thresholds that are dynamically adopted to the circumstances of concrete application contexts.

1.6. Validation Methodology

In the field of software engineering, there are three major research methodologies (Wohlin et al., 2012): *survey*, *case study* and *experiment*. A *survey* aims at collecting information from some subjects, such as knowledge, opinion or behaviour (Fink, 2003). A *case study* is "an empirical enquiry that draws on multiple sources of evidence to investigate one instance [...] of a contemporary software engineering phenomenon within its real-life context [...]" (Runeson et al., 2009). An *experiment* (or controlled experiment) is "an empirical enquiry that manipulates one factor or variable of the studied setting" (Wohlin et al., 2012). While case studies provide more realistic insights, they provide less control than experiments.

In this thesis, we evaluated the APPD approach by means of all three types of investigation, depending on the purpose of validation. According to Wohlin et al., "case studies are very suitable for industrial evaluation of software engineering methods and tools because they can avoid scale-up problems"

(Wohlin et al., 2012). Therefore, we conducted three case studies in which we evaluated the end-to-end applicability of the APPD approach. Thereby, we investigated APPD under various conditions by applying the approach on target systems that differ in several aspects. This includes different types and scales of target systems, different technologies and run times, as well as different set-ups. In the case studies, we investigated the diagnostics accuracy of the APPD approach and explored its strengths and limitations. The case studies show that, independently from the application scenarios, APPD accurately diagnoses performance problems. Moreover, the case studies revealed some characteristics of performance problems in practice that affect the way of applying APPD. To validate the benefits of the SSE concept in the field of experiment-based performance evaluation, we conducted a controlled experiment. In this experiment, we applied the SSE concept on a different performance evaluation scenario (beyond the scope of performance problem diagnostics) and compared it to alternative approaches. In particular, we utilized the SSE concept for automated derivation of resource demands that are fed into an architectural performance model for the purpose of performance predictions. The results of the experiment show that the SSE concept is an enabler of gathering accurate and precise performance data. Finally, in an empirical study, external users applied the APPD approach in a controlled environment. As part of the empirical study, we conducted a survey to capture the perception and opinion of the external users with respect to the APPD approach. Despite some minor issues like potential for better usability and documentation, users evaluated the APPD as a useful means in diagnosing performance problems. Most study participants also demonstrated willingness to use the APPD approach in their own software development projects.

1.7. Outline

The current thesis is structured as follows.

Chapter 2 describes the foundations of the conducted research work. We describe the notion of enterprise software systems, discuss their main characteristics, and elaborate corresponding implications on the performance behaviour of enterprise software systems. Furthermore, we describe common approaches and concepts in the field of software performance analysis. Thereby, we give an overview on relevant concepts of the queueing theory and discuss the essence of measurement-based performance evaluation approaches. As we use the Palladio Component Model (PCM) as an architectural performance model in one of the validation studies in Chapter 7, in Chapter 2, we provide a summary on the Palladio approach. Finally, we describe the notion of Software Performance Anti-patterns (SPAs), their origin and classification, as well as a set of anti-patterns relevant for present research.

Chapter 3 describes the overall approach of this thesis. This chapter provides an overview of the constituent parts of the APPD approach and their interrelation. We introduce the SSE concept and describe the basic concept of the systematic search for performance problems by means of a taxonomy on performance problems. Furthermore, we discuss the assumptions of the APPD approach as well as the intended scope of its applicability. On the basis of the research questions outlined in Section 1.3 and the constituent parts of the APPD approach we derive seven research hypotheses that guide the current research work and serve as validation criteria.

Chapter 4 addresses the challenge of systematically structuring the expert knowledge on performance problems. In this chapter, we elaborate on a systematic process for deriving a taxonomy-based Performance Problem Evaluation Plan (PPEP). Thereto, we develop a categorization scheme for performance anti-patterns, describe the steps to derive a taxonomy, and introduce the transformation of a taxonomy into an augmented PPEP. We apply our process on a set of 27 anti-patterns reported in existing literature and instantiate the PPEP for twelve anti-patterns that are considered in more detail in the remaining chapters of this thesis.

Chapter 5 introduces the P^2D^2M, a meta-model defining a set of domain-specific description languages for the specification of information that is required for automatic diagnostics of performance problems. P^2D^2M comprises four sub-languages that address different aspects of experiment-based performance problem diagnostics: Experimentation Description, Instrumentation and Monitoring Description, Measurement Environment Description, and Data Representation. We describe the interrelation of the sub-languages of P^2D^2M and their roles in the APPD approach. For each sub-language, we describe the design goals, the abstract syntax and the informal semantics of elements from the corresponding meta-models.

Chapter 6 addresses the systematic design of detection heuristics for performance problems. In this chapter, we introduce the notion of a detection heuristic and design a systematic process for the creation of accurate detection heuristics. According to the proposed process, we create 23 micro-benchmark applications for the evaluation of alternative detection heuristics. We develop different detection strategies for the twelve performance problems selected in Chapter 4 and evaluate them by means of the benchmark applications. The best performing heuristics are selected to be integrated into the APPD approach.

Chapter 7 comprises the validation of the APPD approach and its constituent concepts. Based on the hypotheses defined in Chapter 3, we derive more fine-grained validation questions. To investigate the validation questions, we conduct three case studies, one controlled experiment and an empirical study with external participants. In the case studies, we investigate the functionality, strengths and weaknesses of the APPD approach by means of different target systems including a benchmark application, an open-source commercial application, and an industrial large-scale application. The controlled experiment aims at validating the benefit of the SSE concept. Finally, an empirical study investigates the applicability of APPD by external users, as well as their perception of the approach.

Chapter 8 discusses related work. This includes related work in the fields of classifying performance problems, experimentation-based performance evaluation, models and languages for performance testing, as well as detection and diagnostics of performance problems. The latter part is further divided into model-based and measurement-based approaches.

Chapter 9 concludes this thesis by providing a summary, discussing benefits, assumptions and limitations of the APPD approach, and giving an outlook on future work.

2. Foundations

In this chapter, we introduce some foundations that are relevant for the remainder of this work. In Section 2.1, we first describe the essentials of enterprise software systems and corresponding performance-related characteristics. We then give an overview on performance evaluation techniques and concepts. Thereto, we introduce relevant aspects of model-based performance evaluation approaches (Section 2.2) as well as measurement-based performance analysis techniques (Section 2.3). Finally, we describe the notion of performance anti-patterns and introduce the anti-patterns that are considered in this work (Section 2.4).

2.1. Performance of Enterprise Software Systems

Software engineering covers different types of software (Fowler, 2002), from operating systems and desktop applications through mobile applications and embedded systems to enterprise applications and information systems. Though similar software engineering principles apply to different kind of applications, with respect to Quality of Service (QoS), different classes of applications differ in their behaviour as well as aspects that are important to be considered. For instance considering performance, embedded systems have strict real-time requirements that, by contrast, are less important for enterprise software systems. In this work, we focus on the performance of enterprise software systems. There is no explicit definition of the term *enterprise software system* or *enterprise application*. However, Fowler describes enterprise applications as follows:

> "Enterprise applications are about the display, manipulation, and storage of large amounts of often complex data and the support

> or automation of business processes with that data. Examples include reservation systems, financial systems, supply chain systems, and many others that run modern business. Enterprise applications have their own particular challenges and solutions, and they are different from embedded systems, control systems, telecoms, or desktop productivity software." (Fowler, 2002)

According to the three main aspects of displaying, manipulating and storing data, enterprise applications are often designed along a three-tier architecture. The three tiers comprise a *presentation*, an *application* and a *data* tier. The presentation tier is responsible for displaying data to the end users in a client (e.g. Web browser). The application tier encapsulates the business logic of an enterprise application, responsible for processing and manipulation of business data. Finally, the data tier persists data in a database or any other data storage. In all tiers, there are different types of performance problems. In the presentation tier of Web-based applications, there are different performance problems concerning parsing and interpreting of Java Script code (D. J. Westermann, 2014) and transmission of data over Internet. Performance problems in the data tier are often manifested in improper design of database schemes, inappropriate configuration of database management systems and badly designed database queries. In this work, we focus on performance problems in the application tier as well as its communication with the data tier (i.e. including inefficient data access operations). The following characteristics of enterprise software systems are of crucial importance to this work.

Complexity of Software Often, the application tier comprises a great part of the complexity of enterprise applications. Rettig described the complexity of enterprise applications as follows:

> "Much of the seemingly boundless complexity of enterprise software is founded on conditional branching (if-then statements) and a hierarchy of interacting objects, all of which manipulate information in a logical succession of small steps. [...] as enterprise software becomes increasingly comprehensive and complex, the costs and risks involved in changing it increase as well. No single person within an organization could possibly

> know how a change in one part of the software will affect its functioning elsewhere." (Rettig, 2007)

As in most cases no single person can overlook the complexity of an enterprise application, automatic support in analyzing that kind of systems is essential. This applies for all types of analysis, inter alia, including evaluation of performance characteristics and performance problem diagnostics.

Interactivity Most enterprise applications have an interactive nature, meaning that end users are actively interacting with the software system by issuing requests to the system and awaiting a response. This property has an important implication on the understanding of performance requirements in the domain of enterprise software systems. End users expect the systems to respond quickly. Hence the response time of user requests plays a crucial role when evaluating the performance of enterprise applications. Deficiencies in the responsiveness of enterprise applications have a proven, negative effect on the success of business (Kohavi et al., 2007; Compuware 2015). Thereby, the software system is mostly a black box for the end users. As they don't see the complexity of certain interactions, they expect each interaction to be equally responsive. Often, certain classes of end users exhibit a similar behaviour with respect to the usage of the software system. Understanding different classes of users is an important means to enable development-time performance testing through synthetic generation of load.

Scalability While in enterprise systems the degree of parallelization is mostly low for individual user requests, most enterprise systems must be able to manage a high level of concurrency induced by concurrent usage of the system. Often hundreds, thousands or even millions of users are using an enterprise software system concurrently. As the level of concurrency often cannot be estimated in advance, and as it may change rapidly during operation, scalability is a crucial requirement for enterprise applications. Hence, by adding additional hardware resources an enterprise application must be able to manage a higher level of concurrency without noticeable effects on the performance (i.e. responsiveness of the system). Therefore, performance testing of enterprise software systems is closely related with testing the scalability of the application.

2.2. Model-based Performance Evaluation

Performance evaluation of software systems can be conducted along different phases of software development. Depending on the artifacts that are available in corresponding phases of development, different methods for performance evaluation can be applied. In the early 80's, Connie Smith introduced the disciple of Software Performance Engineering (SPE). Smith defined SPE as "a method for constructing software systems to meet performance objectives" (Smith, 1993). SPE, as described by Smith, utilizes system and performance models, prediction methods and quantitative methods to evaluate the performance of software in early development phases. Performance models provide an abstract projection of the performance aspects of a software system under development. Performance models allow to evaluate the performance of software systems in early development phases (e.g. requirements elicitation and design phases) without the need to fully implement the system. In this way, SPE methods provide a means to support architects and software developers in estimating the performance effect of certain design and implementation decisions.

Different modelling approaches are available to conduct model-based performance evaluation. Pure performance models such as *Queueing Networks* (Bolch et al., 2006), *Stochastic Petri Nets* (Marsan et al., 1994) or *Queueing Petri Nets* (Bause, 1993; Kounev, 2006) allow to directly model the performance aspects of software systems. While focusing on capturing the performance aspects of the target system, these kind of models often abstract from the software architecture of the target system. The gap between pure performance models and actual software development constructs (e.g. classes, components, etc.) has been a significant obstacle for the adoption of performance models in industrial software development projects. To bridge this gap, in recent decades, performance models have been progressively hidden behind domain-specific languages that are familiar to software developers. Thereby, modelling languages such as the UML with the UML MARTE profile (Object Management Group, 2015b) and the Palladio Component Model (Becker et al., 2009) allow to enrich architectural models with additional performance annotations. In the background, model-to-model and model-to-code transformations are executed to enable performance evaluation of the corresponding architectural models.

In general, there are two ways of evaluating a performance model: analytically or simulative. With an analytical approach mathematical methods are used to resolve a system of equations and stochastic expressions yielding stochastic results for certain performance metrics of interest. Simulative approaches synthetically execute a performance model by emulating user requests in a specified way while observing the performance behaviour of the model. As the performance models of realistic software systems are far to complex to be solved analytically, in most cases, simulative approaches are used for model-based performance analysis of enterprise software systems.

Besides the modelling and evaluation of concrete software systems, the theory behind model-based performance evaluation constitutes the basis for any kind of performance analysis and understanding, including measurement based analysis techniques. In the following, we introduce some core concepts behind Queueing Networks and the Queueing Theory. Furthermore, we introduce the Palladio approach for component-based software architecture and performance modelling and software performance evaluation.

2.2.1. Queueing Theory

Queueing theory is used to describe and analyze queueing processes in different domains. Gross et al. describe queueing theory as follows: "Queueing theory was developed to provide models to predict the behavior of systems that attempt to provide service for randomly arising demands" (Gross et al., 2011). As software applications fall into this category of systems, the queueing theory constitutes the basis for performance considerations of software systems. In this section, we describe only some selected aspects of the queueing theory. For detailed information on the queueing theory and its usage for evaluating the performance of software systems we refer to Gross et al., 2011 and Menascé et al., 2004, respectively. The following descriptions are based on Gross et al., 2011 and Menascé et al., 2004.

The queueing theory is based on the notion of *queues*. Figure 2.1a schematically shows a queue and important quantities. A *queue* consists of a *waiting line* and one or more *servers*. Servers are responsible for processing requests, whereby only one request can be processed at a time. The time that is needed to process a request is called *service time* S. If the server is busy with the processing of a request, incoming requests have to wait in the waiting line

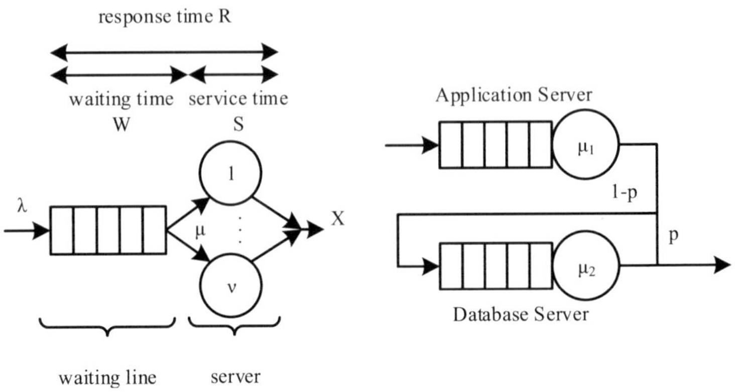

(a) Queue **(b)** Queueing Network

Figure 2.1.: Queue and queueing network

of the queue. The waiting time is denoted by W. The residence time R of a request in a queue is the sum of the waiting time W and the service time S. Characteristics of a queue can be mathematically described by means of the following properties:

- **Arrival Rate:** Requests to a queue are described by means of an arrival process and arrival patterns. Thereby, a probability distribution specifies the inter-arrival times of individual requests. The average number of requests per second arriving at the queue is denoted by the *arrival rate* λ.

- **Service Rate:** In a similar way, the service times of a server are described. A probability distribution specifies the service times of a server, whereby μ denotes the average service rate of a server. Consequently the average service time of a server is $S = 1/\mu$. The arrival rate λ and the service rate μ determine the throughput X of the queue.

- **Scheduling Strategy:** A scheduling strategy describes in which order requests from the waiting line of a queue are served by the server (e.g. First-Come-First-Serve, Round Robin, Processor Sharing, etc.).

- **Capacity:** A queue can be either finite or infinite. In the former case, a capacity specifies the maximum allowed queue length of the waiting line. In the latter case, the queue length can grow to infinity.
- **Number of Servers:** A queue can have either one or multiple servers. In a multi-server queue, requests in the waiting line are assigned to the next server that becomes available.
- **Networks:** Queues as depicted in Figure 2.1a can be composed to more comprehensive networks of queues. Requests that were served by one queue are transmitted for processing to the next queue. Connections between individual queues describe the flow of requests between individual queues. Figure 2.1b shows a simple example of a queueing network modelling an application server and a database server with a cache. First, each request is processed by the Application Server queue. Thereafter, a request is either served by the database cache with a probability of p (i.e. cache hit), or is processed by the Database Server queue with the probability of $1 - p$.

A fully specified queue (or queueing network) can be mathematically solved using methods from operational analysis (Menascé et al., 2004). Operational analysis is an approach that allows to reason on performance quantities based on specified data. Different laws from operational analysis exist that describe dependencies between different operational quantities (e.g. utilization, arrival rate, response time, etc.). In the following, we describe some of the basic principles and laws from operational analysis that are relevant in this thesis.

Steady State Given an average arrival rate λ and an average service rate μ, the utilization of a multi-server queue with ν servers is defined by $\rho = \lambda/(\nu\mu)$. As long $\rho < 1$, in average, the server is able to process requests faster than they arrive. Otherwise ($\rho \geq 1$), the requests arrive more frequently than they can be processed by the server. In this case, the queue length grows infinitely leading to an unstable system. Hence, a queueing system is considered to be in a steady state (or in an *operational equilibrium*), only if $\rho < 1$. Analysis of queueing networks is often based on the assumption of a steady state. Under this assumption, the throughput X of a queueing system is determined by the arrival rate λ of the requests: $X = \lambda$.

Service Demand Law Given a processing resource r, the Service Demand Law describes the relation between the service demand D_r of a request to resource r, the utilization U_r of the resource r and the overall throughput X:

$$D_r = \frac{U_r}{X} \tag{2.1}$$

Hereby, the service demand D_r is defined as the sum of all service times S_r at resource r of the corresponding request. Hence, if a request is served m times by resource r, then the service demand is defined as $D_r = mS_r$. In the particular case that a request is served only once by a resource r, the service demand is equal to the service time of r and the Service Demand Law is turned into: $S_r = U_r/X$.

Little's Law Little's Law is one of the most important and generic laws of operational analysis. Given a self-contained queueing system that is in a steady state, Little's Law describes the dependency between number N of requests in the system, throughput X and residence time R as follows:

$$N = RX \tag{2.2}$$

Little's Law is very generic and can be applied on any black box. For instance, the law holds for the waiting line of a queue, the server of a queue, the entire queue or even an entire queueing network.

Utilization-Response Time Relationship Given an infinite, single-server queue, the average number N of requests in the queue solely depends on the utilization $U = \rho = \frac{\lambda}{\mu}$ of the server:

$$N = \frac{U}{1 - U} \tag{2.3}$$

Combining Equation 2.3 with Little's Law yields the following relation between the residence time R of a request in a queue, the request's service time S, and the server's utilization U.

$$R = \frac{N}{X} = \frac{U}{(1-U)X} = \frac{\frac{\lambda}{\mu}}{(1-U)\lambda} = \frac{\frac{1}{\mu}}{(1-U)} = \frac{S}{1-U} \tag{2.4}$$

Assuming a fix service time S, Figure 2.2 graphically illustrates the relationship between the server utilization and the residence time of a request. If the server is idle, the residence time is equal to the service time. With a server utilization of 50%, the residence time is twice as high as the service time. If the utilization is close to capacity (i.e. 100%), the residence time grows rapidly.

For a multi-server queue with v servers, the average number of requests in the queue is more complex, as shown in the following equation (Menascé et al., 2004):

$$N = \frac{U}{1-U} C(v, U) + Uv \tag{2.5}$$

Hereby, Erlang's C formula calculates the probability that an arriving request has to wait in the waiting line of the queue:

$$C(v, U) = \frac{\left(\frac{(Uv)^v}{v!}\right)\left(\frac{1}{1-U}\right)}{\sum_{i=0}^{v-1} \frac{(Uv)^i}{i!} + \left(\frac{(Uv)^v}{v!}\right)\left(\frac{1}{1-U}\right)} \tag{2.6}$$

Again, combining Equation 2.5 with Little's Law yields the following dependency between utilization, service time and residence time for a multi-server queue with v servers:

$$N = \frac{S}{v(1-U)} C(v, U) + S \tag{2.7}$$

Figure 2.3 shows the corresponding curve for a queue with eight servers. Compared to the curve in Figure 2.2, with a multi-server queue, the residence time stays longer low with an increasing utilization of the servers. However, near to a utilization of 100%, the curve increases more sharply than for a single-server queue. Transferring these considerations to a software system allows to reason about expected response times in dependence on observed utilization of hardware resources.

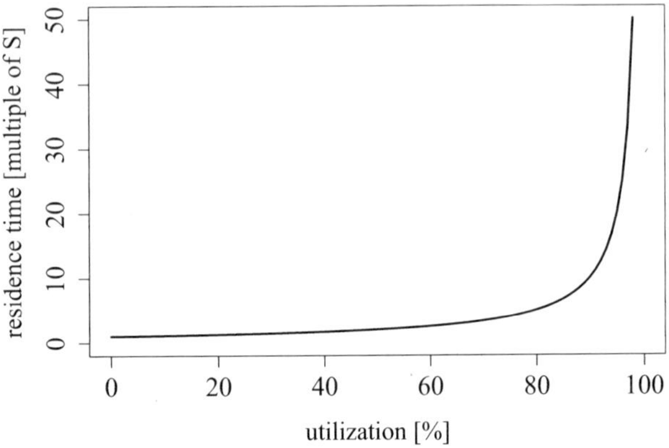

Figure 2.2.: Single-server queue: residence time in dependence on server utilization

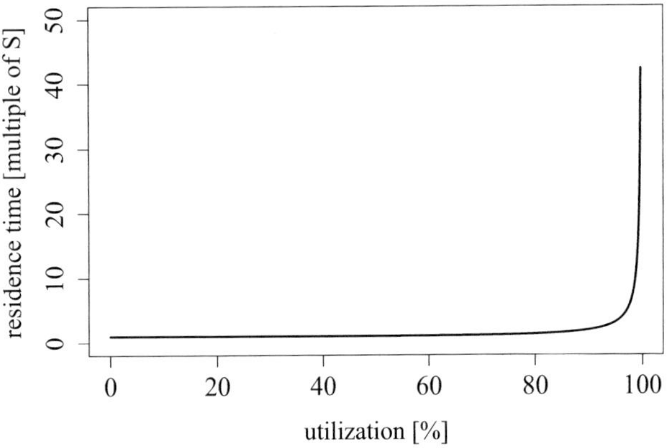

Figure 2.3.: Queue with 8 servers: residence time in dependence on server utilization

2.2.2. Palladio

Palladio (Becker et al., 2009) is an approach for component-based modelling of software architectures and model-based evaluation of QoS attributes (e.g. including performance and reliability). In this section, we give a general overview on Palladio and explain the parts of Palladio that are required to understand the corresponding parts in the work at hand. For a detailed description of Palladio, we refer to Becker et al., 2009.

Palladio comprises a meta-model for architectural modelling, a process, as well as a set of tools that allow for an automatic, model-based prediction and analysis of QoS attributes. The meta-model is called Palladio Component Model (PCM). To support different roles in a software development process, PCM is divided into four sub-models. Figure 2.4 depicts the Palladio process including the different roles and sub-models. *Component Developers* are responsible for specifying and designing individual components. This includes the provided and required interfaces, the dynamic behaviour associated with individual services provided by the components, as well as the performance characteristics of the services. The performance behaviour is specified in a parametric way depending on certain characteristics of input data and the environment. Components are intended to be reusable, that is why they are stored in a repository of components. *System Architects* assemble individual software components to entire software systems. With respect to performance (or QoS in general), an essential concept is the composability of parametric performance behaviour. Hence, knowing low-level performance characteristics of individual components allows to reason about the performance of an assembly of components. As QoS characteristics directly depend on the execution environment of a software system, a *System Deployer* is responsible for providing a model of the execution environment. This includes modelling of available servers with their hardware resources (e.g. CPU, HDD, etc.) and network links. Furthermore, a System Deployer specifies the allocation of the software components to the available system nodes. Finally, a *Domain Expert* describes the usage model of the target system representing typical behaviour of system users.

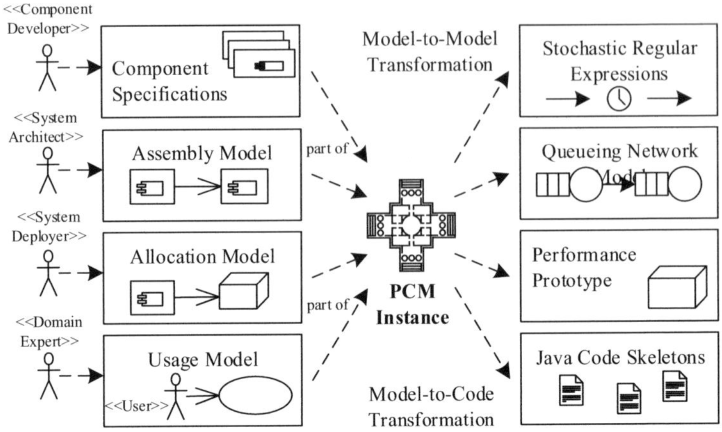

Figure 2.4.: The Palladio process (Becker et al., 2009)

In sum, the four sub-models subsume the entire information to conduct an analysis of QoS attributes. Thereto, Palladio provides different alternatives. Using Model-to-Model Transformations, a PCM instance can be either transformed to a model based on stochastic regular expressions or a queueing network model. The former model needs to be solved analytically, however is limited to single-user scenarios. Queueing network models can be either solved analytically or through simulation. By means of Model-to-Code Transformation a PCM instance can be transformed into a performance prototype, into simulation code, or can be used to generate code skeletons for the initialization of the implementation process. The tooling of Palladio allows to run automatic simulation runs on generated simulation code. During simulation, the tooling gathers simulation data for different performance quantities and metrics. Analyzing the simulation data provides insights on the QoS effects of architectural design decisions.

One of the most central means of specifying the performance behaviour of software components in PCM is the notion of Resource Demanding Service Effect Specification (RD-SEFF)s. An RD-SEFF models a control flow by means of a UML Activity diagram-like representation that is, in addition, annotated with performance characteristics. An RD-SEFF may contain different types of actions including control flow actions (e.g. branch, loop and fork actions), external call actions, and internal actions. While external call actions model calls to other services, internal actions represent component-internal computations. Actions can be annotated with parametric resource demands to different resource types. Thereby, parameters are propagated from the usage model through the RD-SEFFs and allow to describe the performance behaviour of a component in dependence of its usage. Resource demands within RD-SEFFs constitute the core concept in PCM for modeling performance. The compositional interplay of resource demands and their effect on the underlying simulated resources yields the overall performance of the simulated software system. Different techniques can be used to obtain resource demands. In very early stages, service demands can be roughly estimated. If implementations of comparable software components exist, measurement techniques can be used to derive resource demands. In general, the performance prediction accuracy of a PCM instance highly depends on the accuracy of the resource demands used to calibrate the model.

2.3. Measurement-based Performance Evaluation

The definition of SPE by Smith (Smith, 1993) mainly focuses on the usage of models to conduct performance evaluation of software systems. Woodside et al. extend the definition of SPE as follows:

> "Software Performance Engineering (SPE) represents the entire collection of software engineering activities and related analyses used throughout the software development cycle, which are directed to meeting performance requirements."
>
> (Woodside et al., 2007)

In contrast to the definition in (Smith, 1993), the definition by Woodside et al. explicitly includes both model-based and measurement-based approaches. Hence, measurement-based performance evaluation approaches are complementary to the model-based approaches. In particular, model-based approaches often depend on measurements for model calibration or validation. As we have discussed model-based approaches in Section 2.2, in this section, we introduce foundations in the field of performance measurements.

According to Menascé et al., 2001, performance measurements can be divided into passive and active measurements. In the former case, measurements are taken from the software system under a real load. Hence, passive measurements are applied during operations of a software system. Passive measurement approaches are used, for instance, to enable online problem anticipation, reporting of performance problems, understanding of user behaviour or online self-adaptation of systems. Active performance measurements involve synthetic generation of load and, thus, are typically conducted on a test environment. Different types of active measurement approaches exist that differ in their goal and the measurement methodology (Liu, 2011; Menascé et al., 2001):

Performance Regression Testing Performance regression testing has the purpose of comparing the performance of ongoing development versions of a software product with previous versions. In this way, degradations in performance can be promptly identified after their emergence during development.

Performance Optimization Performance optimization is the process of continuously improving the performance of an application. In contrast to performance problem detection and resolution, optimization is not focused on finding severe problems but identify and exhaust potentials for performance improvement.

Performance Benchmarking The primary focus of performance benchmarking is the comparability of the tested systems with a baseline. Thereby, different alternatives are tested under identical conditions to evaluate competing alternatives. This applies for competing products, different versions of software application, etc. Depending on the goal, benchmarks are either created for testing specific aspects (i.e. micro-benchmarks) or entire systems (i.e. macro-benchmarks). Industrial benchmarks are typically created by independent organizations such as the Standard Performance Evaluation Corporation (SPEC 2015) or the Transaction Performance Processing Council (TPC 2015).

Load and Scalability Testing This kind of tests are executed to analyze the target system's ability to meet the performance requirements under high-load situations. Load and scalability tests are often applied as part of detection and diagnostics of performance problems.

Single-user Performance Testing In contrast to load tests, single-user performance tests evaluate the performance of an application under the load of one user. The purpose of such tests is to understand the control flow of user requests and identify segments that consume the major part of the response time. Often, single-user tests are applied manually to get a first impression of an application and its performance. Furthermore, single-user tests are applied to analyze client-side performance of applications (e.g. Java script rendering times, etc.).

Performance Unit Testing Apart from entire system tests, performance tests can be applied on smaller units (e.g. components, classes or even methods) of software systems. This approach is especially useful to test the performance of complex algorithms. Functional unit tests can be reused to conduct performance unit testing. (Heger et al., 2013)

Factor Analysis and systematic experimentation This category encapsulates systematic measurement approaches that aim at providing insights on dependencies between a set of controlled variables (i.e. *factors*) and a set of observed measures. Thereby, a set of experiments is executed while systematically exploring the value space spanned by the controlled variables. Different factorial designs (Menascé et al., 2001) and exploration strategies (D. J. Westermann, 2014) exist that reduce the amount of required experiments. Factor analysis is a generic approach that can be applied to achieve a multitude of different performance evaluation goals.

The different measurement approaches are not mutually exclusive. Often, different measurement approaches are combined to achieve certain analysis goals. For instance, Heger et al., 2013 combine performance regression testing with performance unit testing to realize performance problem detection. Bulej et al., 2005 combine regression testing with benchmarking. In this thesis, we combine load and scalability testing, single-user testing and systematic experimentation to realize systematic performance problem diagnostics. An aspect that is essential in all measurement-based approaches is the gathering of data. Furthermore, an important part of load and scalability testing is the generation of load. As load generation and gathering of measurement data are two essential topics for this work, in the following, we take a closer look onto these aspects.

2.3.1. Workload Generation

The purpose of workload generation is to create a synthetic workload on a target system during testing. Thereby, the goal is to achieve a representative workload that is close to the real workload. As real workloads are highly nondeterministic and complex, synthetic load generation cannot exactly reflect real workloads. Therefore, load generation uses workload models that abstractly represent real workloads. A workload model comprises two main aspects: the *work description* and the *load intensity*. The former, describes type and order of requests to the tested software system that are emitted by simulated users (i.e. *virtual users*). The load intensity determines the frequency of user requests. There are different types of load models and representations of workload. Both aspects are discussed in the following.

Load Type In general, there are two different types of load: *open* and *closed* model type (Liu, 2011). With an open model type, the simulated users are not explicitly part of the modelled system. The load intensity of an open load is specified by means of an arrival rate. The arrival rate determines the frequency of user requests that are entering the system. If the arrival rate is higher than the maximum throughput of the tested system, the system can get into an unsteady state with an infinitely growing backlog of requests to be served by the system (cf. Section 2.2.1). A closed load model explicitly includes users into the modelled system. There is a fix *population size* of users in the modelled system. Each user that creates a request to the tested system and has been served by the system, repeatedly creates a new request. In between two requests, users are idle for a specified time span (i.e. *think time*). In contrast to open load models, systems that are tested with a closed load are inherently in a steady state as there is an upper limit for the number of concurrent users (i.e. population size).

Workload Representations A workload is the sum of all requests emitted by different users. However, different groups of users exhibit similar behaviour. For instance, in an e-commerce system there can be power-shopper, users that prevalently browse products, users that visit the shop rarely, etc. In a workload model, user groups with similar behaviour are represented by workload classes. There are different types of models that reflect the work description for virtual users. A *markov model* (Jain, 1991; van Hoorn et al., 2008; van Hoorn et al., 2014) is a probabilistic way of modelling virtual users. A markov model is a directed graph, whereby the nodes represent user interactions and the edges represent transitions probabilities between individual nodes. Different paths in the markov model represent different workload classes. The big advantage of a markov workload model is the high degree of indeterminism of user behaviour that is very representative for actual workloads. However, creating such models requires a lot of detailed information about the actual behaviour of real users, which however is seldom available. Real user monitoring (Allspaw et al., 2010) during operations can be used to obtain the information required to build a markov workload model.

Record and replay of user behaviour is a common approach in practise (Podelko, 2005). Thereby, either real user sessions are recorded during operation, or a tester records a click sequence based on some assumptions on the actual user behaviour. In both cases, the result is a *load script* comprising a fix sequence of user interactions that form a virtual user session. For load generation, the load scripts are replayed, potentially with a high number of parallel, virtual users. Most professional load generation tools like HP LoadRunner™ or Apache JMeter™ provide means for recording and replaying load scripts.

2.3.2. Gathering Performance Measurement Data

The process of gathering measurement data is called *monitoring*. To describe the essence of software performance monitoring, we first define some basic terms:

Measurement Probe In order to capture the data to be collected, monitoring tools execute program code snippets that conduct measurements and write back data. In this thesis, we denote such code snippets as *measurement probes*. Measurement probes may, for instance, capture time spans of operation executions, retrieve current CPU utilization, intercept certain events, and much more.

Measurement Scope Measurement probes can be placed in different locations of a system (different system nodes, components, classes, etc.).

The sum of all locations where a certain measurement probe has been placed is called *measurement scope*.

Measurement Accuracy The purpose of performance monitoring is to capture the actual performance behaviour of the System Under Test (SUT). Thereby, it is desirable that the measurement values reflect the actual behaviour as good as possible. According to ISO standard 24765, the accuracy of measurement is "the closeness of the agreement between the result of a measurement and the true value of the measurand" (ISO/IEC/IEEE, 2010). Hence, accuracy is an important quality attribute of monitoring approaches and tools.

Measurement Precision In (ISO/IEC/IEEE, 2010) the term *precision* is defined as "the degree of exactness or discrimination with which a quantity is stated" (ISO/IEC/IEEE, 2010). In the context of monitoring software applications, we consider the term *precision* as the level of detail that a monitoring approach or tool achieves. For instance, if monitoring is conducted from the user perspective, we can only observe the response time of the entire system service. Hence, the precision is low. However, if we are able to provide detailed, discriminant execution times of all sub-parts of the system service, the precision is high.

Monitoring Overhead Analogously to Heisenberg's uncertainty principle (Busch et al., 2007), the presence of monitoring probes affects measured data. Each measurement probe that is executed as part of monitoring must be processed by computational resources (e.g. CPU), which entails an overhead on the utilization of the resources as well as on the execution time of the monitored routines. Usually, measurement probes are very light-weight and, per se, introduce only a very small, negligible monitoring overhead. However, if measurement probes are executed very frequently (e.g. for each instruction of the monitored SUT) the monitoring overhead can be very large and, thus, may completely distort the measured data.

Depending on the monitoring target, there are different means to realize monitoring. We distinguish between event-based monitoring, sampling, and control flow monitoring. The former type of monitoring encapsulates all monitoring techniques that intercept asynchronous events that are emitted in the environment of a SUT. Hence, event-based monitoring is a passive type of monitoring. In Java, for instance, the monitoring of garbage collection events falls into this category. Sampling denotes the process of periodically taking a measurement. This approach is typically used to retrieve state information from hardware or software resources. For instance, measuring CPU utilization, the number of free connections in a connection pool, the number of active database requests, etc. is usually conducted by means of sampling. Control flow monitoring, covers all measurements that are triggered within the control flow of a user request. Instrumentation techniques (Angel et al., 2001; Filman et al., 2002) are used to enrich the application code with measurement probes. As soon as the control flow of a thread reaches an instrumented code location, the corresponding measurement probe is executed. In this way, information can be monitored that is directly related to the control flow, such as response times, memory footprints, etc. Instrumentation can be conducted by different means. Static instrumentation is conducted at implementation or compile time. As instrumentation is a cross cutting concern, often, Aspect-oriented Programming (AOP) techniques (Kiczales et al., 1997) are used to weave measurement probes into the application code. As static instrumentation is not flexible, many monitoring tools apply dynamic instrumentation, for instance, by means of dynamic bytecode manipulation (Marek et al., 2012). Thereby, managed programming languages (e.g. Java or .NET) allow to intercept class loading and provide means to manipulate the bytecode of classes before they are used in the application. Furthermore, Java allows to adapt the bytecode of a class at any time in the execution of the application. Utilizing this functionality, the Adaptable Instrumentation and Monitoring (AIM) framework (Wert et al., 2015a) allows to dynamically adapt instrumentation of a SUT. In this thesis, we utilize the adaptive instrumentation of AIM to realize systematic experimentation.

To get a comprehensive and detailed picture of the SUT, ideally, every single, detailed aspect of the system should be monitored. However, due to the monitoring overhead inherent in each monitoring approach, a full monitoring of a system is typically not practical as it would distort the measurement data. In general, within a single measurement run, accuracy, precision and measurement scope are contradicting requirements that cannot be achieved at once. The more precise (i.e. detailed) and broad (i.e wide scope) the measurements are, the lower is the accuracy. Accuracy is only high if either the precision is low or the scope is tight. This consideration is essential, when conducting measurements and relying on measurement data.

2.4. Software Performance Anti-Patterns

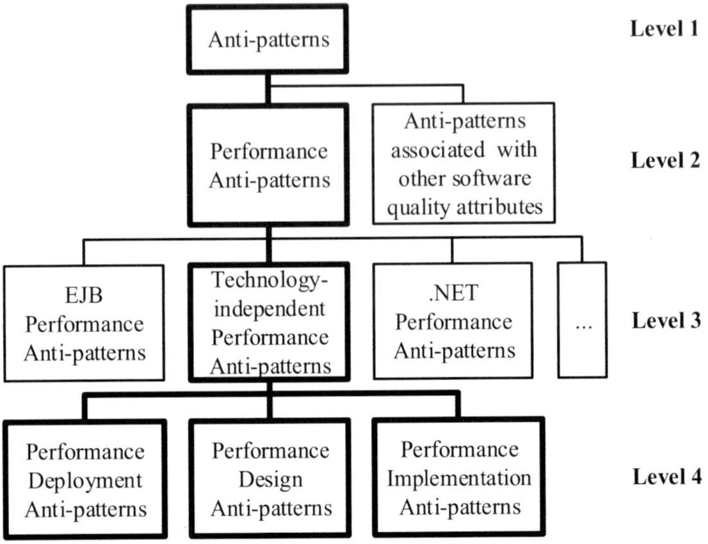

Figure 2.5.: Hierarchy on anti-pattern types (following and adopting Parsons et al., 2008)

In software engineering, design patterns (Gamma et al., 1994) and architectural patterns (Buschmann et al., 2007) constitute established concepts for structuring software. Patterns describe good practices in solving recurrent design problems exhibiting a positive effect on extra-functional software quality attributes such as modularity, maintainability, performance, reliability, etc. Design patterns have their origin in civil engineering. Christopher Alexander introduced a pattern language for describing common solutions to recurrent problems in designing buildings (Alexander, 1982). Design patterns are characterized by a pattern name, a description of the problem to be solved as well as a common solution to the problem. Introducing patterns in the context of software development was a crucial step towards establishing software development as an engineering discipline. Using patterns for design of software brings along multiple benefits. Firstly, patterns explicitly capture expert knowledge in designing software that otherwise is implicit and needs to be learned through years of experience. Secondly, patterns are expressed on an appropriate level of abstraction making it a predestined means for documentation and communication of design decisions. Finally, properly using patterns for the design of software significantly increases software quality along different dimensions.

Koenig, 1998 introduced the notion of *anti-patterns*. Anti-patterns are conceptually similar to patterns, however describe recurrent solutions to design problems which, however, may have a negative effect on different software quality attributes. Brown et al., 1998 describe a number of anti-patterns concerning different software quality attributes. Brown et al. introduce three categories of anti-patterns: *development anti-patterns*, *architecture anti-patterns* and *software project management anti-patterns*. Parsons et al., 2008 extended the classification of anti-patterns as shown in Figure 2.5.

The first level encapsulates all high-level software anti-patterns as, for instance, described by Brown et al., 1998. On Level 2, Parsons et al. distinguish anti-patterns by means of the affected software quality attributes. In this work, we are concerned with anti-patterns that have negative effects on software performance - Software Performance Anti-patterns (SPAs). Within the class of SPAs, Parsons et al. distinguish between technology-specific and technology-independent performance anti-patterns. For instance, in the field of Enterprise Java Beans (EJB), anti-patterns have been described by Tate et al., 2003. In this thesis, we focus on technology-independent SPAs as our goal is to support different target technologies. Technology-independent performance anti-patterns have been introduced by Smith et al., 2000. Finally, performance anti-patterns can be classified into performance *deployment*, *design* or *implementation* anti-patterns. The bold part in Figure 2.5 denotes the scope of anti-patterns that are considered in this work.

The essence of the term *performance anti-pattern* or *SPA* lies in the existence of a description following a certain template, typically including a name, a description and common solutions. In general, any recurrent type of performance problem is a potential SPA. Therefore, in this work we use the terms *performance anti-pattern*, *SPA* and *recurrent performance problem type* as substitutes.

In Table 2.1, we give an overview on SPAs considered in this thesis. Thereby, we provide their names, synonyms, references to their original definitions, as well as short descriptions.

	Name, Reference	Description
(a)	Traffic Jam (Smith et al., 2002b)	The Traffic Jam anti-pattern describes an abstract timing behaviour characterized by a high variance in response times. Overload situations or inefficient computations lead to congestions at software or hardware resources. While some requests get stuck in congestion, others are not affected by the Traffic Jam. The result is a high variance in response times. Corresponding solutions depend on the actual root cause of the Traffic Jam.
(b)	The Ramp (Smith et al., 2002a)	"Any situation in which the amount of processing required to satisfy a request increases over time will produce the behavior [...]" of the Ramp anti-pattern (Smith et al., 2002a). This behaviour leads to degrading performance even if the load does not change over time. Typical causes are manifested in an increasing amount of data, pollution of memory, etc. Solutions to the Ramp anti-pattern depend on concrete root causes.
(c)	Application Hiccups (Tene, 2014)	The Application Hiccups anti-pattern describes a timing behaviour showing a periodic pattern of temporarily increased response times (i.e. hiccups) while during the remaining time the system performance is satisfactory. Hiccups are often caused by periodic tasks that either temporarily overload the system or block other requests (e.g. periodic OS tasks, garbage collection, etc.).

	Name, Reference	Description
(d)	Garbage Collection Hiccups (Tene, 2014)	The Garbage Collection Hiccups anti-pattern is a special form of the Application Hiccups anti-pattern. In this case, garbage collection periods temporarily stop the execution of a virtual machine (e.g. JVM or CLR) leading to a backlog of requests. Processing the backlog leads to increased response times.
(e)	One Lane Bridge Software Bottleneck (Smith et al., 2000)	"One Lane Bridge is a point in the execution where one, or only a few, processes [or threads] may continue to execute concurrently. All other processes must wait. [When an application accesses a database], a lock ensures that only one process may update the associated portion of the database at a time. It may also occur when a set of processes make a synchronous call to another process that is not multi-threaded;" (Smith et al., 2000) In multi-threaded applications, synchronization points (e.g. semaphores) constitute another typical cause for this anti-pattern.
(f)	Tower of Babel (Smith et al., 2003)	This anti-pattern occurs in software systems that need to exchange big amount of data however use different representation formats of data. As format transformation is expensive, data exchange in such contexts may lead to a considerable performance overhead.

	Name, Reference	Description
(g)	Dispensable Synchronization (Grabner, 2010)	"Too often developers make the mistake to over-synchronize, e.g.: excessively-large code sequences are synchronized. Under low load (on the local developers workstation) performance won't be a problem. In a high-load or production environment over-synchronization results in severe performance and scalability problems." (Grabner, 2010) Mitigating Dispensable Synchronization includes reducing the holding time of a resource.
(h)	The Blob God Class (Smith et al., 2000) God Component Bloated Service (Palma et al., 2013)	"A 'god' class [or a Blob] is one that performs most of the work of the system, relegating other classes to minor, supporting roles. [Typically there is] a single, complex controller class [...] that is surrounded by simple classes that serve only as data containers. [...] From a performance perspective, a 'god' class creates problems by causing excessive message traffic. [...] The solution to the 'god' class problem is to refactor the design to distribute intelligence uniformly across the top-level classes in the application." (Smith et al., 2000)

	Name, Reference	Description
(i)	Empty Semi Trucks (Smith et al., 2003) Message Chain (Fowler et al., 2012) Service Chain (Palma et al., 2013)	Empty Semi Trucks is another performance anti-pattern that causes severe messaging behaviour. Besides the actual payload, messages entail data overheads as well as processing overheads (e.g. meta-data and time to process a message). Therefore, sending an aggregated message is often cheaper than sending multiple, small messages. The Empty Semi Trucks anti-pattern describes the problem of sending many small messages instead of conducting an aggregation. Often, this anti-patterns is caused by inefficient use of bandwidth or inefficient interfaces. Message aggregation and interface coupling are typical solutions to this anti-pattern.
(j)	Excessive Dynamic Allocation (Smith et al., 2000)	"With dynamic allocation, objects are created when they are first accessed [...] and then destroyed when they are no longer needed. [...] While the overhead for creating and destroying a single object may be small, when a large number of objects are frequently created and then destroyed, the performance impact may be significant." (Smith et al., 2000) Pooling expensive resources (e.g. database connections, Threads, etc.) is a solution to this anti-pattern. Furthermore, when applicable, resources can be shared among different tasks to avoid unnecessary creation of individual resource instances.

	Name, Reference	Description
(k)	The Stifle (Dudney et al., 2003) n+1 Query Trap (Still, 2013)	The Stifle anti-pattern occurs if data is retrieved from a database by means of many similar (or equal) database queries. This problem often occurs as a result of improperly using an entity framework (or Object-relational Mapping). As each database request entails a considerable overhead, the high amount of database requests leads to a performance problem. In order to resolve a Stifle problem, SQL queries should be adopted to retrieve data by means of some few database requests.
(l)	Circuitous Treasure Hunt (Smith et al., 2000)	With the Circuitous Treasure Hunt anti-pattern, "[...] software retrieves data from a first table, uses those results to search a second table, retrieves data from that table, and so on, until the 'ultimate results' are obtained. [...] The impact on performance is the large amount of database processing required each time the 'ultimate results' are needed." (Smith et al., 2000) In order to solve this anti-pattern, the data organization of the application needs to be refactored to provide simpler access to required ensembles of data.

	Name, Reference	Description
(m)	Dormant References (Rayside et al., 2007)	A *dormant reference* points to an object that will never be used in the future anymore. Hence, the Dormant References anti-pattern constitutes a memory-leak that may lead to increased garbage collection activities. Furthermore, the performance of algorithms that operate on distending collections containing dormant references is impaired by this anti-pattern as well. Hence, resources and objects that are not required anymore should be dereferenced to allow garbage collection to properly clean up memory.
(n)	Session as a Cache (Kopp, 2011)	"The Session caching anti-pattern refers to the misuse of the HTTP session as data cache. The HTTP session is used to store user data or state that needs to survive a single HTTP request." (Kopp, 2011) This anti-pattern can lead to huge memory demands when considering a high amount of parallel users. Instead, developers should use a central, dedicated cache that allows to manage the maximum amount of the memory used for caching.
(o)	Large Temporary Objects (Kopp, 2011)	The creation of large objects in memory may lead to increased memory management activity (swapping or garbage collection) and, thus, impair software performance. Hence, when processing big files, pipelining should be used to avoid loading of huge objects into the main memory.

	Name, Reference	Description
(p)	Sisyphus Database Retrieval (Dugan et al., 2002)	This anti-pattern describes the problem of retrieving a huge amount of data from a database although only a small subset is actually processed by the application. This problem is often due to improper formulation of SQL queries or insufficient fragmentation. With a growing database size, the performance of retrieving the data from the database degrades. Using proper Where-clauses in SQL and applying paging in interactive systems allows to mitigate the effect of the Sisyphus Database Retrieval anti-pattern.
(q)	Spaghetti Query (Karwin, 2010)	The Spaghetti Query (SQL) anti-pattern is a counterpart to the Stifle anti-pattern. Instead of splitting a very complex task into manageable blocks of work, with this anti-pattern developers try to accomplish such complex tasks as one SQL query. However, overly complex database queries may lead to significantly worse processing performance than some few, simpler queries in sum.
(r)	Unnecessary Processing (Smith et al., 2002a)	The Unnecessary Processing anti-pattern describes the problem of conducting computations that are not required at that time, or are unnecessary at all. For instance, conducting a calculation that is required only in one part of a subsequent branching-block is not required if the control flow takes another branch. Hence, any calculations should be conducted when it is clear that they are required.

	Name, Reference	Description
(s)	Spin Wait Busy Waiting (Boroday et al., 2005)	The Spin Wait anti-pattern describes the problem of actively waiting for a condition (i.e. repeatedly checking the condition). Thereby, the actively waiting thread consumes processing resources without conducting any useful task. Consequently, busy waiting has a significant impact on the CPU utilization and, thus, on the performance of the system. Instead, waiting threads should be set into sleep mode and should be notified when any state concerning the corresponding condition has been changed.
(t)	Insufficient Caching (Reitbauer, 2010)	With respect to databases, any database request that can be avoided is a potential improvement in performance. When database requests are repeated again and again, caching is a common means to avoid repeated database requests. However, often caching is not completely understood so that caches are improperly used or omitted at all. Properly setting up caching so that data can be efficiently used is an important factor for software performance.
(u)	Wrong Cache Strategy (Grabner, 2010)	As a counterpart to the Insufficient Caching anti-pattern, the Wrong Caching Strategy anti-pattern describes the problem of memory pollution through improper use of a cache. Hence, if a cache has a high cache-miss rate, objects are permanently created and dropped from the cache. This leads to an increased pollution of memory and, thus, an increased memory management overhead that impairs the performance.

	Name, Reference	Description
(v)	Unbalanced Processing (Smith et al., 2002a)	The Unbalanced Processing anti-pattern describes the problem of unbalanced execution of concurrent tasks leading to an unbalanced utilization of corresponding resources. Long tasks may block a resource for long periods of time. Remaining tasks are distributed among remaining resources degrading the throughput.
(w)	Single-threaded Code (Smith et al., 2002a)	Single-threaded applications cannot make use of concurrent execution, hence, waisting available resources and potential for performance improvement. This anti-pattern is a special case of the Unbalanced Processing anti-pattern. To resolve this anti-pattern, independent tasks of an application should be designed in a way that they can be executed in parallel.
(x)	Pipe and Filter Architecture (Smith et al., 2002a)	In a pipe and filter architecture, the slowest filter determines the throughput of the entire chain. Remaining filters have to "wait" for the slowest filter, leading to unbalanced processing. As a solution, pipe and filter architectures should be designed in a way that individual filters exhibit a similar throughput.
(y)	Chatty Service (Palma et al., 2013) (Dudney et al., 2003)	"Chatty Service corresponds to a set of services that exchange a lot of small data of primitive types, usually with a Data Service antipattern. The Chatty Service is also characterized by a high number of method invocations. Chatty Services chat a lot with each other." (Palma et al., 2013)

	Name, Reference	Description
(z)	The Knot (Palma et al., 2013) (Rotem-Gal-Oz et al., 2012)	"The Knot is a set of very low cohesive services, which are tightly coupled. These services are thus less reusable. Due to this complex architecture, the availability of these services may be low, and their response time high." (Palma et al., 2013)
(aa)	Bottleneck Service (Palma et al., 2013)	"Bottleneck Service is a service that is highly used by other services or clients. It has a high incoming and outgoing coupling. Its response time can be high because it may be used by too many external clients, for which clients may need to wait to get access to the service." (Palma et al., 2013)

Table 2.1.: Software Performance Anti-patterns

3. Automatic Performance Problem Diagnostics

The Automatic Performance Problem Diagnostics (APPD) approach introduced in this thesis automates measurement-based detection and root cause analysis of software performance problems. In this chapter, we provide an overview on the APPD approach and explain its constituent parts. Section 3.1 explains the high-level idea behind the APPD approach. An overview on constituent parts of the APPD approach as well as on their interrelations is given in Section 3.2. In Section 3.3, we discuss the assumptions and the scope of applicability of the APPD approach. Finally, based on the research questions from Section 1.3, we derive seven research hypotheses that guide the remainder of this work. Section 3.5 summarizes this chapter. Early ideas on the APPD approach have been published in (Wert, 2012; Wert, 2013; Wert et al., 2013) and constitute the basis for this thesis and, especially, this chapter.

3.1. Overview

To shape the meaning of the term *software performance problem* (or just *performance problem*) in the work at hand, we provide the following definition:

Definition 1. *A* ***software performance problem*** *is a violation of specified performance requirements aroused by design, implementation or deployment failures that, under certain load situations, propagate through the software system as a chain of causes and symptoms, and are observable as externally visible symptoms.*

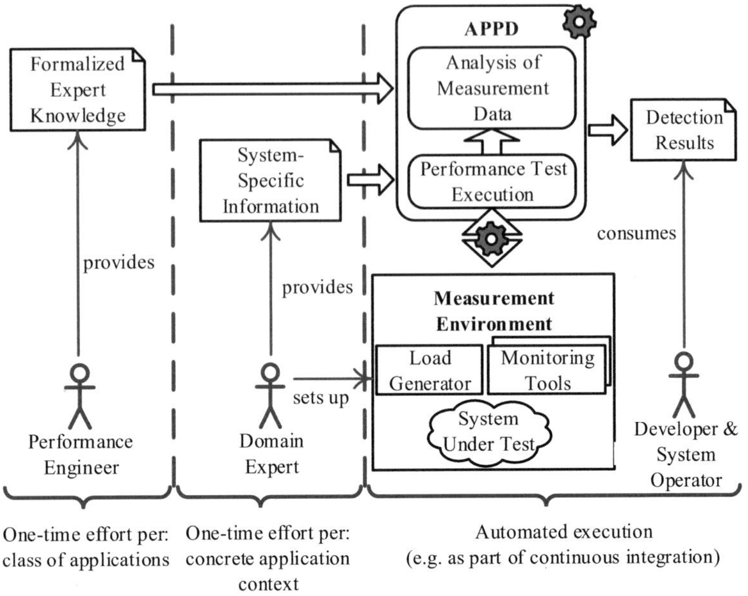

Figure 3.1.: General overview on the approach for automated, experiment-based diagnostics of performance problems

This definition is closely related to the high-level idea of the APPD approach as described in the following. As stated in Definition 1, the root causes of performance problems are manifested in design, implementation or deployment failures. Many of these failures follow certain patterns which are recurrently observable in different contexts. Software Performance Anti-patterns (SPAs) (cf. Section 2.4) describe recurrent types of performance failures and common ways of resolving the failures. APPD leverages the recurrent nature of SPAs as a knowledge base for a generic performance problem diagnostics approach. In particular, recurrent failures imply recurrent processes and rules to detect corresponding failures which lays the foundation for APPD. Figure 3.1 illustrates the high level idea behind APPD.

First, APPD requires *performance engineers* to externalize and formalize their expert knowledge. This includes knowledge about typical SPAs leading to performance problems in different contexts, their symptoms, possible root causes as well as interdependencies between SPAs. Furthermore, the expert knowledge comprises information about proper execution of performance tests for the detection of corresponding performance problems. For instance, applying an appropriate load and measuring the right performance metrics is essential for successful diagnostics of performance problems. Finally, a set of data processing steps and data analysis rules are required to be able to draw conclusions from measurement data collected during the performance tests. While SPAs are specific for certain types of applications, within individual application types (e.g. three-tier enterprise applications) SPAs describe in a generic, system-independent way recurrent patterns of performance problems. Hence, SPAs as well as processes and rules to detect them are generically applicable on most application contexts within a certain type of applications. Thus, for each application type it is only a one-time effort to externalize and formalize the expert knowledge required to detect performance problems that result from corresponding SPAs.

For each concrete context where APPD is applied, a *domain expert* once has to provide system-specific information, such as performance requirements, load scripts describing the user behaviour, expected maximum load, etc. Furthermore, the domain expert is responsible for setting up and providing a description on the *measurement environment*, comprising the System Under Test (SUT), load generators and performance monitoring tools. Both providing system-specific information and setting up the measurement environment needs to be done once per concrete application context of APPD.

Given the formalized expert knowledge, the system-specific information and a set up measurement environment, an implementation of our APPD approach automatically scans the SUT for potential performance problems. Thereto, a series of performance tests is executed utilizing the aforementioned monitoring tools for gathering performance data. Analysis rules, derived from the expert knowledge of performance engineers, are applied to the measurement data in order to identify potential indications for performance problems. The detection results, containing a list of detected performance problems and their root causes, are provided to the stakeholders of the development of the SUT (e.g. developers, system operators, etc.). With that information, stakeholders can directly initiate the solution process to resolve the detected performance problems. Hereby, the stakeholders can be further supported by solution engineering approaches as described by Heger et al., 2014.

3.2. Constituent Parts of Automatic Performance Problem Diagnostics

In this section, we introduce the constituent parts of the APPD approach. The APPD approach combines several concepts each addressing one or more research questions described in Section 1.3. Figure 3.2 shows the different concepts introduced in this thesis as part of APPD and illustrates their orchestration to the overall approach. The bottom of Figure 3.2 illustrates the *Measurement Environment* that encapsulates the specific characteristics of a concrete application context. This includes different specific tools for load generation and monitoring. The upper part of the figure schematically shows the constituent parts of the generic APPD approach.

To bridge the gap between a generic diagnostics approach and specific application contexts, we introduce an *abstraction layer* on top of the target measurement environment (cf. Part I in Figure 3.2). The abstraction layer comprises description languages and data structures which allow to specify performance tests and their results in a generic, system-independent way. In this way, the abstraction layer constitutes the basis for a common interface between our diagnostics approach and the variety of different load generators and monitoring tools. Existing load generators and monitoring tools, which do not directly support the formalisms defined in our abstraction layer, require additional, lightweight adapters for the transformation of our generic formalisms to the corresponding tool-specific specifications.

Precise diagnostics of performance problems requires extraction of fine-grained and detailed performance metrics from a SUT. Furthermore, the measurement data must not be distorted by the monitoring process in order to avoid inaccurate diagnostics. As these are conflicting requirements, they cannot be realized simultaneously in a single performance test (*RQ 3*, Section 1.3). To overcome this problem, we introduce the concept of *Systematic Selective Experimentation (SSE)* (cf. Part II(a)), whereby comprehensive performance tests are broken down to series of multiple tests with selective, lightweight monitoring. In order to realize the SSE concept, a way of adapting monitoring instructions of the target SUT is required. To this end, we use the Adaptable Instrumentation and Monitoring (AIM) approach (Part II(b), Wert et al., 2015a) for target applications based on managed programming languages (such as Java or .NET) which allows to adapt monitoring instruc-

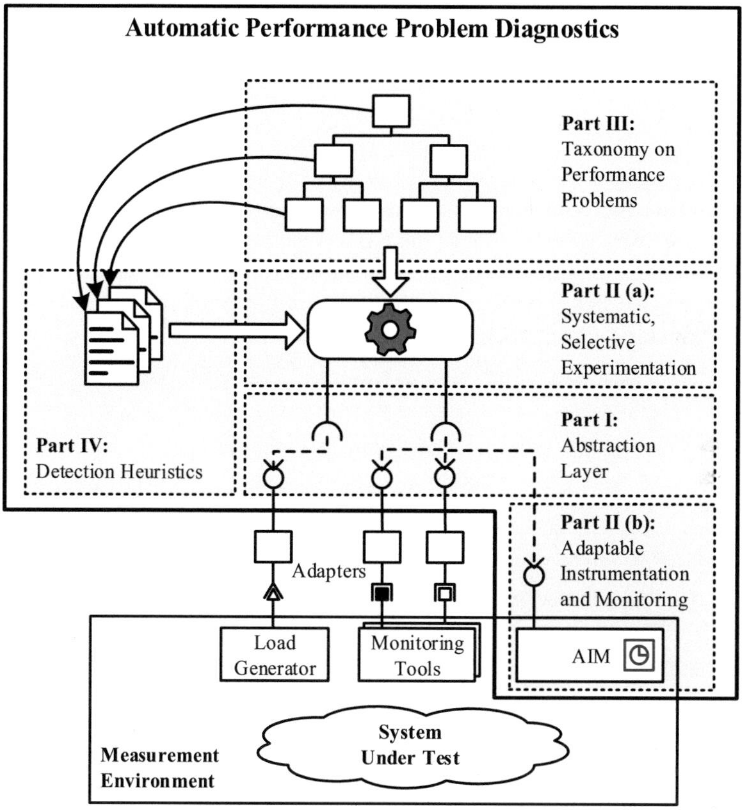

Figure 3.2.: The concepts behind the APPD approach

tions dynamically during run-time of the SUT. Though AIM significantly increases the practicability of our APPD approach, the availability of AIM is not a mandatory criterion for the applicability of APPD as long as the monitoring instructions of the target application can be adapted in another way (e.g. by rebuilding, redeploying and restarting the target application).

A *taxonomy on performance problems* (cf. Part III) and a set of *detection heuristics* (cf. Part IV) constitute the formalized knowledge on performance problem diagnostics provided by performance experts (cf. Figure 3.1). Allowing to describe the knowledge on performance problems in a generic, system-independent way, the taxonomy and the detection heuristics address research questions *RQ 1* and *RQ 6* (cf. Section 1.3). The taxonomy on performance problems provides a means to systematize the search for the root causes of observed performance problems. Serving as a decision tree (Rokach et al., 2008), the taxonomy guides the SSE concept and inherently addresses research question *RQ 8* (cf. Section 1.3) by reducing the amount of required performance tests to find a root cause of a performance problem. For each node in the taxonomy, there is a detection heuristic specifying rules for execution of performance tests and subsequent analysis steps. In particular, the heuristics comprise knowledge about how to detect corresponding performance problem symptoms or root causes.

Finally, we align the APPD approach to the concepts of established software development processes. Thereby, APPD reuses artifacts which already exist in the corresponding development processes. In this way, we minimize the number of tasks which need to be conducted solely for the application of APPD.

3.2.1. Systematic, Selective Experimentation

As mentioned before, all measurement-based performance evaluation approaches face the trade-off between high resolution of measurement data and high measurement accuracy. This trade-off becomes especially critical when performance evaluation approaches require data with a high resolution and at the same time a wide scope of points where data needs to be collected from. Performance problem diagnostics falls into this category of performance evaluation approaches, as it requires high data resolution for the ability to narrow down and pinpoint the root causes of performance problems. At the same time, the location of a performance problem cannot be foreseen, resulting in a wide scope of points where data potentially may be gathered from. In order to realize both requirements within a single performance test, excessive instrumentation is required. This means that the target application has to be comprehensively instrumented on a fine-grained level. However, excessive instrumentation introduces an immense overhead which may distort the measurement data impairing the accuracy of performance problem diagnostics.

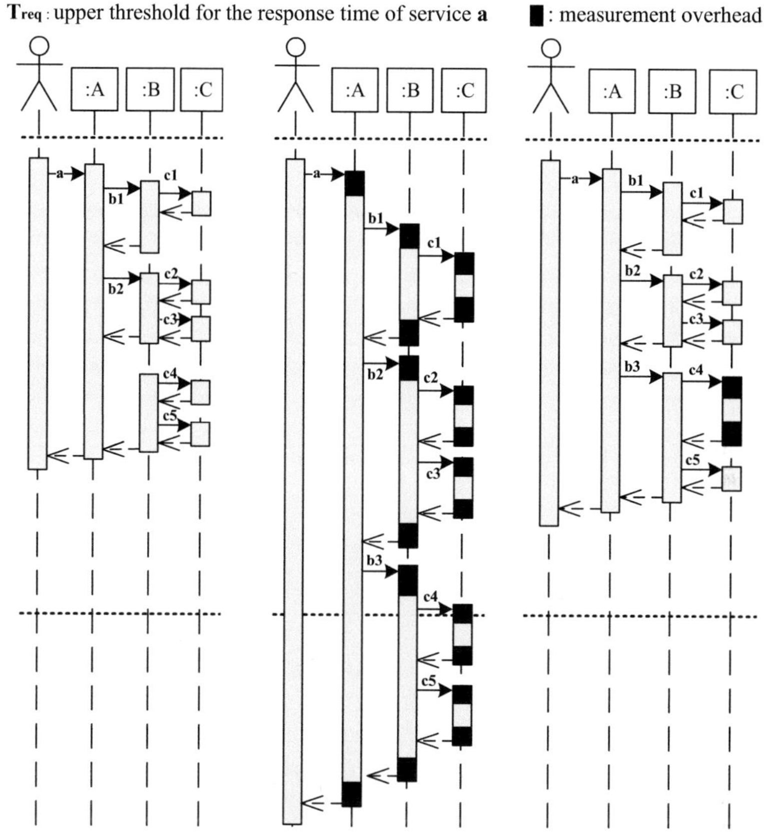

(a) Without instrumentation

(b) Excessive instrumentation

(c) Selective instrumentation

Figure 3.3.: Measurement overhead with excessive and selective instrumentation

Figure 3.3 qualitatively illustrates the measurement overhead introduced by excessive data gathering and selective gathering, and demonstrates how it may impair the accuracy of performance problem diagnostics. Figure 3.3a shows the call hierarchy of a hypothetical system service **a** as a UML sequence diagram. As a performance requirement, the time span T_{req} defines the upper threshold for the response time of service **a**. Let us assume that a performance problem is reported by a performance problem diagnostics approach if the response time of service **a** exceeds T_{req}. Without instrumentation, the service **a** fulfills the requirement T_{req}. Applying excessive instrumentation for performance problem diagnostics introduces a measurement overhead in each sub-call (cf. Figure 3.3b). Though the overhead in each call is relatively small, in sum, the measurement overheads accumulate to a considerable response time overhead of service **a**. As a result, the service **a** violates the performance requirement T_{req} leading to a falsely detected performance problem. By contrast, applying selective instrumentation, as depicted in Figure 3.3c, introduces only a negligible measurement overhead. However, when applying selective instrumentation, in a single performance test the collected data is inherently limited to a very specific, narrow scope.

Our SSE concept combines selective instrumentation with systematic experimentation in order to achieve the possibility of gathering high-resolution measurement data from a wide scope with a minimal measurement overhead. The core idea is to conduct series of independent performance tests with different, goal-oriented, selective instrumentation instructions. The measurement data collected in one experiment can be (automatically) analyzed to take decisions on the experiment configuration and instrumentation of the next experiment. Similar to the CADA (Collect-Analyze-Decide-Act) feedback loop in software engineering (Cheng et al., 2009) and the MAPE loop (Monitor-Analyze-Plan-Execute) in the area of autonomic computing (Kephart et al., 2003), the SSE concept defines an experimentation process for performance analysis tasks as illustrated by the loop in Figure 3.4. The process starts with a goal-oriented, *selective instrumentation* of the target system. During the *measurement* activity, measurement data are gathered that originate from the instrumentation. Subsequently, the measurement data is *analyzed* with respect to the specific overall goal of the corresponding performance analysis task. Based on the analysis results, decisions can be made with respect to further analysis activities that may prescribe an adaptation of the selective instrumentation.

For instance, for performance problem diagnostics, we may start to analyze the high level performance metrics of the SUT with the first experiment.

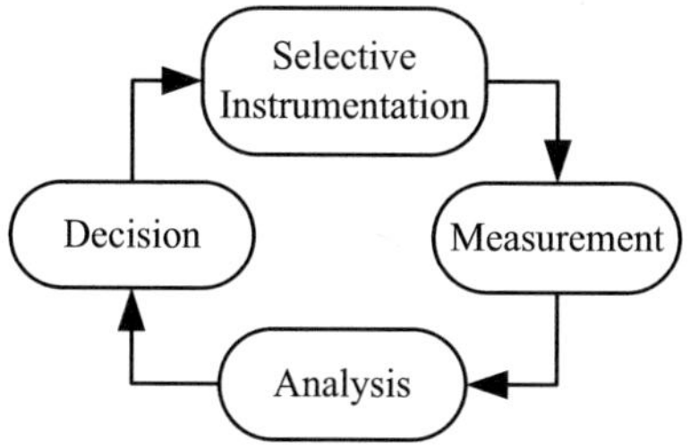

Figure 3.4.: Instrumentation-Measurement-Analysis-Decision loop

Based on the analysis results on the corresponding measurement data, we decide where to search further for the root cause of an occurring performance problem. This systematic diagnostics process is described in more detail in Section 3.2.2.

Compared to a single experiment with excessive instrumentation, the data gathered with SSE may cover the same width of scope, but, the data exhibits a higher accuracy due to a significantly smaller measurement overhead. A consequence of the SSE concept is a different nature of the gathered data. With excessive instrumentation within a single performance test, the gathered measurement values can be correlated on a per-instance basis, which is not possible with data gathered with the SSE concept. Let us illustrate that consideration on an example. In the example of Figure 3.3b, we can calculate the average portion p of sub-call **b1** of the response time of service **a** by simply dividing the response times $R_{b1,i}$ of **b1** by the corresponding response times $R_{a,i}$ of **a**. Thereby, I is the set of call instances of service **a**:

$$p = \frac{1}{|I|} \sum_{i \in I} \frac{R_{b1,i}}{R_{a,i}} \tag{3.1}$$

This simple calculation of p is possible, because, in the case of excessive instrumentation, the values $R_{b1,i}$ and $R_{a,i}$ belong to the same call instance $i \in I$ of service **a**. In particular, the following applies:

$$|R_a| = |R_{b1}|, \quad R_a = \{R_{a,i}\}_i, \quad R_{b1} = \{R_{b1,i}\}_i \tag{3.2}$$

By contrast, with selective instrumentation, we cannot apply Equation 3.1 to calculate p due to the fact that the response times $R_a = \{R_{a,i}\}_i$ of service **a** and the response times $R_{b1} = \{R_{b1,j}\}_j$ of sub-call **b1** are measured in different, independent experiments. Hence, there are no direct correspondences between any elements $r_a \in R_a$ with any element $r_{b1} \in R_{b1}$. However, in enterprise software systems, performance metrics (such as response times) follow different, mostly multi-modal statistical distributions (Rohr et al., 2008; Mielke, 2006). Hence, we can employ measures of descriptive statistics (e.g. average, median, variance, etc.) to conduct calculations and correlations on the measurement values of different performance metrics. For instance in our example, p denotes the *average* portion of sub-call **b1** of the response time of service **a**. Hence, we can use the arithmetic means of R_a, respectively R_{b1}, to calculate p:

$$p = \frac{\overline{R_{b1}}}{\overline{R_a}}, \quad \overline{R_a} = \frac{1}{|R_a|} \sum_{x \in R_a} x, \quad \overline{R_{b1}} = \frac{1}{|R_{b1}|} \sum_{y \in R_{b1}} y \tag{3.3}$$

To sum up, the SSE concept allows to retrieve high resolution data from a wide measurement scope while keeping measurement overhead negligible. SSE entails two implications. First, SSE increases the amount of experiments to be executed and, thus, increases the overall experimentation time. Second, SSE can only be applied if correspondences of individual measurement values from different experiments are not of interest, but the entirety of individual performance metrics is important, represented by statistical distributions. Though the SSE concept introduces two additional implications which need further considerations to circumvent corresponding limitations, SSE provides an elegant solution to combine the requirements for high measurement accuracy and high-resolution measurement data for our APPD approach.

3.2.2. A Taxonomy on Performance Problems as a Decision Tree

There is a large body of literature defining different Software Performance Anti-patterns (SPAs) and typical, corresponding root causes (cf. Section 2.4). The result is a huge set of root causes which may potentially lead to a performance problem in a SUT. As described in the previous section, the SSE concept provides a way to conduct measurement-based root cause analysis without sacrificing measurement accuracy. There are different ways of employing the SSE concept for performance problem diagnostics. A *naive approach* is to conduct a brute-force scan for all potential root causes on the SUT by executing an SSE experiment for each potential root cause. However, this naive approach leads to a huge amount of required experiments, which results in a very long overall experimentation time, rendering the naive diagnostics approach impractical. The alternative is to follow a more systematic approach which is based on the following considerations.

If a software design, implementation or deployment failure in a concrete SUT leads to a performance problem, then a workload configuration exists under which the problem becomes visible in terms of symptoms, such as high end-to-end response times, low throughput, high CPU utilization, etc. Besides the symptoms which are visible from outside the application, performance problems exhibit application-internal indications in form of distinctive performance characteristics. In many cases, following the path from symptoms to the application-internal indications leads to the root cause of the performance problem. Furthermore, many root causes of performance problems exhibit similar application-internal indications and, in turn, application-internal indications result in similar symptoms. Consolidating these considerations yields a taxonomy of symptoms, application-internal indications and root causes. Thereby, there are only some few high-level symptoms, a bigger set of descending application-internal indications which may be spread across multiple layers of the taxonomy and, finally, there is a huge amount of potential root causes. Figure 3.5 illustrates the idea behind structuring performance problems along a taxonomy. At the very top, the category *Performance Problem* constitutes the root of the taxonomy subsuming all behavioural patterns leading to the high-level symptom of violated performance requirements. In the levels below, the taxonomy distinguishes different categories of performance problems, whereby the types of performance problems become more specific the deeper they are located in the taxonomy. The root causes of performance problems are represented by the leaf nodes of the taxonomy. In general, there is no strict separation between symptoms and causes of performance problems. In fact, the terms *symptom* and *cause* describe roles of individual taxonomy nodes in a relationship between two nodes. In particular, each inner node of the taxonomy is a potential cause for the parent node, and a symptom for its descendant nodes, respectively. Let us further consider the exemplary taxonomy branch in Figure 3.5. A *single user performance problem* and a *scalability problem* are two potential causes for a violation of performance requirements. Within the category of scalability problems, we further distinguish between typical *software bottlenecks* and other causes for scalability problems. External calls and software synchronization (i.e. software locks) are some typical root causes for a software bottleneck.

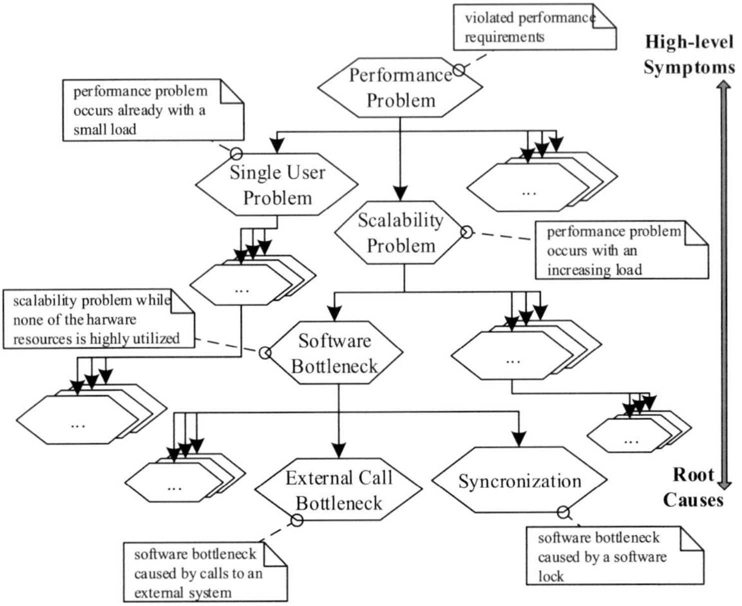

Figure 3.5.: Concept of a Performance Problem Taxonomy

A taxonomy on performance problems has positive aspects in two respects: Firstly, the taxonomy encapsulates explicit knowledge on the relationships between individual symptoms and causes of performance problems. Even aside from automation of performance problem diagnostics, such a taxonomy provides a systematic guidance for (potentially inexperienced) performance engineers when manually diagnosing performance problems. Following such a taxonomy, performance engineers may come more efficiently to a valid diagnostics result, than without any explicit procedure. Secondly, in the context of our APPD approach, the taxonomy constitutes a core part determining the search process for root causes of performance problems. More precisely, the taxonomy guides the execution of experiments while following our SSE concept. Thereby, the taxonomy serves as a decision tree (Rokach et al., 2008). At the beginning, a light-weight, selective experiment (cf. Section 3.2.1) is executed, gathering only the measurement data which is required to take decision on the existence of the high-level symptom of violated requirements in the SUT (i.e. *Performance Problem* in Figure 3.5). In this particular case, end-to-end response times of user transactions are sufficient to decide whether high-level performance requirements are violated. Assuming the case, that a violation of performance requirements is observed, our APPD approach executes further selective experiments for the child nodes of the taxonomy's root node. This process is recursively repeated until a leaf node of the taxonomy is reached, meaning that a root cause of an observed performance problem has been identified. By contrast, if a symptom, which is reflected by a certain taxonomy node, cannot be found in the SUT, the APPD approach skips the whole sub-tree beneath the corresponding taxonomy node. This consideration is based on the following rationale: With APPD, we are searching for actual performance problems instead of potential performance anti-patterns. Hence, APPD looks for *guilty* performance anti-patterns that emerge as performance problems and, thus, are observable from the end-user perspective. Consequently, if a cause for a performance problem is *guilty*, then all taxonomy nodes on the path from the corresponding guilty node to the root node must be observable. Vice versa, if a symptom is not observable, then all descending causes in the taxonomy are not observable, hence, are not *guilty*.

Compared to the naive, brute-force approach, the taxonomy-based approach of applying SSE for performance problem diagnostics is more systematic and, therefore, also more efficient. Reducing the amount of required experiment executions, the taxonomy-based approach significantly increases the practicability of our APPD approach.

For each node of the taxonomy, a *detection heuristic* (cf. Part IV in Figure 3.2) is required that specifies a set of experiments to be executed for the corresponding taxonomy node and an analysis strategy responsible to take decisions on the existence of the performance problem, symptom or cause in the SUT. Thereby, the heuristics utilize the abstraction languages (cf. Part I in Figure 3.2) to specify the execution plan of experiments and the measurement data to be collected. In Chapter 5, we introduce the abstraction languages and describe the detection heuristics in detail in Chapter 6. In Chapter 4, we further elaborate on the formalization and instantiation of the taxonomy, and explain in more detail its role as an integral part of the APPD approach.

3.3. Scope of Applicability

In this section, we discuss the scope of applicability of the APPD approach, including limitations on the application context of APPD and its integration with established software development processes.

3.3.1. Assumptions on the Application Context

Though our APPD approach is designed to be generically applicable on different, independent application cases, its scope of application is limited by some assumptions setting the boundaries for the target domain of software systems APPD can be applied on. In the following, we list and discuss the assumptions on the application contexts of APPD:

Interactive Enterprise Software Systems Typically, software systems from different domains (e.g. enterprise software systems, embedded software systems, operating systems, etc.) encounter different classes of performance problems or different manifestations of performance problems. Consequently, the concepts for performance problem diagnostics vary from one domain of software systems to another. Hence, developing a diagnostics approach which can be generically applied across all domains of software systems is basically impossible. Many types of performance problems considered in this work may occur only in enterprise software systems based on three-tier architectures. Therefore, the APPD approach is designed for diagnosing enterprise software systems. Furthermore, some detection heuristics elaborated in this thesis assume a user-based target system. This means that the workload applied on the SUT is constituted from interactive user requests. Furthermore, we focus on enterprise software systems where the end-to-end response times are higher prioritized than the throughput of user requests. In particular, we abstain from considering systems that need to be optimized for throughput rather than for low response times. The same consideration applies to the types of performance problems. We focus on performance problems that express themselves in high response times rather than in low throughput.

Focus on Application Logic As stated in the previous paragraph, APPD is designed for three-tier software systems. A three-tier software system comprises a presentation layer, an application logic layer, and a persistence layer. Though many performance problems in enterprise software systems occur due to failures in the presentation layer (e.g. inefficient Java script code in Web-based applications) or inefficiencies in the persistence of data (e.g. improper database schemas, missing database indexes, etc.), a fairly big amount of performance problems originates from the application logic, or improper use of the persistence service from the application layer (Grabner, 2010). In this thesis, we focus on performance problems which originate from the application logic layer. In particular, we abstain from improving front-end performance and optimizing database configurations for better performance. However, besides performance problems which are purely manifested in the application logic, we consider types of performance problems which are due to improper use of services (e.g. data persistence).

Common Programming Concepts The focus of APPD on enterprise software systems implies that the programming languages of the target application support common programming concepts which are established in the domain of enterprise software systems (e.g. database APIs, APIs for object relational mapping, Messaging APIs, Garbage Collection, REST APIs, etc.). Moreover, some of the performance problem types investigated in this thesis and the corresponding heuristics rely on the existence of these common concepts in the programming language of the target application. In particular, the abstraction layer on top of different SUTs highly depends on a common understanding of these concepts, for instance in order to specify instrumentation instruction on the target application in an abstract, yet unambiguous way. Consequently, our APPD approach is designed for modern-day managed run-times (e.g. Java (Stärk et al., 2001), .NET (Box et al., 2002), Ruby (Flanagan et al., 2008), etc.) as they support the mentioned concepts.

3.3.2. Alignment with Established Software Development Processes

Usually, the development of a software product follows one of the established software development processes (Sommerville, 2007), or a variations of those. In order to ensure acceptance and practicability of our APPD approach, it must not intervene the underlying development process with additional, significant efforts, manual tasks or even additional process steps. On the contrary, the approach should be aligned with the established software development processes to take advantage of artifacts and tasks which are part of the development process. Reuse of existing artifacts may significantly reduce the manual effort to apply APPD on a software development project. To this end, we have to identify which inputs required by APPD are covered by artifacts of established software development processes. The following inputs are required to apply APPD:

Testing Environment As controlled performance experiments are a crucial part of the APPD approach, a testing environment is required that allows to evaluate the SUT under different load and stress conditions without affecting the real users in operations. The testing environment must comprise a SUT which is a representative projection of the operational setup. Furthermore, for gathering of measurement data, instrumentation and monitoring tools need to be set up. Finally, end users of the target application need to be emulated using a load generator, which is another important part of the testing environment.

Measurement Tool Adapters As mentioned in Section 3.2, on top of concrete SUTs, APPD provides an abstraction layer comprising description languages which abstract from the realization of specific instrumentation and monitoring tools as well as load generators. As existing monitoring tools and load generators do not directly support our description languages, adapters for these monitoring tools need to be set up. Alternatively, our

Adaptable Instrumentation and Monitoring (AIM) approach can be applied, which directly supports the description languages defined in the abstraction layer of APPD (Wert et al., 2015a).

Usage Profile In order to emulate the end user behaviour with a load generator, the user behaviour needs to be explicitly specified in a usage profile. Specifying a deterministic sequence of user interactions in a so-called *user script* is a common approach to describe the usage behaviour (cf. Section 2.3). Besides the deterministic way of describing the usage behaviour, other, probabilistic approaches exist (van Hoorn et al., 2008; van Hoorn et al., 2014). For the application of APPD, the type of the usage profile is irrelevant, however, the usage profile needs to be directly parsable by the used load generator. Furthermore for the application of APPD, we assume that the load intensity during an experiment is stable. In particular, the load intensity must not exhibit periodic patterns like oscillation, burst behaviour or any trends.

Performance Requirements The decision on the existence of a performance problem in a SUT is always relative to the performance requirements for the SUT. In particular, we cannot identify any performance problems without at least knowing the high-level performance requirements for a specific SUT. High-level performance requirements describe from the perspective of the end users the maximum load, and the worst case performance behaviour which must not be exceeded under the maximum load. Hence, high-level performance requirements are an important input for APPD, enabling APPD to take decisions on the existence of performance problems.

Regardless of the type, all software development processes, from the waterfall model through incremental iterative processes to agile methods, cover in one form or another the activities of the five basic phases of the software life cycle: *Requirement Definition, System Design, Implementation, Integration and Testing,* and *Operation and Maintenance* (Sommerville, 2007). The *Requirement Definition* and *Integration and Testing* life cycle phases are particularly important for the application of APPD. The Requirement Definition phase serves for the elicitation of different types of requirements including functional as well as extra-functional requirements. Hence, the result of a thoroughly conducted requirements elicitation should comprise performance requirements which can be used for performance testing. The Integration and Testing phase evaluates the integration of software components to a software system with respect to different functional and extra-functional aspects. In particular, performance testing is a part of the Integration and Testing phase, constituting the basis for the performance experiments of APPD. Consequently, a testing environment as well as usage profiles reflecting the end user behaviour are some artifacts which should exist in a software project which thoroughly follows a software development process. Based on this considerations we may conclude, that except for the measurement tool adapters, all inputs required for the application of APPD are covered by existing artifacts of software projects which strictly follow a development process.

Unfortunately in practice, many software projects follow only to a very limited extent a certain software development process. In particular, many software projects lack awareness for software performance so that performance considerations are omitted at all. In such a case, neither performance requirements nor the testing environment exists. On the one hand, applying APPD in such a case would require additional manual effort to elicit performance requirements, setting up a testing environment and capturing the end user behaviour for the creation of usage profiles. On the other hand, conducting these tasks is required for any performance evaluation approach which is based on performance tests. Furthermore, considering the inputs required by APPD, we may conclude that except for the measurement tool adapters, the inputs required by APPD are not specific to our approach, but, constitute general requirements for all test-based performance evaluation approaches. To sum up, in performance-aware software projects our APPD approach can be integrated into the underlying development process, whereby existing artifacts can be used for most inputs required for APPD. In software projects which are not performance-aware, the application of APPD entails a higher effort which, however, is common in all measurement-based performance evaluation activities. In general, the advantages of APPD are greater in incremental, iterative software development processes, where the stakeholders can benefit from regular executions of APPD as part of continuous integration.

3.4. Research Hypotheses

From the goals and research questions described in Section 1.3 as well as the constituent parts of the APPD approach (cf. Figure 3.2), we derive seven research hypotheses that constitute the basis for the validation of the APPD approach. In Chapter 7, we use these hypotheses to derive refined validation questions for a thorough validation of the APPD approach:

Hypothesis 1 — *There is an adequately big set of performance problem types which are generically detectable by a set of explicit experiments and analysis rules.*

There is a large body of literature describing different types of performance problems (also known as Software Performance Anti-patterns (SPAs)) (cf. Section 2.4). While some of these performance problem types are detectable by applying experimentation and corresponding analysis rules, others may be not suitable to be detected by experimentation or cannot be covered by generic rules. Hence, it is important to conduct a categorization of performance problem types, to identify those, which are per-se detectable by our APPD approach. (*RQ 1*, Section 1.3)

Hypothesis 2 — *Different types of performance problems, their symptoms and causes share common characteristics allowing to structure them hierarchically along a taxonomy.*

Based on the idea that all different types of performance problems lead to some few observable symptoms, we investigate the relationships between different symptoms and causes of performance problems with the goal to create a generic taxonomy on performance problems in the context of enterprise software applications. (*RQ 1*, *RQ 2*, Section 1.3)

Hypothesis 3 — *A taxonomy on performance problems systematizes performance problem diagnostics and increases its efficiency.*

With this research hypothesis, we investigate to which degree a taxonomy on performance problems (cf. *Hypothesis* 2) supports diagnostics of performance problems. (*RQ 8*, *RQ 9*, *RQ 10*, Section 1.3)

Hypothesis 4 — *Performance test specifications can be generalized by a language which allows to describe instrumentation instructions and performance test series in a system-independent and tool-independent way.*

Performance testing comprises a multitude of configuration and description artifacts, including descriptions of instrumentation and monitoring instructions, load descriptions, etc. We investigate which abstraction languages are required to describe the generalizable parts of performance tests in a way that the description instances can be used for automation of performance tests. (*RQ 6*, *RQ 7*, Section 1.3)

Hypothesis 5 — *The conflicting requirements of high measurement accuracy and detailed measurement data can be achieved by a goal-oriented experimentation concept.*

We conceptualize an experimentation methodology (cf. SSE, Part II in Figure 3.2) which allows to gain detailed measurement data with a negligible measurement overhead. Furthermore, we investigate the scope of applicability of SSE on further performance engineering approaches and evaluate its limits. (*RQ 3*, *RQ 4*, Section 1.3)

Hypothesis 6 — *The composition of a taxonomy on performance problems, a language for generic description of instrumentation instructions, monitoring as well as performance test series, and the SSE concept enable full automation of performance problem diagnostics.*

As already discussed, the APPD approach combines multiple concepts and artifacts. The ensemble of these concepts enables a full automation of a systematic diagnostics approach. As automation is the primary goal of APPD, providing a fully automated implementation of the APPD approach is not only a technical realization, but an important validation of the main promise of APPD.

Hypothesis 7 — *Applying our APPD approach in the scope of established software development processes entails a manual effort which is negligible compared to traditional, manual performance problem diagnostics.*

We investigate the applicability of our overall APPD approach by evaluating the approach-specific effort for application of APPD. To this end, we discuss the integration of APPD into established software development processes and conduct an empirical study to gain an insight on the perception of our approach by external participants.

3.5. Summary

In this chapter, we introduced the APPD approach showing a sketch of its constituent parts and their interplay. The high-level idea behind APPD is the formalization, structuring and reuse of expert knowledge on recurrent performance problem types to enable automatic diagnostics of performance problems. Hence, tasks that are currently conducted for each performance problem diagnostics context are automated by means of generalizing and extracting knowledge on recurrent problems and corresponding, recurrent diagnostics activities. The APPD approach comprises four main, constituent parts. Generic knowledge on recurrent performance problems and their interrelation is captured in a taxonomy on performance problems. For each performance problem type, the APPD approach provides for a corresponding, experiment-based detection heuristic. Applying the Systematic Selective Experimentation (SSE) concept, APPD systematically searches for root causes of performance problems by utilizing the taxonomy on performance problems as a decision tree. For each node in the taxonomy, a detection heuristic exists that describes which experiments need to be executed and how corresponding measurement data must be analyzed to make a decision on the existence of the investigated performance problem. In order to keep performance problem diagnostics generic, an abstraction layer provides a set of specification languages that constitute the basis to bridge the gap between specific application contexts and the generic diagnostics algorithms. Discussing the assumptions of the APPD approach, we came to the conclusion that APPD is closely aligned with established software development processes as it relies on artifacts that should be available in common software development projects. Considering the research question stated in Section 1.3 and the constituent parts of the APPD approach, we derived seven research hypotheses. These hypotheses guide the remainder of this thesis and constitute the base for the validation goals of the APPD approach. The following three chapters take a closer look on the constituent parts of APPD. Chapter 4 provides deeper details on the performance problem taxonomy. Chapter 5 introduces a set of description languages that allow to keep the core of APPD generic. Finally, in Chapter 6 we consider detection heuristics in more detail.

4. Systematizing Diagnostics of Performance Problems

Both scientific and industrial literature define a large set of different Software Performance Anti-patterns (SPAs) in the domain of enterprise software systems (cf. Section 2.4). An SPA describes a certain type of design, implementation or deployment failures that may lead to performance problems. Taken into account, SPAs are an effective means to avoid performance problems in advance during development. Nevertheless in practice, due to time restrictions and higher prioritized functional requirements, SPAs are often unconsciously introduced into the architecture and code of a software product. In such cases, the SPAs have to be uncovered and diagnosed, for instance in the testing phase. A description of an SPA is helpful in investigating the existence of the corresponding type of performance problems in a System Under Test (SUT). However, descriptions of SPAs do not convey enough information on the interrelationship between individual SPAs, symptoms and root causes. Hence, in order to conduct a diagnostics of performance problems (i.e. scanning for all types of performance problems), the descriptions on SPAs allow only for an investigation of each SPA in isolation. However, this approach is rather unsystematic, tedious and error-prone. In fact, many SPAs, problem symptoms and root causes are interrelated. In particular, every type of performance problems leads to the same high level symptom of violated performance requirements (e.g. response times exceeding a threshold). Moreover, different SPAs and root causes exhibit similar internal indicators (e.g. high CPU utilization, congestion points, etc.). The interrelationships constitute a potential to support a more systematic approach of diagnosing a SUT for performance problems instead of investigating each SPA individually. In this chapter, we provide a methodology for deriving a systematic guidance in diagnosing performance problems from existing knowledge on different types of performance problems, i.e. SPAs. An explicit guidance in diagnosing performance problems is essential in two respects: First, laying the basis for automating the systematic search for performance problems and their root causes, it is a crucial part of the Automatic Performance Problem Diagnostics (APPD) approach. Second, apart from automating performance problem diagnostics, an explicit guidance facilitates manual diagnostics of performance problems and enables less experienced performance analysts to achieve more accurate diagnostics results. We introduce a process for the systematization of performance problem diagnostics (Section 4.1) and elaborate on the individual process steps (Section 4.2, Section 4.3 and Section 4.4). Preliminary parts of the systematization of performance problems have been published before in (Wert et al., 2013; Wert et al., 2014; Wert, 2012).

4.1. Systematization Process

In this section, we introduce a process that describes the necessary activities to provide systematic guidance in performance problem diagnostics. Figure 4.1 shows the systematization process comprising four activities with corresponding process and artifacts flow.

As mentioned before, our approach is based on the notion of Software Performance Anti-patterns (SPAs). The knowledge about existing SPAs is spread among different sources. While some SPAs are explicitly defined in different sources of scientific and industrial literature, other SPAs remain as implicit knowledge resulting from practical experience of performance experts. Furthermore, some SPAs are explicitly described but not known under that term. Hence, the first essential step to create systematic guidance in performance problem diagnostics is the gathering of knowledge about different SPAs. Based on the resulting definitions of SPAs, the SPAs can be categorized with respect to different dimensions using a predefined categorization template. The resulting, explicit characteristics of SPAs can be used to identify relevant SPAs (e.g. those, which are automatically diagnosable by a measurement-based approach) and structure them hierarchically, yielding a taxonomy. The taxonomy lays the basis for a systematic search for performance problems. However, as the resulting taxonomy covers only static information about the SPAs and their interrelationships, the last activity of the process augments the taxonomy with information about related diagnostics activities. The result of

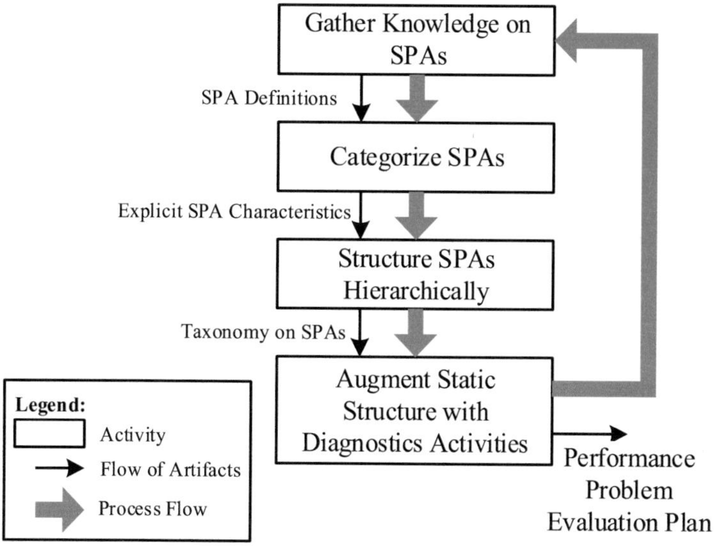

Figure 4.1.: Process for deriving systematic guidance in performance problem diagnostics.

the process is a Performance Problem Evaluation Plan describing how and in which order to evaluate the individual SPAs. The process is intended to be iterated as many times as needed in order to extend the resulting artifacts including the knowledge base of existing SPAs, their categorization, the taxonomy and the final evaluation plan.

For the categorization step, we develop a categorization template (Section 4.2) that supports a better understanding of individual SPAs, allows to identify relevant SPAs and provides the necessary information for creating a corresponding taxonomy. We apply that categorization template on a set of SPAs that we gathered from some selected scientific and industrial sources of literature. Based on the categorization of the selected SPAs, we create a taxonomy (Section 4.3) showing the interrelationships of the corresponding SPAs. We introduce the meta-structure of the evaluation plan (Section 4.4.1) and describe how to derive an instance of the evaluation plan from a given SPAs taxonomy (Section 4.4.2). Based on the evaluation plan, we define an algorithm that automates the systematic search for performance problems and their root causes (Section 4.4.3).

4.2. Categorizing Performance Anti-patterns

To provide a systematic guidance in diagnosing a SUT for potential performance problems, known types of performance problems (i.e. SPAs) need to be analyzed with respect to different aspects. In particular, we aim at identifying conceptional degrees of freedom in existing definitions of known SPAs. Based on the degrees of freedom, we derive a categorization template which helps to understand the nature of different SPAs, including their scope of occurrence and suited methods of analyzing instances of corresponding SPAs. Furthermore, we are interested in the type of stakeholders who are responsible for certain kind of performance problems and, thus, are the target consumer group of the results generated by our overall approach APPD. By applying the categorization template to a set of known SPAs, we identify those SPAs which are relevant for our APPD approach and get an insight on the relationships between individual SPAs. The categorization of the individual SPAs lays the basis for constructing a taxonomy.

4.2.1. Categorization Template

While gathering definitions of SPAs from scientific literature as well as from industrial journals and blogs (cf. Section 2.4), we compared the nature of SPAs with respect to different dimensions. Thereby, we came to the conclusion that definitions of SPAs are not entirely consistent. In particular, we made the following observations:

- Definitions of SPAs exhibit different levels of granularity. This even applies for SPAs which come from the same source of literature. While some SPAs describe high level symptoms (e.g. the Ramp anti-pattern, Smith et al., 2002a), others describe internal symptoms (e.g. the One Lane Bridge anti-pattern, Smith et al., 2000) or even root causes (e.g. the Excessive Dynamic Allocation anti-pattern, Smith et al., 2000).

- Furthermore, the anti-patterns are distinguishable in the pattern type to which they refer. On the one hand, some SPAs describe behavioural patterns (e.g. patterns in the progression of response times, etc.) which can be observed only dynamically during execution of the SUT. On the other hand, some SPAs cover structural and static patterns that may lead to performance problems. Examples are improper constellations of software components or classes and bad sequences of code statements, respectively.
- As mentioned before, SPAs describe design, implementation or deployment failures which may lead to performance problems. Consequently, the abstraction level of the failure constitutes another degree of freedom with the following possible manifestations: architectural failure, design failure (including object-oriented design, database schema design, etc.), implementation failure and deployment failure (including SUT configuration).
- Finally, as mentioned before, SPAs are interrelated, following a cause-effect relationship. SPAs that represent high level symptoms are caused by other SPAs representing internal symptoms or root causes.

Level of Granularity • root cause / • internal symptom / • externally visible symptom	**Type of Pattern** • structural pattern / • static pattern / • behavioural pattern
Level of Abstraction • architecture / • design (OO, DB, etc.) / • implementation / • deployment	**Detection Method** • static analysis / • measurement / • manual analysis
Interrelation	
Symptoms	**Causes**
...	...

Table 4.1.: Categorization: Template

Based on the observations we developed a categorization template for analyzing individual SPAs as depicted in Table 4.1. The template comprises six dimensions of categorization: *Level of Granularity, Type of Pattern, Level of Abstraction, Detection Method, Symptoms* and *Causes*. The former three dimensions are directly derived from the mentioned observations. As the level of abstraction describes the type of the actual failure that may lead to a performance problem, this dimension of categorization can only be applied on SPAs which constitute a root cause (cf. *Level of Granularity*). Regardless of the level of granularity, the type of pattern or the level of abstraction of SPAs, the level of difficulty and possible methods of detecting an anti-pattern as a cause or symptom of a performance problem varies, depending on the individual SPA. Hence, it is important to understand which SPAs are automatically detectable and which methods can be applied to realize the detection. Hereby, we distinguish between automatic detection through static code analysis, automatic detection through measurements, and manual detection requiring human interaction. The latter case applies to SPAs which cannot be detected by automatic application of rules due to complex semantic dependencies which can be only resolved by human interaction. This dimension of categorization is especially important for our APPD approach, as it distills those SPAs that are potentially detectable with our approach.

Finally, the interrelation dimensions *Symptoms* and *Causes* are the most essential categorization dimensions for our goal of providing a systematic guidance in diagnosing performance problems. Identifying which SPAs are potential causes or symptoms for other SPAs is important to develop a holistic view on the set of known SPAs.

4.2.2. Applying the Categorization

To understand how individual SPAs are interrelated and to identify relevant SPAs, it is essential to apply the defined categorization template to a representatively big set of SPAs. In this section, we apply the categorization template to a set of 27 selected SPAs from mentioned scientific and industrial sources of literature (cf. Section 2.4). The selection of considered SPAs is based on the assumptions for the application context described in Section 3.3.1. Many of the SPAs categorized in the following are applicable in different contexts which may result in different categorization results. However, as in this thesis we focus on performance problems in the application logic (cf. Section 3.3.1), the considered SPAs are analyzed from the perspective of the application logic. For instance, we consider a slow database request as a root cause. By contrast, from the database configuration and design perspective, a slow database request is a symptom rather than a root cause.

Though the considered SPAs cover many relevant types of performance problems, we are aware that this set of SPAs is not exhaustive. However, the categorization and taxonomy derivation methodology applied in the following sections can be analogously applied to further SPAs that are not in our list of selected SPAs.

4.2.2.1. Traffic Jam

The evaluation of the Traffic Jam anti-pattern is depicted in Table 4.2. The Traffic Jam describes the symptom of highly varying response times caused by congestion of threads (cf. Table 2.1(a), Chapter 2.4). This symptom can be observed externally from a SUT in the end-to-end response times or as an internal symptom in the response times of internal operations. As the Traffic Jam refers to a behavioural pattern, we cannot specify a value for the level of abstraction.

Level of Granularity • internal symptom • externally visible symptom	**Type of Pattern** behavioural pattern
Level of Abstraction [not applicable]	**Detection Method** measurement
Interrelation	
Symptoms violation of performance requirements under high load	**Causes** • One Lane Bridge • CPU intensive application • congestion on database

Table 4.2.: Categorization: Traffic Jam

Furthermore, the type of pattern implies that the Traffic Jam can only be detected by conducting measurements but not by static code analysis. The Traffic Jam may lead to a violation of performance requirements, especially if the SUT is under high load. A Traffic Jam is typically caused by a software bottleneck (also known as the One Lane Bridge anti-pattern (cf. Table 2.1(e), Chapter 2.4)), CPU intensive computations, or congestion on external services like a database access.

4.2.2.2. The Ramp

Similarly to the Traffic Jam anti-pattern, the Ramp anti-pattern (cf. Table 2.1(b), Chapter 2.4) describes a symptom manifested in the behavioural pattern that response times grow with the operation time (cf. Table 4.3). An existence of a Ramp anti-pattern in a SUT mostly reveals very slowly. It may take weeks or month of operation until an increase in response times becomes noticeable. Hence, though the Ramp anti-pattern is theoretically detectable by conducting performance tests, in practice, typical performance tests are too short to uncover a Ramp behaviour. As the Ramp constitutes a slow growth in response times, typically, it does not immediately results in a violation of performance requirements. The Ramp rather leads to a delayed violation of requirements which, however, gets worse with the operation time. Typical causes are the Sisyphus Database Retrieval anti-pattern (cf. Table 2.1(p), Chapter 2.4) yielding a Ramp because of improper database queries combined with growing database tables, or the Dormant References anti-pattern (cf. Table 2.1(m), Chapter 2.4) resulting in growing data structures.

Level of Granularity	Type of Pattern
• internal symptom • externally visible symptom	behavioural pattern
Level of Abstraction	**Detection Method**
[not applicable]	measurement (long running)
Interrelation	
Symptoms	**Causes**
increasing violation of performance requirements	• Sisyphus Database Retrieval • Dormant References

Table 4.3.: Categorization: The Ramp

4.2.2.3. Application Hiccups

The Application Hiccups anti-pattern (cf. Table 2.1(c), Chapter 2.4) describes the externally visible symptom of periodically occurring phases with high response times that, consequently, may lead to periodic violations of performance requirements (cf. Table 4.4). Hence, it is a behavioural pattern that, analogously to the Traffic Jam anti-pattern, can be detected only dynamically by executing the SUT. Hiccups caused by garbage collection is a typical cause for the Application Hiccups anti-pattern.

Level of Granularity	Type of Pattern
externally visible symptom	behavioural pattern
Level of Abstraction	**Detection Method**
[not applicable]	measurement
Interrelation	
Symptoms	**Causes**
periodical violation of performance requirements	Garbage Collection Hiccups

Table 4.4.: Categorization: Application Hiccups

4.2.2.4. Garbage Collection Hiccups

The anti-pattern Garbage Collection Hiccups (cf. Table 2.1(d), Chapter 2.4) is a special case of the Application Hiccups anti-pattern, however, it is an internal symptom (cf. Table 4.5) as it requires monitoring of garbage collection executions in order to be uncovered. Hence, the behavioural pattern Garbage Collection Hiccups can be detected by measurement. Garbage Collection Hiccups are caused by memory management anti-patterns which may lead to an increased pollution of memory.

Level of Granularity internal symptom	**Type of Pattern** behavioural pattern
Level of Abstraction [not applicable]	**Detection Method** measurement
Interrelation	
Symptoms Application Hiccups	**Causes** • Wrong Cache Usage • Session as a Cache • Large Temporary Objects • Sisyphus Database Retrieval

Table 4.5.: Categorization: Garbage Collection Hiccups

In particular the Wrong Cache Usage anti-pattern, the Session as a Cache anti-pattern, the Large Temporary Objects anti-pattern and the Sisyphus Database Retrieval anti-pattern are typical causes for Garbage Collection Hiccups.

4.2.2.5. One Lane Bridge

The One Lane Bridge (OLB) anti-pattern (cf. Table 2.1(e), Chapter 2.4) is an internal symptom (cf. Table 4.6) describing a behavioural pattern which is similar to the Traffic Jam symptom (cf. Table 2.1(a), Chapter 2.4), however, that is manifested in a software bottleneck. A OLB can be detected in a similar way as the Traffic Jam, by conducting measurements. An OLB is typically caused by synchronization in the application code (e.g. in thread pools, connection pools, etc.), database locking, or external services which become bottlenecks.

Level of Granularity internal symptom	**Type of Pattern** behavioural pattern
Level of Abstraction [not applicable]	**Detection Method** measurement
Interrelation	
Symptoms Traffic Jam	**Causes** • synchronization • database locking • Bottleneck Service

Table 4.6.: Categorization: One Lane Bridge

4.2.2.6. Dispensable Synchronization

Dispensable Synchronization (cf. Table 2.1(g), Chapter 2.4) is a common root cause for the OLB anti-pattern. It is a static pattern that is manifested in an implementation failure (cf. Table 4.7). This root cause is characterized by the location in the application code where threads need to wait for a lock because of unnecessarily long locking areas. While static code analysis may be useful to identify all synchronization points in the target application, measurements are required to reveal those synchronization points which become a bottleneck and, thus, constitute a performance problem.

Level of Granularity	**Type of Pattern**
root cause	static pattern
Level of Abstraction	**Detection Method**
implementation	• static (code) analysis • measurement
Interrelation	
Symptoms	**Causes**
One Lane Bridge	[not applicable]

Table 4.7.: Categorization: Dispensable Synchronization

4.2.2.7. The Blob

The Blob (cf. Table 2.1(h), Chapter 2.4), also known as the God Class anti-pattern, describes a structural pattern on the level of architectural or object-oriented design (cf. Table 4.8), manifested in a central component. The communication between the central component and other components may lead to an excessive messaging which impairs the performance of the SUT. Hence, the Blob is a root cause that is characterized by the instance identifier of the central, guilty component. Though a central component can be statically (i.e. by static code or model analysis) detected as a potential Blob anti-pattern, deciding whether that component constitutes a performance problem or not is not possible by applying static analysis. Hence, measurements are required to be conducted to reveal a central component as a guilty Blob anti-pattern that is resulting in a performance problem.

Level of Granularity	Type of Pattern
root cause	structural pattern
Level of Abstraction	**Detection Method**
• architecture • design	• static analysis (partially) • measurement
Interrelation	
Symptoms	**Causes**
excessive messaging	[not applicable]

Table 4.8.: Categorization: The Blob

4.2.2.8. Empty Semi Trucks

The Empty Semi Trucks anti-pattern (cf. Table 2.1(i), Chapter 2.4) is another potential root cause for excessive messaging, manifested in an unnecessarily high amount of small messages. Empty Semi Trucks describes a behavioural pattern originating from an implementation failure characterized by two communication points (i.e. locations in the source code) where many small messages are transmitted. Analogously to the Blob, the Empty Semi Trucks anti-pattern is detectable by measurement.

Level of Granularity	Type of Pattern
root cause	behavioural pattern
Level of Abstraction	**Detection Method**
implementation	measurement
Interrelation	
Symptoms	**Causes**
excessive messaging	[not applicable]

Table 4.9.: Categorization: Empty Semi Trucks

4.2.2.9. The Stifle

Table 4.10 shows the categorization of the Stifle anti-pattern. Very similar to the Empty Semi Trucks anti-pattern, the Stifle (cf. Table 2.1(k), Chapter 2.4) describes the behavioural pattern of sending too many, fine-grained database queries instead of aggregating them. In particular, the Stifle is a root cause on the implementation level, which is identified by the fine-grained SQL statements and the location in the SUT where the corresponding database queries are emitted. The potential consequences of a Stifle anti-pattern are an increased network utilization or an overloaded database that results in database congestion.

Level of Granularity root cause	**Type of Pattern** behavioural pattern
Level of Abstraction implementation	**Detection Method** measurement
Interrelation	
Symptoms • congestion on database • increased network utilization	**Causes** [not applicable]

Table 4.10.: Categorization: The Stifle

4.2.2.10. Circuitous Treasure Hunt

The Circuitous Treasure Hunt anti-pattern (cf. Table 2.1(l), Chapter 2.4) is similar to the Stifle, as it entails many database requests. However, with Circuitous Treasure Hunt the database requests are interrelated.

Level of Granularity	**Type of Pattern**
root cause	static pattern
Level of Abstraction	**Detection Method**
design	manual analysis
Interrelation	
Symptoms	**Causes**
• congestion on database • increased network utilization	[not applicable]

Table 4.11.: Categorization: Circuitous Treasure Hunt

This anti-pattern constitutes a root cause that is manifested in a bad design of database tables and corresponding SQL statements. Therefore, the Circuitous Treasure Hunt anti-pattern describes a static type of pattern. Analogously to the Stifle, this anti-pattern may lead to a congestion on the database or increased utilization of the network. However, due to the semantic dependency between database requests, the Circuitous Treasure Hunt cannot be detected automatically, neither by measurement nor by static analysis. In particular, the detection of this anti-pattern requires analysis of data flow in order to identify relationships between individual database requests. Therefore, manual analysis is the only way of detecting this anti-pattern.

4.2.2.11. Dormant References

The Dormant References anti-pattern (cf. Table 2.1(m), Chapter 2.4) is a behavioural pattern referring to steadily growing data structures due to missing clean-up operations. Therefore, it is a failure which is manifested in the implementation of the target application. Because of growing response times of operations working on that data structures, the Dormant References anti-pattern constitutes a root cause for the Ramp anti-pattern. However, this anti-pattern may lead to a memory leaks, as well. By tracking the sizes of data structures, the Dormant References anti-pattern can be detected through measurements.

Level of Granularity	Type of Pattern
root cause	behavioural pattern
Level of Abstraction	**Detection Method**
implementation	measurement
Interrelation	
Symptoms	**Causes**
• The Ramp • Memory Leak	[not applicable]

Table 4.12.: Categorization: Dormant References

4.2.2.12. Session as a Cache

Session as a Cache (cf. Table 2.1(n), Chapter 2.4) is a static pattern originating from an implementation failure (cf. Table 4.13), whereby a user session is misused as a data cache. As this anti-pattern leads to an increased pollution of the memory, it constitutes a potential root cause for Garbage Collection Hiccups. Static code analysis may be useful to identify locations in code where data objects are attached to a user session object. Combining static analysis with measurements allows to evaluate whether large-size objects or huge sets of objects are attached to user sessions.

Level of Granularity	Type of Pattern
root cause	static pattern
Level of Abstraction	**Detection Method**
implementation	• static analysis (partially) • measurement
Interrelation	
Symptoms	**Causes**
Garbage Collection Hiccups	[not applicable]

Table 4.13.: Categorization: Session as a Cache

4.2.2.13. Excessive Dynamic Allocation

Describing the process of allocating a huge amount of temporary objects, the Excessive Dynamic Allocation anti-pattern (cf. Table 2.1(j), Chapter 2.4) describes a static pattern resulting from an implementation failure (cf. Table 4.14). The code fragment, where a big amount of memory is allocated, constitutes the root cause of this anti-pattern. As allocation of objects is an expensive task, Excessive Dynamic Allocation may lead to an increased usage of CPU. By applying static code analysis, frequent allocations of temporary objects can be detected (e.g. temporary objects in loops). Measurements may be helpful to retrieve the memory footprint of such code fragments.

Level of Granularity root cause	**Type of Pattern** static pattern
Level of Abstraction implementation	**Detection Method** • static analysis • measurement
Interrelation	
Symptoms increased CPU usage	**Causes** [not applicable]

Table 4.14.: Categorization: Excessive Dynamic Allocation

4.2.2.14. Sisyphus Database Retrieval

Level of Granularity root cause	**Type of Pattern** static pattern
Level of Abstraction implementation	**Detection Method** manual analysis
Interrelation	
Symptoms • Garbage Collection Hiccups • The Ramp • long-running database requests	**Causes** [not applicable]

Table 4.15.: Categorization: Sisyphus Database Retrieval

The Sisyphus Database Retrieval anti-pattern (cf. Table 2.1(p), Chapter 2.4) constitutes a static implementation pattern in the SQL statements of database queries. It leads to big amounts of data that is retrieved from the database, however, is not entirely used in the application logic. In the cases where the database grows over time, the time for processing the database queries increases steadily which may lead to an observation of the Ramp anti-pattern. Furthermore, if data is dropped immediately after it has been retrieved from the database, it may lead to an increased pollution of memory and, thus, may result in Garbage Collection Hiccups. An exposure of a Sisyphus Database Retrieval anti-pattern requires analysis of data flow in order to decide which parts of the retrieved data are actually used in the application logic. However, this task entails semantic interpretation of data usage and data transformation. Therefore, the detection of the Sisyphus Database Retrieval requires manual human interaction.

4.2.2.15. Tower of Babel

The Tower of Babel anti-pattern (cf. Table 2.1(f), Chapter 2.4) describes the problem of conducting too many, expensive transformations of data between different representation formats. As data transformation code is typically very CPU intensive, this anti-pattern may lead to a massive increase in the

CPU utilization (cf. Table 4.16), especially, if large amounts of data have to be transformed. As decisions on which data formats to use are made during implementation, the Tower of Babel is an implementation failure manifested as a static pattern. The code fragments in the target application which are responsible for transforming data into different formats constitute the root cause of the Tower of Babel anti-pattern. However, in order to identify such code fragments, semantic interpretation of the source code is required. Hence, the Tower of Babel anti-pattern cannot be detected in an automatic way, neither by static code analysis nor by measurements. Consequently, the detection of the Tower of Babel depends on manual analysis.

Level of Granularity	**Type of Pattern**
root cause	static pattern
Level of Abstraction	**Detection Method**
implementation	manual analysis
Interrelation	
Symptoms	**Causes**
increased CPU utilization	[not applicable]

Table 4.16.: Categorization: Tower of Babel

4.2.2.16. Unnecessary Processing

The Unnecessary Processing anti-pattern (cf. Table 2.1(r), Chapter 2.4) refers to code fragments whose processing is not required for the correct execution of the target application. The code fragments constitute a static root cause on the implementation layer which may lead to an unnecessary increase in the CPU utilization (cf. Table 4.17). In order to identify an Unnecessary Processing anti-pattern, one must be able to decide whether a certain piece of code is necessary at that point in time of execution or not. However, this kind of decision, again, requires semantic interpretation of the tasks realized by the corresponding code fragment and, thus, depends on manual analysis. Though measurements can be applied to identify code fragments which are especially CPU intensive, deciding whether these code fragments constitute an Unnecessary Processing anti-pattern requires human interaction.

Level of Granularity root cause	**Type of Pattern** static pattern
Level of Abstraction implementation	**Detection Method** • measurement (partially) • manual analysis
Interrelation	
Symptoms increased CPU utilization	**Causes** [not applicable]

Table 4.17.: Categorization: Unnecessary Processing

4.2.2.17. Spin Wait

Table 4.18 shows the categorization of the Spin Wait anti-pattern (cf. Table 2.1(s), Chapter 2.4). Spin Wait describes the static pattern of misusing an empty loop for synchronization of threads. As an empty loop consumes CPU time without conducting any useful computations, the Spin Wait anti-pattern constitutes a potential, implementation-level root cause for an unnecessarily high utilization of the CPU. The empty loop of a Spin Wait can be easily detected by conducting static code analysis.

Level of Granularity root cause	**Type of Pattern** static pattern
Level of Abstraction implementation	**Detection Method** static code analysis
Interrelation	
Symptoms increased CPU utilization	**Causes** [not applicable]

Table 4.18.: Categorization: Spin Wait

4.2.2.18. Insufficient Caching

Introducing caching is often a solution to reduce the performance impact of repeated, CPU-intensive computations or repeated database requests. The Insufficient Caching anti-pattern (cf. Table 2.1(t), Chapter 2.4) describes the problem of a missing or undersized cache. Depending on whether a cache is missing for the database access or in the application logic, its absence may lead to a congestion on the database, or to a high CPU utilization at the application server, respectively (cf. Table 4.19). As decisions on the utilization of a cache can be made on different abstraction levels (architecture, design, implementation), the Insufficient Caching anti-pattern is a root cause which may be manifested on any of these levels. In cases where a cache is missing at all, the Insufficient Caching anti-pattern describes a structural pattern. If a cache is undersized, this anti-pattern describes the behavioural pattern of frequent cache misses. A missing cache can be detected by identifying repeated, CPU-intensive methods which produce unique results for given inputs. Monitoring CPU times of methods and the corresponding relationships between input and output values allows to identify such methods. An undersized cache can be identified by monitoring its cache miss rate.

Level of Granularity root cause	**Type of Pattern** • structural pattern • behavioural pattern
Level of Abstraction • architecture • design • implementation	**Detection Method** measurement
Interrelation	
Symptoms • congestion on database • increased CPU utilization	**Causes** [not applicable]

Table 4.19.: Categorization: Insufficient Caching

4.2.2.19. Wrong Cache Strategy

Using a cache is not always beneficial in terms of performance. The Wrong Cache Strategy anti-pattern (cf. Table 2.1(u), Chapter 2.4) describes the opposite structural pattern to the Insufficient Caching anti-pattern (cf. Table 4.20). In particular, if a cache is used in inappropriate situations, it may lead to an increased pollution of the memory and, thus, may result in hiccups which are caused by garbage collections. Analogously to the Insufficient Caching anti-pattern, the Wrong Cache Strategy anti-pattern can be found on any abstraction level (architecture, design, implementation). An improperly used cache can be detected through measurement by monitoring the cache miss rate.

Level of Granularity root cause	**Type of Pattern** structural pattern
Level of Abstraction • architecture • design • implementation	**Detection Method** measurement
Interrelation	
Symptoms Garbage Collection Hiccups	**Causes** [not applicable]

Table 4.20.: Categorization: Wrong Cache Strategy

4.2.2.20. Unbalanced Processing

The Unbalanced Processing anti-pattern (cf. Table 2.1(v), Chapter 2.4) occurs when the work is not evenly distributed among available processors. Hence, it is a symptom which is only visible from the interior of the SUT, but not from the end-user perspective (cf. Table 4.21). This behavioural pattern can be detected by monitoring the utilization of available CPUs and analyzing the distribution. The Unbalanced Processing anti-pattern may lead to a bottleneck (i.e. Traffic Jam) due to inefficient use of available resources. Single-threaded code or an unevenly distributed Pipe and Filter Architecture are typical causes for the Unbalanced Processing symptom.

Level of Granularity	Type of Pattern
internal symptom	behavioural pattern
Level of Abstraction	**Detection Method**
[not applicable]	measurement
Interrelation	
Symptoms	**Causes**
Traffic Jam	• Single-threaded Code • Pipe and Filter Architecture

Table 4.21.: Categorization: Unbalanced Processing

4.2.2.21. Single-threaded Code

Table 4.22 shows the categorization of the Single-threaded Code anti-pattern (cf. Table 2.1(w), Chapter 2.4). Single-threaded Code is one of the potential, implementation-level root causes for an Unbalanced Processing anti-pattern. This static pattern can be identified by static code analysis or by monitoring the amount of active threads.

Level of Granularity	Type of Pattern
root cause	static pattern
Level of Abstraction	**Detection Method**
implementation	• static code analysis • measurement
Interrelation	
Symptoms	**Causes**
Unbalanced Processing	[not applicable]

Table 4.22.: Categorization: Single-Threaded Code

4.2.2.22. Pipe and Filter Architecture

If a Pipe and Filter Architecture is distributed unevenly, one of the filters may become a bottleneck which impairs the performance of the entire chain (cf.

Table 2.1(x), Chapter 2.4). Describing a structural failure on the architecture level, the Pipe and Filter Architecture anti-pattern is a root cause for Unbalanced Processing (cf. Table **??**). While a static analysis is helpful to identify a Pipe and Filter Architecture, in order to reveal that such an architecture is unevenly distributed, monitoring the execution of the individual filters is essential.

Level of Granularity	**Type of Pattern**
root cause	structural pattern
Level of Abstraction	**Detection Method**
architecture	• static analysis • measurement
Interrelation	
Symptoms	**Causes**
Unbalanced Processing	[not applicable]

Table 4.23.: Categorization: Pipe and Filter Architecture

4.2.2.23. Large Temporary Objects

The creation of Large Temporary Objects (cf. Table 2.1(o), Chapter 2.4) is a potential root cause for an increased pollution of the memory and, thus, may lead to Garbage Collection Hiccups (cf. Table 4.24). As the allocation of objects is an implementation issue, this anti-pattern needs to be solved at the implementation level. Identifying large objects can be conducted by monitoring object allocations. However, in order to decide whether an object is used temporarily, static code analysis has to be applied.

Level of Granularity	**Type of Pattern**
root cause	behavioural pattern
Level of Abstraction	**Detection Method**
implementation	• measurement • static code analysis
Interrelation	
Symptoms	**Causes**
Garbage Collection Hiccups	[not applicable]

Table 4.24.: Categorization: Large Temporary Objects

4.2.2.24. Chatty Service

The Chatty Service anti-pattern (cf. Table 2.1(y), Chapter 2.4) describes the behavioural pattern of emitting a big amount of service calls in order to perform a task. While from the perspective of the service consumer this anti-pattern constitutes a behavioural pattern, from the service provider side, the Chatty Service is a static pattern that usually originates from an improper design of the service interface (cf. Table 4.25). As calls to external services are very expensive in terms of performance, for the service consumer the Chatty Service anti-pattern may be a root cause for high response times, even in cases of low load on the SUT. A sequence of external service calls can be identified either by conducting static code analysis or by monitoring the interaction with external services.

Level of Granularity	Type of Pattern
root cause	• behavioural pattern • static pattern
Level of Abstraction	**Detection Method**
design	• static code analysis • measurement
Interrelation	
Symptoms	**Causes**
high response times	[not applicable]

Table 4.25.: Categorization: Chatty Service

4.2.2.25. The Knot

Table 4.26 shows the categorization of the Knot anti-pattern (cf. Table 2.1(z), Chapter 2.4). Similarly to the Chatty Service anti-pattern, the Knot anti-pattern is a potential root cause for high end-to-end response times. The Knot describes the problem of emitting an expensive call to an external, complex service in order to perform a simple task. For the service consumer the Knot constitutes a behavioural pattern. However, for the service provider, the Knot is a structural design failure that is manifested in tightly coupled sub-services. Expensive, external services can be easily detected by monitoring the response times of external service calls.

Level of Granularity	Type of Pattern
root cause	• behavioural pattern • structural pattern
Level of Abstraction	**Detection Method**
design	measurement
Interrelation	
Symptoms	**Causes**
high response times	[not applicable]

Table 4.26.: Categorization: The Knot

4.2.2.26. Bottleneck Service

A Bottleneck Service (cf. Table 2.1(aa), Section 2.4) is a potential root cause for an observation of an OLB. As the Bottleneck Service anti-pattern constitutes a behavioural pattern, it can be detected in a similar way as an OLB, by monitoring the relationship between load and the response times of the external service. From the perspective of the service provider, the Bottleneck Service is a symptom rather than a root cause. In particular, at the provider side, a Bottleneck Service may have different root causes from all possible levels of abstraction (architecture, design, implementation, deployment). However, as our focus is on the application logic of the service consumer, we consider a Bottleneck Service as a root cause rather than a symptom.

Level of Granularity root cause	**Type of Pattern** behavioural pattern
Level of Abstraction any	**Detection Method** measurement
Interrelation	
Symptoms One Lane Bridge	**Causes** [not applicable]

Table 4.27.: Categorization: Bottleneck Service

4.2.2.27. Spaghetti Query

The Spaghetti Query anti-pattern (cf. Table 2.1(q), Chapter 2.4) describes the static pattern of an overly complex SQL statement. Often this can lead to unnecessarily complex computations on the database resulting in a congestion on the database. As the SQL query design is an implementation issue, the Spaghetti Query anti-pattern constitutes an implementation-level root cause. This anti-pattern can be detected by applying static code analysis for identification of overly complex SQL statements. However, measurements are required to decide whether a corresponding query has a negative impact on performance.

Level of Granularity root cause	**Type of Pattern** static pattern
Level of Abstraction implementation	**Detection Method** • static code analysis • measurement
Interrelation	
Symptoms congestion on database	**Causes** [not applicable]

Table 4.28.: Categorization: Spaghetti Query

4.3. Deriving a Taxonomy

Based on the categorization from the previous section, we derive a taxonomy which provides a holistic view on the considered SPAs and their relationships. Figure 4.2 shows the resulting taxonomy. For the construction of the taxonomy, we primarily utilize the categorization dimensions *Symptoms* and *Causes* (cf. Section 4.2.1). In particular, we use these dimensions to derive hierarchical links between individual SPAs. Hence, the taxonomy reflects the cause-effect relationships of the considered SPAs. While high-level symptoms, such as the Ramp (cf. Section 4.2.2.2), the Traffic Jam (cf. Section 4.2.2.1) or the Application Hiccups (cf. Section 4.2.2.3) anti-patterns are located at the top levels of the taxonomy, internal symptoms and causes constitute inner nodes and leaf nodes of the taxonomy, respectively. In addition to the 27 SPAs considered in the previous section, we introduce some taxonomy nodes representing common symptoms that are not reflected by defined SPAs.

The *Performance Problem* node constitutes the root node of the taxonomy serving as a grouping of all potential types of performance problems. On the first level of the taxonomy, the high-level symptoms separate different patterns of the end-to-end response time progression under a constant, high load. Hereby, we distinguish between continuously growing response times (i.e the Ramp anti-pattern), periodically high response times (i.e. the Application Hiccups anti-pattern) and continuously high response times. In contrast to the Traffic Jam anti-pattern, the *Single User Problem* node subsumes all types of performance problems that exhibit high response times under single-user load and the response times do not get worse under increasing load. Typically, such performance problems are related to communication with system-external services. The additionally introduced *Database Congestion* node constitutes an internal symptom that groups all SPAs resulting in congestion due to inefficient communication and usage of the database. Hereby, the *Expensive Database Call* subsumes SPAs that are manifested in single, expensive calls to the database. The *Excessive Messaging* node constitutes an internal symptom which results from SPAs related to inefficient communication between software components and system nodes. Finally, the *CPU-intensive Application* node groups all types of performance problems that lead to a high CPU utilization on the application servers.

Although most SPAs have a unique path from the corresponding node in the taxonomy to the root node, some SPAs may have different or multiple effects on the performance of a SUT, depending on the runtime environment (e.g. sizing of hardware resources) and the manifestation of the corresponding SPA. For instance, on the one side, the Sisyphus Database Retrieval anti-pattern (cf. Section 4.2.2.14) may lead to Garbage Collection Hiccups (cf. Section 4.2.2.4) because of an increased pollution of memory. On the other side, Sisyphus Database Retrieval may lead to a Ramp (cf. Section 4.2.2.2) if the database content grows over time. Furthermore, the Sisyphus Database Retrieval may result in Database Congestion due to an expensive, long-running database call. Hence, according to our definition in Section 3.1, the essence of a performance problem is characterized by a chain of causes and symptoms, as reflected by a path in the taxonomy from the root node to a leaf node.

Except for the anti-patterns Tower of Babel, Circuitous Treasure Hunt and Sisyphus Database Retrieval, the considered SPAs are automatically detectable by applying rules in the context of static analysis, performance measurements or combination of both. Hence, there is a solid base of anti-patterns that can be addressed by our APPD approach. Furthermore, as we considered only a subset of potential, explicitly or implicitly known SPAs, the taxonomy shown in Figure 4.2 can be extended with additional SPAs by applying the categorization methodology described in these sections.

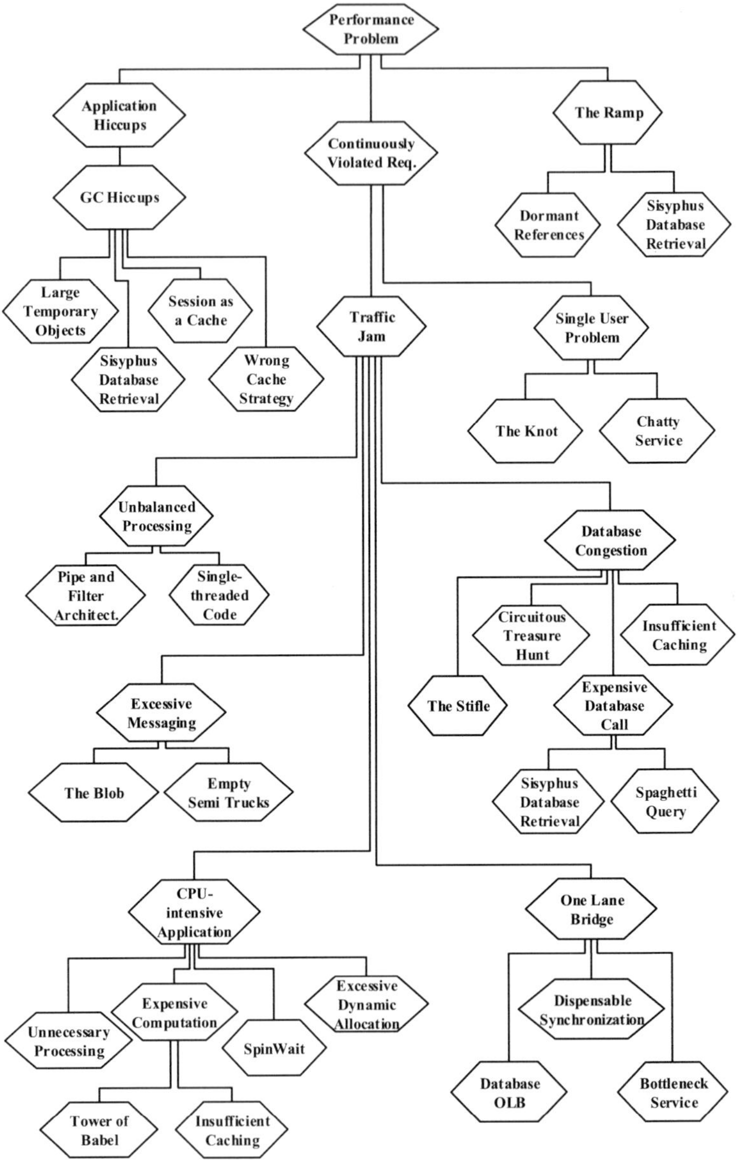

Figure 4.2.: Taxonomy on performance problems

4.4. Evaluation Plan for Performance Problem Diagnostics

A taxonomy as derived in the previous section lays the basis for a better understanding of the interrelationships between individual anti-patterns. As the taxonomy is based on the principle of cause-effect chains, it can be considered as a kind of a decision tree (Rokach et al., 2008) for diagnostics of performance problems (cf. Section 3.2.2). For instance in Figure 4.2, we do not need to investigate the Blob anti-pattern if we have not observed Excessive Messaging, yet. With respect to the evaluation of performance problems we can skip the entire sub-tree under the Traffic Jam node, if a Traffic Jam anti-pattern is not present. Hence, the taxonomy describes the order for the evaluation of individual types of performance problems and can be used to avoid unnecessary evaluation steps.

As mentioned in the beginning of this chapter, our goal is to provide a systematic guidance in diagnosing performance problems. However, the taxonomy structure as derived up to now does not provide sufficient guidance in diagnosing performance problems, yet. In particular, it is unclear what are the concrete activities to evaluate the corresponding performance problems. Therefore, in this section, we augment the taxonomy by additional constructs to provide a Performance Problem Evaluation Plan (PPEP) which can be either used manually by non-experts to analyse performance problems or can be utilized as a guiding process in APPD. We instantiate the PPEP for the SPAs that we considere in more detail in this thesis and for which we provide detection strategies in Chapter 6. Based on the PPEP structure, we provide an algorithm describing the usage of PPEP as a guiding process.

4.4.1. Augmenting the Taxonomy

The taxonomy derived in Section 4.3 consists of nodes which separate different categories and sub-categories of SPAs. In this way, the taxonomy provides only a static view on the interrelationships of individual SPAs. In order to create a guiding process for performance problem diagnostics, we derive a PPEP from the taxonomy. Therefore, we augment the meta-structure of the taxonomy by additional types of nodes that provide additional

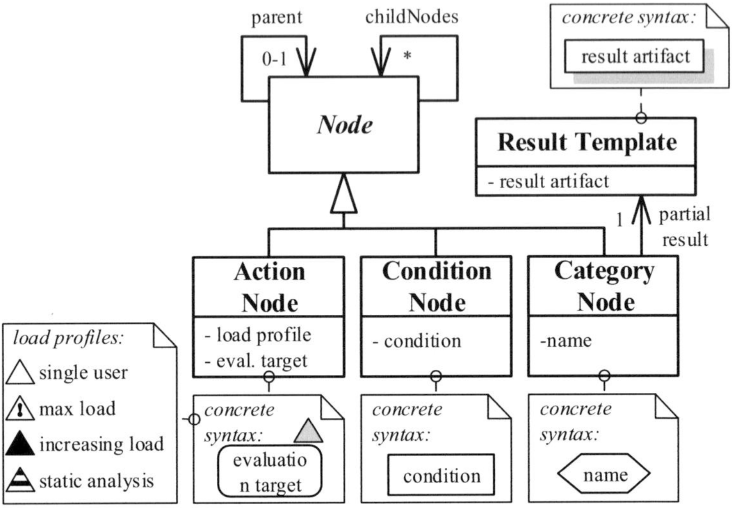

Figure 4.3.: Meta-structure for the Performance Problem Evaluation Plan (PPEP)

semantics on how to utilize the taxonomy as a decision tree for performance problem diagnostics. Figure 4.3 shows the abstract syntax of the PPEP and the concrete, graphical syntax we use to represent an instance of PPEP.

The abstract *Node* class with its associations represents a tree structure, whereby each node (except for the root node of the PPEP) has a parent node and a (potentially empty) set of child nodes. In the PPEP, we distinguish three types of nodes: *Category Node*, *Condition Node* and *Action Node*. Identified by SPA names, the *Category Nodes* reflect the nodes from the taxonomy and serve as a static categorization of SPAs detected during the diagnostics process. Additionally, a *Category Node* refers to a *Result Template* which describes the type of the detection result artifact for the corresponding SPA. An *Action Node* describes which evaluation activities need to be executed in order to take decisions on further evaluation of the corresponding descending branch in the PPEP. An *Action Node* comprises a *load profile* and an *evaluation target*. The *load profile* determines whether performance tests need to be executed or static analysis has to be conducted. In the former case, the *load profile* describes the load pattern to be applied during a series of performance tests. Hereby, we distinguish between a *single-user* test, a load test with a high load, and a series of performance tests with an *increasing load* from one test to the next. With the *evaluation target*, the *Action Node* defines which performance metrics or more complex aspects should be evaluated under the corresponding *load profile*. Based on the evaluation data (e.g. measurement data, static analysis insights, etc.) gained from preceding *Action Nodes*, a *Condition Node* defines a boolean term evaluating the existence of the SPA represented by the subsequent *Category Node*. Hence, a *Condition Node* constitutes a guard for further descending in the corresponding branch of the evaluation plan. The existence of an SPA is specified by the AND-concatenation of all conditions in the *Condition Nodes* along the path from the corresponding *Category Node* to the root node of the PPEP instance (comparable to rule induction in decision trees, (Rokach et al., 2008)).

In addition to the meta-structure, a set of Object Constraint Language (OCL) rules specifies a correct instantiation of the PPEP (cf. Listing 4.1). First, there is exactly one root node, characterized by an undefined parent(cf. Listing 4.1, l. 2-3). Second, a PPEP must start with an initial *Action Node* that generates measurement data for subsequent evaluation decisions (cf. Listing 4.1, l. 4-5). Each *Category Node* must have a preceding *Condition Node* that evaluates the existence of the SPA referred to by the subsequent *Category Node* (cf. Listing 4.1, l. 6-7). *Action Nodes* and *Condition Nodes* that have no descending *Category Nodes* are useless, as they cannot lead to an additional diagnostics result. Consequently, all leaf nodes of the PPEP must be of the type *Category Node* (cf. Listing 4.1, l. 8-9). Finally, as consecutive nodes of same type can be merged to one node, sequences of equally typed nodes are not allowed ((cf. Listing 4.1, l. 10)).

Listing 4.1: OCL rules for the meta-structure of the augmented taxonomy on performance problems

```
context: Node
inv: Node.allInstances()->select(t |
     t.parent.oclIsUndefined())->size() = 1
inv: self.parent.oclIsUndefined()
     implies self.oclIsTypeOf(ActionNode)
inv: self.oclIsTypeOf(CategoryNode)
     implies self.parent.oclIsTypeOf(ConditionNode)
inv: self.childNodes->isEmpty()
     implies self.oclIsTypeOf(CategoryNode)
inv: not self.getType().conformsTo(self.parent.getType())
```

In the following, we introduce necessary steps to derive a PPEP instance from a performance problem taxonomy and create an instance for a selected part of the taxonomy shown in Figure 4.2.

4.4.2. Instantiating the Evaluation Plan

Based on the meta-structure explained before and shown in Figure 4.3, we instantiate the PPEP for a selected set of SPAs that we consider in more detail in the following chapters. To this end, we augment the grey part of the taxonomy depicted in Figure 4.2. The selected part of the taxonomy, covers database related performance problems as well as software bottlenecks. Both classes of performance problems occur very frequently in practice (Grabner, 2010). Furthermore, the selected part of the taxonomy contains conceptually different performance problems. This allows us, in the following chapters of this thesis, to evaluate the APPD approach with respect to different types of performance problems.

For the derivation of a concrete PPEP instance from a given taxonomy, we define four steps based on the following considerations:

1. **Characterization of Categories:** Each node from the original taxonomy is specified by a unique set of characteristics that differentiates the corresponding SPA from others. For each taxonomy node we capture these characteristics as boolean expressions. In this way, we create for each *Category Node* a preceding *Condition Node*. Parts of conditions

can be moved to preceding *Condition Nodes*, if the corresponding partial condition is common in all sibling *Condition Nodes*.

2. **Derivation of Experiments:** Based on the metrics used in the *Condition Nodes* we derive the definitions of experiments required to obtain these metrics. Primarily, we get for each *Condition Node* an *Action Node* describing the experiments to retrieve the data required for the subsequent *Condition Node*.

3. **Optimization:** As experiment execution is expensive in terms of time, we try to reduce the amount of *Action Nodes* in the PPEP instance. Therefore, we remove *Action Nodes* with redundant experiments and merge similar, light-weight experiments by moving and aggregating corresponding *Action Nodes* up to the next ancestor *Action Node*.

4. **Result Definition:** Finally, we define for each *Category Node* the template for the partial result by listing the artifact types that precisely specify an instance of the corresponding SPA.

Applying these steps to the grey part of the taxonomy in Figure 4.2 yields a PPEP instance as depicted in Figures 4.4-4.6.

Though a PPEP describes the high-level process for performance problem diagnostics, the *Action* and *Condition Nodes* of a PPEP may represent comprehensive executions of performance tests and complex evaluations of corresponding measurement data, respectively. Therefore, in the shown instance of the PPEP, we describe the *Action* and *Condition Nodes* on a high level of abstraction, whereby a detailed consideration of the actions and evaluation of conditions is covered by corresponding detection heuristics discussed in Chapter 6.

The root node of the PPEP is an Action Node describing the evaluation of the end-to-end response times R_{e2e} of all system services under a constant, high load (cf. Figure 4.4). If a time frame exists in which the response times R_{e2e} exceed the threshold T_{req} defined in the performance requirements, then a *Performance Problem* exists in the SUT. The result template of a *Performance Problem* allows for specifying the *guilty* system services that are responsible for the violation of performance requirements. Additionally, the rate of cases can be specified that violate the performance requirements.

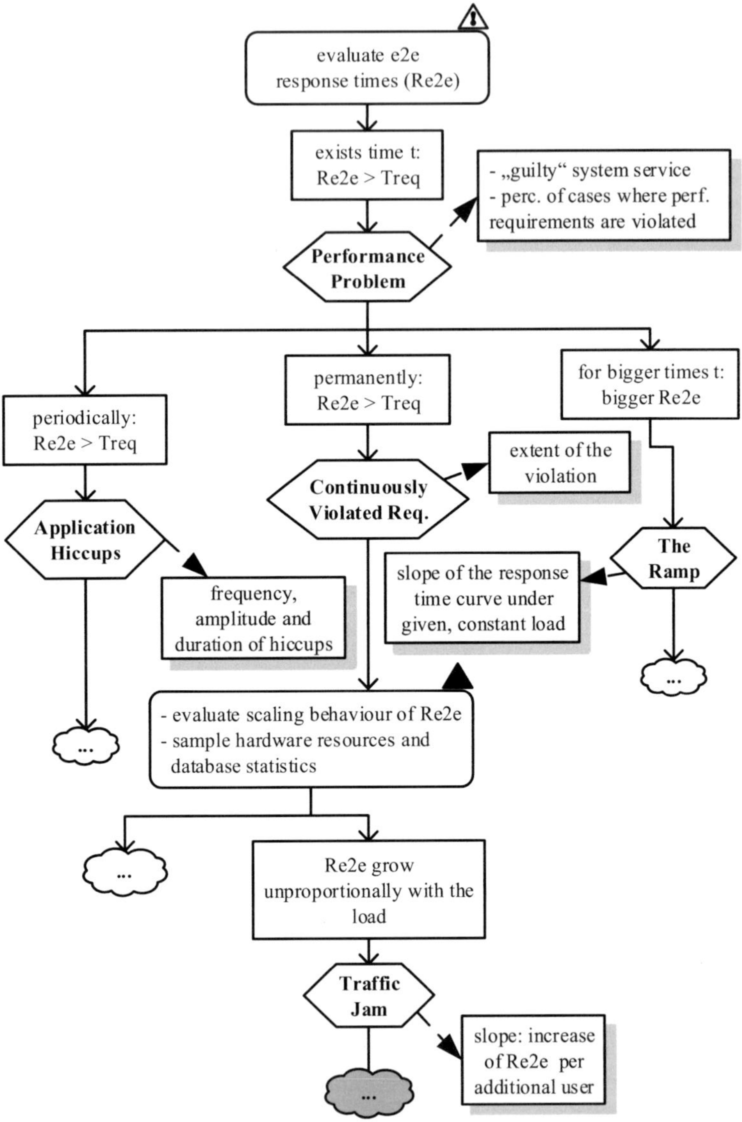

Figure 4.4.: Performance Problem Evaluation Plan - Part 1

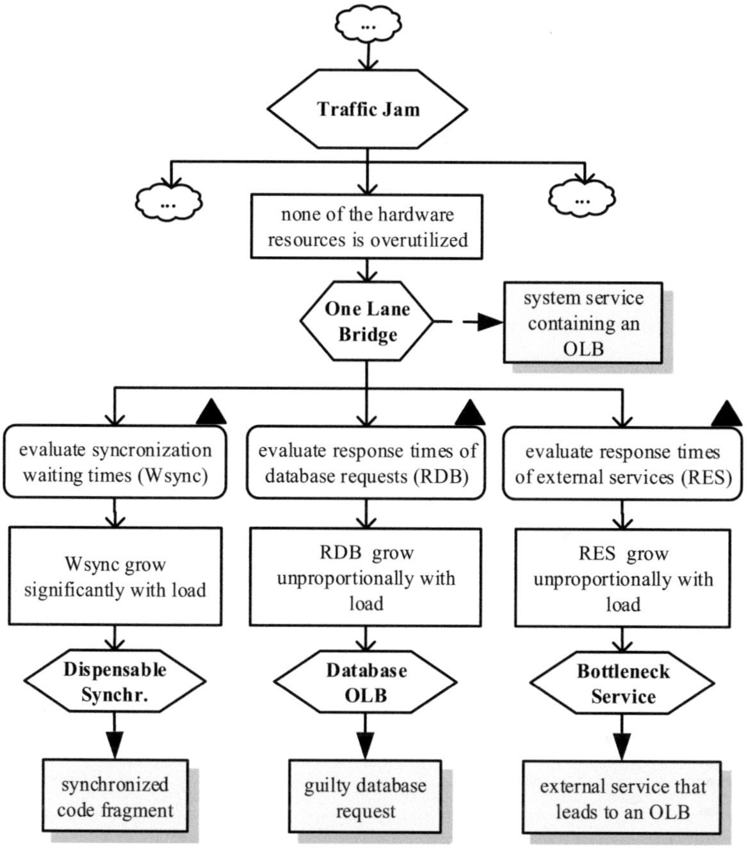

Figure 4.5.: Performance Problem Evaluation Plan - Part 2

If performance requirements are violated in periodic time frames, an *Application Hiccups* anti-pattern is present in the SUT. In this case, the partial result template allows to specify the frequency, amplitude and duration of the hiccups. If the end-to-end response times R_{e2e} grow with the operation time, then a *Ramp* anti-pattern has been observed specified by the slope of the increasing response time curve. Finally, if the response times R_{e2e} exceed the threshold T_{req} permanently, without any particular pattern, we observe

Continuously Violated Requirements. In this case, the result template allows for specifying the extent of violation by providing the average difference between the measured response times and the threshold T_{req}. In the case of continuously violated requirements, we need to distinguish between *Single User Problems* and scale-based problems (i.e. *Traffic Jam*) (cf. Figure 4.2). To this end, the end-to-end response times, utilizations of different hardware resources, and server statistics (e.g. database server, messaging server, etc.) have to be evaluated under different load situations. If single-user response times R_{e2e} do not violate performance requirements, however, the response times exceed the threshold T_{req} under higher load because of an unproportional growth of R_{e2e} with the load, then a *Traffic Jam* is detected in the SUT. A *Traffic Jam* is specified by the slope of the growing response times, i.e. the increase of R_{e2e} per additional user.

Figure 4.5 shows the continuation of the PPEP instance beneath the *Traffic Jam* node. An OLB is a special case of a *Traffic Jam* that occurs if none of the hardware resources exhibits a critical utilization (e.g. CPUs, Network, etc.) and at the same time response times R_{e2e} grow unproportionally with the load. The result template allows for specifying the system services that exhibit an OLB. Application-internal synchronization is a possible cause for an OLB. In order to evaluate that alternative, we need to measure the synchronization waiting times W_{sync} under different load intensities. If W_{sync} grow significantly with the load, then the *Dispensable Synchronization* anti-pattern is the root cause for the observed OLB. This root cause is specified by the location of the synchronized code fragment, which can be specified in the result template for the *Dispensable Synchronization* node. Database requests constitute another potential root cause for an occurrence of an OLB. Measuring the response times R_{DB} of database requests under different load intensities allows to evaluate whether the response times R_{DB} grow unproportionally with the load. If this is the case, then the database requests are most likely the root cause for an observed OLB. A *Databse OLB* result is characterized by the guilty SQL statement and the code location where the corresponding database query is emitted. Finally, external services constitute the third alternative root cause for an OLB. The evaluation of the *Bottleneck Service* is similar to the *Database OLB*. If response times R_{ES} of external services grow unproportionally with the load, then the corresponding external service is the root cause for the occurrence of the OLB. For the three root cause alternatives of the OLB we created three separate *Action Nodes* in the PPEP, as an aggregated *Action Node* may lead to a high measurement overhead in the corresponding performance tests because of the detailed retrieval of measurement data for each of the three *Action Nodes*.

Figure 4.6 shows the last part of the PPEP instance considered in this thesis. Based on the measurement data retrieved in the experiments of the *Action Node* preceding the *Traffic Jam* (cf. Figure 4.4), we can evaluate whether the network or a messaging server are critically utilized. In this case, the messaging behaviour of the SUT has to be evaluated under a scaling load intensity. If the message throughput stagnates with an increasing load, we can assume *Excessive Messaging*. *The Blob* and the *Empty Semi Trucks* anti-patterns as potential root causes for *Excessive Messaging* need to be evaluated in separation. For *the Blob* the participation in messaging p_C needs to be captured for each software component C under a constantly high load intensity. If a component C^* exists that has a significantly higher participation p_{C^*} than all other components, then, in terms of messaging, C^* is a Blob component that causes *Excessive Messaging*. The result template for *the Blob* allows to specify the guilty component as the root cause. For the evaluation of the *Empty Semi Trucks* anti-pattern the messaging patterns needs to be evaluated under single-user load. If many small messages are transmitted per user transaction, then we observe the *Empty Semi Trucks* anti-pattern. In this case, the partial diagnostics result is specified by the location of the code fragment that emits many small messages.

The right branch in Figure 4.6 shows another potential chain of causes for the *Traffic Jam* anti-pattern. If a high utilization of the database CPU (CPU_{DB}) is observed, or any tables of the database are excessively locked, then we observe *Database Congestion*. Observing the database access patterns under single-user load allows to evaluate the *Stifle* anti-pattern as a potential root cause for *Database Congestion*. To this end, we investigate whether many database requests are emitted with the same SQL query pattern. In the corresponding result template, an occurrence of a *Stifle* is specified by the SQL query pattern and the location of the code fragment that emits the corresponding database requests. An *Expensive Database Call* anti-pattern is identified if single database calls have a long execution time.

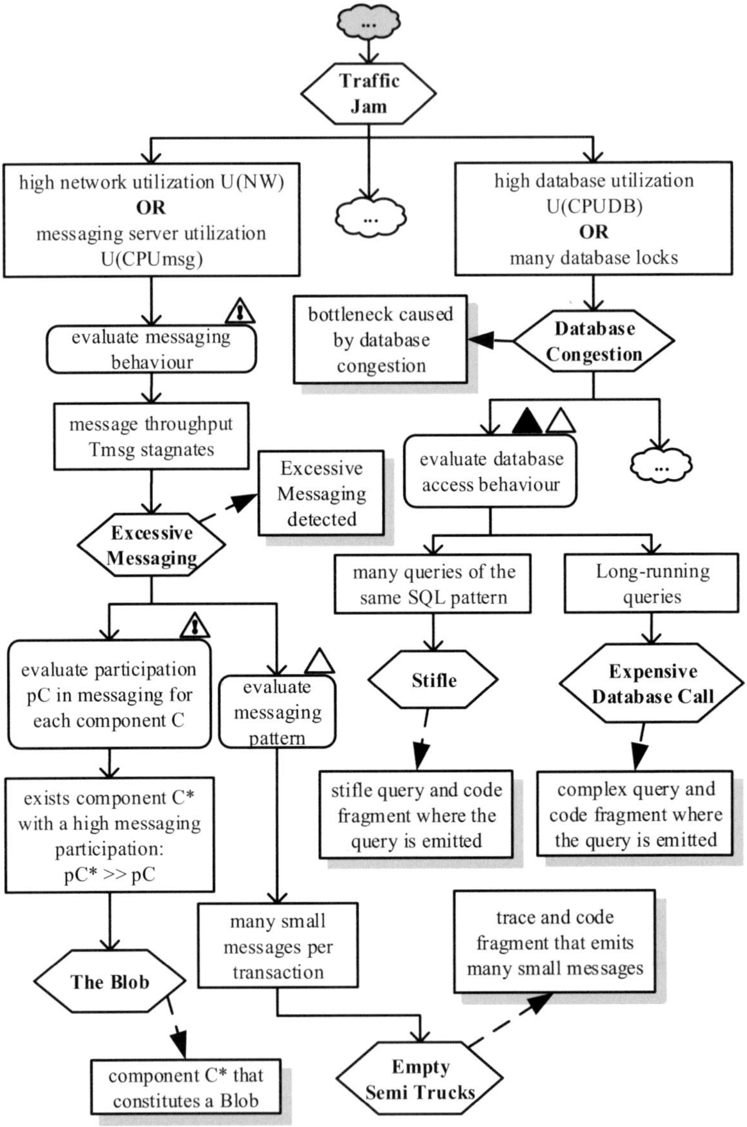

Figure 4.6.: Performance Problem Evaluation Plan - Part 3

4.4.3. Systematic Search Using an Evaluation Plan

The PPEP provides a means to describes a process for performance problem diagnostics. In this section, we explain a complimentary algorithm that uses a PPEP instance to automate the systematic diagnostics of performance problems.

4.4.3.1. Systematic Search Algorithm

The systematic search for performance problems and their root causes is depicted in Algorithm 1. The algorithm is based on a breadth-first search on a PPEP instance. Therefore, the algorithm is initiated with a PPEP instance $\mathcal{T}_a$ (Algorithm 1, line 2). The result tree $\mathcal{R}$ (cf. line 4) is a projection of $\mathcal{T}_a$ containing only *Category Nodes*. Hence initially, $\mathcal{R}$ reflects the original taxonomy that was used to derive $\mathcal{T}_a$. In the algorithm, $\mathcal{R}$ serves as a structured container for the diagnostics results. In particular, a final diagnostics result is an instance of the original taxonomy, whereby each taxonomy node is annotated either with `'detected'` or `'not-detected'`, respectively. For SPAs that have been detected in the SUT, specific detection artifacts are attached to the corresponding nodes in the result tree $\mathcal{R}$. Hence, the diagnostics result for a specific performance problem is the concatenation of the partial results (cf. Figure 4.3) along the path from the problem's deepest detected cause to the root node of the taxonomy. $\mathcal{Q}$ constitutes a processing queue for PPEP nodes used for breadth-first search (cf. line 7). Initially, $\mathcal{Q}$ contains only the root node of the PPEP instance $\mathcal{T}_a$. The set $\mathcal{M}$ is a repository for the measurement data gathered during execution of the performance tests (cf. line 8).

In the lines 11-13, all nodes of the result tree $\mathcal{R}$ are initially annotated with `'not-detected'`. The subsequent loop (cf. lines 15-32) iterates over the PPEP nodes in a breadth-first search manner. Depending on the type of the node in process η, different activities are conducted (cf. lines 18-28) before all children of η are enqueued to $\mathcal{Q}$ for processing (cf. lines 29-31). If the node in process is an *Action Node*, the algorithm executes the performance experiments defined in the corresponding node, and appends the gathered measurement data to the data repository $\mathcal{M}$ (cf. lines 18-20). The data repository $\mathcal{M}$ is used to evaluate the condition of a subsequent node of type

Algorithm 1 Systematic Search Algorithm

`Input:`
$\mathcal{T}_a$ *// an instance of the PPEP*
`Result:`
$\mathcal{R}$ *// the result tree $\mathcal{R}$ reflects $\mathcal{T}_a$, but contains only Category Nodes annotated with diagnostics results*
`Init:`
$\mathcal{R} \leftarrow$ simplified $\mathcal{T}_a$
$Q \leftarrow$ {root node of $\mathcal{T}_a$} *// queue on PPEP nodes to be processed*
$\mathcal{M} \leftarrow \{\}$ *// set of measurement data*
`Algorithm:`
for all $\tau \in \mathcal{R}$ **do**
  annotate τ as `'not-detected'`
end for

while Q is not empty **do**
  $\eta \leftarrow$ pull first element of Q
  $\zeta \leftarrow$ *true* *// ζ is a guard, indicating whether to descend into the sub-tree beneath η*
  if η is Action Node **then**
    $\mu \leftarrow$ *executeExperiments(η)* *// returns measured data*
    $\mathcal{M} \leftarrow \mathcal{M} \cup \{\mu\}$
  else if η is Condition Node **then**
    $\zeta \leftarrow$ *evaluateCondition(η , $\mathcal{M}$)* *// returns the boolean value of the evaluated condition*
  else if η is Category Node **then**
    $\tau \leftarrow$ corresponding node in $\mathcal{R}$ for η
    annotate τ as `'detected'`
    $\rho \leftarrow$ *calculatePartialResult(η , $\mathcal{M}$)* *// fill result template with concrete information*
    attach ρ to τ
  end if
  if ζ is true **then**
    enqueue all child nodes of η to Q
  end if
end while
return $\mathcal{R}$

Condition Node (cf. lines 21-22). If a condition for a node η is evaluated to `false`, the guard ζ ensures that the child nodes of η are not enqueued for processing in lines 29-31. In this way, the entire sub-tree beneath η is skipped and all *Category Nodes* of that sub-tree remain annotated as `'not-detected'`. However, if a condition is evaluated to `true` the descending *Category Node* η will reach the lines 24-27 of the algorithm, meaning that the SPA represented by η has been detected in the SUT. In this case, the algorithm annotates the corresponding result node τ in $\mathcal{R}$ with `'detected'`. Furthermore, based on the measurement data $\mathcal{M}$ and the result template of the *Category Node* η (cf. Figure 4.3), the algorithm calculates the specific result artifact ρ and attaches it to the result node τ. As soon as the queue Q is empty, the algorithm terminates, returning the result tree $\mathcal{R}$ that contains information about detected SPAs, and additional diagnostics information according to the result templates.

Summing up, Algorithm 1 describes a high-level procedure of using a PPEP for diagnostics of performance problems. In particular, the main complexity of diagnosing performance problems is hidden behind the three tasks *executeExperiments()*, *evaluateCondition()* and *calculatePartialResult()*. For each SPA these tasks are encapsulated in a corresponding detection heuristic. In Chapter 6, we discuss the detection heuristics in more detail and explain how these tasks are conducted for the individual SPAs.

4.4.3.2. Complexity Considerations

Execution of performance experiments is very time consuming and, thus, the critical factor that determines the time complexity of a performance problem diagnostics approach. Hence, during diagnostics of performance problems it is important to avoid execution of unnecessary experiments. The introduced algorithm (cf. Algorithm 1) realizes a systematic search for performance problems and their root causes while avoiding unnecessary experiments. Without a systematic approach, the only alternative to diagnose performance problems is the brute-force scan for all known SPAs. Therefore, we qualitatively compare the computational complexity of the systematic search algorithm against a brute-force diagnostics approach.

Let us assume that the set of all known SPAs has a cardinality of n. For that n SPAs we would apply the described categorization, taxonomy derivation and augmentation steps to obtain a PPEP instance. For simplicity, let us further assume that

- the resulting PPEP instance is a balanced tree with a height h and width b that defines the number of child nodes per tree node.
- each *Category Node* has exactly one preceding *Condition Node* and *Action Node*.

Hence, the number of *Action Nodes* in the PPEP instance is:

$$n = \sum_{i=0}^{h-1} b^i = 1 + b \sum_{i=0}^{h-2} b^i \tag{4.1}$$

Applying the brute-force diagnostics approach means that each SPA is analyzed individually. Independently whether and how many performance problems (i.e. in this context: root causes) exist in the SUT, the brute-force approach implies n evaluation steps, resulting in the following time complexity:

$$C_{BF} = n = 1 + b \sum_{i=0}^{h-2} b^i \tag{4.2}$$

The complexity of the Systematic Search Algorithm depends on the number of existing performance problems in the SUT and their location in the PPEP instance. Hence, depending on the number of performance problems we can calculate a best-case and a worst-case complexity of the Systematic Search Algorithm.

No performance problem In the case that no performance problem exists in the SUT, no symptoms are visible from outside the SUT. Hence, the first *Condition Node* in the PPEP would be evaluated to `false`, so that the Systematic Search Algorithm terminates after **one** evaluation step. In this case, the Systematic Search Algorithm is obviously significantly superior to a brute-force diagnostics approach.

One performance problem If the SUT contains exactly one root cause of a performance problem, the algorithm would evaluate b alternatives on each level of the PPEP instance and descend into the one branch that leads to the root cause of the performance problems. The resulting complexity $C_{SSA}(1)$ for one problem is:

$$C_{SSA}(1) = 1 + \sum_{i=1}^{h-1} b = 1 + b\,(h-1) \tag{4.3}$$

For a PPEP instance with a height $h > 2$ and width $b > 1$ the complexity of the Systematic Search Algorithm is smaller than the complexity of the brute-force approach:

$$C_{SSA}(1) = 1 + \sum_{i=1}^{h-1} b < 1 + \sum_{i=1}^{h-1} b^i = C_{BF} \tag{4.4}$$

The benefit in time complexity of the Systematic Search Algorithm shown in Equation 4.4 becomes more significant the wider and higher the instance of the PPEP is. For instance, with a width of $b = 2$ and a height of $h = 4$ the Systematic Search Algorithm is more than double as efficient as the brute-force approach with the complexities of $C_{SSA}(1) = 7$ and $C_{BF} = 15$, respectively.

Multiple performance problems Given the case that the SUT contains x root causes of performance problems, whereby $1 < x \leq b$, the complexity $C_{SSA}(x)$ depends on the distribution of the root causes in the PPEP instance. In the best case, the x root causes are located in the same PPEP branch, so that the corresponding *Category Nodes* in the PPEP have the same ancestor *Category Node*. In this case, the best-case time complexity $C^{bc}_{SSA}(x)$ of the algorithm is the same as for one root cause (cf. Equation 4.4). By contrast, if the root causes are equally distributed among different PPEP branches, the Systematic Search Algorithm has to descend the entire depth of the tree x times. Consequently, the worst-case complexity $C^{wc}_{SSA}(x)$ can be calculated as follows:

$$C^{wc}_{SSA}(x) = 1 + b + xb\,(h-2) \quad , \quad 1 < x \leq b \tag{4.5}$$

Given the extreme case that $x = b$, the complexity $C^{wc}_{SSA}(x)$ is still smaller than the brute-force complexity C_{BF}:

$$\begin{aligned} C^{wc}_{SSA}(b) = 1 + b + b^2 (h-2) &= 1 + b + b^2 + b^2 + \ldots + b^2 \\ &< 1 + b + b^2 + b^3 + \ldots + b^{h-1} \\ &= 1 + b \sum_{i=0}^{h-2} b^i = C_{BF} \end{aligned} \tag{4.6}$$

Many performance problems In the case, that the SUT contains a performance problem instance for each leaf node of the PPEP instance, the Systematic Search Algorithm would need to traverse the entire PPEP instance resulting in a time complexity C^{wc}_{SSA} that is equal to the complexity C_{BF} of the brute-force approach.

To sum up, the time complexity C_{SSA} of the Systematic Search Algorithm is never worse than the brute-force complexity C_{BF}. Assuming that diagnostics of performance problems is conducted on a regular, frequent basis, the SUT should not contain many root causes for performance problems at the same time. The SUT would contain only a few, if at all, different performance problems. In such a case, the Systematic Search Algorithm is significantly more efficient than a naive, brute-force diagnostics approach (cf. Equations 4.4,4.6) and, therefore, increases the practicability of the APPD approach.

4.5. Summary

In this chapter, we introduced a methodology to systematize the diagnostics of performance problems. The core idea is to utilize the explicit knowledge about recurrent types of performance problems, known as Software Performance Anti-patterns (SPAs), and to structure that knowledge in order to provide an explicit, systematic guidance in diagnosing performance problems. We defined a process that describes by means of four activities how to create a Performance Problem Evaluation Plan (PPEP) from a set of SPA definitions. The first activity describes the step of gathering knowledge about existing SPAs. Next, SPAs have to be categorized to gain a better understanding of the characteristics of individual SPAs. Based on some observations regarding the definitions of SPAs, we developed a categorization template and applied the template to 27 selected SPAs. Based on the categorization results, we were able to identify SPAs that are relevant for our measurement-based diagnostics approach. Furthermore, we used the insights from the categorization to create a taxonomy on performance problems for the selected set of relevant SPAs. Augmenting the taxonomy structure by additional information on diagnostics activities, we introduced the meta-structure of the PPEP. We described the steps to be conducted in order to derive a PPEP instance from a performance problem taxonomy and demonstrated the instantiation on a selected part of the previously created taxonomy. Finally, we introduced the Systematic Search Algorithm that utilizes a PPEP to systematically search for performance problems and their root causes. Conducting a theoretical analysis of the complexity of the Systematic Search Algorithm, we have shown that in most cases the Systematic Search Algorithm exhibits a significantly higher efficiency than a brute-force diagnostics approach.

5. Specification Languages for Performance Problem Diagnostics

As described in Section 3.1, the main benefit of the Automatic Performance Problem Diagnostics (APPD) approach results from the decoupling of generic, context-independent knowledge about performance problem diagnostics and the context-specific information required for diagnostics of performance problems. While the context-specific information needs to be provided for every application context of APPD, the generic knowledge is intended to be captured once in a generic way so that it can be reused independently from the specific context. Both types of information need to be captured in a proper, goal-oriented way facilitating the usage of the APPD approach for the knowledge providers (i.e. performance experts) as well as the end users of APPD (e.g. developers, system operators, etc.). Hence, besides a language that allows to specify necessary context-specific information for problem diagnostics, we need generic languages that allow to capture experimentation rules in a system-, tool- and context-independent, as well as reusable way.

In this chapter, we introduce the Performance Problem Diagnostics Description Model (P^2D^2M) that comprises four sub-meta-models for the definition of context-specific information as well as generic experimentation descriptions for performance problem diagnostics. Section 5.1 discusses the motivation for a new description language for performance problem diagnostics. The sub-meta-model for the specification of context-specific information for the APPD approach is introduced in Section 5.2. In Section 5.3, we introduce languages for the specification of generic experimentation rules, instrumentation instructions and corresponding data formats for the resulting measurement data. Finally, this chapter is summarized in Section 5.4.

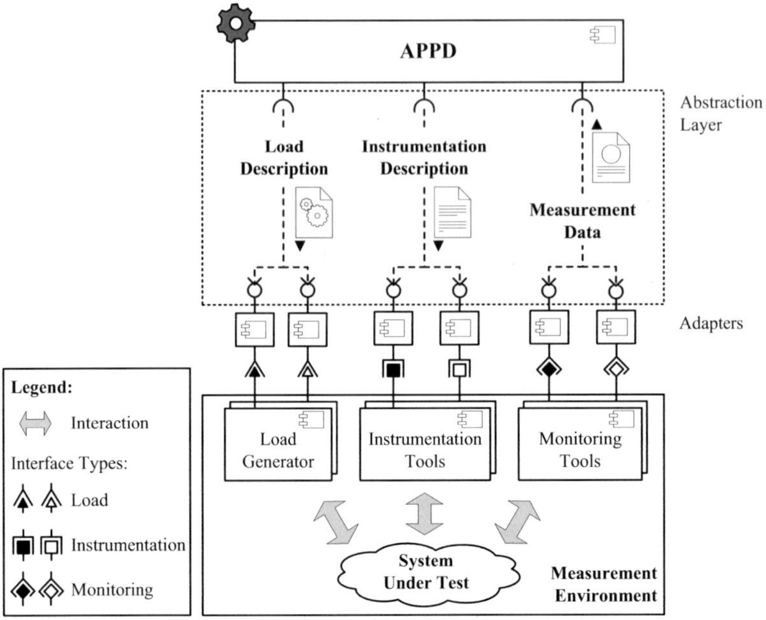

Figure 5.1.: Abstraction Layer Context

5.1. The Abstraction Layer

As mentioned in Section 3.2, an abstraction layer between a specific measurement environment (including the System Under Test (SUT) and used measurement tools) and our APPD approach is an essential part in order to enable the development of generic, context-independent *detection heuristics* for individual Software Performance Anti-patterns (SPAs). A properly defined abstraction layer allows to specify detection heuristics in a generic way while the specific application contexts (i.e. SUT, measurement tools, etc.) can vary without the need to adapt the detection heuristics to the specific contexts. In this section, we discuss the requirements on the abstraction layer in order to identify its essential, constituent parts.

Figure 5.1 shows the context for the abstraction layer. The *Measurement Environment* comprises the SUT as well as all tools used for conducting measurements, including *Load Generators*, *Instrumentation Tools* and *Monitoring Tools*. The Load Generators are responsible for emulating virtual users that apply a load on the SUT. Instrumentation Tools are used to enrich the SUT with measurement probes that retrieve measurement data from the internals of the target application (e.g. response times of individual methods) as well as the corresponding landscape (e.g. utilization of hardware resources). Finally, the Monitoring Tools are responsible to collect data from the placed measurement probes. With respect to performance testing, the measurement tools constitute the interface to the SUT. In particular, a measurement-based diagnostics approach (such as our APPD approach) does not interact directly with the SUT but over the measurement tools. Corresponding to the different types of measurement tools, we distinguish three relevant *interface types* in the Measurement Environment, as illustrated by the different interface symbols (triangle, square, and diamond) in Figure 5.1. Moreover, within an interface type the interfaces may differ depending on the concrete tool implementations used in the specific context. For instance, HP LoadRunner™ (LoadRunner 2014) and Apache JMeter™ (JMeter 2014) provide different interfaces though both tools are load generators. The big variety of existing measurement tools that can be used in specific contexts constitutes a challenge that needs to be dealt with in order to create a generic, automatic diagnostics approach.

The most top box in Figure 5.1 represents an implementation of the APPD approach, comprising the systematic search for performance problems and their root causes (cf. Chapter 4), as well as generically defined detection heuristics for individual SPAs (described in detail in Chapter 6). In order to bridge the gap between generically defined detection heuristics of the APPD approach and specific Measurement Environments, two additional layers are required in between: First, an *Abstraction Layer* enables the generic definition of detection heuristics based on a common understanding of underlying, specific contexts (i.e. SUTs and measurement tools). Second, a layer of tool *Adapters* transforms the generic concepts defined by the Abstraction Layer to corresponding, tool-specific interpretations. Hence, instead of defining detection heuristics specifically for each available combination of measurement tools, with these two layers we reduce the complexity by shifting the transformation of generic to specific knowledge to a more elementary layer (Adapters layer) that is close to the individual measurement tools. The essence of the Abstraction Layer is to provide generic languages and data

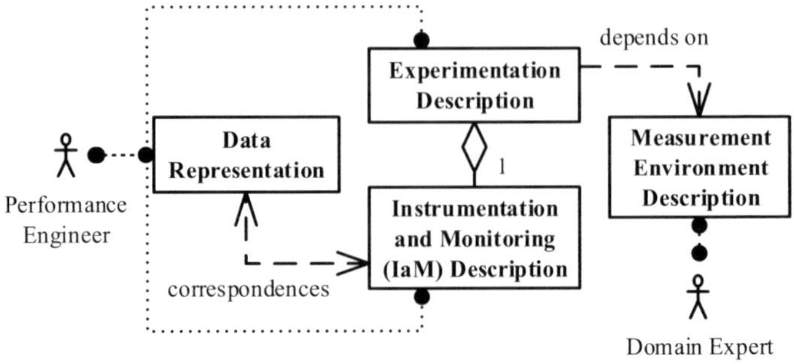

Figure 5.2.: meta-models and their interrelationships

formats that cover the core concepts of the corresponding interface types and at the same time provide the basis for a generic specification of detection heuristics for different SPAs. Consequently, we identified the following three requirements for the Abstraction Layer:

- The Abstraction Layer must provide a language that allows to generically specify which performance tests should be executed by the underlying load generators and how to execute them (cf. *Load Description* in Figure 5.1).
- An *Instrumentation Description* language is required that enables to specify instrumentation instructions (i.e. where and what to measure) independently from the SUT and the used instrumentation tools.
- Finally, a *Measurement Data* format is required to provide a common understanding of the measurement data returned by used monitoring tools.

Based on these considerations, we develop the P^2D^2M that comprises four sub-meta-models that constitute the Abstraction Layer and its binding to a specific application context. Thereby, we specify the abstract syntax and informal semantics of the languages. Figure 5.2 shows the four sub-meta-models, their interrelationships, and their assignment to corresponding stakeholder roles.

As mentioned in Chapter 3, in the context of our APPD approach, the performance engineer is responsible for providing generic knowledge about diagnostics of performance problems. We further have shown that this knowledge covers two aspects: knowledge about the generic process of diagnosing performance problems and the knowledge on the detection heuristics for individual SPAs. In Chapter 4, we discussed in detail the former aspect, whereas, for the formalization of the knowledge on specific detection heuristics the abstraction layer plays a crucial role. In particular, in order to describe detection heuristics that follow the Systematic Selective Experimentation (SSE) concept (cf. Section 3.2.1), the performance engineer requires languages that allow him to generically specify experiment series and the corresponding measurement data to be retrieved . To this end, we provide the *Experimentation Description* meta-model and the *Instrumentation and Monitoring (IaM) Description* meta-model. For each detection heuristic that a performance engineer creates fo an SPA, he provides an experimentation description that specifies which experiments need to be executed. Furthermore, the performance engineer specifies an IaM Description that specifies which measurement data needs to be retrieved from the SUT for the detection heuristic of the corresponding SPA. The IaM Description is attached to the Experimentation Description for the SPA under investigation. Finally, the performance engineer has to specify analysis strategies to be applied on the measurement data gathered during corresponding experiments. Thereto, he requires a common, context-independent way to access the measurement data. To this end, we provide the *Data Representation* meta-model that provides a common representation of performance measurement data, as well as its binding to corresponding entities of the IaM Description. By means of the Experimentation Description, IaM Description and Data Representation meta-models the performance engineer is able to define generic, context-independent detection heuristics for individual SPAs. However in most cases, the circumstances under which SPAs emerge as performance problems are relative to the characteristics of a specific SUT (e.g. size or load of the SUT). On the one hand, in order to support this relativity, the detection heuristics must be defined in a way that they allow to be parametrized with context-specific characteristics. On the other hand, a language is required that allows a domain expert to provide the necessary, context-specific information for a concrete SUT (e.g. the performance requirements for the SUT, or a description of the measurement environment components, etc.). To this end, we introduce the *Measurement Environment (ME) Description* meta-model. Corresponding model instances bind generic detection heuristics to specific application contexts of APPD by providing context-specific information for the parametrization of the detection heuristics. While ME Descriptions are created by domain experts for each individual application context of APPD, the remaining models are assigned to the performance expert and are intended to be created once for each individual, generic detection heuristic of an SPA (cf. Section 3.1).

In the following, we introduce the abstract syntax of the four meta-models and describe the corresponding informal semantics. We use UML Class diagrams to present the abstract syntax of the languages.

5.2. Context-specific Description of the Measurement Environment

In this section, we introduce the meta-model for the specification of context-specific characteristics of concrete measurement environments and experimentation related properties. We discuss the design goals for the meta-model (Section 5.2.1) and describe the abstract syntax with the corresponding informal syntax (Section 5.2.2).

5.2.1. Design Goals

The following goals guide the design of the ME Description meta-model:

Simplicity The ME Description is the only meta-model a domain experts has to deal with in the context of using APPD. As discussed in Section 3.1, the manual effort to provide context-specific information by the domain expert as well as the effort for setting up the measurement environment mainly constitute the *per-project-effort* of APPD and, thus, significantly affect the cost-benefit ratio of APPD. Hence, it is important that the ME Description meta-model allows a domain expert to provide the necessary, context-specific information in a simple way so that the overhead for using APPD is kept to a minimum. Consequently, the meta-model should be designed as simple as possible in order to keep the complexity of creating corresponding model instances low.

Focus Experiment specification languages that support multiple-purposes (such as D. Westermann et al., 2013) exhibit a high level of abstraction with the costs of sacrificing specificity of semantics, i.e. the semantics of individual meta-model elements are generic and, thus, context-independent. By contrast, the ME Description language has the specific purpose of specifying context-specific information for automatic, measurement-based performance problem diagnostics. Hence, the corresponding meta-model should be tailored for this purpose, comprising elements with clear, specific semantics. A tailored meta-model fosters simplicity due to a better understanding of the specific semantics.

Re-use In order to reduce the additional modelling effort for the domain experts, the ME Description meta-model must not cover information that is explicitly captured by other, existing artifacts or models. In particular, necessary artifacts that typically exist in performance-aware software development projects (cf. Section 3.3) should be re-used for APPD by referencing them in the ME Description, but, the meta-model must not provide redundant modelling constructs for the information covered by these artifacts.

Extensibility As mentioned before, the purpose of the ME Description language is to cover context-specific information (e.g. specification of the measurement environment) for performance problem diagnostics. However, the information space in the scope of specific application contexts for APPD is typically highly diverse and evolves over time (for instance, due to a high variety of existing measurement tools, evolution of tools and releases of new tools). Therefore, the meta-model for the ME Description must allow for flexible extensibility. In particular, evolution or usage of a new measurement tools must not imply changes on the meta-model.

5.2.2. Abstract Syntax

Figure 5.3 shows the abstract syntax of the ME Description meta-model. The ME Description element is the root of the meta-model, comprising a set of *Environment Entities* and exactly one *Experimentation Configuration.* As described in Section 5.1, for APPD the set of measurement tools constitutes

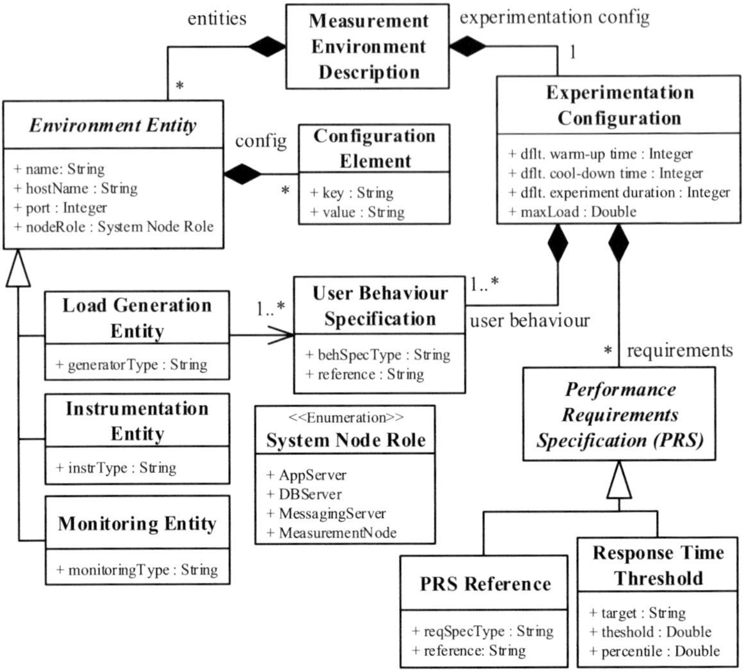

Figure 5.3.: Measurement Environment Description meta-model

the interface to the SUT as all interactions with the SUT are conducted over the measurement tools. The set of Environment Entities reflects the set of measurement tools used in a specific application context. More precisely, each Environment Entity instance represents a deployed adapter to a measurement tool (cf. Figure 5.1). Thus, assuming that the underlying adapters conform to the corresponding, common interfaces, each Environment Entity is identified by a *name* and specifies under which *hostName* (or IP) and *port* the corresponding adapter is accessible. Furthermore, an Environment Entity has a *nodeRole* that describes the role of the corresponding system node in the measurement environment. Possible roles are: *AppServer, DBServer, MessagingServer* and *MeasurementNode*. While the first three roles represent nodes of the SUT, the MeasurementNode role stands for all nodes that are part of the measurement environment, however, that do not belong to the

SUT (e.g. a load generator node). The Environment Entity meta-model element itself is an abstract class. As mentioned in Section 5.1, we distinguish three different roles of measurement tools: monitoring, instrumentation and load generation tools. Often, the instrumentation and monitoring roles are implemented in a single tool. Nevertheless, due to separation of concerns, we consider load generation, instrumentation and measurement as separate roles with individual types of interface. Corresponding to the measurement tool roles, we distinguish three concrete Environment Entity types in the meta-model: *Monitoring Entities*, *Instrumentation Entities* and *Load Generation Entities* represent adapters to monitoring tools, instrumentation tools, and load generators, respectively. Each concrete Environment Entity is characterized by a corresponding type (*monitoringType, instrType* and *generatorType*), modelled as a String attribute. These types refer to the actual tool implementations used in the specific application context. For instance, the *generatorType* of a Load Generation Entity may refer to an HP LoadRunner™ (LoadRunner 2014) instance or an Apache JMeter™ (JMeter 2014) installation. The *instrType* and *monitoringType* may refer to monitoring and instrumentation tools like Kieker (van Hoorn et al., 2012), DiSL (Marek et al., 2012) or our Adaptable Instrumentation and Monitoring (AIM) tool (Wert et al., 2015a). For the purpose of extensibility, we do not explicitly include all available measurement tool types into the meta-model. As a ME Description model is intended to be automatically parsed by an implementation of the APPD approach (e.g. DynamicSpotter (Wert, 2015)), it is the responsibility of the implementation to validate the *type* attributes of the Environment Entities and to evaluate whether corresponding tool adapters exist. As different measurement tools may have tool-specific configuration parameters, the meta-model allows to specify a set of key-value pairs (cf. *Configuration Element*) for each Environment Entity. The Configuration Elements are intended to be passed to corresponding measurement tool adapters that interpret the configurations and apply them to the underlying measurement tools. A *Load Generation Entity* must be assigned with at least one *User Behaviour Specification* that describes the behaviour of the virtual users to be emulated by the corresponding load generator. There are sophisticating approaches to describe user behaviour for specific load generator tools (e.g. HP LoadRunner™ VUser scripts, or Apache JMeter™ test scripts) or in a generic way (van Hoorn et al., 2008; Shams et al., 2006). Due to the re-use and extensibility design goals (cf. Section 5.2.1), we abstain from providing detailed modelling constructs for specifying user behaviour.

Therefore, the User Behaviour Specification element is only a reference to an existing artifact describing the user behaviour. The User Behaviour Specification is characterized by a behaviour specification type (*behSpecType*) and a *reference* String. While the *behSpecType* specifies the type of the external artifact (e.g. HP LoadRunner™ VUser script), the *reference* constitutes a pointer to the actual artifact. Depending on the artifact type, the *reference* may contain a file name (e.g. path to a VUser script file), a pointer to another, external model element (e.g. a User Behaviour Model element as described in van Hoorn et al., 2008), or any other type of pointer. Again, it is the responsibility of the APPD implementation to resolve the User Behaviour Specification references and to ensure that the *behSpecType* matches the *generatorType* of the Load Generation Entity using the corresponding User Behaviour Specification.

The Experimentation Configuration element covers all boundary conditions on the experiment execution implied by the specific application context. First, the Experimentation Configuration serves as a container for all User Behaviour Specifications that should be used in the application context potentially by different load generators. As proper experiment timings highly depend on the characteristics of the specific SUT, the Experimentation Configuration allows a domain expert to specify common experimentation times: *default warm-up time*, *default cool-down time*, and *default experiment duration*. The *maxLoad* attribute specifies the maximum load that the SUT should be able to handle without running into performance problems. Finally, the Experimentation Configuration comprises a set of *Performance Requirements Specifications (PRS)* that determine under which circumstances the performance requirements can be considered as violated in the specific application context. Hence, the Performance Requirements Specifications determines under which circumstances a performance problem is present and, thus, when APPD should resume with deeper diagnostics. We provide two concrete Performance Requirements Specifications: the *Response Time Threshold* and the *PRS Reference*. The Response Time Threshold allows to specify performance requirements in a very simple way by providing a fix *threshold* for the response time of a *target* service and a corresponding *percentile* that specifies in how many percent of cases the threshold must not be exceeded. The PRS Reference allows to reference an external performance requirements artifact that may be specified using sophisticated performance requirements and Service Level Agreement (SLA) specification languages (Frølund et al., 1998; Leue, 1995; Ren et al., 1997; Lamanna et al., 2003; Keller et al., 2003). With the requirements specification type (*reqSpecType*) and *reference* attributes, the PRS Reference uses the same reference mechanism as explained for the User Behaviour Specification element. Examples of instances for this part of the P^2D^2M are shown in Section 6.2.2 and Section 7.2.

5.3. Generic Specification of Performance Tests

In this section, we introduce three interdependent meta-models describing languages for generic specification of performance test series, including an *Experimentation Description* characterizing the load series, an IaM Description specifying the data to be measured (Wert et al., 2015b), and a Data Representation model describing the data format for measured data. While the ME Description introduced in the previous section is intended to be used by domain experts to provide context-specific information, the languages introduces in this section constitute the basis for the definition of generic detection heuristics by performance engineers. Explicit definitions of detection heuristics imply some important benefits: First, explicit definitions of performance tests can be more easily maintained and improved over time. Second, generic, explicitly written down detection heuristics support interchange of knowledge in performance problem diagnostics and propagation of best practices. In this way, common mistakes in performance evaluation as described by Jain, 1991 can be reduced. Finally, the most important aspect for this thesis is that generic, explicit detection heuristics are automatable. As key enabler for generic, explicit definitions of detection heuristics, the languages introduced in this section constitute an important part of the APPD approach. In the following, we introduce the design goals for the meta-models and introduce their abstract syntax while discussing the corresponding, informal semantics. Note that parts of this section are based on our publication (Wert et al., 2015b) and the supervised Master's Thesis (Schulz, 2014).

5.3.1. Design Goals

The following three design goals apply to all three meta-models introduced in this section:

Abstraction In order to enable generic definition of detection heuristics, the languages used for their definition have to abstract from any context-specific information. In particular, the languages must abstract from concrete target applications, programming languages of the target application, used measurement tools as well as performance requirements of the specific context. Hereby, we assume that the programming languages are from the set of modern-day managed runtimes (cf. Section 3.3.1).

Focus Description languages with a clear focus on a certain domain allow to define expressive models with specific semantics while reducing complexity and effort of model creation. Though the meta-models introduced in this section are intended to be generic with respect to SUTs and measurement tools, they nevertheless are designed for a particular purpose. The focus of the meta-models lies on the definition of performance test plans for diagnostics of performance problems.

Declarativity We propose a declarative description of the execution of experiments and the SUT instrumentation in order to decouple the *What* from the *How*. More precisely, while the description languages declaratively describe which experiments to execute, what data to measure, and what the desired data format is, they abstain from determining the realization.

From the three meta-models introduced in this section, the IaM Description meta-model is the most complex and challenging with respect to conceptualization and design. The process of instrumenting a target application is per se application-specific. Hence, we have to develop new instrumentation description concepts in order to enable a generic IaM Description language. Furthermore, the design of the IaM Description may influence the measurement overhead of the realized instrumentation instructions. Therefore, we identified the following additional design goals for the IaM Description meta-model:

Orthogonality An instrumentation instruction describes two different aspects: *Where* to measure, and *What* to measure (cf. Section 2.3). In general, both aspects are independent from each other and can be comprehensive and complex. In order to be independently reusable, these aspects need to be defined independently from each other.

Composability In order to provide a flexible and expressive way of describing instrumentation instructions, the meta-model needs to be composable. Besides the orthogonality of *Where* and *What* to measure, individual model elements should cover basic, minimalistic aspects of the SUT and the measurement data of interest. In this way, instrumentation descriptions can be kept simple (e.g. in order to keep the measurement overhead low), while advanced descriptions can be composed from elementary parts, when needed.

5.3.2. Abstract Syntax

In this section, we introduce the abstract syntax and the informal semantics of the three meta-models Experimentation Description, IaM Description and Data Representation (cf. Figure 5.2).

5.3.2.1. Experimentation Description

As described in Section 3.2.1, the APPD approach is based on the Systematic Selective Experimentation (SSE) concept. Hence, each detection heuristic implies execution of at least one, mostly multiple, experiments, whereby individual experiments differ in the load and the instrumentation of the SUT during the experiments. A performance engineer that defines detection heuristics requires a specification language that allows him to describe such series of experiments in a context-independent way. To this end, we provide the Experimentation Description meta-model whose abstract syntax is depicted in Figure 5.4.

An Experimentation Description is intended to be instantiated for the definition of each individual detection heuristic developed for an SPA. Constituting the root element of the meta-model, the Experimentation Description element consists of an *Experiment Plan* and a reference to an IaM Description.

While the Experiment Plan describes the experiments to be executed for the corresponding detection heuristic, the attached IaM Description specifies the measurement data to be retrieved from the SUT during the execution of the Experiment Plan. An Experiment Plan is specified in a generic way that, however, is relative to the context-specific information provided in the ME Description meta-model (cf. Section 5.2). For instance, the semantics of the *«depends»* relationship includes that during the execution of the specified Experiment Plan, the load generators specified in the ME Description model execute the virtual user behaviours specified in the corresponding User Behaviour Specifications (cf. Figure 5.3). We distinguish two different types of Experiment Plans: *Experiment* and *Experiment Series*. While an Experiment describes a single performance test, an Experiment Series represents a sequence of different performance tests. An Experiment can have an arbitrary set of experiment specifying parameter values that appear in the final measurement data as additional specification of data. The *Parameter Value* element is further defined in the Data Representation meta-model explained further below in Section 5.3.2.3. The meta-model provides three different, concrete Experiment types. The *Load Test* element represents a performance test with the maximum allowed load intensity. Hence, the concrete semantics of this element depends on the *maxLoad* attribute of the Experimentation Configuration element in the ME Description model. The *Single-user Test* describes a performance test with a minimum load intensity (i.e. one user in the case of a closed workload), whereby no concurrent user requests are allowed. The default, context-specific experimentation times specified in the Experimentation Configuration element of the ME Description model should be used for both the Load Test and the Single-user Test. Furthermore, both the Load Test and the Single-user Test have an implicit experiment specifying Parameter Value that captures the corresponding load intensity. Finally, the *Custom Test* allows to specify a performance test with custom experimentation timings and custom load. However, all value specifications of the Custom Test are relative to the default values of the Experimentation Configuration, too. In particular, the attributes of the Custom Test allow to specify a multiplication factor for the corresponding default values. As experimentation timings and performance requirements are defined by the domain expert in the ME Description model, the performance engineer does not need to think about absolute values when using the Experimentation Description meta-model for defining generic detection heuristics, but, provides relative scales for the individual attributes. Besides the three Experiment types, the

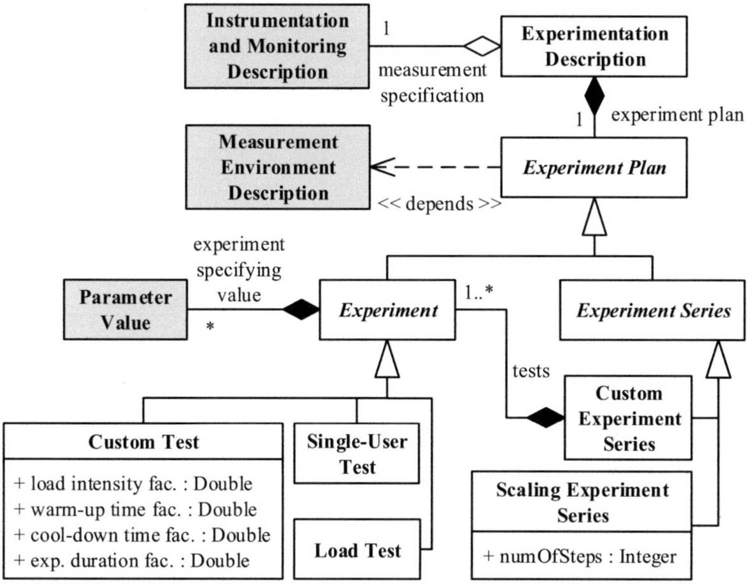

Figure 5.4.: Meta-model for the Description of Experiment Series

meta-model provides two types of *Experiment Series*. The *Custom Experiment Series* allows to explicitly specify an arbitrary sequence of *Experiments*. In contrast, the *Scaling Experiment Series* describes an implicit sequence of performance tests, whereby the load intensity is evenly increased from one experiment to the next. The first experiment starts with the minimum load (i.e. one concurrent user), and the last experiment is executed with the maximum load that is specified in the Experimentation Configuration element of the ME Description model. The *numOfSteps* attribute specifies the number of experiments (with a minimum of 2) to be executed as part of the Scaling Experiment Series and, thus, determines the interval of the increase in load between two consecutive experiments.

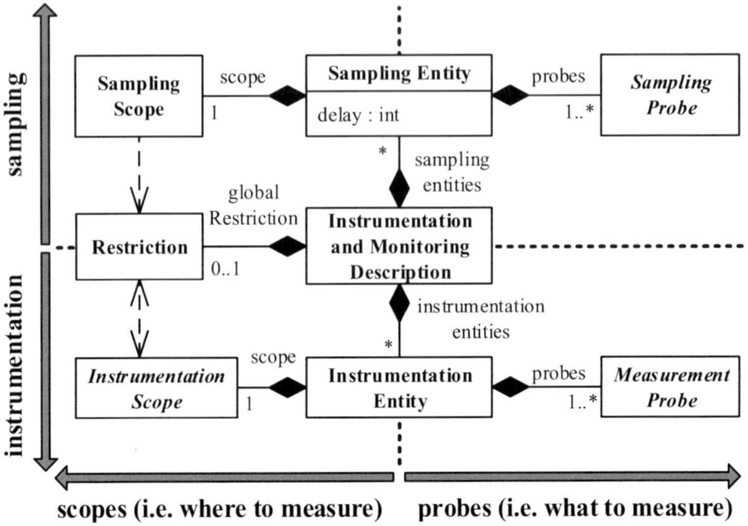

Figure 5.5.: Overview on the Instrumentation and Monitoring Description meta-model

5.3.2.2. Instrumentation and Monitoring Description

As discussed in the previous section, an IaM Description is an essential complement to an Experimentation Description, specifying which data should be retrieved from the SUT during the execution of the specified experiments. In this section, we describe the abstract syntax and the informal semantics of the IaM Description meta-model. Note that this section is closely based on our publication (Wert et al., 2015b).

Overview Following the three general design goals and the two specific design goals (cf. Section 5.3.1), we created a meta-model for the IaM Description as depicted in Figures 5.5-5.9. Figure 5.5 shows an overview of the IaM Description meta-model. The IaM Description element constitutes the root element of the model. As stipulated in the *Orthogonality* design goal (cf. Section 5.3.1), we divided the meta-model along two dimensions. On the one hand, we distinguish between *scopes* (i.e. *where* to measure) and *probes* (i.e. *what* to measure). On the other hand, we distinguish between *instrumentation* and *sampling*. Hereby, instrumentation is the process of enriching the target application with measurement probes to retrieve measurement data directly from the execution of the target application (i.e. monitoring of the control flow within the target application). The IaM Description does not specify *how* instrumentation should be realized in a concrete target application, but, declaratively describes *where* and *what* to measure. Consequently, specific instrumentation tools may choose from different instrumentation techniques applicable in the specific application contexts, as long as they achieve the desired instrumentation state specified in the IaM Description. For instance in Java, instrumentation can be realized by bytecode manipulation (Dahm, 1999), augmentation of source code or even by hooking of events emitted by the Java Virtual Machine (JVM). Similar, techniques exist in the area of .NET. In contrast to instrumentation, sampling constitutes the process of periodically retrieving measurement data from target resources. Hereby, resources may be either hardware resources (e.g. CPU, Memory, Network Interface, etc.) or software processes with managed statistics that can be queried periodically (e.g. Database server statistics, JVM Heap statistics, etc.). Accordingly to the two dimensions of differentiation, an IaM Description element comprises a set of *Sampling Entities* and a set of *Instrumentation Entities*. A Sampling Entity consists of a *Sampling Scope* describing where to sample measurement data for resources, and a set of *Sampling Probes* specifying which resources to sample. Analogously, an Instrumentation Entity comprises an *Instrumentation Scope* specifying where to inject measurement probes, and a set of *Measurement Probes* specifying what to measure in the corresponding scope, respectively. Finally, a IaM Description may contain a *global Restriction* that restricts the scope of all attached Sampling and Instrumentation Entities. Furthermore, both Sampling and Instrumentation Entities may have local *Restrictions* as denoted by the corresponding dependency association in Figure 5.5. We explain the local restrictions further below.

Instrumentation Scopes Figure 5.6 shows a detailed view on the Instrumentation Scope. The Instrumentation Scope element, per se, is an abstract class with two specializations: *Method Enclosing Scope* and *Synchronization Scope*. The Synchronization Scope represents all points in the execution of the target application where one or more threads have to wait for the

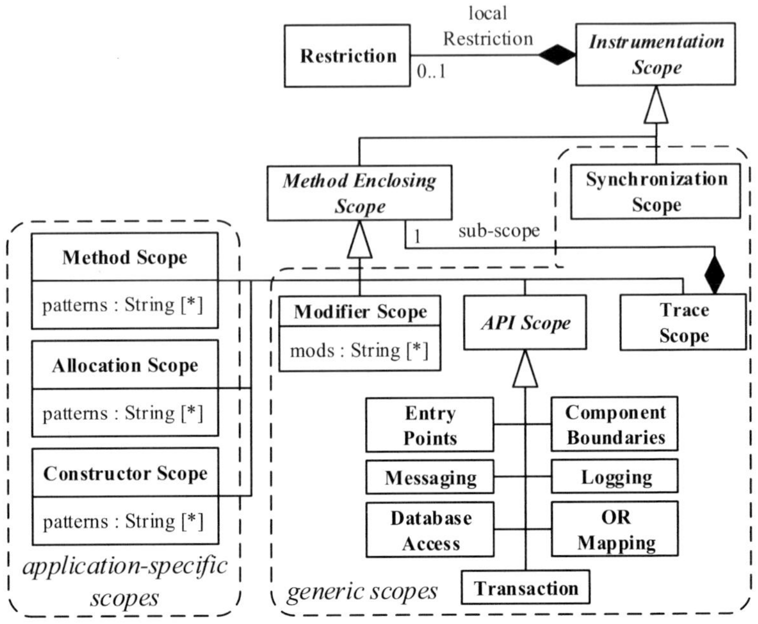

Figure 5.6.: Instrumentation and Monitoring Description meta-model: scopes

availability of a software resource that is locked by other threads. Connection pools, thread pools, concurrent file accesses, or semaphores are typical places where synchronization occurs. From a technical perspective, the Synchronization Scope covers all events when a lock is acquired or released.

The Method Enclosing Scope is an abstract class that subsumes all scopes that, in modern-day managed programming languages (e.g. Java, .NET, etc.), can be resolved to a set of methods or method invocations. Hereby, we distinguish six scope types:

Method Scope The *Method Scope* can be used to directly specify a set of methods to be instrumented. The methods are specified by a set of name *patterns*, whereby the patterns may contain wild-cards. Each method whose full qualified name matches at least one of the patterns is covered by the corresponding Method Scope element.

Constructor Scope The *Constructor Scope* is conceptually similar to the Method Scope, however, explicitly covers only class constructors. The patterns, specified in a Constructor Scope element, represent names of classes whose constructors should be instrumented. Hence, all class constructors whose class names match at least one of the patterns are within the corresponding Constructor Scope.

Allocation Scope The *Allocation Scope* is closely related to the Constructor Scope, however, constitutes a wider scope. The intention of the Allocation Scope is to cover invocations of class constructors, instead of directly instrumenting constructors. Furthermore, the allocation scope covers all instantiations of objects, even if they cannot be covered by the Constructor Scope because of technical reasons (e.g. instantiation through reflection in Java).

For the specification of the Method, Constructor and Allocation Scopes the name patterns must be specified. Hence, knowledge about the specific application is required to specify these type of scopes. Therefore, we categorize these scopes as *application-specific scopes*. Besides the application-specific scopes, the meta-model provides three *generic scopes* of the Method Enclosing Scope type:

API Scope The *Application Programming Interface (API) Scope* element is an abstract class subsuming all scopes that cover *abstract APIs*. Abstract APIs represent generic concepts that are common in modern-day, managed programming languages in the domain of enterprise software development. The database access API is a typical example for an abstract API that exists in all programming languages that are used for developing enterprise software systems. Though the concepts behind abstract APIs are common in these programming languages, the way the individual APIs are realized in the different languages and runtimes may strongly vary. In order to enable a generic language for instrumentation description, we use abstract APIs in the meta-model of the IaM Description instead of referring to concrete APIs that may very from context to context. Conversely, this means that the individual instrumentation tools and their adapters (cf. Figure 5.1) take over the responsibility of mapping abstract APIs to concrete APIs of the corresponding application contexts. In the following, we describe the seven API Scopes that are supported by our IaM Description meta-model and introduce examples how the corresponding abstract APIs are usually realized in Java (Stärk et al., 2001) and .NET (Box et al., 2002).

The *Entry Points* API scope covers all points in the target application where the control flow enters the application. In Java, the Entry Points scope covers all Java Servlets (Hunter et al., 2001) as well as all interface implementations related to the Java API for RESTful Web Services (JAX-RS) (Burke, 2009) or the Java API for XML Web Services (JAX-WS) (Vohra, 2012). In .NET, the Windows Communication Foundation (WCF) (Lowy, 2010) contains all concrete APIs that are necessary to realize application entry points, such as Web Services or REST interfaces. Prior to WCF, .NET provided the ASP.NET Web Services API (Tabor, 2001).

The *Messaging* API scope subsumes all code fragments of the target application, where remote communication (i.e. communication beyond simple method invocations) between individual software components is conducted. In Java, this scope covers all code fragments where messages (or procedure invocations) are sent or received using the concrete APIs Java Message Service (JMS) (Richards et al., 2009) or Remote Method Invocation (RMI) (Grosso, 2002). In .NET, messaging and remote procedure calls are typically realized using the Microsoft Message Queue (MSMQ) middleware (Redkar et al., 2004) and the WCF or .NET Remoting APIs (Szpuszta et al., 2005), respectively. Hence, MSMQ, WCF and .NET Remoting define the concrete scope that the abstract Messaging API scope needs to be mapped to by a .NET instrumentation tool.

All modern-day languages provide a way to access a relational database. For instance, the Java Database Connectivity (JDBC) interface (Reese, 2000) is usually used to access a database from Java code. ADO.NET (Holzner et al., 2003) provides corresponding set of classes for accessing a database in the world of .NET. In our IaM Description meta-model, the *Database Access* scope represents the abstract concept of a common database access layer. Hence, this abstract API is intended to be mapped to JDBC and ADO.NET elements in the world of Java and .NET, respectively.

The *Logging* API scope covers all code lines of the target application that are related to logging and, thus, are not critical for the functionality of the target application. In modern-languages, usually common frameworks are used for logging, constituting the concrete APIs that the abstract Logging API is intended to be mapped to by corresponding instrumentation tools. While the Java Logging API (Java Logging 2014), Apache log4J™ (Gupta, 2005), slf4J™ (SLF4J 2014) or Apache Commons Logging (Commons Logging 2014) are the most used logging frameworks in Java, in the world of .NET the following frameworks and libraries are available for logging: NLog™ (NLog 2014), SmartInspect™ (SmartInspect 2014), Apache log4net™ (Log4Net 2013), and Microsoft Enterprise Library (Enterprise Library 2015).

The *Object-Relational (OR) Mapping* scope represents all frameworks that are used to map relational database structures to object-oriented constructs. In Java, the Java Persistence API (JPA) (Keith et al., 2006) constitutes a standard interface for OR Mapping frameworks. In .NET, the ADO.NET Entity Framework (Holzner et al., 2003), LINQ (Calvert et al., 2009) are the mostly used frameworks for realizing OR Mapping.

The *Transaction* API scope covers all standard APIs that are used to implement business transactions. The Java Transaction API (JTA) (Sriganesh et al., 2006) and the Lightweight Transaction Manager (LTM) (Lowy, 2010) (i.e. System.Transactions namespace in .NET) constitute the standard APIs for transaction handling in Java and .NET, respectively.

Finally, the *Component Boundaries* scope covers all entry points into individual software components. In Java, public methods of Enterprise JavaBeans (Monson-Haefel, 2004) or exported packages of OSGI bundles (McAffer et al., 2010) represent component boundaries of the corresponding software component models. In .NET the component model is natively integrated into the the .NET framework.

Trace Scope The *Trace Scope* covers all methods along the dynamic traces originating from the specified *sub-scope*. Hereby, the dynamic traces are the call trees whose root nodes are from the set of methods that are covered by the sub-scope.

Modifier Scope The *Modifier Scope* allows to specify a set of method modifiers as strings (e.g. public, private, etc.). This scope covers all methods of the target application whose modifiers match all modifiers specified in the Modifier Scope.

As shown in Figure 5.6, the IaM Description meta-model allows both definition of application-specific scopes as well as generic scopes. Despite the requirement for an *abstract* meta-model (cf. Section 5.3.1), for the definition of detection heuristics both kinds of scopes (i.e. application-specific and generic scopes) are essential. The generic scopes can be used to get a first insight on a concrete SUT without knowing any internals of it. Based on the measurement data gained from experiments using generic scopes, the detection heuristics may retrieve application-specific information. The application-specific information can then be used with application-specific scopes to dig deeper into the internals of the SUT. Note that the definitions of detection heuristics still remain generic, as long as the usage of application-specific scopes is parametrized. In particular, for the specification of application-specific scopes one must not use concrete values (e.g. no concrete method names for the patterns of the Method Scope) but use parameters whose values are derived from previous experiments.

In addition to the different types of scopes, a local Restriction (cf. Figure 5.6) allows to specify further restrictions to an Instrumentation Scope. In the following paragraph, we describe the *Restriction* element in more detail.

Restrictions Figure 5.7 shows the part of the IaM Description meta-model that contains the Restriction class and related elements. The purpose of the Restriction is to provide a way to limit the extent of an Instrumentation Scope or a Sampling Scope (cf. Figure 5.5). A Restriction comprises three levels: The *System Node* allows to restrict the instrumentation or sampling to specific nodes of the SUT. Such nodes can be specified in a specific way using a *hostName* and *IP* (*SpecificNode*) or the the *NodeByRole* element can be used to cover all system nodes that correspond to the corresponding *role* value. In the latter case, the roles are mapped to the *System Node Role* of the ME Description (cf. Section 5.2.2). The *Process* element allows to limit the instrumentation scope to certain operating system processes identified by a *processName* or a *processID*. Finally, the *includes* and *excludes* sets restrict the scopes on the application level. While the specification of Process restrictions is SUT-specific, the application-level restrictions refer to Instrumentation Scope elements that can be both application-specific or generic as explained in the previous paragraph. Hereby, the application-level restriction has the following semantics: Let us assume that M is the set of all methods in the target application, S is the set of methods defined by a scope X (without regarding the restrictions), and In_i, Ex_j are the inclusive, respectively exclusive, scopes of the local Restriction (cf. Figure 5.6) for X. Then, the scope X is resolved to the following set of methods:

$$X = S \cap \left(\bigcap_i In_i \right) \cap \left(\bigcap_j M \setminus Ex_j \right) \tag{5.1}$$

Hence, the Restriction realizes the composability design goal. On the one hand, the Restriction allows to compose elementary Instrumentation Scopes to comprehensive scope constructs enabling description of complex scopes. On the other hand, definitions of Instrumentation Scopes remain simple, if complex scopes are not required.

All parts of the Restriction element are optional. Hence, if no restrictions are defined for a certain type of element, then the scope on that level is unlimited. For instance, if no System Node restriction is specified, then the corresponding Instrumentation Entity or Sampling Entity (cf. Figure 5.5) is applied to all nodes of the SUT. Additionally to the local Restrictions of individual *Instrumentation Entities*, an *IaM Description* can have a global *Restriction* which applies to all *Instrumentation Entities* and *Sampling Entities* (cf. Figure 5.5).

Measurement Probes While Instrumentation Scopes describe *where* to instrument, Measurement Probes define *what* to measure. Measurement Probes are closely related to the result types of measurement data that are expected to be returned for a measurement. Therefore, as shown in Figure 5.8, a Measurement Probe corresponds to a *Record Type* and vice versa. A *Record*

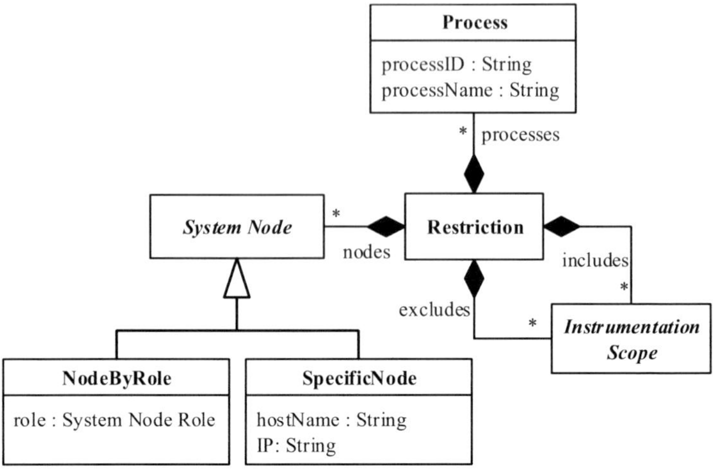

Figure 5.7.: Instrumentation and Monitoring Description meta-model: restriction

Type is an element from the Data Representation meta-model (explained in more detail in Section 5.3.2.3) and describes the structure of measurement data that is expected for the corresponding Measurement Probe.

The Measurement Probe is an abstract class that has several concrete specializations. In general, measurement probes are not specific to individual scopes. Hence, where reasonable, we keep measurement probes independent from instrumentation scopes so that a measurement probe can be combined with a possibly wide range of instrumentation scopes. However, some measurement data is very specific to the type of location where it is retrieved from. For instance, an SQL statement can only be retrieved from database related scopes. In this cases, we limit the applicability of the measurement probes by specifying corresponding Object Constraint Language (OCL) constraints. The IaM Description meta-model comprises five probe types that are applicable to all instrumentation scopes (cf. Figure 5.6): The *Response Time* probe captures the response time of the correspondingly instrumented methods (i.e. the difference in time between the control flow entering and leaving the method). A Response Time probe has a time unit (*tu*) attribute that specifies the time unit of the measured response time. The *CPU Time* probe measures the CPU demand of the target method. Hereby, the CPU

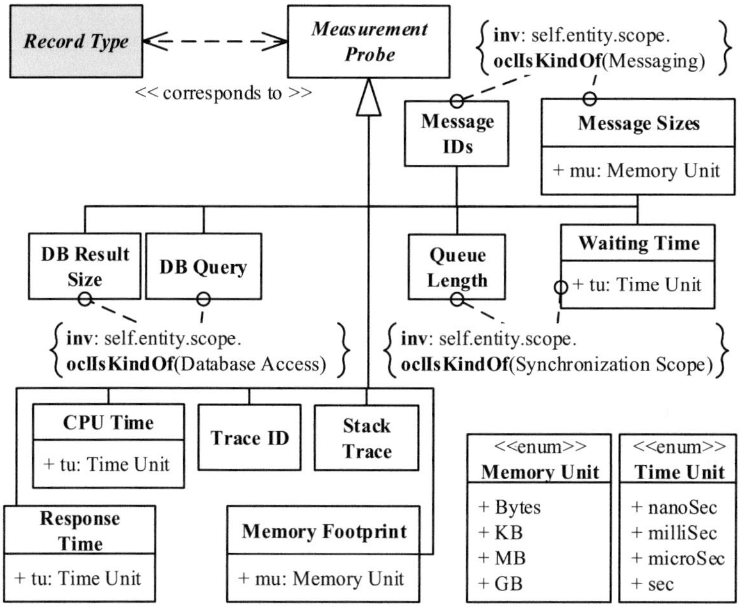

Figure 5.8.: Instrumentation and Monitoring Description meta-model: probes

demand is the time a thread consumes on the CPU while processing the corresponding method. Analogously to the Response Time probe, a time unit can be specified for a CPU Time probe. The *Trace ID* probe captures an identifier for the current trace. Typically, the thread ID constitutes the trace identifier within an application instance. In the case of remote communication, the trace ID needs to be transferred from one system node to the other in order to be able to reconstruct traces from corresponding measurement data. The *Stack Trace* probe allows to capture the entire stack trace of a method execution. As retrieving the stack trace is typically a relatively expensive operation with respect to performance overhead, the Stack Trace probe should be used with caution. Finally, the *Memory Footprint* probe measures the difference in memory that a thread consumes when processing the target method. The memory unit attribute (*mu*) specifies the unit of memory for the measured footprint.

Besides the generically applicable measurement probes, the meta-model comprises some probes that are specific to some selected scope types. As database requests often have a significant impact on the overall performance of an SUT, for some performance problem detection heuristics it is essential to capture measurement data related to database requests. To this end the meta-model provides the *DB Result Size* and *DB Query* probes. While, the DB Query probe captures the SQL statement executed in a database request, the DB Result Size probe measures the size (i.e. number of rows) of the corresponding database result. The usage of these two probes is limited to the *Database Access* API scope. The *Message IDs* and *Message Sizes* probes are applicable only with the Messaging API scope. The Message IDs probe captures the ID of transmitted messages in order to correlate transmissions of messages with their receptions. The Message Sizes probe captures different sizes of messages, including payload sizes as well as meta-data sizes of messages. The message sizes are measured using the specified memory unit (*mu*). Finally, the *Queue Length* and *Waiting Time* probes are intended for the Synchronization Scope, measuring the number of threads waiting for a locked software resource and the corresponding waiting times, respectively. The time unit (*tu*), for measuring the waiting time, can be specified in the corresponding Waiting Time probe.

Sampling A *Sampling Entity* is structured in a similar way as an Instrumentation Entity, comprising a *Sampling Scope* and a set of *Sampling Probes* (cf. Figure 5.9). Furthermore, a Sampling Entity specifies a delay (in milliseconds) determining the frequency of the sampling routine for the corresponding entity. The Sampling Scope comprises an optional set of System Nodes and an optional set of Processes. Analogously to the Restriction element (cf. Figure 5.7) the System Nodes and Processes restrict the sampling of the corresponding Sampling Entity to certain SUT nodes and operating system processes. In this way for instance, the CPU consumption of individual processes can be measured. Orthogonally to the Sampling Scope element, the set of Sampling Probes defines which resource characteristics shell be sampled. Analogously to the Measurement Probe element, a Sampling Probe corresponds to a Record Type that defines the structure for the data to be sampled by the corresponding probe. Sampling probes may cover characteristics of hardware resources, such as *Network Utilization*, *CPU Utilization*, *Disk I/O* and *Memory Usage*, as well as statistics on software resources, such as *Database Statistics* or *Messaging Statistics*. The Network Utilization probe periodically captures the bandwidth utilization of each available network interface. Hereby the utilization is defined by the ratio of transmitted data per time unit and the available bandwidth. Analogously, the CPU Utilization probe captures the utilization of each CPU core that is covered by the corresponding Sampling Scope. The Memory Usage periodically retrieves the usage characteristics of the Heap memory for the corresponding SUT processes (i.e. used space divided by available space). The Disk I/O probe measures the frequency of disk reads and writes for the corresponding processes. Both Messaging Statics and Database Statistics probes retrieve statistical information from the corresponding servers. For instance, the Database Statistics probe periodically retrieves from the database management system how many locks are currently hold, how many queries are processed and what is the current lock holding time. The Messaging Statics probe captures the capacities and lengths of messaging queues as well as the corresponding message throughputs.

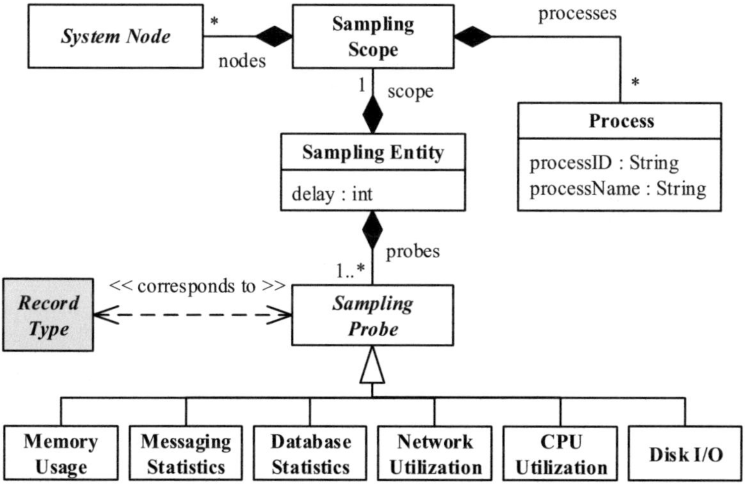

Figure 5.9.: Instrumentation and Monitoring Description meta-model: sampling

5.3.2.3. Measurement Data Representation

The Experimentation Description and IaM Description meta-models provide means to specify for a detection heuristic which experiments should be executed and what kind of measurement data should be gathered during the execution (cf. Section 5.3.2.1 and Section 5.3.2.2). However, in order to complete a detection heuristic a performance engineer has to provide generic analysis algorithms that operate on the gathered measurement data. In order to specify generic analysis algorithms, the performance engineer must be able to rely on common measurement data structures (i.e. independent from monitoring tools) that correspond to the applied IaM Description instance. To this end, we provide the Data Representation meta-model as shown in Figure 5.10.

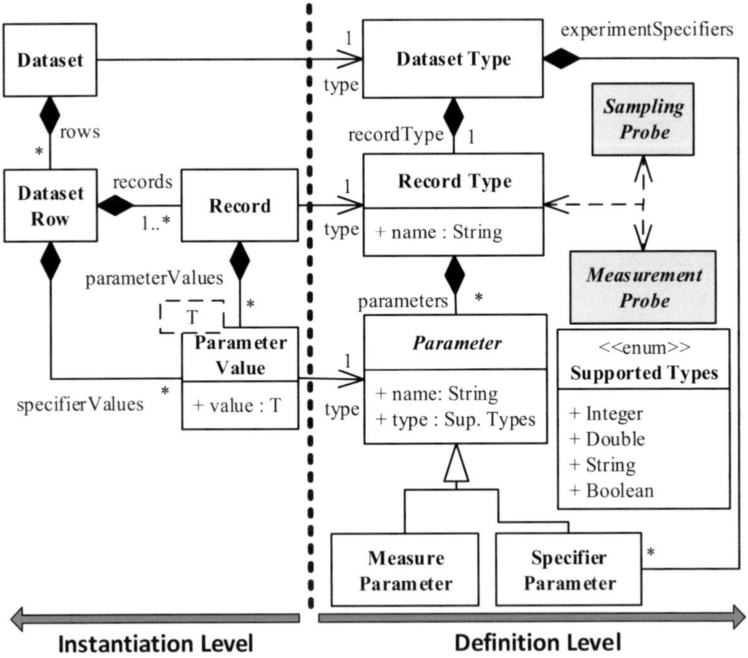

Figure 5.10.: Measurement Data Representation

Following the multi-level modelling approach (Atkinson et al., 2001; Atkinson et al., 2011), we divide our Data Representation meta-model into two levels (i.e. *ontological level* in Atkinson et al., 2011): *Definition Level* and *Instantiation Level*. The Definition Level of the meta-model provides modelling elements that allow to describe structures of measurement data. Hence, the Definition Level is intended to be used by performance engineers for the development of analysis algorithms as part of creating detection heuristics. By contrast, the Instantiation Level comprises elements that represent concrete measurement data instances as they are returned by the monitoring tools. Thereby, some of the elements on the Instantiation Level can be considered as ontological instances (Atkinson et al., 2011) of the Definition Level elements.

Listing 5.1: OCL rules for the Data Representation meta-model

```
// unique parameter names in a Record Type
context: Record Type
inv: self.parameters->isUnique(p:Parameter | p.name)
// unique parameter names in a Dataset Type
context: Dataset Type
inv: self.experimentSpecifiers->
     union(self.recordType.parameters)->
     isUnique(p:Parameter | p.name)

// correspondence of record's Parameter Values
// and Record Type Parameters
context: Record
inv: self.parameterValues->
     collect(pv:Parameter Value | pv.type).asBag()
     = self.type.parameters.asBag()

// specifier Parameter Values are unique in a Dataset Row
context: Dataset Row
inv: self.records->first().type.parameters->select
     (par:Parameter | par.oclIsTypeOf(Specifier Parameter))
     ->forAll(
        sp:Specifier Parameter | self.records->
        collect(rec:Record | rec.parameterValues)->
        flatten()->
        select(pv:Parameter Value | pv.type = sp)->
        collect(pv:Parameter Value | pv.value)->
        asSet()->size() = 1)

// 1) Record Type is unique for a Dataset
// 2) correspondence of dataset's specifier values
//    and Dataset Type experiment specifiers
context: Dataset
inv: self.rows->collect(row:Dataset Row |
     row.records->collect(rec:Record | rec.type))
     ->flatten()->asSet()->size() = 1
inv: self.rows->collect(row : Dataset Row |
     row.specifierValues->
     collect(pv:Parameter Value | pv.type))
     ->flatten() = self.type.experimentSpecifiers
```

As mentioned in Section 5.3.2.2, sampling probes and measurement probes have corresponding *Record Types* that describe the structures of the measurement data that is captured by the probes. A Record Type is identified by a *name* and comprises a set of *Parameters*. A Parameter is characterised by a *name* and a *type*, whereby the *type* is from the *Supported Types* enumeration that comprises basic data types. The *parameters* collection of a Record Type must not have parameters with the same name (cf. OCL constraint in Listing 5.1, lines 1-3). We distinguish two concrete specializations of the abstract Parameter element: *Measure Parameter* and *Specifier Parameter*. While a Specifier Parameter describes the circumstances under which a measurement has been taken, a Measure Parameter describes what has been measured. For instance, if we measure the response time of a method at a certain point in time, then the method name and the timestamp of the measurement are potential Specifier Parameters and the response time is a Measure Parameter, respectively. The Specifier Parameters and Measure Parameters are comparable to the notion of Input Parameters and Observation Parameters, respectively, in the work of D. J. Westermann, 2014. However, in (D. J. Westermann, 2014), Input Parameters are controllable while our Specifier Parameters do not necessarily need to be controllable. For instance, a measurement timestamp is a Specifier Parameter that is not controllable.

Record Types determine the structure of data to be returned by monitoring tools. However, for diagnostics of performance problems, measurement data often needs to be annotated with additional, experiment-related information that cannot be provided by the monitoring tools. For instance, if a monitoring tool returns a set of response time records for a certain experiment, the records do not convey the information about the load intensity applied during the experiment. In order to provide such additional information, the Data Representation meta-model provides the Dataset Type element. A Dataset Type decorates a Record Type with additional specifier parameters (cf. *experimentSpecifiers* in Figure 5.10) that do not correspond to any measurement or sampling probes. As specified by the OCL constraint in Listing 5.1 (lines 6-9), all parameters of a Dataset Type must have a unique parameter name, including all Record Type parameters and all experiment specifiers.

On the Instantiation Level, the *Parameter Value*, *Record* and *Dataset* elements constitute ontological instances (Atkinson et al., 2011) of the Parameter, Record Type and Dataset Type, respectively. The Parameter Value captures a single *value* for the corresponding Parameter (referred to by the *type* reference). The value attribute has a parametrized type *T* that corresponds to the type attribute value of the corresponding Parameter. A Record bundles the parameter values for the corresponding Record Type. Hence, a Record can be seen as an instance of a Record Type, whereby the corresponding parameters are filled with values. Consequently, between all parameter values of a Record and the parameters of the corresponding Record Type there must be a unique one-to-one correspondences (cf. Listing 5.1, lines 11-16). A *Dataset* captures a set of equally typed records and additional parameter values for the experiment specifiers of the corresponding Dataset Type (cf. Listing 5.1, lines 31-41). A Dataset is partitioned into a set of *Dataset Rows*, whereby each Dataset Row comprises a set of Records (cf. *records* reference) and a set of Parameter Values for the experiment specifiers (cf. specifierValues reference). A Dataset Row is characterized by a unique value assignment of the tuple that comprises all Specifier Parameters of the corresponding Dataset Type. This constraint is specified in Listing 5.1, lines 18-29. In contrast, with respect to Measure Parameters the records within a Dataset Row may contain different values for the same Measure Parameters. Hence, a Dataset virtually constitutes a table-like structure, whereby the columns represent different Record Type parameters and experiment Specifier Parameters of the corresponding Dataset Type. While the table cells of Specifier Parameter columns are single-valued, the cells of Measure Parameter columns contain collections of measured values. In this way, the Datasets structure the measurement data in a reasonable way, allowing for intuitive retrieval of data of interest. Hence, in order to access the required data for individual analysis algorithms, during development time, performance engineers may specify queries in a generic way using the elements from the Definition Level. At execution time of the analysis algorithms, the queries are applied to the corresponding Instantiation Level elements to retrieve the specified data of interest for the specific context.

5.4. Summary

In this chapter, we introduced the P^2D^2M, a domain-specific language for the description of performance problem diagnostics. P^2D^2M is specified by means of a meta-modelling and comprises four sub-models. An Experimentation Description language allows to compose different constellations of performance experiments. For the experiments, an Instrumentation and Monitoring (IaM) Description language allows to specify instrumentation and monitoring instructions in a generic, context-independent way. Thereby, the IaM Description language encapsulates domain-specific knowledge about typical concepts in technologies for enterprise software development, and common measures that are gathered for the purpose of performance evaluation. A Data Representation language prescribes a common format for the measurement data gathered by the instrumentation and monitoring instructions. The Experimentation Description, IaM Description, and the Data Representation languages prove generic, context-independent means to describe experiments. These languages constitute the basis for specifying generic detection heuristics as elaborated in the following chapter. In order to bridge the gap between generic diagnostics algorithms and specific application contexts, a fourth language, the Measurement Environment Description language, allows to specify context-specific information for APPD in a light-weight way.

6. Detection Heuristics

In Chapter 4, we introduced a methodology to derive a systematic plan for performance problem diagnostics (cf. Performance Problem Evaluation Plan (PPEP) in Section 4.4) from unstructured and spread knowledge about recurrent types of performance problems (i.e. Software Performance Antipatterns (SPAs)). While a PPEP lays the basis for a high level diagnostics algorithm that guides the overall diagnostics process of the Automatic Performance Problem Diagnostics (APPD) approach, detailed detection heuristics are required for individual SPAs within the PPEP instance. In particular, detection heuristics describe concrete diagnostics strategies for individual SPAs and, thus, constitute a complementary part to the high level algorithm.

In this chapter, we introduce a methodology for the design of accurate detection heuristics for individual SPAs (Section 6.1). For a selected set of SPAs, we create detection heuristics following the described methodology. Thereby, we create a set of test cases (Section 6.2) that are used to evaluate different heuristics and select the best performing detection strategies (Section 6.3). Section 6.4 concludes this chapter. Parts of this chapter are build upon some of our publications (Wert et al., 2013; Wert, 2012; Wert et al., 2014), as well as the supervised Bachelor's Thesis of Oehler, 2014.

6.1. A Methodology for Systematic Design of Detection Heuristics

In this section, we introduce the notion of a *detection heuristic*. Thereby, we explain the essence of detection heuristics and their role in the overall APPD approach. Furthermore, we introduce a methodology for the systematic design of accurate detection heuristics.

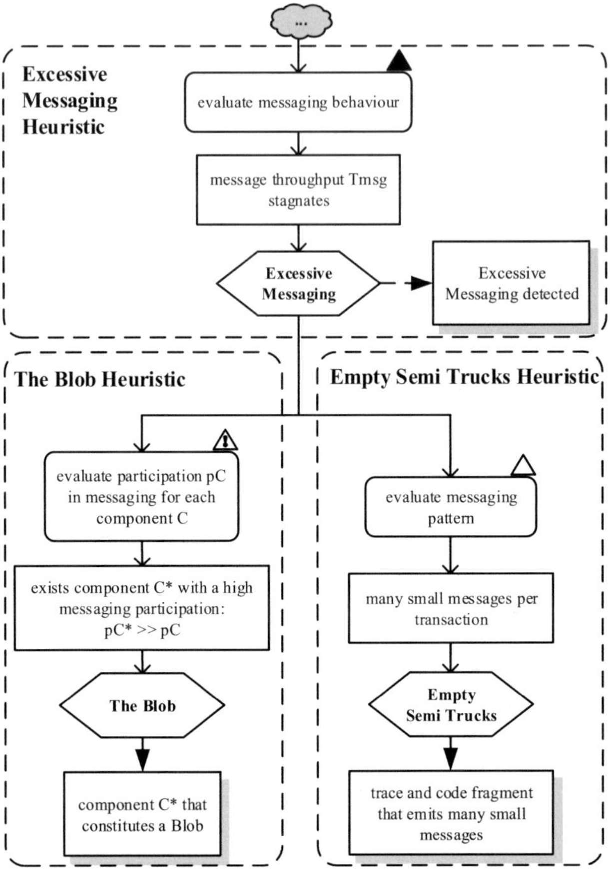

Figure 6.1.: Relationship between heuristics and the evaluation plan

6.1.1. The Essence of Detection Heuristics

The purpose of a detection heuristic is to provide an experimentation and data analysis strategy that is able to take decisions on the existence of a specific SPA in the System Under Test (SUT). Figure 6.1 shows a part of the PPEP instance introduced in Section 4.4.2 and the incorporation of corresponding detection heuristics. Considered from the perspective of the

PPEP and the Systematic Search Algorithm, a detection heuristic refines the *experiment execution*, *condition evaluation*, and *result calculation* tasks (cf. Section 4.4.3). Hence, as illustrated in Figure 6.1, a detection heuristic covers a sequence of an Action Node, a Condition Node, a Category Node, and a Result Template in a PPEP instance (cf. Section 4.4.1). In particular, a detection heuristic provides an experimentation strategy represented in the Action Node and an analysis strategy of measurement data to evaluate the condition of the Condition Node. In case that the condition is evaluated to true, a detection heuristic fills the Result Template for the corresponding Category Node. Each SPA that is represented by a Category Node in the PPEP must have its own detection heuristic that is solely responsible for evaluating the related condition. The hierarchical structure of the PPEP implies a hierarchical structure of the detection heuristics, whereby heuristics have an implicit dependency to the ancestor heuristics. Hence, according to the Systematic Search Algorithm (cf. Section 4.4.3) a detection heuristic will only be executed if the parent heuristic detects the corresponding parent SPA as a performance problem. Consequently, the detection of a specific SPA as a problem is the outcome of the joint work of all heuristics along the path to the root of the hierarchy of heuristics.

Regarding the structure of a detection heuristic, a heuristic comprises two parts: a definition of experiments and a detection strategy. The experiments and the corresponding instrumentation are defined using the Experimentation Description model (cf. Section 5.3.2.1) and the Instrumentation and Monitoring (IaM) Description model (cf. Section 5.3.2.2), respectively. A detection strategy is an algorithm that processes the measurement data which is available in the data format as described by the Data Representation model (cf. Section 5.3.2.3).

6.1.2. Design Methodology for Heuristics

The design of generic detection heuristics constitutes a major part of the initial, one-time effort for the overall APPD approach (cf. Section 3.1, Figure 3.1). As detection heuristics are intended to be re-used in different contexts, they must be able to provide accurate results for a high variety of different application contexts. Hence, it is important to invest an adequate amount of time and effort for the design of generic, flexible and accurate detection heuristics. However, due to the re-use of detection heuristics in different contexts the effort for their creation amortizes over time. To support performance engineers in reliably designing accurate detection heuristics, in the following, we introduce a methodology for a systematic design of heuristics including a set of design guidelines and a design process.

6.1.2.1. Design Guidelines

Alignment with Evaluation Plan As discussed in the previous section (Section 6.1.1), in the APPD approach detection heuristics are tightly coupled to the PPEP. Hence, creation of detection heuristics must be aligned and integrated with the corresponding PPEP instance. In particular, SPAs of interest must be integrated into a PPEP instance before detection heuristics for that SPAs can be created. Furthermore, as detection heuristics have a hierarchical dependency structure implied by the corresponding PPEP instance (cf. Figure 6.1), design of detection heuristics should be conducted in a top-down manner. Hence, a heuristic for a certain SPA should be created only if heuristics for all ancestors of the corresponding SPA already exist.

Reasonable Use of Systematic Experimentation Detection heuristics should reasonably use the Systematic Selective Experimentation (SSE) concept (cf. Section 3.2.1). In particular, excessive and, with respect to measurement overhead, expensive instrumentation should be avoided. Instead, expensive instrumentation should be split into several parts that can be collected as part of individual, separate experiments. Often, detection heuristics require different kind of information from the SUT that can be gathered in separate experiments, too. For instance, structural information about the SUT can be retrieved by means of low-load experiments, as the corresponding instrumentation instructions usually are expensive in terms of measurement overhead. By contrast, behavioural information and especially load-related performance metrics can be gathered in high-load experiments while applying light-weight instrumentation. Furthermore, SSE may be useful to avoid time-based correlations between different metrics that often involve uncertainties and inaccuracy. For instance, all time-based correlations between the load intensity and any other performance metric can be replaced by a set of experiments with different load intensities. Thereby, the target metric can be directly observed for the corresponding load intensity of the experiment.

Avoidance of Absolute Values The values for different performance metrics observed during experiment execution are absolute. For instance, the response time is measured in an absolute time unit (e.g. milliseconds), the memory footprint is measured in Bytes, etc. Hence, when designing detection heuristics it seems to be intuitive to derive absolute thresholds that are used to decide about the existence of individual SPAs. However, the existence of performance problems is by definition (cf. Definition 1 in Section 3.1) always relative to the specific application context and the corresponding performance requirements. Hence, in most cases absolute thresholds cannot be generically applied to a high variety of different SUTs. An exception are "rules of thumb" and best practices providing generic reference values that apply to a wide range of different systems. In Section 5.2, we introduced the Measurement Environment (ME) Description model that, inter alia, allows for the specification of performance requirements for the system services. For the design of detection heuristics these performance requirements can be used in a parametrized way as a reference value for the derivation of thresholds for end-to-end performance behaviour. Besides the specified performance requirements, the detection heuristics should avoid absolute thresholds, where possible. Instead, analysis algorithms should apply relative considerations of values that are independent of specific SUTs.

6.1.2.2. Design Process

In order to ensure high quality detection heuristics that are able to deal with a high variety of SUTs, detection heuristics must be tested properly during the design time. Therefore, we propose a design process for detection heuristics as depicted in Figure 6.2. The process comprises two main parts: *Creation of Test Cases* and *Selection of a Detection Strategy*. In the test cases creation part, a set of test cases is created that is then used to select an accurate and generic detection strategy.

The design process of each detection heuristic should always start with the creation of test cases that are tailored for the SPA for which the detection

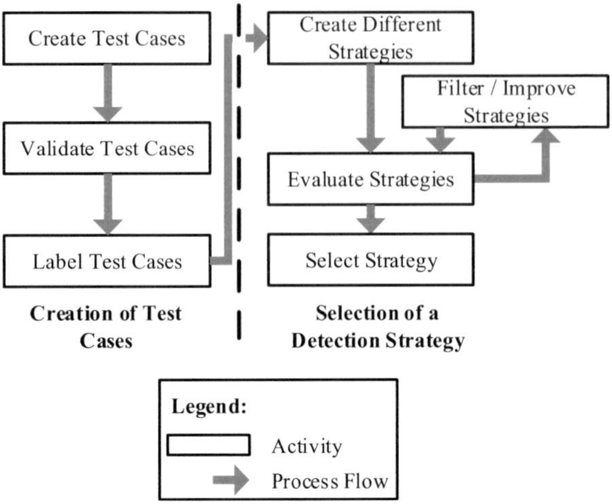

Figure 6.2.: Design Process for Detection Heuristics

heuristic should be created (micro-benchmarks). The set of different, potentially synthetic, test cases are used to investigate the accuracy of the created detection heuristic under different circumstances. Thereby, the test cases should cover both possible types of test cases: *positive test cases* that contain the corresponding SPA and emit the corresponding performance behaviour, and *negative test cases* that do not contain the target SPA. Furthermore, the test cases should cover a preferably big variety of circumstances, including different technologies used to implement the corresponding SPA, different forms of the performance behaviour, as well as different manifestations of the target SPA. In order to avoid biased test cases, the creation of test cases should be separated from the realization of corresponding detection heuristic. To this end, corresponding to the two parts of the process, we distinguish two roles (*Test Case Engineer* and *Heuristics Engineer*) that preferable should be represented by separate persons in order to avoid biasing effects. Due to the top-down order of heuristics creation (cf. Section 6.1.2.1), during design of a new detection heuristic we can assume that all ancestor heuristics (corresponding to the PPEP) have already been created. This assumption is important for the second step of the design process: validation of the created test cases. Due to the Systematic Search Algorithm (cf. Section 4.4.3) guiding the APPD approach, all test cases for a new detection heuristic are invalid, if they are not detected by all ancestor heuristics of the new heuristic. In this case, the Systematic Search Algorithm would skip the execution of the new heuristic, anyway. Hence, all test cases created for a new detection heuristic must be *positive test cases* for all ancestor heuristics as implied by the corresponding PPEP instance. In the second design step, this precondition must be validated. Finally, all valid test cases must be labeled either as *positive* or *negative test cases*.

For most SPAs, different ways exist how to detect an individual SPA (in the following referred to as *detection strategies*). Alternative strategies may differ in the experimentation strategies, in the type of measurement data that needs to be collected or in the data analysis algorithms. Furthermore, individual detection strategies may have some configuration parameters that span a multi-dimensional configuration space. In such a case, efficient, experiment-based optimization approaches (like the Adaptive Breakdown approach by D. J. Westermann, 2014) can be used to find an optimal parameter configuration for a detection strategy. If individual detection strategies cannot be discarded in advance by means of some logical considerations, all potential detection strategies need to be realized. The alternative strategies are then applied to the created test cases in order to find the detection strategy with the highest detection accuracy. The test case results can be used to discard badly performing detection strategies or to improve individual detection strategies if the evaluation results show potential improvement. Hence, the design of detection heuristics contains an iterative step of evaluating, filtering and improving the detection strategies. Finally, a single detection strategy with the highest accuracy needs to be selected for the corresponding detection heuristic. In the following, we formally explain how we derive the accuracy of detection strategies that is used to compare different detection strategies.

Assuming that we are designing a detection heuristic for an *SPA A*, the vector $\vec{c_A}$ comprises a set of n test cases $c_{A,i}$ for *SPA A*:

$$\vec{c_A} = (c_{A,1}, \ldots, c_{A,n}) \tag{6.1}$$

Labeling the test cases yields an *expectation vector* $\vec{v_A}$ describing for each test case whether it is a *positive* or a *negative test case*:

$$\vec{v_A} = (v_{A,1}, \ldots, v_{A,n}) \tag{6.2}$$

$$v_{A,i} = \begin{cases} 1 & \text{, test case } c_{A,i} \text{ contains anti-pattern } A \text{ (positive test case)} \\ 0 & \text{, otherwise (negative test case)} \end{cases} \tag{6.3}$$

The number of *positive test cases* n_A^p and the number of *negative test cases* n_A^n are defined as follows:

$$n_A^p = \vec{v_A} * \vec{1} \tag{6.4}$$

$$n_A^n = (\vec{1} - \vec{v_A}) * \vec{1} \tag{6.5}$$

Given a vector $\vec{s_A} = (s_{A,1}, \ldots, s_{A,m})$ of m alternative detection strategies for SPA A, we are looking for the detection strategy $s_{A,X}$ that has the highest detection accuracy. To this end, we apply the detection strategies to the set of labeled test cases yielding for each detection strategy $s_{A,k}$ a *detection vector* $\vec{d_{A,k}}$. The detection vector describes in which test cases the considered SPA A has been detected by the applied detection strategy s_k:

$$\vec{d_{A,k}} = (d_{A,k,1}, \ldots, d_{A,k,n}) \tag{6.6}$$

$$d_{A,k,i} = \begin{cases} 1 & \text{, detection strategy } s_{A,k} \text{ detected } A \text{ in test case } c_{A,i} \\ 0 & \text{, otherwise} \end{cases} \tag{6.7}$$

Based on the expectation vector $\vec{v_A}$ and the detection vector $\vec{d_{A,k}}$ for detection strategy $s_{A,k}$, we calculate the error vector $\vec{e_{A,k}}$:

$$\vec{e_{A,k}} = \vec{d_{A,k}} - \vec{v_A} \tag{6.8}$$

Hereby, the error vector has the following semantics:

$$\vec{e_{A,k,i}} = \begin{cases} -1 & \text{, strategy } s_{A,k} \text{ falsely neglected } A \text{ in } c_{A,i} \text{ (false negative)} \\ 1 & \text{, strategy } s_{A,k} \text{ falsely identified } A \text{ in } c_{A,i} \text{ (false positive)} \\ 0 & \text{, otherwise (true positive or true negative)} \end{cases} \tag{6.9}$$

Following Swets, 1988, we use the number of *false positives* and *false negatives* to calculate the accuracy of a detection strategy. To this end, we calculate the number of false positives and false negatives as follows. Let f be a function that counts the number of scalars in a vector that are equal to one:

$$f : \{-1, 0, 1\} \times \ldots \times \{-1, 0, 1\} \rightarrow \mathbb{N}, \qquad f(\vec{x}) = \left\lfloor \frac{1}{2} * \left(\vec{x} + \vec{1}\right) \right\rfloor * \vec{1} \tag{6.10}$$

Using function $f(\vec{x})$, we calculate for each detection strategy $s_{A,k}$ the number of *false positives* ($n^{fp}_{A,k}$), *false negatives* ($n^{fn}_{A,k}$), *true positives* ($n^{tp}_{A,k}$), and *true negatives* ($n^{tn}_{A,k}$) from the error vector $\vec{e_{A,k}}$:

$$n^{fp}_{A,k} = f(\vec{e_{A,k,i}}) \tag{6.11}$$

$$n^{fn}_{A,k} = f(-1 * \vec{e_{A,k,i}}) \tag{6.12}$$

$$n^{tp}_{A,k} = n^{p}_{A} - n^{fn}_{A,k} \tag{6.13}$$

$$n^{tn}_{A,k} = n^{n}_{A} - n^{fp}_{A,k} \tag{6.14}$$

Consequently, the *false positive rate* $r^{fp}_{A,k}$ and the *true positive rate* $r^{tp}_{A,k}$ of detection strategy $s_{A,k}$ are defined as follows:

$$r^{fp}_{A,k} = \frac{n^{fp}_{A,k}}{n^{n}_{A}} \quad , \quad r^{tp}_{A,k} = \frac{n^{tp}_{A,k}}{n^{p}_{A}} \tag{6.15}$$

Following Swets, 1988, we utilize the Receiver Operating Characteristics (ROC) curve in order to calculate an accuracy measure based on the *false positive rate* and the *true positive rate*. For a tuple (r^{fp}, r^{tp}) the corresponding ROC curve is depicted in Figure 6.3, showing the *true positive rate* over the *false positive rate*. The area beneath the curve constitutes a measure for the accuracy (Swets, 1988). The diagonal line represents a random process with an accuracy value of 0.5. Hence, detection strategies with an accuracy near to 0.5 are comparable to random guessing. Detection strategies with accuracies smaller than 0.5 have a systematic error, that makes the result accuracy worse than a random guessing approach. Finally, detection strategies that are in all cases correct ($(r^{fp}, r^{tp}) = (0, 1)$) have a maximum accuracy of 1.0.

For a tuple of a *false positive rate* and a *true positive rate* the function $a(r^{fp}, r^{tp})$ calculates the area under the corresponding ROC curve and, thus, provides an accuracy measure:

$$a : \mathbb{R} \times \mathbb{R} \rightarrow \mathbb{R} \tag{6.16}$$

$$a(r^{fp}, r^{tp}) = \left(1 - r^{fp}\right) + \frac{1}{2} * \left(r^{tp} * r^{fp} - \left(1 - r^{tp}\right) * \left(1 - r^{fp}\right)\right) \tag{6.17}$$

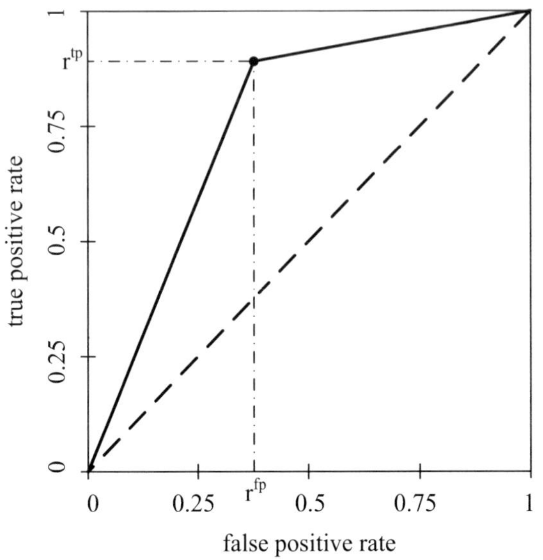

Figure 6.3.: ROC Curve

Hence, a detection strategy $s_{A,k}$ for SPA A performs better than an alternative strategy $s_{A,l}$, if the following applies:

$$a(r^{fp}_{A,k}, r^{tp}_{A,k}) > a(r^{fp}_{A,l}, r^{tp}_{A,l}) \tag{6.18}$$

The more test cases are created for an SPA and the higher the variety in the test cases, the more representative is the calculated accuracy for the individual detection strategies. Hence, the *Test Cases Creation* part of the design process is essential to ensure accurate and at the same time generic detection heuristics. In the following, we apply the described methodology to design detection heuristics for the SPAs covered by the PPEP instance that we discussed in Section 4.4.2.

6.2. Heuristics Evaluation Setup

In the following, we design twelve detection heuristics for the set of SPAs covered by the PPEP instance shown in Section 4.4.2. Corresponding to the design process explained in the previous section, we divide the design of heuristics into a test cases creation part and a heuristics creation part. In Section 6.2.1, we introduce a set of test cases that cover different scenarios for the individual SPAs. The corresponding experiment setup is described in Section 6.2.2.

6.2.1. Test Cases

Table 6.1 shows an overview on the test cases that we use in Section 6.3 to evaluate alternative detection strategies for individual SPAs.

In the header row, twelve SPAs are listed for which we are going to design detection heuristics. Hereby, the last column covers all manifestations of the One Lane Bridge anti-pattern (cf. Section 4.3). In the rows, 22 test cases are listed with corresponding labeling for the individual SPAs. While a flag (⚐) means that the corresponding performance problem exists in the test case, the checkmark (✓) represents the opposite, meaning that the corresponding performance problem is not present in the given test case. Finally, a minus sign (—) means that the test case is not applicable on the corresponding performance problem due to the hierarchical structure of SPAs. The columns of Table 6.1 represent the *expectation vectors* $\vec{v_A}$ for the individual anti-patterns A (cf. Section 6.1.2.2). Note that cells with a minus sign (—) are not part of the corresponding expectation vector. Consequently, the expectation vectors have different sizes depending on the corresponding SPA.

We create two *negative test cases* for the high level *Performance Problem* (TC 1, TC 2). While the response times in TC 1 are steadily under the defined performance requirement threshold, in TC 2, the response times contain some rare outliers that exceed the threshold. However, according to the percentile specification of performance requirements, both test cases meet the performance requirements. The remaining test cases (TC 3 - TC 22) contain different manifestations of performance problems.

Test Cases	Performance Problem	Application Hiccups	The Ramp	Cont. Violated Req.	Traffic Jam	Database Congestion	The Stifle	Expensive DB Call	Excessive Messaging	The Blob	Empty Semi Trucks	One Lane Bridge
	Software Performance Anti-patterns											
TC 1	✓	—	—	—	—	—	—	—	—	—	—	—
TC 2	✓	—	—	—	—	—	—	—	—	—	—	—
TC 3	⚐	⚐	✓	✓	—	—	—	—	—	—	—	—
TC 4	⚐	⚐	✓	✓	—	—	—	—	—	—	—	—
TC 5	⚐	⚐	✓	✓	—	—	—	—	—	—	—	—
TC 6	⚐	✓	⚐	✓	—	—	—	—	—	—	—	—
TC 7	⚐	✓	⚐	✓	—	—	—	—	—	—	—	—
TC 8	⚐	✓	✓	⚐	✓	—	—	—	—	—	—	—
TC 9	⚐	✓	✓	⚐	✓	—	—	—	—	—	—	—
TC 10	⚐	✓	✓	⚐	⚐	✓	—	—	✓	—	—	✓
TC 11	⚐	✓	✓	⚐	⚐	⚐	✓	✓	✓	—	—	✓
TC 12	⚐	✓	✓	⚐	⚐	⚐	⚐	✓	✓	—	—	⚐
TC 13	⚐	✓	✓	⚐	⚐	⚐	⚐	✓	✓	—	—	⚐
TC 14	⚐	✓	✓	⚐	⚐	⚐	✓	⚐	✓	—	—	✓
TC 15	⚐	✓	✓	⚐	⚐	⚐	✓	⚐	✓	—	—	⚐
TC 16	⚐	✓	✓	⚐	⚐	✓	—	—	⚐	✓	✓	✓
TC 17	⚐	✓	✓	⚐	⚐	✓	—	—	⚐	⚐	✓	✓
TC 18	⚐	✓	✓	⚐	⚐	✓	—	—	⚐	⚐	✓	✓
TC 19	⚐	✓	✓	⚐	⚐	✓	—	—	⚐	✓	⚐	✓
TC 20	⚐	✓	✓	⚐	⚐	✓	—	—	⚐	✓	⚐	✓
TC 21	⚐	✓	✓	⚐	⚐	✓	—	—	✓	—	—	⚐
TC 22	⚐	✓	✓	⚐	⚐	✓	—	—	✓	—	—	⚐
TC 23	⚐	✓	✓	⚐	⚐	✓	—	—	✓	—	—	✓

Legend: ⚐ = test case contains the problem, ✓ = test case does not contain the problem, — = test case cannot be applied to the problem

TC 1: No Problem w/o Outliers, TC 2: No Problem with Outliers, TC 3: Clear Hiccups, TC 4: Rising Hiccups, TC 5: Blurred Hiccups, TC 6: Monotone Ramp, TC 7: Blurred Ramp, TC 8: Stable External Call, TC 9: Varying External Call, TC 10: CPU-intensive App., TC 11: Many Diff. DB calls, TC 12: Many Equal DB call, TC 13: Many Similar DB calls, TC 14: CPU-inten. DB calls, TC 15: Locking DB calls, TC 16: JMS File Transfer, TC 17: Clear Blob, TC 18: Blurred Blob, TC 19: Direct Message Loop, TC 20: Cascading Message Loo, TC 21: Clear Sync, TC 22: Blurred Sync, TC 23: Increase Without Sync

Table 6.1.: Overview on test cases and corresponding expectation vectors

The test cases TC 3 - TC 5 represent different manifestation of the *Application Hiccups* SPA and at the same time constitute *negative test cases* for the *Continuously Violated Requirements* and the *Ramp* anti-patterns. Test case TC 3 comprises clear hiccups, whereby in the hiccup phases the response times clearly exceed the performance requirements. In test case TC 4, the hiccups steadily arise from low response times instead of an impulse-like jump of response times. Finally, in TC 5 the response times in the hiccup phases vary significantly, including response times that exceed and that do not exceed the performance requirements threshold.

TC 6 and TC 7 are *positive test cases* for the the *Ramp* SPA. The *Monotone Ramp* test case represents a quite artificial scenario where response times grow strictly with the operation time. By contrast, the ramp behaviour in test case TC 7 is more realistic, comprising varying response times that have an increasing long-term trend.

The test cases TC 8 and TC 9 simulate an expensive, external service call that leads to a continuous violation of performance requirements, however, does not constitute a *Traffic Jam* anti-pattern as the performance does not get worse with increasing load. Hence, both TC 8 and TC 9 constitute *positive test cases* for the *Performance Problem* and the *Continuously Violated Requirements* anti-patterns. For the *Application Hiccups, the Ramp* and the *Traffic Jam* anti-patterns, TC 8 and TC 9 constitute *negative test cases.* In TC 8, all requests to the external service exceed the response time threshold of the performance requirements. By contrast, in TC 9 the response times exhibit a high variance varying from small response times that meet performance requirements to high response times that exceed the threshold.

Test case TC 10 simulates a CPU-intensive application that leads to a *Traffic Jam* anti-pattern due to limitations of hardware resources (i.e. CPU). As implied by the taxonomy on SPAs (cf. Section 4.3), besides the *Traffic Jam* anti-pattern, TC 10 is a *positive test case* for the *Performance Problem* and the *Continuously Violated Requirements* anti-patterns. However, as TC 10 does not cause *Database Congestion, Excessive Messaging* or a *One Lane Bridge*, it is considered as a *negative test case* for those anti-patterns.

Test case TC 11 simulates a *Database Congestion* anti-pattern that is caused by many different database requests that overload the database. As the definition of a *Stifle* anti-pattern implies that similar database requests are repeated, TC 11 does not include a *Stifle* due to its variety of the database requests. Furthermore, as TC 11 comprises many small database requests, it does not represent an *Expensive Database Call* anti-pattern.

The test cases TC 12 and TC 13 are very similar to test case TC 11, however in TC 12 and TC 13, multiple similar database queries are sent per user request. Consequently, the labeling of TC 12 and TC 13 is equal to the labeling of TC 11 except that TC 12 and TC 13 are *positive test cases* for the *Stifle* anti-pattern. The difference between TC 12 and TC 13 lies in the level of similarity of the multiple database queries. While in TC 12 the queries are repeated identically, in TC 13 the database queries are slightly modified from one request to the next. While TC 12 represents unintended repetitions of queries in practice, TC 13 simulates an improper use of SQL's *Where* clause, i.e., data filtering on application level instead of specifying proper *Where-conditions* in the SQL statement.

TC 14 and TC 15 simulate an *Expensive Database Call* by issuing CPU-intensive database requests and emitting database requests that lead to excessive locking, respectively. According to the SPA taxonomy (cf. Section 4.3), a *positive test case* for the *Expensive Database Call* is implicitly a *positive test case* for the *Performance Problem*, *Continuously Violated Requirements*, and *Database Congestion* anti-patterns. For all other SPAs (except for the *Blob* and the *Empty Semi Trucks* anti-patterns), TC 14 is labeled as a *negative test case*. As TC 15 leads to a *Traffic Jam* without saturating any hardware resources, the performance problem in TC 15 is at the same time a database manifestation of the *One Lane Bridge* anti-pattern.

The test cases TC 16 - TC 20 cover messaging related scenarios. TC 16 represents an *Excessive Messaging* scenario that neither contains a *Blob* anti-pattern nor an *Empty semi Trucks* anti-pattern. Thereby a messaging service is misused to transfer big files leading to a highly utilized network. TC 17 and TC 18 are *positive test cases* for the *Blob* anti-pattern. In TC 17, all software components communicate with each other over a central broker that constitutes the *Blob* component. By contrast, in TC 18, in addition to the excessive communication with the *Blob* component, individual components conduct peer-to-peer communication. Instead of a *Blob*, the test cases TC 19 and TC 20 contain an *Empty Semi Trucks* anti-pattern. In TC 19, many small messages are sent via a messaging service in a loop. TC 20 is very similar to TC 19, however, the loop containing the repeated sending of small messages is more complex comprising multiple levels of indirection.

The test cases TC 21 to TC 22 represent different manifestations of the *One Lane Bridge* anti-pattern. TC 21 contains a synchronization point on application level that applies to all user requests. By contrast, the synchronization point in TC 22 is passed only by a subset of user requests, leading to a blurred *One Lane Bridge* behaviour. Finally, TC 23 is a test case that is similar to test case TC 10, yielding the same labeling. However, while TC 10 leads to a very high utilization of the CPU at the application server, TC 23 comes with a moderate CPU utilization, while still constituting a Traffic Jam anti-pattern.

6.2.2. Measurement Environment Setup

Each test case described in Section 6.2.1 is designed as a micro-benchmark, emulating the desired behaviour without performing any specific task. In order to apply an implementation of a generic detection heuristic on a specific test case, the specific scenario must be described using the Measurement Environment Description model (cf. Section 5.2). For all test cases from Section 6.2.1, we use the measurement environment as specified by the Measurement Environment Description instance in Figure 6.4. The measurement environment comprises seven system nodes including a load driver node, a database node, a messaging node, as well as four application nodes. Depending on the test case, the distributed Application Components (*App Comp. A - D*) communicate either only with the Database, or among each other via the *Messaging Broker* (e.g. in the cases of messaging related test cases). We denote each application node with the node role *AppServer* and for each of these nodes we specify an Instrumentation Entity for application code instrumentation, as well as a Monitoring Entity for gathering of measurement data. For the evaluation of our detection heuristics we use the Adaptable Instrumentation and Monitoring (AIM) framework (Wert et al., 2015a) for instrumentation and monitoring, allowing to dynamically adapt instrumentation of the target applications. At the database node and the messaging node, we deploy only a Monitoring Entity for the sampling of resource statistics (e.g. CPU utilization, network I/O, etc.). Finally, the virtual load is generated by a dedicated Load Generation Entity. For our test cases, we use a custom load driver that is basically a simple Java program emitting virtual requests to the target application. Consequently, in the corresponding User Behaviour Specification we specify a Java class name of the class that

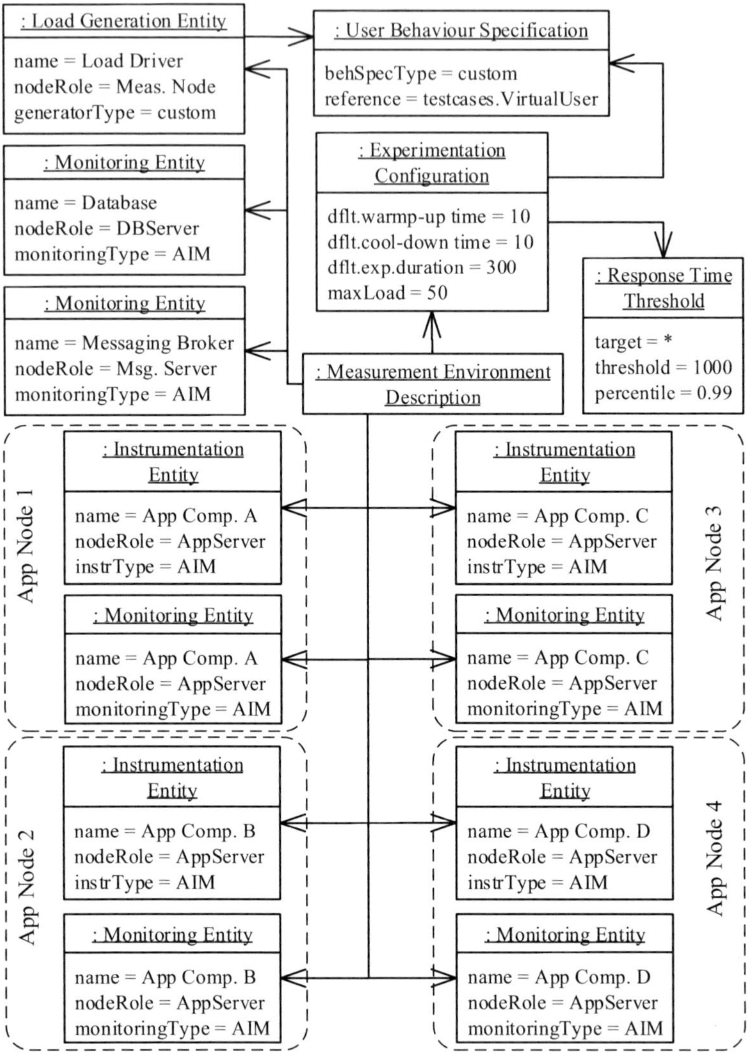

Figure 6.4.: Measurement environment and experimentation configuration for evaluation of heuristics

represents a virtual user script (*testcases.VirtualUser* in Figure 6.4). For the Experimentation Configuration we specify a default experiment duration of five minutes (300 seconds) and ten seconds for each of both the warm-up and the cool-down phase. The maximum load is limited to 50 concurrent users utilizing a closed workload. Finally, for the performance requirements we use a Response Time Threshold specification. Thereby, all system services (*) are not allowed to exceed the one second (1000 ms) response time threshold in 99% of cases.

6.3. Design of Detection Heuristics

In this section, we introduce different detection heuristics for the selected set of performance problems. Thereby, we discuss different, alternative detection strategies for some of the performance anti-patterns. The detection heuristics are described by means of the corresponding sub-models of Performance Problem Diagnostics Description Model (P^2D^2M) (cf. Chapter 5) and textual description of the detection strategies. Furthermore, for each detection strategy, the Appendix Section A.1 provides the corresponding algorithms as pseudo code. We evaluate the detection strategies and heuristics by means of the created test cases (cf. Section 6.2.1). Note that the evaluation of the detection heuristics in this section is part of the heuristics design process and does not constitute the final validation of the APPD approach nor of the heuristics. A comprehensive validation of the APPD approach and the heuristics is conducted on real software systems and is discussed in detail in Chapter 7.

6.3.1. High-level Performance Problem Heuristic

The top level heuristic (cf. PPEP instance in Section 4.4.2) is responsible for identifying any type of performance problem. By definition a performance problem exists if performance requirements are violated (cf. Definition 1 in Section 3.1). Hence, the Performance Problem heuristic just has to investigate if the end-to-end response times exceed the requirements defined by the domain expert in the corresponding ME Description model (cf. Section 5.2).

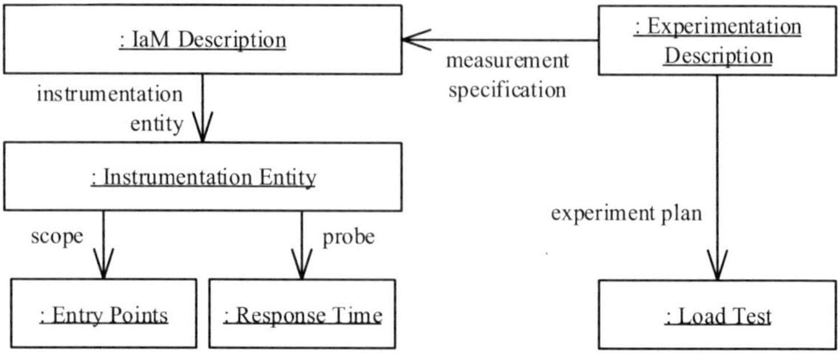

Figure 6.5.: Experiment and instrumentation description for the Performance Problem Heuristic

Assuming that the *Response Time Threshold* element of the ME Description model is used for the definition of the performance requirements, the detection heuristic is unambiguous as it only needs to evaluate the response time distributions of individual system services. As there is only one reasonable, conceptual way of evaluating that, we introduce only one detection strategy for the Performance Problem anti-pattern that we evaluate against the corresponding test cases.

6.3.1.1. Detection Strategy

Figure 6.5 shows the instance of the Experimentation Description model for the Performance Problem heuristic with an attached IaM Description (cf. Section 5.2). If a performance problem exists in the SUT, then the problem must become visible under a high load intensity. Therefore, for the detection of a performance problem we apply a single *Load Test* as the experiment plan. With respect to instrumentation, in this high level detection step, we are interested in the server-side end-to-end response times. To this end, the IaM Description contains one *Instrumentation Entity* covering the *Entry Point* scope with a *Response Time* probe. Applying the specified experiment with the corresponding instrumentation description on a SUT yields measurement data that correspond to the data format depicted in Figure 6.6. Figure 6.6 shows an instance of the Definition Level part of the Data Representation model (cf. Section 5.3.2.3). The corresponding Dataset Type is determined

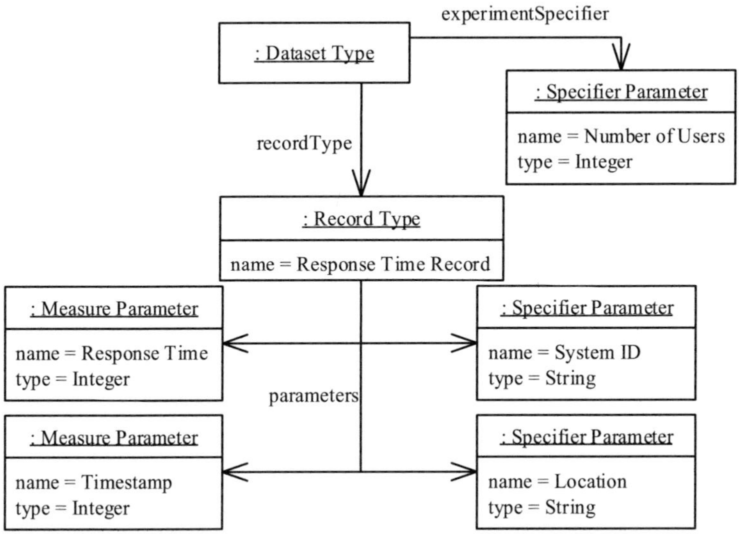

Figure 6.6.: Data representation format for the Performance Problem Heuristic

by the *Response Time Record* type as well as an additional *Specifier Parameter*. For the *Load Test* experiment the *Number of Users* parameter is implicitly set to the *maxLoad* value specified in the *Experimentation Configuration* element of the ME Description model (cf. Section 5.2). The Response Time Record type comprises two *Measure Parameters* and two Specifier Parameters. The *Response Time* and the *Timestamp* parameters capture the response time of the target method in milliseconds and the absolute timestamp (in milliseconds) of the corresponding method call, respectively. The *System ID* and the *Location* parameters specify the system node of the method call and the name of the called method (or service), respectively.

Based on this data format, we define a detection strategy for the Performance Problem SPA (cf. Algorithm 2, Appendix A.1.1). The inputs of the detection strategy are a Dataset $\mathcal{D}$ of defined Dataset Type containing the measurement data (cf. Figure 6.6) as well as the provided performance requirements from the ME Description model specified by a response time threshold ρ and a corresponding cumulative probability π (percentile) that determines the portion of requests that must not exceed the response time threshold.

The detection strategy returns a set $\mathcal{L}$ of system services that violate the performance requirements. For each system service $\omega \in O$ (e.g. Servlet names in Java, etc.) the algorithm retrieves the set $\mathcal{V}$ of response times and evaluates whether the corresponding percentile υ_{π} of response times from $\mathcal{V}$ exceeds the provided response time threshold ρ. In this case, the system service ω is added to the result set $\mathcal{L}$. If the algorithm returns an empty result set, then no performance problem has been detected. Otherwise, the detection heuristic reports the violating system services $\mathcal{L}$ as the detection result for the corresponding node of the PPEP.

6.3.1.2. Evaluation

The detection strategy of the Performance Problem heuristic is rather simple, as it only evaluates whether the response time distribution of each system service meets the percentile specification of the performance requirements. In particular, the detection strategy of the Performance Problem heuristic is directly derived from the definition of a Performance Problem (cf. Definition 1, Section 3.1). Consequently, applying the detection heuristic on all 23 test cases from Table 6.1 yields a detection accuracy of $a = 1.0$, as the 21 positive test cases as well as both negative test cases have been correctly detected or passed, respectively. As the test cases TC 3 - TC 23 have been successfully detected by the Performance Problem heuristic, they have passed the test case validation step in the process of Figure 6.2 (cf. Section 6.1.2.2) and, thus, can be further used to evaluate the heuristics for the Application Hiccups, the Ramp, and the Continuously Violated Requirements anti-patterns.

6.3.2. Application Hiccups Heuristic

As indicated by the PPEP instance in Section 4.4.2, the detection heuristic for the Application Hiccups SPA (cf. Table 2.1(c), Chapter 2.4) may reuse the measurement data from the Performance Problem heuristic as its analysis is based on the same type of data. Hence, the Application Hiccups Heuristic uses the same Experimentation and IaM Description as the Performance Problem heuristic (cf. Section 6.3.1). Consequently, the resulting data format of the measurement data is the same, too. Based on that data format, in the following we define and evaluate two alternative detection strategies for Application Hiccups.

6.3.2.1. Detection Strategies

We design and investigate three different analysis strategies for the detection of hiccups in a time series of response times: *Moving Percentile Strategy* and *Bucket Strategy*. These analysis strategies are based on a common strategy (cf. Algorithm 3 in Appendix A.1.2).

Analogously to the Performance Problem heuristic, the core detection strategy for the Application Hiccups anti-pattern takes a data set $\mathcal{D}$ and the specification of performance requirements (ρ and π) as input. Furthermore, it requires a configuration parameter ϕ that specifies the maximum allowed proportion that the cumulative hiccup time may cover of the experiment duration. If this proportion is exceeded, the violations of performance requirements are not considered as occurring periodically, but, are considered to constitute a continuous violation of performance requirements. The algorithm returns a set $\mathcal{L}$ of system services that exhibit a hiccup behaviour in their response time series. To this end, analogously to the Performance Problem heuristic, the core detection strategy iterates over all system services $\omega \in \mathcal{O}$ while retrieving a chronologically ordered response time series $\mathcal{P}$. In the response time series $\mathcal{P}$ the algorithm searches for hiccups $\mathcal{H}$, whereby each hiccup is specified by a start and an end timestamp. The hiccup identification task (*findHiccups()* in Algorithm 3, Appendix A.1.2) is the only part where the different analysis strategies differ. Based on the response time series $\mathcal{P}$ and the set of hiccups $\mathcal{H}$, the algorithm calculates the experiment duration δ and the cumulative duration of hiccups β. If the set of hiccups $\mathcal{H}$ is not empty and the cumulative hiccup duration β does not exceed the specified proportion of the experiment duration ($\delta\phi$), then the corresponding system service ω is added to the result set $\mathcal{L}$. Hence, the system service is considered as a service that exhibits a response time hiccup behaviour. The essential part of this algorithm is the hiccup identification task. Hence, in the following, we investigate the different strategies for the hiccup identification task.

Moving Percentile Strategy The idea behind the Moving Percentile strategy is to utilize a moving percentile time series for the detection of hiccups. Analogously to a moving average (Chou et al., 1975), a moving percentile time series is derived by calculating the percentile of a window that moves over the time series. Algorithm 4 (cf. Appendix A.1.2) shows how the moving percentile technique is used to detect hiccups in a response time series. Besides the performance requirement parameters (ρ and π), the Moving Percentile strategy takes a response time series $\mathcal{P}$ as input where the hiccups shell be searched in. Furthermore, these strategy requires an additional configuration parameter χ that specifies the window size (in number of elements) of the moving window. The strategy returns a set $\mathcal{H}$ of detected hiccups for further processing in the core strategy (cf. Algorithm 3, Appendix A.1.2). In the first step, the algorithm calculates a moving percentile time series $\mathcal{M}$ based on the passed response time series $\mathcal{P}$. Hereby, the strategy uses the specified window size χ and the cumulative probability π for the calculation of the percentiles. While iterating over the chronologically ordered data points $\mu \in \mathcal{M}$ the algorithm evaluates whether the response time of the corresponding percentile data point exceeds the provided response time threshold ρ. In the case that the response time threshold ρ is exceeded and no current hiccup is recorded ($\theta = NULL$), the algorithm signals the beginning of a new hiccup. Hereby, the current hiccup stores the start timestamp of the hiccup. A hiccup θ ends, if the response time percentile does not exceed the response time threshold ρ anymore. In this case, the end timestamp is added to the current hiccup θ, the hiccup is added to the set of detected hiccups $\mathcal{H}$, and the current hiccup variable θ is set to NULL in order to enable the recording of a subsequent hiccup. After all data points of the percentile series $\mathcal{M}$ have been processed, the algorithm returns a list of identified hiccups.

Bucket Strategy The Bucket strategy is similar to the Moving Percentile strategy, however, instead of using a moving window we divide the response time series into buckets with a fixed, time-based width (Algorithm 5 in Appendix A.1.2). Except for the missing window size χ, the Bucket strategy has the same inputs and the same type of output as the Moving Percentile strategy. As the first step, this strategy dynamically calculates a bucket width ξ based on the mean time τ between two subsequent requests. Using the bucket width ξ, the strategy divides the response time series $\mathcal{P}$ into a set of buckets $\mathcal{B}$. Iterating over the chronologically ordered buckets the strategy evaluates for each bucket $\beta \in \mathcal{B}$ whether it violates the performance requirements defined by ρ and π. Thereby the same calculation as described for the Performance Problem heuristic (cf. Section 6.3.1) is applied to the response times of the corresponding buckets. If a bucket violates the requirements and no current hiccup is recorded ($\theta = NULL$), then a new hiccup θ is instantiated and the left border of the current bucket β is used as the start timestamp for the hiccup. A hiccup ends if a bucket β meets the performance requirements or the last bucket is processed. In this case the right border of β is used as the end timestamp of the hiccup θ, the hiccup is added to the result set $\mathcal{H}$, and the hiccup variable is again set to NULL.

6.3.2.2. Evaluation

The detection strategies for the Application Hiccups anti-pattern are evaluated by means of the test cases TC 3 - TC 23. While the Bucket strategy is independent of any configuration parameter (except for the context specific performance requirement specification ρ and π), the Moving Percentile strategy has the window size χ as configuration parameter. Hence, we evaluate the Moving Percentile strategy for four different window sizes (5, 11, 51, and 501). Table 6.2 shows the evaluation results for both detection strategies. While the first column shows the expectation vector for the 21 test cases, the remaining columns show the detection vectors for both detection strategies. For the Moving Percentile strategy, the detection vectors are shown for each examined configuration value of the window size parameter. The last three rows show the calculation of the detection accuracy a for the individual configurations of detection strategies by means of the false positives rate r^{fp} and true positives rate r^{tp} (cf. Equation 6.17 in Section 6.1.2.2).

The Bucket strategy as well as the Moving Percentile strategy with moderate windows sizes (i.e. $10 < \chi < 500$) have a false positive rate of zero and a true positive rate of one. Hence, in this cases an optimal value of $a = 1.0$ is achieved for the detection accuracy. The Moving Percentile strategy with a windows size of $\chi = 5$ falsely detected Application Hiccups in test case TC 10, yielding a false positive rate of $r^{fp} = 0.055$ and, thus, an accuracy of $a = 0.972$. Due to a very high utilization of the application node's CPU, the response times in TC 10 exhibit a high variance including frequent outliers.

Test Cases	expectation vector	detection vectors: Moving Percentile 5	11	51	501	Bucket
TC 3	⚐	⚐	⚐	⚐	⚐	⚐
TC 4	⚐	⚐	⚐	⚐	⚐	⚐
TC 5	⚐	⚐	⚐	⚐	✓	⚐
TC 6	✓	✓	✓	✓	✓	✓
TC 7	✓	✓	✓	✓	✓	✓
TC 8	✓	✓	✓	✓	✓	✓
TC 9	✓	✓	✓	✓	✓	✓
TC 10	✓	⚐	✓	✓	✓	✓
TC 11	✓	✓	✓	✓	✓	✓
TC 12	✓	✓	✓	✓	✓	✓
TC 13	✓	✓	✓	✓	✓	✓
TC 14	✓	✓	✓	✓	✓	✓
TC 15	✓	✓	✓	✓	✓	✓
TC 16	✓	✓	✓	✓	✓	✓
TC 17	✓	✓	✓	✓	✓	✓
TC 18	✓	✓	✓	✓	✓	✓
TC 19	✓	✓	✓	✓	✓	✓
TC 20	✓	✓	✓	✓	✓	✓
TC 21	✓	✓	✓	✓	✓	✓
TC 22	✓	✓	✓	✓	✓	✓
TC 23	✓	✓	✓	✓	✓	✓
false positives rate r^{fp}:		0.055	0.0	0.0	0.000	0.0
true positives rate r^{tp}:		1.000	1.0	1.0	0.667	1.0
accuracy $a(r^{fp}, r^{tp})$:		0.972	**1.0**	**1.0**	0.833	**1.0**

Table 6.2.: Evaluation results on the Appplication Hiccups detection strategies

With a small window size (e.g. $\chi = 5$), the Moving Percentile strategy falsely detects very short outlier phases (in the range of milliseconds) as hiccups. Conversely, using an extremely high window size (e.g. $\chi > 500$) may lead to the effect that Application Hiccups are smoothed out by the moving window, resulting in false negatives. This effect especially occurs on coarse-grained measurement data, i.e. only few measurements per time unit. To sum up, the Bucket strategy and the Moving Percentile strategy with moderate windows sizes perform equally good on our test cases. However, as finding a proper value for the window size parameter χ may depend on the resolution of the measurement data, the Moving Percentile strategy is less generalizable as the Bucket strategy. Therefore, we select the Bucket strategy for further detection of the Application Hiccups anti-pattern in the remainder of this work.

6.3.3. The Ramp Heuristic

The essence of the Ramp anti-pattern (cf. Table 2.1(b), Chapter 2.4) is an increase in response times over operation time. We create three different detection strategies for the Ramp that differ not only in their analysis strategies but also in the experimentation strategies.

6.3.3.1. Detection Strategies

We provide two detection strategies for the Ramp anti-pattern that rely on the same measurement data that has been used for the high-level Performance Problem detection heuristic: *Linear Regression* strategy and *Direct Growth* strategy. Hence, for these two detection strategies the instrumentation, experimentation and data representation descriptions are the same as for the Performance Problem detection heuristic (cf. Section 6.3.1). Furthermore, we provide a third detection strategy (*Time Window* strategy) that is based on a different experimentation strategy.

Linear Regression Strategy When it comes to identifying whether a set of data points in a time series shows an increasing trend, the most intuitive way is an evaluation of the corresponding slope. To this end, the Linear Regression strategy applies a linear regression on the data points to derive the slope for evaluation (Algorithm 6 in Appendix A.1.3). This detection strategy takes a data set $\mathcal{D}$ as well as a slope threshold τ as input, and returns a set $\mathcal{L}$ of system services containing a Ramp anti-pattern. For each system service $\omega \in O$, this detection strategy applies a linear regression on the time series of response times $\mathcal{P}$ yielding a slope κ of the corresponding linear curve. If the slope κ is greater than the specified threshold τ, the corresponding system service ω is considered to contain the Ramp anti-pattern.

Direct Growth Strategy The Direct Growth strategy compares response times measured in the beginning of the load test to response times that have been measured at the end of the test. This detection strategy reports an occurrence of a Ramp if the comparison yields a significant difference between the response times from the beginning of the load test and the response times from the end. As this detection strategy is based on the same type of measurement data as the Performance Problem detection heuristic, one single load test is used to derive the end-to-end response times of the individual system services. Based on that data, the Direct Growth strategy applies the following analysis strategy (Algorithm 7 in Appendix A.1.3). In addition to the response time data set $\mathcal{D}$, this detection strategy takes an additional parameter α as input, that specifies the significance level for statistical tests used in the algorithm. Again, the algorithm returns a list $\mathcal{L}$ of system services that exhibit a ramp behaviour. While iterating over the system services $\omega \in \mathcal{O}$, the detection strategy chronologically divides the response time series $\mathcal{P}$ into two subsets $\mathcal{R}_1$ and $\mathcal{R}_2$ for which the mean values μ_1 and μ_2 are calculated. In order to decide whether response times increase over time, the samples $\mathcal{R}_1$ and $\mathcal{R}_2$ are compared applying a t-test (Downing et al., 2003). However, as the values in $\mathcal{R}_1$ and $\mathcal{R}_2$ may be not normally distributed, we first bootstrap the values according to the *Central Limit Theorem* (Downing et al., 2003) which yields the normally distributed bootstrapped sets $\mathcal{B}_1$ and $\mathcal{B}_2$. Applying a t-test to $\mathcal{B}_1$ and $\mathcal{B}_2$, we get a *p-value* p providing the information on the significance of difference between the mean values of $\mathcal{B}_1$ and $\mathcal{B}_2$. If p is smaller than the specified significance level α and at the same time $\mu_1 < \mu_2$, then the response times in $\mathcal{R}_2$ are smaller than in $\mathcal{R}_1$. In this case, the Direct Growth detection strategy assumes that response times increased from beginning to the end and reports the system service ω as a Ramp.

Time Window Strategy While both the Linear Regression strategy and the Direct Growth strategy are based on the same type of data as the Performance Problem heuristic, the Time Window strategy applies a different experimentation strategy. Figure 6.7 shows the Experimentation Description instance for the Time Window detection strategy. The IaM Description is the same as for the Performance Problem heuristic, including the *Entry Points* scope and the *Response Time* probe. With respect to the experiment plan, we use a *Custom Experiment Series* comprising four *Single-User Tests* and

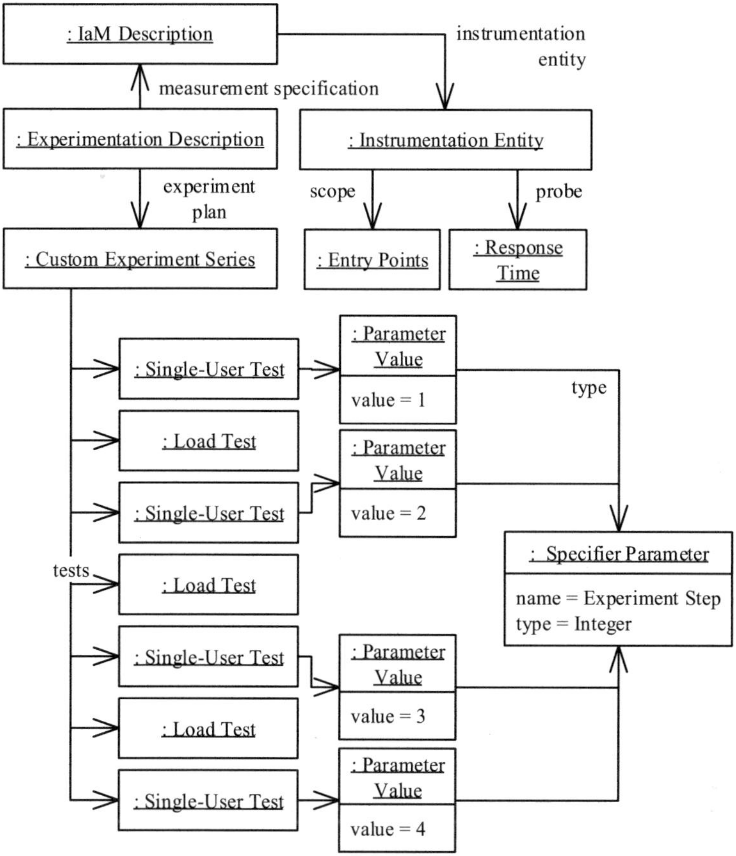

Figure 6.7.: Experiment and instrumentation description for the Time Window strategy

three intermediate *Load Tests*. The Time Window strategy is based on the idea that a Ramp grows faster with a higher load intensity than with a low intensity. Thus, we use the Load Tests to stimulate a potential Ramp anti-pattern, whereby, no measurements are taken in these experiments. Hence, the Load Tests serve as intermediate stimulation phases between the Single-User Tests that constitute the actual tests including gathering of measurement

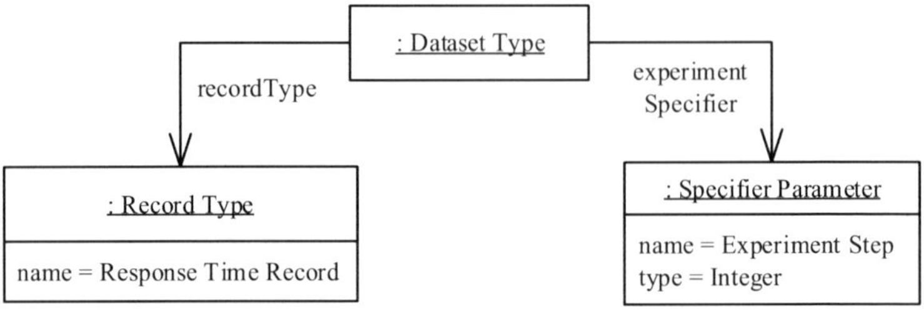

Figure 6.8.: Data representation format for the Time Window strategy

data. In order to reconstruct the sequence of the Single-User Tests in the analysis phase from the measurement data, each Single-User Test refers to a Specifier Parameter *Experiment Step* with an increasing parameter value. Consequently, apart from the Response Time Record type, the corresponding Dataset Type comprises that Specifier Parameter (cf. Figure 6.8). Based on that Dataset Type, the Time Window strategy applies the following analysis (Algorithm 8 in Appendix A.1.3). Besides the dataset $\mathcal{D}$, the detection strategy takes a statistical significance level α as input. The result is, again, a list $\mathcal{L}$ of system services that contain a Ramp anti-pattern. For each system service $\omega \in O$ a pairwise comparison of the response times series of neighbouring experiments is conducted. To this end, for each single-user experiment $\eta \in \{2, 3, 4\}$ the response time sets $\mathcal{R}_\eta$ and $\mathcal{R}_{\eta-1}$ are retrieved and bootstrapped, yielding normally distributed sets $\mathcal{B}_\eta$ and $\mathcal{B}_{\eta-1}$. Applying a t-test (Downing et al., 2003) on $\mathcal{B}_\eta$ and $\mathcal{B}_{\eta-1}$ provides a p-value p. If p is smaller than the specified significance level α, and the mean value μ_η of $\mathcal{R}_\eta$ is greater than the mean value $\mu_{\eta-1}$ of $\mathcal{R}_{\eta-1}$, then the response times in $\mathcal{R}_\eta$ are considered to be significantly greater than in $\mathcal{R}_{\eta-1}$. If this applies for all $\eta \in 2, 3, 4$, then the corresponding system service ω is considered to contain a Ramp anti-pattern and, thus, is added to the result list $\mathcal{L}$.

6.3.3.2. Evaluation

Both the Direct Growth and the Time Window strategies require a significance level α as configuration parameter for the t-tests. For α, we use the commonly used value of 0.05 (corresponding to 95% confidence). The de-

	expectation vector	detection vectors					
		Direct Growth	Linear Regression				Time Window
Test Cases			10^{-5}	10^{-4}	10^{-3}	10^{-2}	
TC 3	✓	⚐	⚐	✓	✓	✓	✓
TC 4	✓	✓	✓	✓	✓	✓	✓
TC 5	✓	✓	✓	✓	✓	✓	✓
TC 6	⚐	⚐	⚐	⚐	⚐	✓	⚐
TC 7	⚐	⚐	⚐	⚐	✓	✓	⚐
TC 8	✓	✓	✓	✓	✓	✓	✓
TC 9	✓	✓	✓	✓	✓	✓	✓
TC 10	✓	⚐	⚐	⚐	✓	✓	✓
TC 11	✓	✓	⚐	⚐	✓	✓	✓
TC 12	✓	✓	✓	✓	✓	✓	✓
TC 13	✓	✓	✓	✓	✓	✓	✓
TC 14	✓	✓	⚐	✓	✓	✓	✓
TC 15	✓	✓	⚐	⚐	✓	✓	✓
TC 16	✓	✓	✓	✓	✓	✓	✓
TC 17	✓	✓	✓	✓	✓	✓	✓
TC 18	✓	⚐	⚐	✓	✓	✓	✓
TC 19	✓	⚐	⚐	⚐	✓	✓	✓
TC 20	✓	✓	✓	✓	✓	✓	✓
TC 21	✓	✓	✓	✓	✓	✓	✓
TC 22	✓	✓	✓	✓	✓	✓	✓
TC 23	✓	✓	✓	✓	✓	✓	✓
false positives rate r^{fp}:		0.210	0.368	0.210	0.00	0.0	0.0
true positives rate r^{tp}:		1.000	1.000	1.000	0.50	0.0	1.0
accuracy $a(r^{fp}, r^{tp})$:		0.895	0.815	0.895	0.75	0.5	**1.0**

Table 6.3.: Evaluation results on the detection strategies for the Ramp anti-pattern

tection results of the Linear Regression strategy highly depend on the linear slope threshold τ. Therefore, we analyze the Linear Regression strategy for four different magnitudes of the configuration value for τ (10^{-5} – 10^{-2}). Table 6.3 shows the evaluation results for the three detection strategies including four configuration alternatives of the Linear Regression strategy. The Direct Growth strategy has a true positives rate $r^{tp} = 1.0$, however, 4 of 19 test cases have been falsely detected leading to a false positives rate of $r^{fp} = 0.21$. Hence, tending to falsely detect a Ramp in negative scenarios, the Direct Growth strategy exhibits a detection accuracy of $a = 0.895$ on our test cases. The Linear Regression strategy behaves very differently depending on the value for the slope threshold τ. For small values of τ ($\tau <= 10^{-4}$), the Linear Regression strategy tends to falsely detect a Ramp anti-pattern in scenarios that, actually, do not contain a Ramp behaviour. With a optimal true positives rate and a false positives rate of $r^{fp} = 0.368$ the Linear Regression strategy has an accuracy of $a = 0.815$ with a slope threshold $\tau = 10^{-5}$. A larger threshold τ decreases the false positive rate, for instance a threshold value $\tau = 10^{-4}$ yields a false positive rate of $r^{fp} = 0.315$, leading to a higher accuracy $a = 0.842$. However, still 4 of 19 test cases have been falsely detected. For a higher threshold $10^{-3} \leq \tau \leq 10^{-2}$, the Linear Regression strategy achieves a optimal false positives rate of zero on our test cases. However, in that cases the true positive rate decreases to 0.5 and 0.0 for a threshold $\tau = 10^{-3}$ and $\tau = 10^{-2}$, respectively. The resulting detection accuracies are $a = 0.75$ and $a = 0.5$, respectively. In the latter case, the detection results are as good as with a random guessing approach. From the evaluation results for the Linear Regression strategy we can conclude that a reasonable configuration of this strategy highly depends on the concrete context. Hence, the Linear Regression strategy is not suitable as part of a generic detection heuristic for the Ramp anti-pattern. The Time Window strategy yields the best detection results on our test cases with an optimal accuracy of $a = 1.0$. Hence, we select the Time Windows strategy for further detection of the Ramp anti-pattern.

Apart from the evaluation on the test cases considered in this chapter, the Ramp anti-pattern and, with that, all potential detection strategies for the Ramp have an inherent obstacle. The test cases TC 6 and TC 7 contain a rather aggressive Ramp behaviour, so that response times increase considerably within minutes when applying a high load intensity. However, in practice occurrences of the Ramp anti-pattern are much more protracted, so that response time increases become noticeable only after days or even months of operation. Hence, the detection results for the Ramp anti-pattern are always relative to the experimentation duration and, thus, should be treated with caution.

6.3.4. Continuously Violated Requirements Heuristic

The Continuously Violated Requirements (CVR) anti-pattern (cf. Section 4.3) is to a certain degree complementary to the Application Hiccups anti-pattern. While in the later case the response times exceed the performance requirements threshold periodically, in the former case, the response time continuously violate the requirements. Hence, it seems reasonable to apply similar detection strategies for the CVR anti-pattern as for the Application Hiccups anti-pattern while reverting some detection conditions. Analogously to the Application Hiccups Heuristic, this heuristic requires the same type of measurement data as the Performance Problem Heuristic. Hence, for this heuristic we use the same experimentation, instrumentation and data representation descriptions as shown in Section 6.3.1. Analogously to the Application Hiccups heuristic, we investigate two different detection strategies.

6.3.4.1. Detection Strategies

For the detection of continuously violated requirements we apply the same basic techniques as for the detection of application hiccups: moving percentile and bucket analysis. Similar to the core strategy of the *Application Hiccups* heuristic, the algorithm retrieves the set $\mathcal{O}$ of system services $\omega \in \mathcal{O}$ for subsequent iteration (Algorithm 9 in Appendix A.1.4). For each system service ω, the strategy applies the corresponding detection strategy that returns a boolean value indicating whether the corresponding response time series $\mathcal{P}$ of system service ω continuously violates the performance requirements. In the following, we explain the different detection strategies and evaluate them on the corresponding test cases.

Moving Percentile Strategy The algorithm for the *Moving Percentile Strategy* (Algorithm 10 in Appendix A.1.4) calculates a percentile time series $\mathcal{M}$ for a given response time series $\mathcal{P}$. While iterating over the percentile data points $\mu \in \mathcal{M}$, the detection strategy evaluates whether the response time of the percentile data point (μ[`'Response Time'`]) exceeds the response time threshold ρ from the performance requirements specification. If all data points $\mu \in \mathcal{M}$ exceed the threshold ρ, then ω is classified as a service that continuously violates the performance requirements under the applied load intensity. By contrast, if at minimum one $\mu \in \mathcal{M}$ does not exceed the response time threshold, then the algorithm does not detect ω as a CVR instance.

Bucket Strategy The *Bucket Strategy* for the detection of continuously violated performance requirements (cf. Algorithm 11 in Appendix A.1.4) is very similar to the corresponding strategy in Section 6.3.2. It requires a configuration parameter ϕ as input. ϕ specifies the minimum proportion of the experiment time in which the response time of ω must exceed the requirements threshold ρ in order that $\mathcal{P}$ is classified as a response time series that continuously violates performance requirements. This strategy divides the given response time series $\mathcal{P}$ into buckets with a fix width, in a similar way as described in Section 6.3.2. For the resulting set of buckets $\mathcal{B}$, this strategy counts the number η of buckets that violate the performance requirements. If the proportion of buckets that violate the performance requirements is bigger then the specified proportion ϕ, then the corresponding system service ω is detected as an instance of the CVR anti-pattern.

6.3.4.2. Evaluation

As the detection strategies for the CVR anti-pattern are conceptually very similar to the Application Hiccups detection strategies (cf. Section 6.3.2), we evaluate the CVR detection strategies in a similar way. For the window size of the Moving Percentile strategy we again use four configuration alternatives (5, 11, 51, and 501), while the Bucket strategy does not have any configuration parameters. Table 6.4 shows the evaluation results for the CVR detection strategies. Although all alternatives exhibit a false positive rate of zero, the Moving Percentile strategy has a true positive rate r^{tp} that is less than 1.0 for all configuration alternatives. Hereby, the true positive rate increases with a larger window size χ. In general, the Moving Percentile strategy for the CVR anti-pattern detection has the same problems as the Moving Percentile strategy in Section 6.3.2. By contrast, the Bucket strategy yields an accuracy of 1.0 on the 21 test cases it has been tested on. Therefore, in the remainder of this thesis, the Bucket strategy is used for the CVR detection heuristic. The positive test cases for the CVR anti-pattern are used to evaluate the Traffic Jam anti-pattern in the following.

Test Cases	expectation vector	detection vectors: Moving Percentile 5	11	51	501	Bucket
TC 3	✓	✓	✓	✓	✓	✓
TC 4	✓	✓	✓	✓	✓	✓
TC 5	✓	✓	✓	✓	✓	✓
TC 6	✓	✓	✓	✓	✓	✓
TC 7	✓	✓	✓	✓	✓	✓
TC 8	⚐	✓	⚐	⚐	⚐	⚐
TC 9	⚐	✓	✓	✓	⚐	⚐
TC 10	⚐	✓	✓	✓	✓	⚐
TC 11	⚐	✓	✓	⚐	⚐	⚐
TC 12	⚐	⚐	⚐	⚐	⚐	⚐
TC 13	⚐	⚐	⚐	⚐	⚐	⚐
TC 14	⚐	✓	✓	✓	⚐	⚐
TC 15	⚐	✓	✓	⚐	⚐	⚐
TC 16	⚐	✓	✓	✓	⚐	⚐
TC 17	⚐	✓	✓	⚐	⚐	⚐
TC 18	⚐	✓	✓	⚐	⚐	⚐
TC 19	⚐	⚐	⚐	⚐	⚐	⚐
TC 20	⚐	✓	⚐	⚐	⚐	⚐
TC 21	⚐	⚐	⚐	⚐	⚐	⚐
TC 22	⚐	✓	✓	✓	⚐	⚐
TC 23	⚐	⚐	⚐	⚐	⚐	⚐
false positives rate r^{fp}:		0.000	0.000	0.000	0.000	0.0
true positives rate r^{tp}:		0.312	0.437	0.687	0.937	1.0
accuracy $a(r^{fp}, r^{tp})$:		0.656	0.718	0.843	0.968	**1.0**

Table 6.4.: Evaluation results on the detection strategies for continuous violation of performance requirements

6.3.5. Traffic Jam Heuristic

As shown in the PPEP instance (cf. 4.4.2), the Traffic Jam anti-pattern (cf. Section Table 2.1(a), Chapter 2.4) subsumes a sub-class of performance problems under the Continuously Violated Requirements anti-pattern. Hereby, the dependency between response times and the load is an essential part of the Traffic Jam anti-pattern. In the following, we provide two different strategies for detecting a Traffic Jam.

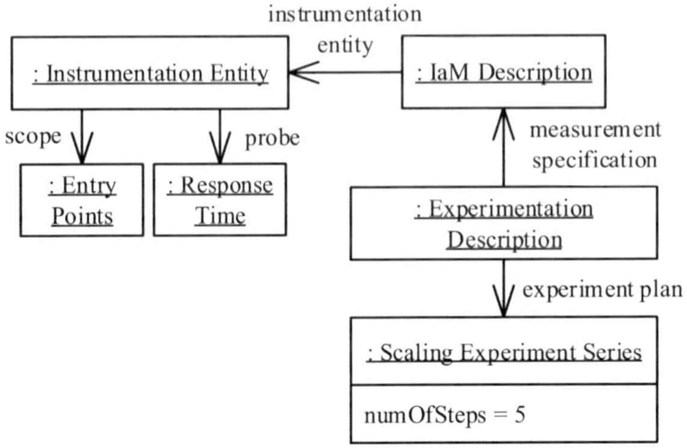

Figure 6.9.: Experiment and instrumentation description for the Traffic Jam detection

6.3.5.1. Detection Strategies

In order to investigate the Traffic Jam anti-pattern, response times need to be evaluated in dependence to different load intensities. Hence, for the detection of the Traffic Jam anti-pattern we need an experimentation strategy that provides means to gather response times under different load intensities. Figure 6.9 shows the Experimentation Description instance for the Traffic Jame detection heuristic. With respect to the instrumentation and monitoring part, we again capture the response times from the *Entry Points* scope. As experiment plan, we use the *Scaling Experiment Series* with five experiment steps. Hence, five experiments are executed, whereby the load is increased from one experiment to the next, starting with a single user and finishing with the specified maximum load intensity. The resulting data representation has the same format as shown in Figure 6.6. Based on that data representation we provide two different detection strategies for the detection of a Traffic Jam anti-pattern: the *Linear Regression* strategy and the *t-Test* strategy.

Linear Regression Strategy The Linear Regression strategy requires two inputs: a dataset $\mathcal{D}$ containing response times for different load intensities, and a parameter τ specifying a slope threshold (Algorithm 12, Appendix A.1.5). The strategy returns a set $\mathcal{L}$ of system services that contain a Traffic Jam behaviour. For each system service $\omega \in O$, the strategy retrieves a set $\mathcal{P}_u$ of pairs comprising number of users and response times. Applying a linear regression on $\mathcal{P}_u$ yields the slope κ of the corresponding linear curve. A system service ω is considered to contain a Traffic Jam if the corresponding regression slope κ is greater than the specified threshold τ.

t-Test Strategy Instead of conducting a linear regression, the t-Test strategy applies a statistical test (similar to the Time Window strategy of the Ramp heuristic in Section 6.3.3) in order to identify a significant increase in data points. This strategy requires the dataset $\mathcal{D}$, a significance parameter α, and the performance requirements (ρ, π) as input. The result is a list $\mathcal{L}$ of system services containing a Traffic Jam and a set $\mathcal{I}$ of load intensities under which the SUT violates the performance requirements. For each system service ω, the strategy conducts the following analysis in order to investigate whether ω contains a Traffic Jam anti-pattern. Given the sets of response times $\mathcal{R}_\eta$ ($\eta \in \{1, 2, 3, 4, 5\}$), this strategy evaluates for each neighbouring pair $(\mathcal{R}_\eta, \mathcal{R}_{\eta-1})$ whether $\mathcal{R}_{\eta-1}$ contains significantly smaller response times than $\mathcal{R}_\eta$. Thereby, t-tests are applied (Downing et al., 2003) in the same way as in the Time Window strategy of the Ramp heuristic (cf. Section 6.3.3). Note, the higher the index η the higher the load during the corresponding experiment. A system service ω is considered to contain a Traffic Jam, if the response times significantly increase for all experiment steps η whose response times $\mathcal{R}_\eta$ violate the performance requirements (ρ, π).

6.3.5.2. Evaluation

The Linear Regression strategy is parametrized with a threshold τ for the linear slope. Hereby, the threshold defines the maximum allowed increase in average response time per additional user in the load intensity such that no Traffic Jam anti-pattern is reported. We evaluate the Linear Regression strategy for four different values of τ. We vary the magnitude of τ from 0.1 ms/user to 100 ms/user. For the t-Test strategy we use a fix significance level of $\alpha = 0.05$. The evaluation results for the Traffic Jam detection strategies are shown in Table 6.5. Again, we see that the Linear Regression strategy performs very differently depending on the threshold τ. With a large threshold $\tau = 100$, the detection strategy performs worst yielding only one true positive of 14 positive test cases. Due to the large slope threshold even

			detection vectors				
		expectation vector	Linear Regression				t-Test
			0.1	1	10	100	
Test Cases	TC 8	✓	✓	✓	✓	✓	✓
	TC 9	✓	✓	✓	✓	✓	✓
	TC 10	⚐	⚐	⚐	⚐	✓	⚐
	TC 11	⚐	⚐	⚐	⚐	✓	⚐
	TC 12	⚐	⚐	⚐	⚐	✓	⚐
	TC 13	⚐	⚐	⚐	⚐	✓	⚐
	TC 14	⚐	⚐	⚐	⚐	✓	⚐
	TC 15	⚐	⚐	⚐	⚐	✓	⚐
	TC 16	⚐	⚐	⚐	⚐	✓	⚐
	TC 17	⚐	⚐	⚐	⚐	✓	⚐
	TC 18	⚐	⚐	⚐	⚐	✓	⚐
	TC 19	⚐	⚐	⚐	⚐	✓	⚐
	TC 20	⚐	⚐	⚐	⚐	✓	⚐
	TC 21	⚐	⚐	⚐	⚐	⚐	⚐
	TC 22	⚐	⚐	⚐	⚐	✓	⚐
	TC 23	⚐	⚐	⚐	✓	✓	⚐
	false positives rate r^{fp}:		0.0	0.0	0.000	0.000	0.0
	true positives rate r^{tp}:		1.0	1.0	0.928	0.071	1.0
	accuracy $a(r^{fp}, r^{tp})$:		**1.0**	**1.0**	0.964	0.535	**1.0**

Table 6.5.: Evaluation results on the Traffic Jam detection strategies

significant increases in response time are neglected. Consequently, in this case the accuracy is very low with a value of 0.535. With $\tau = 10$, the Linear Regression strategy yields only for one test case a wrong detection result. Finally, for small threshold values ($0.1 \leq \tau \leq 1$) the Linear Regression strategy provides optimal detection results with an accuracy of 1.0. These results show that compared to the Linear Regression strategy for the Ramp anti-pattern (cf. Section 6.3.3), in this case the Linear Regression strategy provides more robust detection results for a reasonable range of the threshold τ. As explained before, the Linear Regression strategy for the Traffic Jam anti-pattern executes for each load intensity an individual experiment that provides a robust set of measurement points for each value of the load intensity. These sets of measurement data compensate any outliers leading to a robust linear regression curve. By contrast, in the case of the Ramp detection, the measurement points for the Linear Regression strategy came from a single experiment. Hence, each value on the abscissa has only one corresponding value on the ordinate. Therefore, the Linear Regression strategy for the Ramp anti-pattern is more sensitive to outliers and, thus, is less robust. The t-Test strategy detects all test cases correctly and, thus, achieves a detection accuracy of $a = 1.0$. Although, the Linear Regression strategy with a small threshold τ performs as good as the t-Test strategy on our test cases, it still remains an unintuitive task to provide a proper value for the slope threshold. Therefore, in the remainder of this work, we use the t-Test strategy for the detection of the Traffic Jam anti-pattern. As the test cases TC 10 to TC 23 have been correctly identified as positive test cases for the Traffic Jam anti-pattern, in the following, they are used as test cases for the One Lane Bridge, Database Congestion and Excessive Messaging anti-patterns.

6.3.6. One Lane Bridge Heuristic

The One Lane Bridge (OLB) anti-pattern (cf. Table 2.1(e), Chapter 2.4) constitutes a software bottleneck leading to request congestion due to a limited software resource instead of a saturation of a hardware resource. We distinguish different types of OLB anti-patterns: general OLB, Dispensable Synchronization, Database OLB or Bottleneck Service (cf. Section 4.3). As all types of OLBs can be detected in the same way (apart from the instrumentation scope), in this section, we subsume the detection of all the different types of OLBs under a single detection heuristic.

6.3.6.1. Detection Strategies

The OLB anti-pattern is closely related to the Traffic Jam. While a Traffic Jam refers to a congestion in general, an OLB subsumes all Traffic Jams that are caused by a software resource. Hence, in order to identify an OLB, response times need to be analyzed in correspondence with the utilization of CPUs under different load situations. We create two detection strategies that take both aspects into account in order to investigate the OLB anti-pattern: the *Fix Threshold* strategy and the *Queueing Theory* strategy. Both detection strategies are based on the same experimentation strategy described by the Experimentation Description instance shown in Figure 6.10. Analogously to

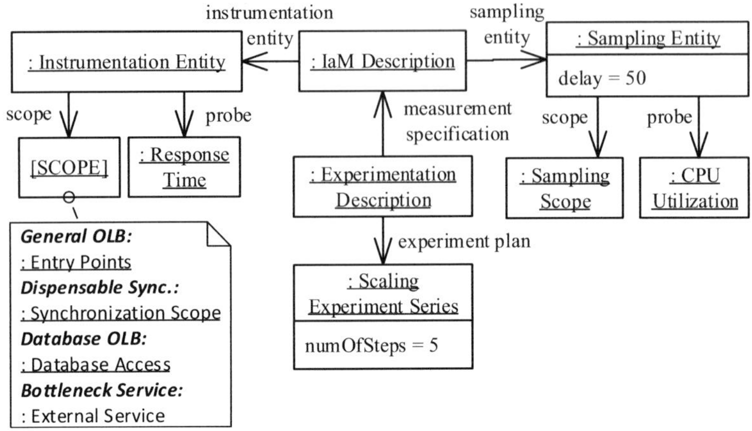

Figure 6.10.: Experiment and instrumentation description for the OLB detection

the Traffic Jam heuristic (cf. Section 6.3.5), we use a *Scaling Experiment Series* with five experiments. With respect to the IaM Description, we add a Sampling Entity with an unlimited scope and *CPU Utilization* as probe. The scope of the Instrumentation Entity depends on the type of OLB (general OLB, Dispensable Synchronization, Database OLB or Bottleneck Service) to be analyzed. Accordingly to the IaM Description, in addition to the response time dataset (cf. Figure 6.6) the experiments yield a CPU utilization dataset as shown in Figure 6.11. Besides the *Number of Users* parameter as experiment specifier, the dataset refers to a *CPU Utilization Record* as Record Type. The CPU Utilization Record contains a Specifier Parameter for the specification of the system node where the CPU utilization is measured, as well as two Measure Parameter that allow to capture the timestamp and the CPU utilization.

Fix Threshold Strategy The Fix Threshold strategy leverages the fact that the OLB anti-pattern is a special case of the Traffic Jam anti-pattern characterized by not saturated utilization of CPU resources. Hence, the Fix Threshold strategy builds upon the t-Test strategy of the Traffic Jam Heuristic (cf. Section 6.3.5) adding an analysis of CPU utilizations (cf. Algorithm 14, Appendix A.1.6). This strategy takes a CPU utilization dataset $\mathcal{D}_{CPU}$ and a

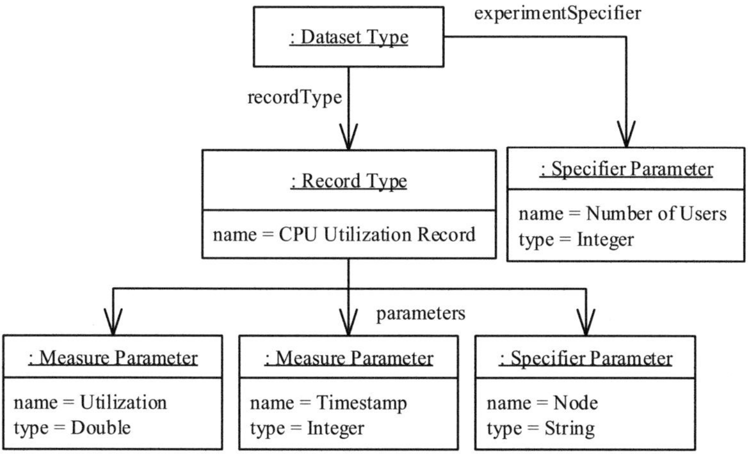

Figure 6.11.: Data representation format for the OLB detection

CPU utilization threshold θ as input and returns a boolean value. The return value indicates whether the Traffic Jams identified in the system services by the Traffic Jam Heuristic are caused by the OLB anti-pattern or not. While iterating over all system nodes $\zeta \in C$ and all experiments with different load intensities $\upsilon \in \mathcal{U}$, the algorithm investigates whether the mean CPU utilization U of the corresponding system node ζ exceeds the CPU threshold θ. If none of the utilizations exceeds the threshold, corresponding services that have been detected by the Traffic Jam Heuristic are considered to contain an OLB anti-pattern.

Queueing Theory Strategy The Queueing Theory strategy utilizes laws from the queueing theory (cf. Section 2.2.1) in order to identify an anomalous balance between CPU utilization and response times. Following Menascé et al., 2004, the average number N of requests in a multi-server queue system is given by Equation 6.19. Hereby, v denotes the number of servers, U the average utilization of the servers, and $C(v, U)$ is *Erlang's C formula* (Menascé et al., 2004) describing the probability that an arriving request must wait in a multi-server queue. Combining Equation 6.19 with *Little's Law* and the *Service Demand Law* (cf. Section 2.2.1) allows to derive a theoretical response time R that depends on the mean CPU utilization U, the number of CPU cores ν and the service demand D of the corresponding request. Equations 6.23-6.25 show the derivation of R from the given laws.

$$\text{Avg. number of requests:} \quad N = \frac{U}{1-U} C(\nu, U) + \nu U \tag{6.19}$$

$$\text{Utilization:} \quad U = \frac{\lambda}{\nu \mu} \tag{6.20}$$

$$\text{Little's Law:} \quad N = \lambda R \tag{6.21}$$

$$\text{Service Demand:} \quad D = \frac{1}{\mu} \tag{6.22}$$

$$(6.19) + (6.20) \Rightarrow \quad N = \frac{\lambda}{\nu \mu} \frac{1}{1-U} C(\nu, U) + \frac{\lambda}{\mu} \tag{6.23}$$

$$(6.21) \Rightarrow \quad R = \frac{1}{\nu \mu} \frac{1}{1-U} C(\nu, U) + \frac{1}{\mu} \tag{6.24}$$

$$(6.22) \Rightarrow \quad R = \frac{D}{\nu} \frac{1}{1-U} C(\nu, U) + D \tag{6.25}$$

The Queueing Theory strategy utilizes this formula to derive an upper threshold τ for the response times that can be described by queueing theory. If an average response time exceeds that threshold, we can assume that a Traffic Jam occurs that cannot be explained by CPU congestion, hence, constituting an OLB anti-pattern. Under very low utilization the average service demand D of a request can be approximated with its average response time ϱ_s. To this end, this detection heuristic calculates for each instrumented location $\omega \in O$ the average single-user response time ϱ_s, as well as the number of CPU cores ν for all system nodes. For each tuple of an instrumented location $\omega \in O$, a load intensity $\upsilon \in \mathcal{U}$, and a system node $\zeta \in C$, this detection strategy calculates the response time threshold $\tau_{\omega,\upsilon,\zeta}$ utilizing Equation 6.25. Hereby, the algorithm uses the number of cores ν on system node ζ, the aggregated average utilization U of the corresponding CPUs on node ζ, and the average single-user response time ϱ_s as an approximation for the service demand D of operation ω. If at least one average response time ϱ_m of operation ω exceeds the corresponding threshold $\tau_{\omega,\upsilon,\zeta}$ then this violation cannot be explained by the queueing theory, leading to the assumption that ω contains an OLB anti-pattern.

	expectation vector	detection vectors: Fix Threshold 60	70	80	90	95	Queueing Theory
Test Cases TC 10	✓	✓	✓	✓	✓	✓	✓
TC 11	✓	✓	✓	✓	✓	✓	✓
TC 12	⚐	⚐	⚐	⚐	⚐	⚐	⚐
TC 13	⚐	⚐	⚐	⚐	⚐	⚐	⚐
TC 14	✓	✓	✓	✓	✓	✓	✓
TC 15	⚐	⚐	⚐	⚐	⚐	⚐	⚐
TC 16	✓	⚐	⚐	⚐	⚐	⚐	✓
TC 17	✓	⚐	⚐	⚐	⚐	⚐	✓
TC 18	✓	⚐	⚐	⚐	⚐	⚐	✓
TC 19	✓	⚐	⚐	⚐	⚐	⚐	⚐
TC 20	✓	⚐	⚐	⚐	⚐	⚐	⚐
TC 21	⚐	⚐	⚐	⚐	⚐	⚐	⚐
TC 22	⚐	⚐	⚐	⚐	⚐	⚐	⚐
TC 23	✓	✓	⚐	⚐	⚐	⚐	✓
false positives rate r^{fp}:		0.556	0.667	0.667	0.667	0.667	0.222
true positives rate r^{tp}:		1.000	1.000	1.000	1.000	1.000	1.000
accuracy $a(r^{fp}, r^{tp})$:		0.722	0.667	0.667	0.667	0.667	**0.889**

Table 6.6.: Evaluation results on the One Lane Bridge detection strategies

6.3.6.2. Evaluation

In this section, we evaluate the Queueing Theory strategy and five configuration alternatives (CPU threshold $\theta \in \{60\%, 70\%, 80\%, 90\%, 95\%\}$) of the Fix Threshold strategy by means of the test cases TC 10 - TC 23. Table 6.6 shows that none of the strategies achieved an optimal detection accuracy. For the CPU threshold values $70 \leq \theta \leq 95$, the Fix Threshold strategy yields constant detection results with an accuracy of $a = 0.667$. Although all positive test cases have been detected correctly, 6 of 9 negative test cases have been falsely detected. In the test cases TC 16 - TC 20, the throughput is limited by the capacity of the network and corresponding transmission protocols. However, the Fix Threshold strategy neglects network utilization. As in these test cases all CPU utilizations are very low, however, the response times grow with the load intensity (due to network limitations), the Fix Threshold strategy falsely detects an OLB anti-pattern in these test cases.

In test case TC 23, the response times increase with the load intensity due to a moderate utilization of the CPU. However, with a high CPU utilization threshold that moderate utilization is missed and results in a false positive. A CPU threshold of $\theta = 60$ resolves the false positive in TC 23, yielding a detection accuracy of $a = 0.722$. The Queueing Theory strategy performs best with an accuracy of $a = 0.889$. First, as indicated by the name and described before, the Queueing Theory strategy is based on queueing theory (cf Section 2.2.1) and, thus, correctly identifies scenarios where response times grow due to moderate utilization of resources (e.g. TC 23). Furthermore, besides the utilization of the CPU, the Queueing Theory strategy takes the network utilization into account. In this way, this strategy provides correct detection results for the test cases TC 16 - TC 18. However, in test cases TC 19 and TC 20, the Queueing Theory strategy still falsely detects an *OLB* anti-pattern. In these cases, the problem is that network utilization cannot be that easily treated as the CPU utilization. In particular, it is very difficult to predict the maximum throughput of a network connection without having detailed information about the characteristics of the transmitted data (e.g. size of messages), configuration of different transmission protocols (e.g. TCP) as well as the usage patterns of the network by the target application (e.g. number of connections). As estimating the maximum throughput of network connections is a topic on its own, in this thesis, we abstain from providing a solution to that problem. As the Queueing Theory strategy performed best, in the remainder of this work it is used for the detection of the OLB anti-pattern.

Besides the correct classification of the positive test cases, the Queueing Theory strategy correctly pointed to the root causes of the observed OLB anti-patterns. In particular, in test cases TC 12 and TC 13, this strategy identified the methods that issued the high amount of database requests as the points of congestion. In TC 15, the detection strategy reported the database call method (with corresponding query) as the guilty method. Finally, in the test cases TC 21 and TC 22 the corresponding synchronized methods have been identified correctly as the root cause.

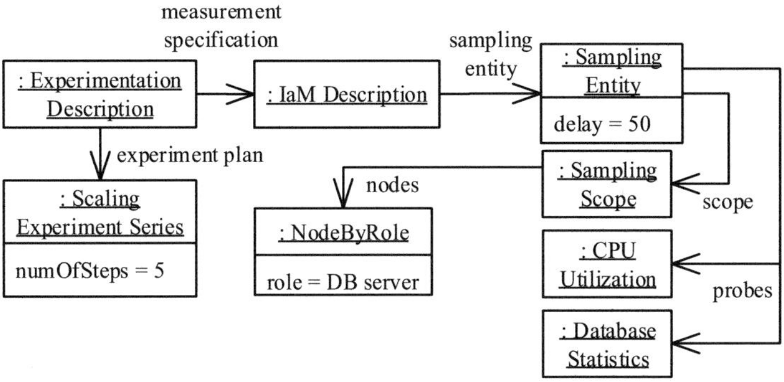

Figure 6.12.: Experiment and instrumentation description for the Database Congestion detection

6.3.7. Database Congestion Heuristic

Besides the OLB anti-pattern, the Database Congestion anti-pattern constitutes another sub-category of performance problems under the Traffic Jam anti-pattern. In this section, we provide detection strategies for the identification of database-intensive performance problems.

6.3.7.1. Detection Strategies

Database-intensive performance problems result either in a high resource utilization of the database server (i.e. CPU utilization) or in excessive locking of the database requests. Hence, for the detection of the Database Congestion problem, the IaM Description must contain both sampling of the CPU utilization as well as sampling of database statistics (cf. Figure 6.12). Hereby the scope is limited to all system nodes that correspond to the *DB server* role. Similar to the response time considerations in the Traffic Jam Heuristic, for the Database Congestion Heuristic we are interested in the progress of CPU utilization and the database's locking behaviour in dependency of the load. Therefore, this heuristic utilizes the same experimentation plan as the Traffic Jam Heuristic, executing a Scaling Experiment Series with five experiment steps (cf. Figure 6.12). The execution of the experiments described by the experiment specification in Figure 6.12 yields two dataset types: a

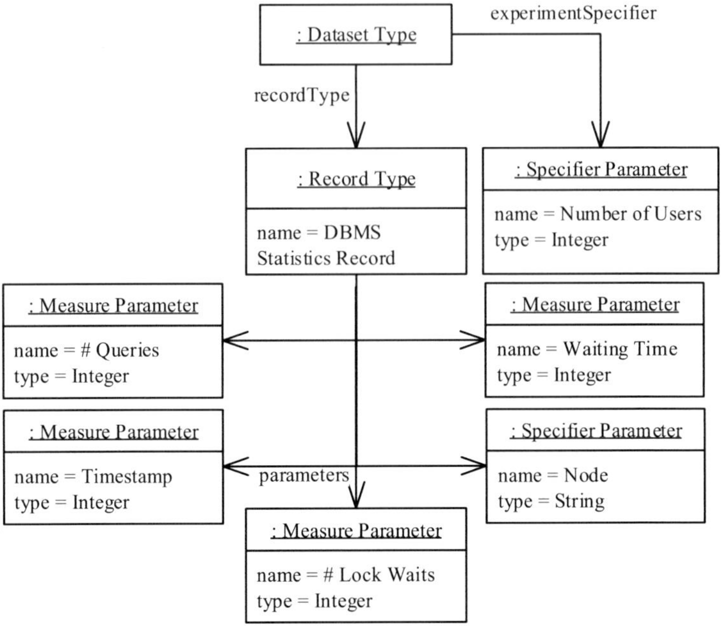

Figure 6.13.: Data representation format for the Database Congestion detection

CPU utilization dataset $\mathcal{D}_{CPU}$ as already shown in Figure 6.11 for the OLB Heuristic, and a database statistics dataset $\mathcal{D}_{DB}$ (cf. Figure 6.13). The latter dataset contains two Specification Parameters capturing the Number of Users during the corresponding experiments and the system Node where the measurements have been taken from. Furthermore, four Measure Parameters capture the measurement's Timestamps, the number of Queries, the number of Lock Waits, as well as the corresponding Waiting Times. Based on this data types, we provide two alternative detection strategies.

Fix Threshold Strategy The Fix Threshold strategy (cf. Algorithm 16, Appendix A.1.7) evaluates two aspects: the utilization of the database server as well as the progression of locking behaviour. For the utilization analysis this strategy uses a defined threshold t_{CPU} that specifies when a database server has to be considered as overloaded. For each load situation v and each database node ζ this strategy evaluates whether the utilization U exceeds the specified threshold t_{CPU}. If U exceeds t_{CPU} for any tuple (υ, ζ), then this strategy reports the presence of a Database Congestion anti-pattern. Otherwise, the Fix Threshold strategy evaluates the growth of locking times over load intensity. To this end, the algorithm calculates for each tuple (υ, ζ) the lock waiting times Q' per database request. By conducting pairwise t-tests (Downing et al., 2003) on the neighbouring sets of waiting times Q' and Q'_p (Q'_p are the waiting times with the next smaller load intensity than in Q') this detection strategy examines whether the locking times increase with the load. If the t-tests yield statistically significant differences for all Q' whose corresponding load intensities υ lead to violating performance requirements in the Traffic Jam heuristic, then this detection strategy considers the SUT to contain a Database Congestion anti-pattern. If neither the CPU threshold t_{CPU} is exceeded nor the locking times grow significantly with the load, then the Fix Threshold strategy assumes that the Database Congestion anti-pattern is not present in the SUT.

Queueing Theory Strategy The Queueing Theory strategy (cf. Algorithm 17, Appendix A.1.7) is equal to the Fix Threshold strategy except for the fact that no fix threshold t_{CPU} is used for the analysis of the database utilization. In order to avoid the need to specify an absolute, potentially context-specific threshold, this strategy dynamically calculates a threshold t^{qt}_{CPU} based on the number of CPU cores n_C and a relative response time increase factor f_R that is context independent. Thereby, this detection strategy inverts the *Erlang's C formula* (Menascé et al., 2004) in order to find the CPU utilization t^{qt}_{CPU} (for a CPU with n_C cores) under which the response times increase by a factor of f_R compared to a low-utilization scenario. The Queueing Theory strategy then applies the same algorithm as the Fix Threshold strategy, however, uses the dynamically calculated threshold t^{qt}_{CPU} instead of the fix threshold t_{CPU}.

6.3.7.2. Evaluation

The evaluation results of the Database Congestion detection strategies (cf. Table 6.7) show that both detection strategies (Fix Threshold and Queueing

	expectation vector	detection vectors: Fix Threshold 60	70	80	90	95	Queueing Theory
Test Cases TC 10	✓	✓	✓	✓	✓	✓	✓
TC 11	⚐	⚐	⚐	⚐	⚐	⚐	⚐
TC 12	⚐	⚐	⚐	⚐	⚐	⚐	⚐
TC 13	⚐	⚐	⚐	⚐	⚐	⚐	⚐
TC 14	⚐	⚐	⚐	⚐	⚐	⚐	⚐
TC 15	⚐	⚐	⚐	⚐	⚐	⚐	⚐
TC 16	✓	✓	✓	✓	✓	✓	✓
TC 17	✓	✓	✓	✓	✓	✓	✓
TC 18	✓	✓	✓	✓	✓	✓	✓
TC 19	✓	✓	✓	✓	✓	✓	✓
TC 20	✓	✓	✓	✓	✓	✓	✓
TC 21	✓	✓	✓	✓	✓	✓	✓
TC 22	✓	✓	✓	✓	✓	✓	✓
TC 23	✓	✓	✓	✓	✓	✓	✓
	false positives rate r^{fp}:	0.0	0.0	0.0	0.0	0.0	0.0
	true positives rate r^{tp}:	1.0	1.0	1.0	1.0	1.0	1.0
	accuracy $a(r^{fp}, r^{tp})$:	**1.0**	**1.0**	**1.0**	**1.0**	**1.0**	**1.0**

Table 6.7.: Evaluation results on the DB congestion detection strategies

Theory), provide optimal detection results with an accuracy of 1.0. With reasonable CPU thresholds between 60% and 95% utilization, the Fix Threshold strategy is equally good independent of the threshold. In the negative test cases (TC 10, TC 16-TC 23) both the database's CPU utilization as well as the database locking times are very low, leading to a correct classification by the detection strategies. The positive test cases exhibit either a significantly growing locking times behaviour or a very high CPU utilization (near to 100%). In the former case, both detection strategies use the same substrategy to identify growing locking times. Hence both strategies provide correct results in those cases. In the case of very high CPU utilization at the database server, both detection strategies managed to identify that situation. None of the negative test cases exhibit a moderate CPU utilization at the database server. Therefore, we cannot make any statements on how the detection strategies would perform in such cases. For further detection of the Database Congestion anti-pattern we select the Queueing Theory strategy as it is independent of any configuration parameters.

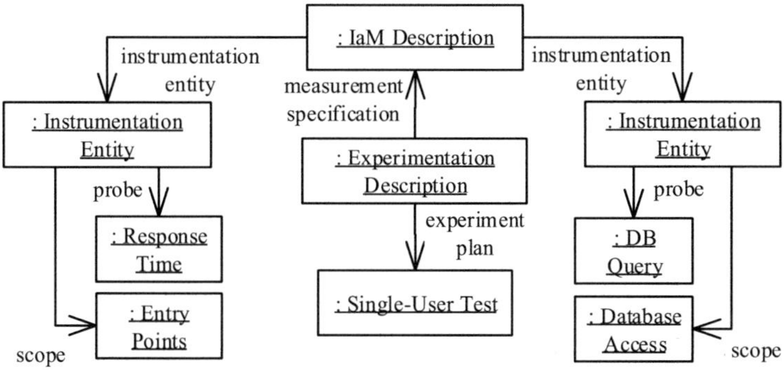

Figure 6.14.: Experiment and instrumentation description for the Stifle detection

6.3.8. The Stifle Heuristic

The Stifle anti-pattern (cf. Table 2.1(k), Chapter 2.4) is a root cause of the Database Congestion problem manifested in a high amount of small, similar database queries. Hence, in order to detect a Stifle anti-pattern the corresponding heuristic must capture the database access behaviour of the application logic components. In this section, we provide a detection strategy for the Stifle anti-pattern and evaluate its detection accuracy based on the corresponding test cases.

6.3.8.1. Detection Strategy

In order to uncover a Stifle anti-pattern, the detection strategy has to analyze the database access of the application for individual system services. Therefore, the Stifle heuristic applies a Single-User test while capturing the Response Times of the application's Entry Points as well as the Database Queries at the database access level (cf. Figure 6.14). In this way, measurement data can be captured that allows to reconstruct the relationship between individual system services and according database requests without distorting effects of concurrent user requests.

The experiment defined in Figure 6.14 yields measurement data that is structured along two dataset types: a Response Time dataset $\mathcal{D}_R$ as already used

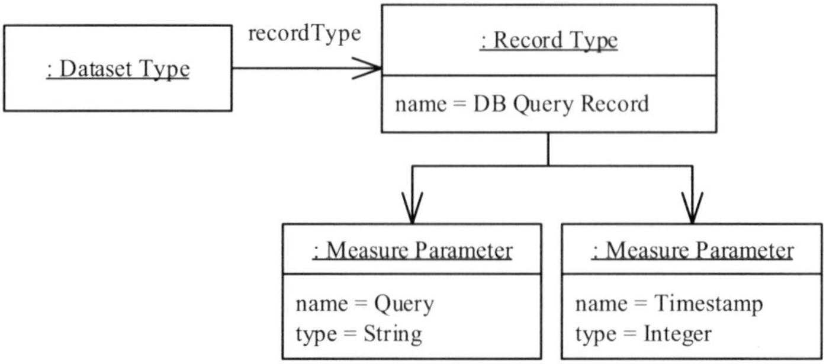

Figure 6.15.: Data representation format for the Stifle detection

for previous heuristics (cf. Figure 6.6), and a Database Query dataset $\mathcal{D}_{SQL}$ capturing the queries of individual database requests (cf. Figure 6.15).

As first analysis step, the detection strategy correlates both datasets $\mathcal{D}_R$ and $\mathcal{D}_{SQL}$ yielding a grouping $\mathcal{D}_C$ of system service calls and corresponding database requests. For each system service ω, the Stifle detection strategy retrieves the set Q of emitted database queries. Applying a clustering on Q provides a set of clusters $\zeta \in Q'$, whereby each cluster represents a set of structurally equal database queries. Clusters ζ with a size that is greater than one indicate queries that have been issued multiple times per user request, hence, constituting a Stifle anti-pattern. Clusters with an extremely large size (e.g. hundreds or thousands of database requests per user) very likely cause a high Database Congestion problem by introducing I/O overhead at the database server as well as significant communication overhead. The Stifle heuristic reports all queries (with the corresponding system services) as potential Stifle anti-patterns whose corresponding clusters have a size greater than one, while sorting the Stifle candidates by their number of repetitions (i.e. cluster sizes) in descending order.

6.3.8.2. Evaluation

Five test cases have passed the Database Congestion heuristic as positive test cases (TC 11 - TC 15). Hence, the Stifle heuristic is evaluated by means of that five test cases comprising two positive scenarios and three

		expectation vector	detection vectors
Test Cases	TC 11	✓	✓
	TC 12	⚐	⚐
	TC 13	⚐	⚐
	TC 14	✓	✓
	TC 15	✓	✓
	false positives rate r^{fp}:		0.0
	true positives rate r^{tp}:		1.0
	accuracy $a(r^{fp}, r^{tp})$:		**1.0**

Table 6.8.: Evaluation results on the Stifle detection strategy

negative scenarios. Applying the Stifle heuristic on these test cases yields an accuracy of 1.0 as shown in Table 6.8. Both positive test cases (TC 12 and TC 14) containing repetitions of equal or similar database requests per user request have been correctly identified as a Stifle anti-pattern. In this cases the heuristic where able to extract the corresponding system service as well as the guilty SQL statement. Test cases TC 14 and TC 15 contain only one database request per user request, hence, as correctly classified by the Stifle heuristic, this test cases do not contain a Stifle. Finally, in test case TC 11, many database requests are issued per user request, however, they are all different with respect to the query structure. Hence, this heuristic correctly classified this test case as a negative test case for the Stifle anti-pattern.

6.3.9. Expensive Database Call Heuristic

The Expensive Database Call (EDC) anti-pattern leads to a similar symptom as the Stifle anti-pattern, resulting in a high overhead at the database, either due to high locking times or high utilization of processing resources. However, while the Stifle anti-pattern is manifested in many small database requests, the EDC anti-pattern constitutes the opposite behaviour of a single, long-running database request. In the following, we provide and evaluate a detection strategy for the EDC anti-pattern.

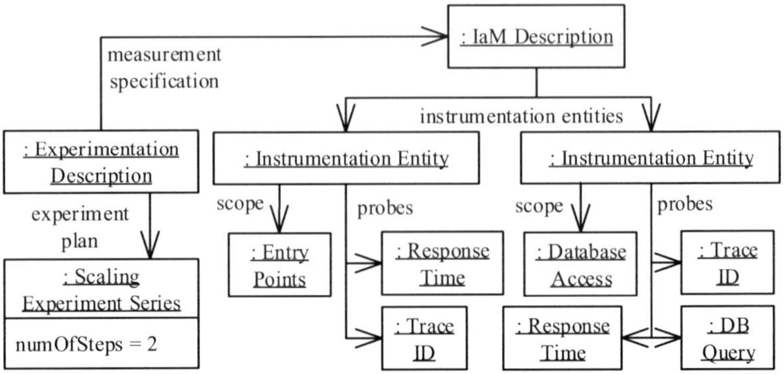

Figure 6.16.: Experiment and instrumentation description for the Expensive Database Call detection

6.3.9.1. Detection Strategy

Typically, EDC instances only reveal under high load, while they remain unnoticed under low load. Furthermore, the higher the load intensity, the more the EDC execution time dominates the overall response time of the system service. In order to analyze this behaviour at the SUT, the EDC detection heuristic executes two experiments, one with a low and one with a high load intensity. Therefore, we define for the experiment plan a Scaling Experiment Series with two experiment steps comprising a Single-User Test and a Load Test (cf. Figure 6.16). In order to enable analysis of the response time proportions between database query times and system service times, the detection strategy instruments the Entry Points and the Database Access scopes with a Response Time probe and a Tracing probe. Additionally, the Database Access scope is instrumented with the Database Query probe to retrieve the SQL statements of expensive database calls (cf. Figure 6.16). The instrumentation specification yields measurement data structured along three dataset types: a Response Time dataset as already used by the Performance Problem Heuristic (cf. Section 6.3.1), a Database Query dataset as used by the Stifle heuristic (cf. Section 6.3.8), and a Tracing dataset shown in Figure 6.17. The Tracing dataset captures the Trace ID, the Enter - and Exit Timestamps, and the operation name (i.e. Location) for the corresponding operation calls. Besides the datasets, the EDC detection

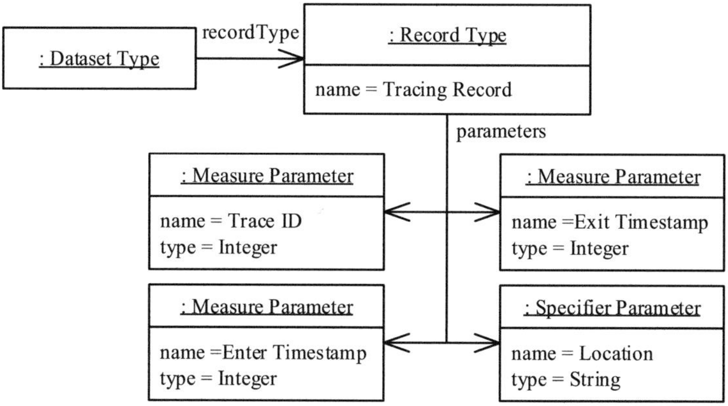

Figure 6.17.: Data representation format for the Expensive Database Call detection

strategy (Algorithm 19, Appendix A.1.9) takes a set $\mathcal{V} = \{(\varsigma_i, \varrho_i, \varphi_i)\}_i$ as input. The elements of $\mathcal{V}$ represent system services ς_i that violate the performance requirements (detected by the Performance Problem heuristic, cf. Section 6.3.1) as well as the corresponding, average single-user response times ϱ_i and high-load response times φ_i. The trace information is used to correlate system service calls with the corresponding database requests (i.e. DB Queries). For each query η that has been executed as part of a system service ς this detection strategy calculates the mean execution time ν_s under single-user load and the execution time ν_h under the maximum specified load intensity. A database request ς is considered as an EDC instance, if the proportion of the execution time ν_h (query time under high load) and the response time φ (response time of corresponding system service under high load) exceeds a specified threshold τ ($\nu_h > \tau\varphi$), the proportion grows with the load:

$$\frac{\nu_h}{\varphi} > \tau \wedge \frac{\nu_h}{\varphi} > \frac{\nu_s}{\varrho} \tag{6.26}$$

Equation 6.26 means that the execution time of the corresponding database request increasingly dominates the overall response time the higher the load is, which is an indicator for an EDC instance.

		expectation vector	detection vectors
Test Cases	TC 11	✓	✓
	TC 12	✓	✓
	TC 13	✓	✓
	TC 14	⚐	⚐
	TC 15	⚐	⚐
	false positives rate r^{fp}:		0.0
	true positives rate r^{tp}:		1.0
	accuracy $a(r^{fp}, r^{tp})$:		**1.0**

Table 6.9.: Evaluation results on the Expensive Database Call detection strategy

6.3.9.2. Evaluation

The EDC heuristic is evaluated on the same test cases as the Stifle heuristic (cf. Table 6.9). From the five test cases, the EDC heuristic correctly identified the two positive test cases (TC 14 and TC 15) that contain long running database calls, either due to long locking times or high database utilization. The heuristic also correctly classifies the test cases TC 11 - TC 13 as negative test cases for the EDC anti-pattern, although they also lead to a Database Congestion problem. In these cases, the heuristic successfully distinguished several short requests from some few long running requests. Furthermore, similar to the Stifle heuristic, the EDC heuristic correctly pinpointed to the queries that took a long time to be processed by the database.

6.3.10. Excessive Messaging Heuristic

The Excessive Messaging anti-pattern is manifested in a high communication overhead on the network induced by inter-component communication of distributed software components. In this section, we introduce and test different detection strategies for the Excessive Messaging anti-pattern.

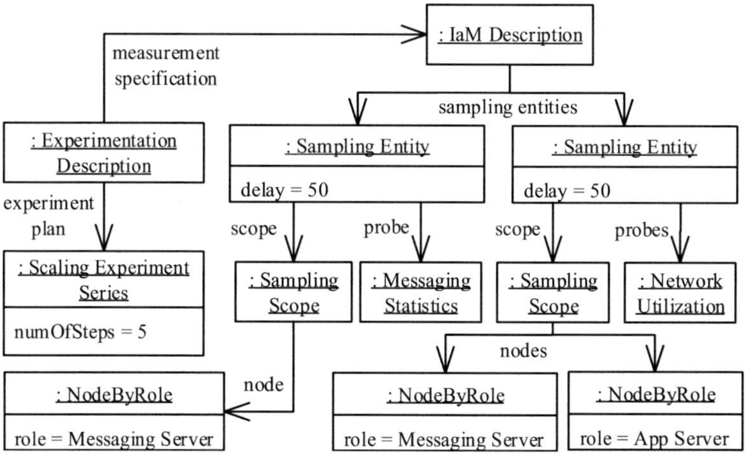

Figure 6.18.: Experiment and instrumentation description for the Excessive Messaging detection

6.3.10.1. Detection Strategies

The detection of the Excessive Messaging anti-pattern requires analysis of the message transmission behaviour as well as the network utilization. The detection strategies introduced in the following are based on the same experimentation and instrumentation specification, while applying different analysis algorithms on the corresponding measurement data. The experimentation description is depicted in Figure 6.18. As Excessive Messaging is a cause of the Traffic Jam anti-pattern (cf. Taxonomy in Figure 4.2), its negative effect on performance increases with the load intensity. Hence, the detection heuristic has to analyze the messaging behaviour and the network utilization in dependency of the load intensity. Therefore, analogously to the Traffic Jam heuristic, a Scaling Experiment Series with five experiment steps is used. Thereby, the heuristic samples Network Utilization of all application nodes and the messaging server, as well as the Messaging Statistics from the Messaging Server (cf. Figure 6.18). Corresponding to the two Sampling entities in Figure 6.18, the Excessive Messaging experiments yield two datasets for the resulting measurement data. The Network I/O dataset (cf. Figure 6.19) captures statistics like network bandwidth (*Speed*), number

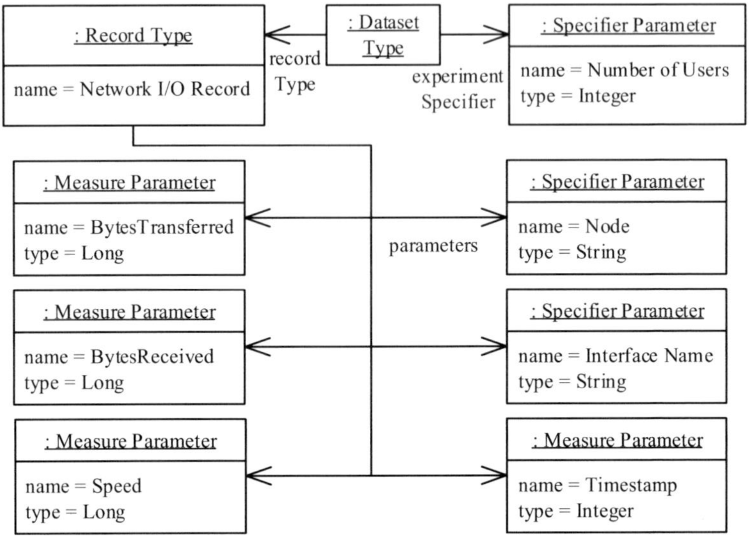

Figure 6.19.: Network I/O dataset format

of *transferred and received bytes* from corresponding network interfaces identified by the Specifier Parameters *Node* and *Interface Name*. As already explained for previous dataset types, the Number of Users parameter captures the load intensity during the corresponding experiment. The Messaging Statistics dataset (cf. Figure 6.20) captures sampled values for the average message size and the sizes of message queues that are specified by a queue name. These two datasets provide the measurement data that is required to analyze an existence of an Excessive Messaging anti-pattern in a SUT. In the following, we explain three different analysis strategies that process this data.

Network Utilization Threshold Strategy Besides an analysis of the queue sizes, the Network Utilization Threshold strategy (cf. Algorithm 20, Appendix A.1.7) analyzes the network utilization measured on the network interfaces of the individual system nodes. Therefore, this strategy calculates a utilization threshold τ that depends on the average message size μ. If the message size is larger than a TCP packet, then the detection strategy uses

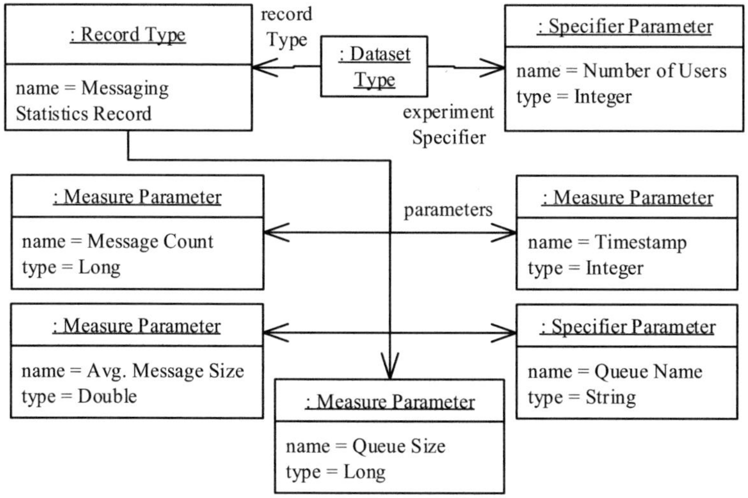

Figure 6.20.: Messaging statistics dataset format

90% of the network interface's bandwidth as the threshold τ. In the case of small messages (μ smaller than a TCP packet), we use the following formula (Huang, 2003) that, based on Nagle's congestion control algorithm (Minshall et al., 2000), describes the maximum network throughput in dependence of the message size:

$$\tau = 0.9\rho \left(\left\lfloor \frac{\pi}{\mu} \right\rfloor + 1 \right) \frac{\mu}{2} \tag{6.27}$$

Hereby, R_p is the TCP packet rate, π the TCP packet size (usually 1460 -1500 bytes), and μ is the average message size. Using the network throughput threshold τ, for each tuple (ν, υ) of a system node ν and a load intensity υ, this detection strategy examines whether the network throughput θ exceeds the threshold τ. In the case that θ exceeds τ, this detection strategy reports an excessive messaging problem. Otherwise, the strategy further analyzes the progression of the queue sizes (cf. Algorithm 21, Appendix A.1.7) in dependency of the load intensity. Therefore, the strategy conducts pairwise t-Tests (Downing et al., 2003) on sampled queue size sets $\mathcal{S}$ and $\mathcal{S}_p$, whereby $\mathcal{S}_p$ contains the sampled queue sizes for the next smaller load intensity than in $\mathcal{S}$. If the mean value of of $\mathcal{S}$ is larger than the mean value of $\mathcal{S}_p$, and the corresponding t-Test shows a significant difference of the samples $\mathcal{S}$ and $\mathcal{S}_p$, the strategy concludes that the values in $\mathcal{S}$ are significantly larger than in $\mathcal{S}_p$. If this applies for all $\mathcal{S}$ whose corresponding load intensity lead to a violation of performance requirements in the Traffic Jam heuristic, then this detection strategy reports an occurrence of Excessive Messaging.

Network Utilization Stagnation Strategy The Network Utilization Stagnation strategy (cf. Algorithm 22, Appendix A.1.7) does the same analysis of the queue sizes as the Network Utilization Threshold strategy. However, with respect to the evaluation of the network throughput, this detection strategy avoids to use a fix threshold. Instead, this strategy examines whether the network throughput stagnates at a certain level with an increasing load. A stagnation of the network throughput indicates a saturation of the maximal possible throughput, limited either by the physical bandwidth or effects of different algorithms implemented as part of certain transmission protocols (such as Nagel's congestion control, flow control, etc. with TCP). For each network interface of the system nodes, this strategy compares the network throughput θ under load intensity υ with the network throughput θ_p under the next smaller load υ_p. If $\theta < \theta_p + \epsilon$ for a specified tolerance value ϵ, then the throughput θ is considered as not significantly higher than θ_p. If this applies for all experiment steps (i.e. load intensities) which resulted in performance requirements violation in the Traffic Jam heuristic (cf. Section 6.3.5), then this detection strategy identifies the network throughput behaviour as an Excessive Messaging problem.

Message Throughput Strategy The Message Throughput strategy (cf. Algorithm 23, Appendix A.1.7) renounces the analysis of the network throughput and utilization. Instead, this detection strategy analyzes the throughput of messages that pass the messaging server in dependency of the load intensity. Therefore, the Message Throughput strategy applies a similar analysis algorithm on the message throughput measures as the Network Utilization Stagnation strategy does on the network throughput values. In particular, for each load intensity υ, the strategy compares the message throughput μ with the throughput μ_p under the next smaller load intensity.

Test Cases	expectation vector	detection vectors		
		Threshold	Stagnation	Message Throughput
TC 10	✓	✓	✓	✓
TC 11	✓	✓	✓	✓
TC 12	✓	✓	✓	✓
TC 13	✓	✓	✓	✓
TC 14	✓	✓	✓	✓
TC 15	✓	✓	✓	✓
TC 16	⚐	✓	⚐	⚐
TC 17	⚐	✓	⚐	⚐
TC 18	⚐	✓	⚐	⚐
TC 19	⚐	✓	✓	⚐
TC 20	⚐	✓	✓	⚐
TC 21	✓	✓	✓	✓
TC 22	✓	✓	✓	✓
TC 23	✓	✓	✓	✓
false positives rate r^{fp}:		0.0	0.0	0.0
true positives rate r^{tp}:		0.0	0.6	1.0
accuracy $a(r^{fp}, r^{tp})$:		0.5	0.8	**1.0**

Table 6.10.: Evaluation results on the Excessive Messaging detection strategy

Again, if $\mu < \mu_p + \epsilon$ for all critical load intensities (i.e. load intensities that lead to performance requirements violation in the Traffic Jam evaluation), then this detection strategy reports an occurrence of the Excessive Messaging anti-pattern.

6.3.10.2. Evaluation

In this section, we evaluate the detection strategies for the Excessive Messaging anti-pattern by means of 14 test cases (TC 10 - TC 23). Table 6.10 shows the detection results for the Excessive Messaging detection strategies. The Network Utilization Threshold strategy classifies all test cases as negative test cases, yielding an accuracy of 0.5. The problem with this strategy is that the calculated thresholds miss to incorporate some important details of network technologies that further limit the maximal network throughput. Therefore, in all positive test cases the calculated utilization threshold τ was to large. The Network Utilization Stagnation strategy has a higher accuracy

(a = 0.8), however, in the test cases TC 19 and TC 20 the Stagnation strategy fails to detect Excessive Messaging. The Message Throughput strategy provides the most accurate results (a = 1.0). The benefit of that strategy is the independence of complex networking considerations. Focusing on the actual goal to detect excessive messaging, this strategy classifies all corresponding test cases correctly.

6.3.11. The Blob Heuristic

An existing Blob anti-pattern (cf. Table 2.1(h), Chapter 2.4) generates a high communication overhead through remote communication between a central Blob component and other components, hence, constituting a cause for the Excessive Messaging anti-pattern. A detection heuristic for the Blob anti-pattern must be able to identify such Blob components by analyzing the messaging behaviour of individual software components. In the following, we introduce two alternative detection strategies for the Blob and evaluate them by means of the corresponding test cases.

6.3.11.1. Detection Strategies

As the Blob anti-pattern is a descendant node of the Traffic Jam anti-pattern (cf. Figure 4.2, Section 4.3), the effect of the communication overhead induced by the Blob component increases with the load intensity. Therefore, the Blob heuristic analyzes the messaging behaviour of software components under a high load, applying a load test as experiment plan (cf. Figure 6.21). Instrumenting the Messaging scope on all application servers, the detection heuristic captures information about transmitted messages. Figure 6.22 shows the data format for the measurement data gathered for the Blob detection. The dataset is based on the Messaging Record that captures for each sent or received message the *Message ID*, the *Timestamp* of reception or dispatch, the *ID of the involved software component*, as well as a boolean flag indicating whether the record represents a message dispatch or a message reception. Based on that measurement data format, we provide two different detection strategies for the Blob anti-pattern.

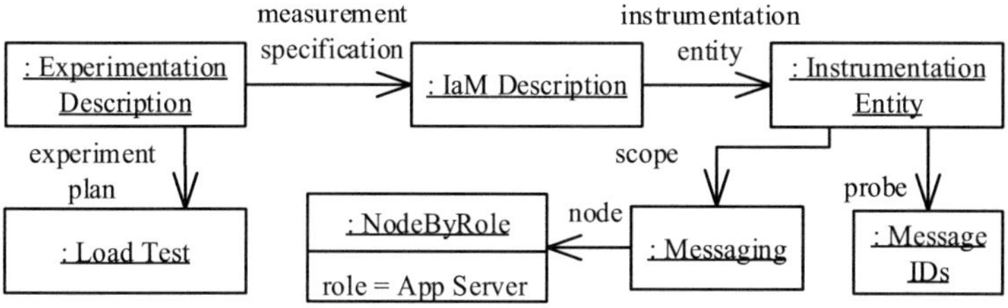

Figure 6.21.: Experiment and instrumentation description for the Blob detection

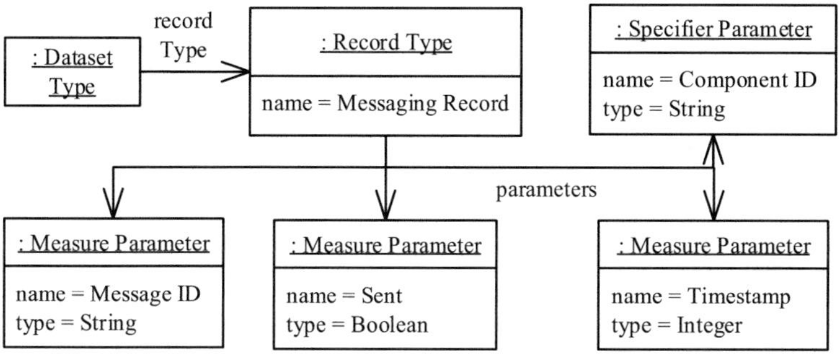

Figure 6.22.: Data representation format for the Blob detection

Mean Analysis Strategy This detection strategy calculates for each component its contributing part π to the overall messaging time and compares π to the mean contribution over all components. Therefore, the detection strategy correlates all message dispatches and receptions using the Message ID. Let C be the set of components involved in messaging. For each message transmission $a \rightarrow b$ from component $a \in C$ to component $b \in C$ the transmission time is calculated using the timestamps. This data processing step yields for each component $\zeta \in C$ a cumulative message transmission time $\nu \in \mathcal{M}$ including the transmission times of messages that have been dispatched as well as received by component ζ. Let μ and σ be the mean of the set $\mathcal{M}$ and the standard deviation, respectively. Applying the Three Sigma Rule (Pukelsheim, 1994), the Mean Analysis strategy examines for each component $\zeta \in C$ whether the corresponding messaging contribution π exceeds the threshold $\tau = \mu + 3\sigma$. A messaging contribution that exceeds τ indicates that the corresponding component exhibits excessive messaging compared to other components. In this case, this detection strategy reports the corresponding component as a Blob component.

Component Exclusion Strategy The Component Exclusion strategy is based on a similar idea as the Mean Analysis strategy, however, applies another way of calculating the messaging contribution. In particular, this strategy calculates the set C of components involved in messaging, and the set of messaging times $\mathcal{M}$ in the same way as the Mean Analysis strategy. Each message transmission involves two components (i.e. the sender and the receiver). Hence, each message dispatch or reception of a Blob component ζ_b contributes to the messaging time of another component ζ such that the messaging contribution measure for ζ is distorted. In order to avoid this effect, the Component Exclusion strategy calculates the messaging contribution for a component ζ by comparing the overall messaging time $\omega = \sum_{\nu \in \mathcal{M}} (\nu)$ to the overall messaging time ω_ζ excluding component ζ. Let $\mathcal{M}_\zeta \subset \mathcal{M}$ be the set of all messaging times excluding the message transmission times where component ζ were involved. Then, ω_ζ is defined as the sum over $\mathcal{M}_\zeta$:

$$\mathcal{M}_\zeta = \bigcup_{c \in C \setminus \{\zeta\}} (\mathcal{M}(c)) \tag{6.28}$$

$$\omega_\zeta = \sum_{\nu \in \mathcal{M}_\zeta} (\nu) \tag{6.29}$$

From the cumulative messaging times ω and ω_ζ, for the Component Exclusion strategy we define the messaging contribution π_ζ of component ζ as follows:

$$\pi_\zeta = 1 - \frac{\omega_\zeta}{\omega} \tag{6.30}$$

Furthermore, the Component Exclusion strategy calculates for each component ζ an individual Three Sigma threshold τ_ζ utilizing the messaging time set $\mathcal{M}_\zeta$. Assuming that μ_ζ and σ_ζ are the mean and the standard deviation of $\mathcal{M}_\zeta$, respectively, then the individual threshold is:

$$\tau_\zeta = \mu_\zeta + 3\sigma_\zeta \tag{6.31}$$

The Component Exclusion strategy identifies a component ζ as a Blob, if its contribution π_ζ exceeds the threshold τ_ζ ($\pi_\zeta > \tau_\zeta$).

		expectation vector	detection vectors: Mean Analysis	detection vectors: Component Exclusion Analysis
Test Cases	TC 16	✓	⚐	✓
	TC 17	⚐	✓	⚐
	TC 18	⚐	✓	⚐
	TC 19	✓	⚐	✓
	TC 20	✓	⚐	✓
	false positives rate r^{fp}:		1.0	0.0
	true positives rate r^{tp}:		0.0	1.0
	accuracy $a(r^{fp}, r^{tp})$:		0.0	**1.0**

Table 6.11.: Evaluation results on the Blob detection strategies

6.3.11.2. Evaluation

Both Blob detection heuristics are free of configuration parameters. We evaluate the detection strategies on five messaging-related test cases (TC 16 - TC 20) that have been successfully detected by the Excessive Messaging heuristic. Table 6.11 shows the evaluation results. Remarkable is the fact that the detection strategies yield completely contrary detection results. While the Component Exclusion Analysis strategy achieves the optimal accuracy of $a = 1.0$, the Mean Analysis strategy is incorrect in all test cases, exhibiting an accuracy of $a = 0.0$. In the test cases TC 16, TC 19 and TC 20 only two software components are involved in messaging. For the Mean Analysis strategy this means that the messaging contribution of each component equals to the overall messaging time. Hence, the standard deviation σ of messaging contributions is zero and each individual messaging contribution $\nu \in \mathcal{M}$ equals to the mean contribution μ. Consequently, both components that are involved in messaging are identified as Blob components. Moreover, the Mean Analysis strategy uses the messaging contributions of all components involved in messaging to calculate a common threshold τ. In the test cases TC 17 and TC 18, however, the messaging contribution of the Blob component biases the mean value μ and the standard deviation σ. Thus, the resulting 3-Sigma threshold τ is to large to detect the messaging contribution of the Blob component as critical. The Component Exclusion Analysis strategy overcomes both problems by calculating an individual threshold τ_ζ for each component $\zeta \in C$ by excluding its messaging contribution from the common set of messaging contributions. Due to the high accuracy, in the remainder of this work we use the Component Exclusion Analysis strategy to detect the Blob anti-pattern.

6.3.12. Empty Semi Trucks Heuristic

The Empty Semi Trucks (EST) anti-pattern (cf. Table 2.1(i), Chapter 2.4) is characterized by a high amount of small messages transmitted between two components as part of a single user request. However, if a component exhibits a high message transmission rate due to a high load, whereas the frequency of message transmissions per user request is low, we do not consider it as an EST anti-pattern. Thus, in order to detect an EST anti-pattern we need to analyze the messaging behaviour of single user requests. In the following, we describe a detection strategy for the EST anti-pattern and evaluate it using the corresponding test cases.

6.3.12.1. Detection Strategy

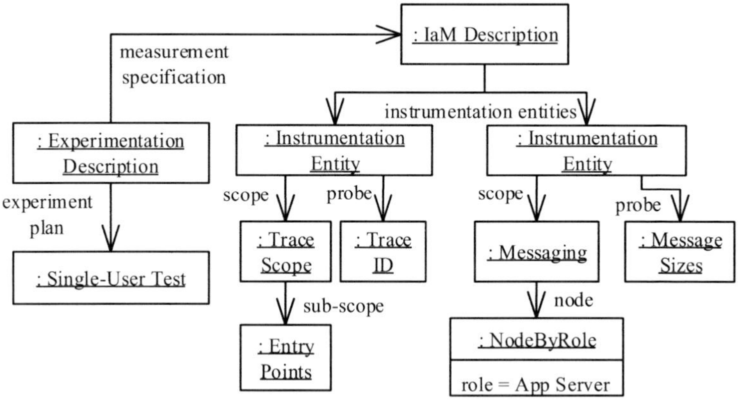

Figure 6.23.: Experiment and instrumentation description for the Empty Semi Trucks detection

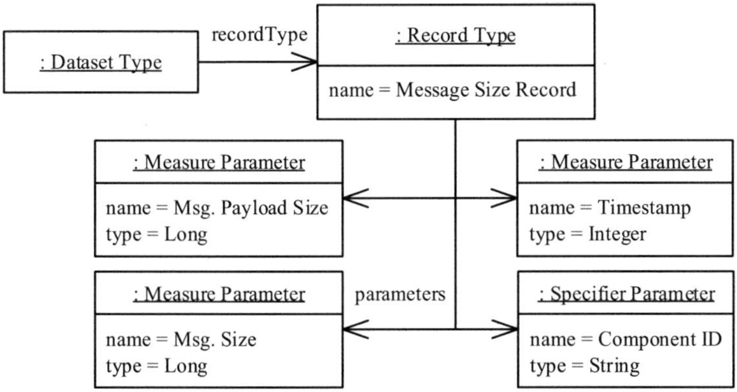

Figure 6.24.: Data representation format for the Empty Semi Trucks detection

Conducting a Single-User Test, the EST detection strategy measures the Message Sizes at all application servers involved in Messaging, as well as the Trace IDs along a dynamic Trace originating from the Entry Points scope (cf. Figure 6.23).

In this way, measurement data can be gathered that allows to reconstruct the call trees from system services to the message dispatch operations. Although the Trace Scope yields a very fine grained and broad instrumentation of the target application, the resulting high measurement overhead is not critical for this detection strategy, because the EST heuristic does not depend on performance measures (e.g. response times) to detect an EST anti-pattern. The specified instrumentation yields two types of datasets: a Tracing dataset (as already used by the Expensive Database call heuristic in Figure 6.17) and a Message Size dataset (cf. Figure 6.24).

For each method called along the dynamic trace, the Tracing dataset captures the *Trace ID*, the method name (cf. *Location*), as well as the *Enter* and *Exit Timestamps*. The Message Size dataset captures for each sent message the overall *Message Size*, the *Size of the Payload*, the software *Component ID*, and again a *Timestamp*.

The EST detection strategy uses the Trace IDs and the Enter and Exit Timestamps to reconstruct a trace instance $\tau \in \mathcal{T}$ for each single user request.

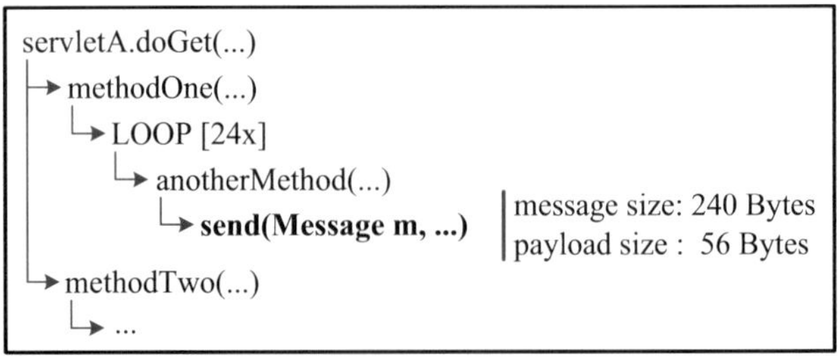

Figure 6.25.: Exemplary Trace (Wert et al., 2014)

Information on the message size and the corresponding payload size are attached to each message-dispatching method in the trace τ. Repeating parts of the trace are aggregated and represented as *loops* while counting the number ν of executions of the corresponding loop body. Finally, trace instances with the same structure are clustered and aggregated with respect to the message size information. This step yields a set of clusters C with representative traces $\zeta \in C$. An example of such a trace is depicted in Figure 6.25. Hereby, the `send` operation occurs in a branch of the call tree within a `LOOP` which has been iterated 24 times. Messages that are repeatedly sent in a loop are candidates for aggregation. The saving potential π in network overhead can be calculated using the number ν of loop iterations, the average overall message size σ and the payload size β:

$$\pi \leftarrow (\nu - 1)(\sigma - \beta) \tag{6.32}$$

The higher the saving potential π the more critical is the corresponding EST instance. This detection heuristic reports all traces containing a message dispatch method in a loop as an EST occurrence, ordering the instances descending by their saving potential.

6.3.12.2. Evaluation

The EST detection heuristic is evaluated on the same test cases as the Blob heuristic (TC 16 - TC 20). Table 6.12 shows that the detection heuristic classified all test cases correctly, yielding a detection accuracy of $a = 1.0$.

		expectation vector	detection vector
Test Cases	TC 16	✓	✓
	TC 17	✓	✓
	TC 18	✓	✓
	TC 19	⚐	⚐
	TC 20	⚐	⚐
	false positives rate r^{fp}:		0.0
	true positives rate r^{tp}:		1.0
	accuracy $a(r^{fp}, r^{tp})$:		**1.0**

Table 6.12.: Evaluation results on the Empty Semi Trucks detection strategy

For the positive test cases the EST heuristic correctly pinpointed to the loops in the stack traces that are responsible for the EST behaviour.

6.4. Summary

In this chapter, we described the notion of a detection heuristic for APPD. We elaborated a process for the development of accurate detection heuristics that are generically applicable on different scenarios. Thereto, we proposed to create a set of micro-benchmarks (i.e. test cases) that are used to compare alternative detection strategies. Based on a set of test cases, we derived a measure for the accuracy of alternative detection strategies. For a selected set of performance problems, we created several detection strategies and evaluated their accuracy on a set of test cases. The evaluation of detection strategies confirmed our presumption that strategies that are based on fix, absolute thresholds cannot be generically applied on different scenarios as they lack the ability of abstraction.

7. Validation

In this chapter, we evaluate the research goals of this thesis to automate performance problem diagnostics and, thus, enable non-experts to uncover performance problems. Thereby, we evaluate each research hypothesis that has been described in Section 3.4 along five studies and discuss the evaluation results. On the one hand, the studies cover the evaluation of individual parts of our Automatic Performance Problem Diagnostics (APPD) approach, such as the Systematic Selective Experimentation (SSE) concept, the performance problem taxonomy, the Performance Problem Diagnostics Description Model (P^2D^2M), and the detection heuristics. On the other hand, some of the studies constitute an end-to-end validation of the APPD approach. Some of the validations described in this chapter have been published in Wert et al., 2014; Wert et al., 2015a.

The remainder of this chapter is structured as follows. In Section 7.1, we describe the design of the validation of APPD. In particular, we derive validation questions from the research hypotheses described in Section 3.4, give an overview on conducted studies and discuss to which degree the cases studies cover the mentioned validation questions. Subsequently, we describe three end-to-end case studies with APPD (Section 7.2 - Section 7.4), a controlled experiment on the SSE concept (Section 7.5), and an empirical study (Section 7.6). In Section 7.7, we summarize and discuss the results from the individual studies and examine the threats to validity to our conclusions. This chapter is concluded with a summary in Section 7.8.

7.1. Design of Validation

As elaborated in the Chapters 3-6, the APPD approach comprises different integral parts including the SSE concept, the performance problem taxonomy, the P^2D^2M, and the detection heuristics. Hence, with respect to validation, there are different aspects that must be covered by the validation. Besides the dimension of validation aspects, the validation should preferably cover multiple different cases in order to increase the significance of the validation results. Furthermore, according to Böhme et al., 2008 and H. Koziolek, 2008, there are different types of validation in the area of mode-based prediction methods. Adopting the validation types from Böhme et al., 2008 and H. Koziolek, 2008 to the area of measurement-based diagnostics of performance problems allows us to further differentiate the depth of validation for individual aspects of validation. In this section, we explain the different aspects of APPD that need to be validated, introduce the conducted studies, and describe how the studies cover the validation aspects.

7.1.1. Validation Goals and Questions

In Section 3.4, we introduced the research hypotheses that guided the contributions of the thesis at hand. In the following, we take up each individual hypothesis to derive corresponding goals of validation. Thereby, we break down the research hypothesis into more fine-grained validation questions that represent the aspects of validation. According to the seven research hypothesis (cf. Section 3.4), we define the following seven validation goals.

Validation Goal 1 — *Functionality of APPD*

The first validation goal aims at evaluating the functionality of the APPD approach. This validation goal is derived from the following research hypothesis:

> *Hypothesis 1*: There is an adequately big set of performance problem types which are generically detectable by a set of explicit experiments and analysis rules. (Section 3.4)

This hypothesis comprises three aspects that are represented by the following validation questions:

VQ 1.1 – *Problem Types:* Are the types of performance problems identified for the performance problem taxonomy automatically detectable by measurement?

VQ 1.2 – *APPD Generalisability:* Along which dimensions of case variability and to what extent is APPD generically applicable?

VQ 1.3 – *Diagnostics Accuracy:* How accurate are the diagnostics results provided by the APPD approach?

Validation Goal 2 — *Appropriateness of the Performance Problem Taxonomy*

In Chapter 4, we conducted a categorization of Software Performance Antipatterns (SPAs) to identify interrelationships between different problem types that allow to structure SPAs hierarchically along a taxonomy. For the overall APPD approach it is an essential point to evaluate whether the identified interrelationships reflect the performance problem constellations in real scenarios. Thereto, we derived the following validation question from *Hypothesis 2*:

> *Hypothesis 2*: Different types of performance problems, their symptoms and causes share common characteristics allowing to structure them along a taxonomy. (Section 3.4)

VQ 2.1 – *Taxonomy Representativeness:* Are the interrelationships captured in the performance problem taxonomy representative for real performance problems encountered in practice, in the area of enterprise software systems?

Validation Goal 3 — *Efficiency of APPD*

In *Hypothesis 3*, we state that a taxonomy potentially increases the efficiency of performance problem diagnostics:

> *Hypothesis 3*: A taxonomy on performance problems systematizes performance problem diagnostics and increases its efficiency. (Section 3.4)

This statement can be evaluated on two different levels, by theoretical elaboration or measurement of the efficiency. Accordingly, we derive two validation questions for this validation goal:

VQ 3.1 – *Theoretical Complexity:* Does the Systematic Search Algorithm of APPD increase the efficiency of the diagnostics process?

VQ 3.2 – *Actual Time Complexity:* What is the real time complexity of the APPD approach when applying it to enterprise software systems?

Validation Goal 4 — *Appropriateness of P^2D^2M*

Investigating the research challenge behind *Hypothesis 4* (Section 3.4), in Chapter 5 we introduced P^2D^2M, a language for describing context specific measurement environments as well as generic specification of performance test plans for diagnostics of performance problems. A generic description language comprises two aspects that need to be evaluated. On the one hand, the expressiveness of the language has to be investigated. On the other hand, we have to evaluate how generic the language is. Based on these considerations, we derive the following two validation questions from the corresponding hypothesis:

> *Hypothesis 4*: Performance test specifications can be generalized by a language which allows to describe instrumentation instructions and performance test series in a system-independent and monitoring tool-independent way. (Section 3.4)

VQ 4.1 – *P^2D^2M Expressiveness:* Is the expressiveness of the P^2D^2M model sufficient to describe real performance problem diagnostics scenarios?

VQ 4.2 – *P^2D^2M Generalization:* To which extent are heuristics, described with P^2D^2M, generically applicable to various performance problem diagnostics scenarios?

Validation Goal 5 — *Necessity of SSE*

In Section 3.2.1, we claim that, in certain scenarios, the SSE approach constitutes a solution to the trade-off between measurement accuracy and measurement resolution:

> *Hypothesis 5*: The conflicting requirements of high measurement accuracy and detailed measurement data can be achieved by a sophisticated experimentation concept. (Section 3.4)

As SSE is an essential part of the APPD approach, a validation of this hypothesis is important. Hence, we have to investigate whether the SSE concept is beneficial compared to alternative experimentation approaches.

Per se, the SSE concept is independent of the APPD approach. Hence, investigating the scope of applicability of SSE is another interesting aspect. For this validation goal we derived the following two validation questions:

VQ 5.1 – *SSE Benefit:* Does the SSE concept provide any benefit in performance analysis scenarios compared to alternative concepts?

VQ 5.2 – *SSE Scope:* Is the SSE concept applicable beyond performance problem diagnostics?

Validation Goal 6 — *Automation of APPD*

While *Hypothesis 1* – *Hypothesis 5* guided the research in this thesis and the conceptualization of all the integral parts of APPD (i.e. SSE, taxonomy, P^2D^2M, detection heuristics), *Hypothesis 6* aims at the main goal of the work at hand: automation of performance problem diagnostics.

> *Hypothesis 6*: The composition of a taxonomy on performance problems, a language for generic description of instrumentation instructions, monitoring as well as performance test series, and the SSE concept enable full automation of performance problem diagnostics. (Section 3.4)

Evaluating the automation of an approach comprises two aspects that are covered by the following validation questions:

VQ 6.1 – *Automation:* Given all required inputs, is a realization of the APPD approach able to automatically diagnose performance problems?

VQ 6.2 – *Up-front Effort:* What are the up-front efforts in practice to enable an automatic diagnosis?

Validation Goal 7 — *Practicability of APPD*

Although a fully automated diagnostics approach does not require human interaction to provide corresponding diagnostics results, humans are involved in providing required inputs and in interpreting the generated results. As covered by *Hypothesis 7*, this aspect is especially important with respect to the question of applicability in real software development projects.

> *Hypothesis 7*: Applying our APPD approach in the scope of established software development processes entails a manual effort which is negligible compared to traditional, manual performance problem diagnostics. (Section 3.4)

Evaluation of the external applicability of APPD includes three aspects that are represented by the following validation questions:

VQ 7.1 – *External Perception:* How do external (non-expert) users of the APPD approach perceive the complexity and the associated manual effort to use APPD?

VQ 7.2 – *Result Interpretability:* Are external (non-expert) users able to correctly interpret the results of APPD?

VQ 7.3 – *Cost Reduction:* Does the APPD approach reduce the costs for performance problem diagnostics in real, industrial software development projects?

7.1.2. Studies

For the investigation of the validation goals and the corresponding validation questions introduced in the previous section, we conducted multiple studies that, on the one hand, investigate individual parts of APPD, and on the other hand, constitute end-to-end validations of the APPD approach. Overall, we conducted five studies, one of which aims at evaluating the SSE concept in isolation through a controlled experiment, three case studies for the end-to-end validation of the APPD approach, and one empirical study that involves external users. As most of these studies depend on a realization of APPD, in the following we shortly introduce DynamicSpotter, an implementation of APPD.

7.1.2.1. Realization of the Automatic Performance Problem Diagnostics Approach

Except for the SSE evaluation study, the remaining four studies assume a full realization of the APPD approach. Hence, to show the applicability of our APPD approach and to enable the practical evaluation of the validation questions, we developed the performance problem diagnostics framework DynamicSpotter (Wert, 2015) that is a realization of the APPD approach. In particular, DynamicSpotter encapsulates the SSE concept, the Systematic Search Algorithm (cf. Section 4.4.3) and P^2D^2M (cf. Chapter 5). Furthermore, DynamicSpotter allows for providing detection heuristics and measurement tool adapters as extensions. For the studies conducted in this chapter, we fed DynamicSpotter with the Performance Problem Evaluation Plan (PPEP) instance elaborated in Section 4.4.2, realized the detection heuristics selected in Chapter 6 as corresponding DynamicSpotter extensions, and developed adapters for different measurement and load generation tools. Furthermore, we created an Eclipse-based graphical user interface (GUI) for DynamicSpotter in order to increase the usability. A GUI is especially important for an empirical study where external users should be as little as possible distracted by an insufficient user interface. Note, though the development of the DynamicSpotter extensions (e.g. heuristic implementations and measurement tool adapters) entailed a significant manual up-front effort, all extensions are generic, publicly available and, thus, can be reused for further performance problem diagnostics scenarios without the need to invest the manual up-front efforts, again.

7.1.2.2. Overview on Conducted Studies

In the following, we give a short overview on the studies conducted in this chapter:

Study 1 — *TPC-W*

In this case study, we conduct an end-to-end validation of the APPD approach. Thereby, we apply APPD to a Java implementation (TPC-W Java 2015) of the e-commerce benchmark TCP-W (Menascé, 2002) that represents a Web-based bookstore. The used realization of the TPC-W benchmark is a typical three tier application that comprises a Web-based representation layer, an application layer written in Java, and a database layer that is accessed through JDBC. We conduct the case study on TPC-W in two parts. In the first part, we take the TPC-W implementation provided by the University of Wisconsin (TPC-W Java 2015) as is and deploy the application as described in the corresponding documentation. We apply DynamicSpotter to investigate the original TPC-W implementation for existing performance problems. We then solve the performance problems identified by DynamicSpotter to show that the diagnosed performance problems constitute true positives, instead of false positives. In the second part of the case study, we extend the TPC-W implementation and setup in order to investigate the ability of DynamicSpotter to diagnose communication related performance problems (i.e. problems related to messaging and database access). Thereby, we consciously inject performance problems into the previously resolved implementation of TPC-W. Based on the injected performance problems we are able to analyze the accuracy of the diagnostics results of DynamicSpotter with respect to false positives and true positives. The TPC-W case study is described in detail in Section 7.2.

Study 2 — *nopCommerce*

The goal of the nopCommerce case study is to investigate the scope of applicability of DynamicSpotter and, thus, to analyze the ability of the APPD approach to generalize from concrete Systems Under Test (SUTs) including involved technologies (e.g. programming languages and run-time environments). nopCommerce (NopCommerce 2015) is an open-source e-commerce software that is based on the .NET framework. In order to investigate whether our APPD approach is able to analyze SUTs that are not Java-based, we inject performance problems into the nopCommerce application and let DynamicSpotter search for that problems. Thereby, we show, that DynamicSpotter and, thus, APPD is independent of the programming language and run-time environment of the target system, as long as corresponding measurement tool adapters are able to support the introduced abstraction layer covered by P^2D^2M (cf. Section 5.1). The nopCommerce case study is described in more detail in Section 7.3.

Study 3 — *Industrial Large-scale System (ILS)*

While TPC-W and nopCommerce constitute e-commerce systems with a low to moderate complexity (TPC-W has approx. 4 thousand of lines of code (LOC) and nopCommerce approx. 700 thousand, respectively), the goal of this case study is to investigate whether DynamicSpotter (and inherently the APPD approach) is able to handle the complexity of large-scale software systems. Therefore, we apply DynamicSpotter on an Industrial Large-scale System (ILS). ILS is a closed-source enterprise resource management software that has a user base in the range of millions and a code extent of more than 5 millions of LOC. We show that DynamicSpotter is able to identify a performance bottleneck in one service of ILS. Section 7.4 describes this case study in more detail.

Study 4 — *Systematic, Selective Experimentation for Resource Demand Estimation (SSE-4-RDE)*

This controlled experiment aims at evaluating the SSE concept in isolation. In order to show both the benefits of SSE compared to alternative experimentation approaches, and the scope of applicability of SSE, we apply SSE to a scenario beyond performance problem diagnostics. In particular, we use SSE to automate resource demand estimation for the calibration of architectural performance models (cf. Section 2.2.2). Using our framework for dynamically adaptable instrumentation and monitoring (AIM, Wert et al., 2015a), we compare the accuracy of the resource demands derived with the SSE concept against the resource demands derived using alternative approaches. We show that *SSE* yields more accurate resource demands than alternative approaches. This experiment is described in detail in Section 7.5.

Study 5 — *Empirical Study*

While the primary goal of *Study 1* to *Study 3* is to apply the APPD approach on representative software systems to evaluate its functionality and technical applicability, these studies do not cover the validation of the practicability (i.e. applicability by external, non-expert users) of the APPD approach. Therefore, we conduct an empirical study in which external participants have to use DynamicSpotter to analyze a SUT for potential performance problems. The empirical study is of a mixed-type including a case study where the test persons have to use DynamicSpotter directly, and a questionnaire-based interview to capture the perception and opinion of the test persons about the APPD approach. The study shows that users prevailingly perceive the complexity of applying the APPD approach as low and rate the results of APPD as useful. The empirical study is described in more detail in Section 7.6.

7.1.3. Overview on Validation

In the previous two sections, we defined the validation questions for the validation (Section 7.1.1) and gave an overview on the studies that are described in this chapter (Section 7.1.2). In this section, we discuss the correspondence between individual studies and the validation questions, giving an overview on the coverage of the validation questions by the investigations in the studies. Furthermore, for each validation question, we differentiate between different levels of validation by adopting the validation types from Böhme et al., 2008 and H. Koziolek, 2008 to our domain.

7.1.3.1. Types of Validation

Böhme et al. (Böhme et al., 2008) and Koziolek (H. Koziolek, 2008) introduced three types of validation in the area of evaluating a model-based performance prediction approach. The validation types indicate how deep the relevance of the approach under validation is evaluated. In H. Koziolek, 2008, a *Type 1 Validation* aims at evaluating the *Feasibility* of a performance prediction approach. Hereby, the prediction accuracy is investigated while the approach is applied by its authors. *Type 2 Validation* evaluates the *Practicability* of an approach, whereby external users (i.e. not the authors of the approach) apply the corresponding approach to get the performance predictions. Finally, *Type 3 Validation* takes into consideration *Costs* and *Benefits* when applying the corresponding approach in real software development projects. Usually, validations of *Type 3* are very expensive and lengthy and, thus, are conducted only in exceptional cases. The validation types have been already adopted to different areas of research, such as design decision research (Durdik, 2014), improvement of software architecture models (A. Koziolek, 2014), or business process simulations (Heinrich et al., 2014).

In the following, we extend the validation types from Böhme et al., 2008 and H. Koziolek, 2008, and explain their relation to the context of this thesis.

Validation Type 0 — Appropriateness Validation Type 0 aims at evaluating the appropriateness of theoretical concepts and description languages by theoretical considerations (such as qualitative analyses or logical conclusions). In the case of languages, the appropriateness is shown by exemplary, reasonable instantiations using corresponding language constructs. In particular, this type of validation is conducted without practical execution of an approach. Consequently, Type 0 validations are limited to the evaluation of concepts, and are not suitable to evaluate approaches that need to be executed to provide meaningful results. In the context of this thesis, we apply validations of this type to show the appropriateness of our description language P^2D^2M and to discuss the appropriateness of our performance problem taxonomy.

Validation Type 1 — Feasibility Similar to H. Koziolek, 2008, validations of Type 1 provide that authors apply their problem diagnostics approach on certain target systems in order to evaluate the diagnostics accuracy. Hereby, performance problems can be either consciously injected into the target system, or the approach is applied to uncover unknown instances of performance problems. In the former case, the diagnostics results are compared to the expectations derived from the problem injection phase to analyze the accuracy of the diagnostics approach. In the latter case, the accuracy of the diagnostics approach can be analyzed with respect to false positives and true positives rates by resolving detected performance problems and showing the resulting improvement in performance. However, statements regarding false negatives and true negatives rates cannot be made because, in advance to the execution of the diagnostics approach, it is unclear which performance problems exist in the target system.

A Type 1, end-to-end validation of a diagnostics approach implies a Type 1 validation of all integral parts and concepts of the diagnostics approach. With respect to modelling languages, a Type 1 validation investigates whether circumstances of real cases can be sufficiently reflected (i.e. modelled) with the corresponding modelling language. Procedure models (such as SSE) are tested on their applicability to real problems and classifications (e.g. performance problem taxonomy) are evaluated with respect to their representativeness of real occurrences of performance problems.

In the field of performance problem diagnostics, validations of this type have been conducted for various approaches (Parsons, 2007; Trubiani et al., 2011; Grechanik et al., 2012; Nistor et al., 2013).

Validation Type 2 — Practicability Similar to H. Koziolek, 2008, validations of Type 1 provide that authors apply their problem diagnostics approach Analogously to H. Koziolek, 2008, the practicability of a performance problem diagnostics approach can only be evaluated by involving external test persons that preferably are software developers without deep expertise in performance problem diagnostics. The test persons apply the diagnostics approach to analyze a target system for performance problems and interpret corresponding diagnostics results. Evaluating the ability of non-expert users to correctly apply the diagnostics approach and reasonably interpret corresponding diagnostics results allows to draw conclusions about the practicability of the diagnostics approach. In the field of performance valuation, Martens et al., 2008 conducted an empirical study to investigate the effort of creating reusable, component-based performance models.

Validation Type 3 — Cost-Benefit Similar to H. Koziolek, 2008, validations of Type 1 provide that authors apply their problem diagnostics approach Type 3 validation of a performance problem diagnostics approach assumes that the approach is used in real, industrial software development projects. Thereby, benefits of the diagnostics approach, such as savings in costs of repeated tasks, are confronted with additional up-front costs and efforts that are induced by the application of the diagnostics approach. In order to get an adequate estimate of the cost-benefit ratio, an expert knowledge-based diagnostics approach needs to be applied over a long period of time and, preferably, in different software development projects in order to amortize the initial costs of externalizing and formalizing the knowledge on performance problems. Consequently, validations of Type 3 are extremely expensive with respect to effort and time. Martens et al., 2011 conducted an empirical study to evaluate the benefits and costs of component-based performance evaluation compared to monolithic evaluation. To the best of our knowledge, for performance problem diagnostics approaches, validations of Type 3 have not been conducted in research, yet.

7.1.3.2. Coverage of Validation

Having introduced the research goals, an overview on the studies and the validation types, in this section, we discuss the coverage of research goals and validation types by the studies. Table 7.1 gives an overview on validation questions (first column), studies (columns 2-6) and corresponding validation types (last column). For validation questions that partly have been answered by theoretical elaborations in this thesis, the second last column points to the corresponding Chapters.

In Section 4.2, we analyzed different SPAs from literature and conducted a categorization to identify SPAs that are detectable by measurement. Hence, the theoretical elaboration in Section 4.2 constitutes a Type 0 validation for question *VQ 1.1*. Furthermore, the end-to-end case studies (TPC-W, nopCommerce and ILS) cover a Type 1 validation of question *VQ 1.1* by confirming the findings from Section 4.2 through practical application on representative target systems. Validation question *VQ 1.2* aims at evaluating the generalisability of the APPD approach. Hence, we need to investigate whether the realization of APPD (DynamicSpotter) can handle diversity along multiple dimensions like type and size of target systems, programming languages and run-time environments of target systems, as well as different measurement tools and load generators. In the three end-to-end case studies we cover diversity in all mentioned dimensions. Hence, these case studies constitute a Type 1 validation of *VQ 1.2*. By investigating the accuracy of

Goal	Validation Questions	Studies: TPC-W	nop Commerce	ILS	SSE-4-RDE	Empirical Experiment	Theoretical Elaboration	Validation Type
Goal 1	VQ 1.1	✓	✓	✓	—	—	Section 4.2	Type 0,1
	VQ 1.2	✓	✓	✓	—	—	—	Type 1
	VQ 1.3	✓	✓	✓	—	—	—	Type 1
Goal 2	VQ 2.1	✓	✓	✓	—	—	—	Type 1
Goal 3	VQ 3.1	—	—	—	—	—	Section 4.4.3	Type 0
	VQ 3.2	(✓)	(✓)	(✓)	—	—	—	Type 1
Goal 4	VQ 4.1	✓	✓	✓	—	—	Section 6.3	Type 0,1
	VQ 4.2	✓	✓	✓	—	—	—	Type 1
Goal 5	VQ 5.1	—	—	—	✓	—	—	Type 1
	VQ 5.2	✓	✓	✓	✓	—	—	Type 1
Goal 6	VQ 6.1	✓	✓	✓	—	—	—	Type 1
	VQ 6.2	(✓)	(✓)	(✓)	—	✓	—	Type 2
Goal 7	VQ 7.1	—	—	—	—	✓	—	Type 2
	VQ 7.2	—	—	—	—	✓	—	Type 2
	VQ 7.3	—	—	—	—	—	Section 9.2.1	Type 3

VQ 1.1: Problem Types, *VQ 1.2*: Generalisability, *VQ 1.3*: Diagnostics Accuracy, *VQ 2.1*: Taxonomy Representativeness, *VQ 3.1*: Theoretical Complexity, *VQ 3.2*: Actual Time Complexity, *VQ 4.1*: P^2D^2M Expressiveness, *VQ 4.2*: P^2D^2M Generalization, *VQ 5.1*: SSE Benefit, *VQ 5.2*: SSE Scope, *VQ 6.1*: Automation, *VQ 6.2*: Up-front Effort, *VQ 7.1*: External Perception, *VQ 7.2*: Result Interpretability, *VQ 7.3*: Cost Reduction

Table 7.1.: Overview on the coverage of validation

APPD in the end-to-end case studies, we conduct a Type 1 validation of validation question *VQ 1.3*.

A correct diagnosis by APPD on representative target systems implies that the underlying taxonomy on performance problems is appropriate and reasonably represents the relationships between performance problem types in real scenarios. Conversely, if APPD uses a performance problem taxonomy that does not adequately represent performance problems in real scenarios, then APPD cannot provide accurate diagnostics results. Based on this consideration, we can conclude that the end-to-end case studies constitute a Type 1 validation of *VQ 2.1*, too.

In Section 4.4.3.2, we qualitatively analyzed the complexity of the Systematic Search Algorithm that, basically, determines the time complexity of an APPD diagnostics run. There, we have shown that, a systematic search on a performance problem taxonomy is more efficient than a naive diagnostics process without a taxonomy. Hence, the theoretical time complexity (*VQ 3.1*) has been evaluated by a theoretical elaboration (Type 0 validation) in Section 4.4.3.2. Validation question *VQ 3.2* aims at investigating whether the findings of Section 4.4.3.2 can be confirmed by measurement. By taking the execution time of DynamicSpotter in the end-to-end case studies we can investigate whether the diagnostics can be conducted in a reasonable time (i.e. multiple hours, in order to be integrable as part of nightly checks in continuous integration). However, as we do not apply an alternative (e.g. naive) diagnostics approach in the corresponding case studies, we cannot compare the execution time of DynamicSpotter to any baseline. Hence, validation question *VQ 3.2* is only partly evaluated as part of a Type 1 validation.

In Section 6.3, we used P^2D^2M to describe detection heuristics in a generic way. Hence, Section 6.3 inherently contains a Type 0 validation of *VQ 4.1* showing that the language defined by P^2D^2M has a sufficient expressiveness to specify the corresponding heuristics. Furthermore, the end-to-end case studies show that the context-specific Measurement Environment (ME) Description part of P^2D^2M is appropriate to describe the different scenarios (Type 1 validation). As the target systems in the case studies vary with respect to different aspects, the case studies cover a Type 1 validation of validation question *VQ 4.2*, as APPD and the integral detection heuristics are applied in different scenarios without adopting the detection heuristics.

Validation Goal 5 aims at validating the benefits and the scope of the SSE concept. The SSE-4-RDE experiment completely covers the evaluation of this validation goal. As we apply the SSE concept in an entirely different context, the SSE-4-RDE experiment constitutes a Type 1 validation of both validation questions, *VQ 5.1* and *VQ 5.2*. As *SSE* is a part of the APPD approach, the application of APPD in the end-to-end case studies (TPC-W, nopCommerce and ILS) further evaluates the scope of SSE (*VQ 5.2*).

In the end-to-end case studies, DynamicSpotter runs fully automatically, once configured. Hence, the TPC-W, nopCommerce and ILS case studies contain a Type 1 validation of *VQ 6.1*. By discussing the efforts that were required to get DynamicSpotter running in the different case studies, we partly evaluate *VQ 6.2*. However, as in the end-to-end case studies all up-front efforts are executed by us, the evaluation of validation question *VQ 6.2* may be biased by our insider knowledge. Therefore, we additionally evaluate that validation question in the empirical study that constitutes a Type 2 validation.

Finally, both the external perception (*VQ 7.1*) and the interpretability of DynamicSpotter results by external users (*VQ 7.2*) are covered by the empirical study (Type 2 validation). The costs and benefits of the APPD are qualitatively discussed in the Conclusion of this thesis (Section 9.2.1). However, as a corresponding practical evaluation would imply a disproportionately expensive validation of Type 3, in this thesis, we abstain from quantitatively evaluating the long-term costs and benefits of APPD.

7.2. Case Study: TPC-W

In this case study, we apply DynamicSpotter on TPC-W, an e-commerce benchmark provided by the Transaction Performance Processing Council (TPC) (TPC 2015). This case study is divided into two parts. In the first part, we take the original implementation of the TPC-W benchmark provided by the University of Wisconsin (TPC-W Java 2015) and deploy it as is. We then configure and apply DynamicSpotter to that setup. DynamicSpotter identifies multiple performance problems in the original version of the TPC-W implementation and configuration. By resolving these problems, we show that the detected problems are no false positives, but, constitute actual performance problems. As the first part of this case study does not cover inter-component communication, in the second part of this case study, we extend the TPC-W scenario using the resolved implementation of TPC-W. Thereby, we create a distributed scenario of TPC-W that comprises multiple, distributed software components that communicate with each other using messaging. In contrast to the first part, in the second part we consciously inject performance problems into the SUT in order to (i) analyze whether DynamicSpotter is able to detect communication-related performance problems and (ii) to be able to investigate the false negative rate of DynamicSpotter in this scenario.

In the following, we introduce TPC-W as the target application (Section 7.2.1) followed by detailed descriptions of the two case study parts (Section 7.2.2 and Section 7.2.3). The results and insights of this case study are summarized in Section 7.2.4.

7.2.1. The Application Under Test: TPC-W

TPC-W (TPC-W 2015) is a benchmark created by TPC for the purpose of evaluating and comparing the scalability behaviour of different e-commerce solutions including database, middleware and the web infrastructure. TPC-W is a typical 3-tier application comprising a Web-based presentation layer, an application layer and a persistence layer. The primary intention of TPC-W is to emulate a typical e-commerce application in a representative way, especially focusing on a representative performance behaviour. Therefore, TPC-W emulates a Web-based book store that provides typical services like search functions for books, displaying details of products, ordering processes, customer registration, etc. The TPC-W specification prescribes three main aspects: rules for setting up the SUT, workload specifications and performance metrics to use for comparison of different solutions. Although TPC-W has been deprecated by TPC as a benchmark, it is negligible for our case study as we do not use TPC-W as a benchmark in the original sense. In particular, we do not evaluate or compare different e-commerce solutions. Rather, we use TPC-W as a representative target application for the evaluation of our APPD approach. However, as TPC-W is a performance benchmark that, according to the specification, is tailored for high performance, for the evaluation of APPD it is especially interesting to analyze whether the used implementation of TPC-W meets that requirement.

As the performance metrics defined in the TPC-W specification refer to the underlying infrastructure (servers, network, etc.) rather than to the application, they are of little relevance for our case study. In contrast, the workload specification is an interesting aspect for our case study. In particular, we use the Remote Browser Emulator (RBE) specified by TPC-W as a load generator in the first part of the case study. The RBE emulates a set of browsers that represent virtual users. Hence, the workload generated by the RBE is a closed workload with a fix number of virtual users and a think time distribution that is prescribed by the TPC-W benchmark specification. In the TPC-W specification, a workload is described by a Customer Behaviour Model Graph (CBMG) that is basically a Markov Model describing the transition probabilities between individual transactions (Menascé, 2002). TPC defines three types of workload for TPC-W: *Browsing, Shopping* and *Ordering Mix*. The difference between the workload types is the distribution of transition probabilities between individual transactions.

In this case study, we use a Java implementation of the TPC-W created by the University of Wisconsin (TPC-W Java 2015). The implementation is based on the Java Servlet technology (Hunter et al., 2001) for the representation layer and entry point to the application layer. Hence, each system service is represented by a corresponding Java Servlet. For the communication with the database, this implementation uses plain SQL over JDBC (Reese, 2000). Besides the implementation of the TPC-W application, the used bundle (TPC-W Java 2015) contains an implementation for the RBE. We use this RBE implementation as a load driver in the first part of this case study.

7.2.2. Part I - Standard TPC-W

In this part of the case study, we analyze the TPC-W implementation without previous modifications of the target application. Hence, we investigate whether DynamicSpotter is able to identify instances of performance problems that we (as experimenters) were not aware of in advance.

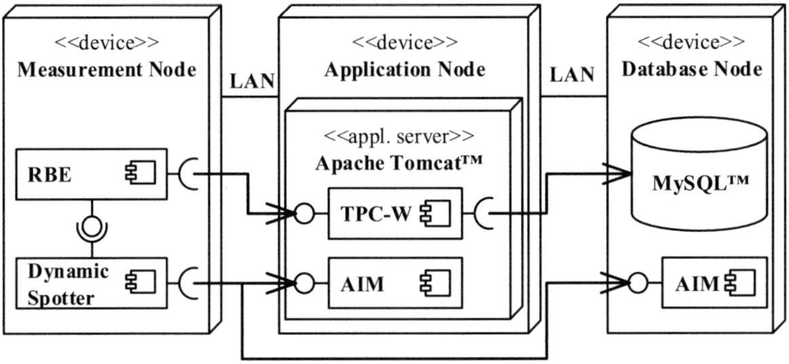

Figure 7.1.: Standard TPC-W: experiment setup

7.2.2.1. Experiment Setup

The experiment setup for the first part of the TPC-W case study is shown in Figure 7.1. The measurement environment comprises three nodes: Application Node, Database Node and Measurement Node. The TPC-W application component runs within an Apache Tomcat™ application server on the Application Node. Besides TPC-W, an Adaptable Instrumentation and Monitoring (AIM) agent (Wert et al., 2015a) runs within the application server that provides the means for DynamicSpotter to dynamically instrument the Java bytecode of the target application and, as needed, to adapt the instrumentation. Furthermore, the AIM component is responsible for collecting the measurement data from the instrumented bytecode as well as the sampled statistics of the hardware resources (e.g. CPU utilization, network I/O, etc.). The TPC-W component access a MySQL™ database that runs on the Database Node via a 100Mbit Ethernet network connection. The AIM component that is co-located with MySQL™ is responsible for sampling statistics of hardware resources on the Database Node. The Measurement Node hosts DynamicSpotter as well as the RBE as a workload generator for TPC-W. The emulated browsers of RBE access the services provided by the TPC-W application via HTTP. For detailed information on the measurement environment we refer to Table A.1 in Appendix A.2.1.

As TPC-W is a database-intensive application, the amount of generated test data is an essential aspect that affects the performance behaviour of the overall TPC-W application. We use the test data generator that is part of the TPC-W implementation to generate 288 thousand customers and 100 thousand items for the initial database content. For the experiments conducted by DynamicSpotter we use the following configuration of the RBE:

- The emulated browsers are started incrementally during the ramp-up phase in order to avoid an oscillating performance behaviour due to a temporary overload situation.
- As workload type, we use the Shopping Mix as it contains both read as well as write accesses to the database.
- Using a think time factor of 0.1, according to the TPC-W specification (TPC-W 2015), the think time for each emulated user varies between 0.7 and 7 seconds.

As described in Section 5.2, to apply the APPD approach through DynamicSpotter we have to describe the context specific information by means of the ME Description part of P^2D^2M. Figure 7.2 shows the corresponding ME Description instance covering all context specific information that is needed to start an automatic diagnostics run of DynamicSpotter. First, the ME Description contains an Experiment Configuration that specifies a ramp-up and a cool-down phase of 100 seconds, an experiment duration of 10 minutes (600 seconds), and a maximal load of 100 users. With respect to the performance requirements, we prescribe for all services of TPC-W a response time threshold of 1 second that, in 99% of cases, must not be exceeded. As already mentioned, as workload specification we use the Shopping Mix as defined by the RBE specification of TPC-W. The AIM component on the Application Node (cf. Figure 7.1) has two corresponding entities in the ME Description model: an Instrumentation Entity and a Monitoring Entity. Although AIM encapsulates both functionalities, due to separation of concerns, we have to distinguish the entity roles in the ME Description model. In contrast, the AIM component at the Database Node is represented only by a Monitoring Entity in the ME Description model, as instrumenting the code of the database management system (here: MySQL™) is not possible and not required for APPD. Finally, the Measurement Node has a Load Generation Entity with corresponding configurations (i.e. *thinkTimeFactor* and *rampUpBehaviour*) and a Monitoring Entity that samples statistics of

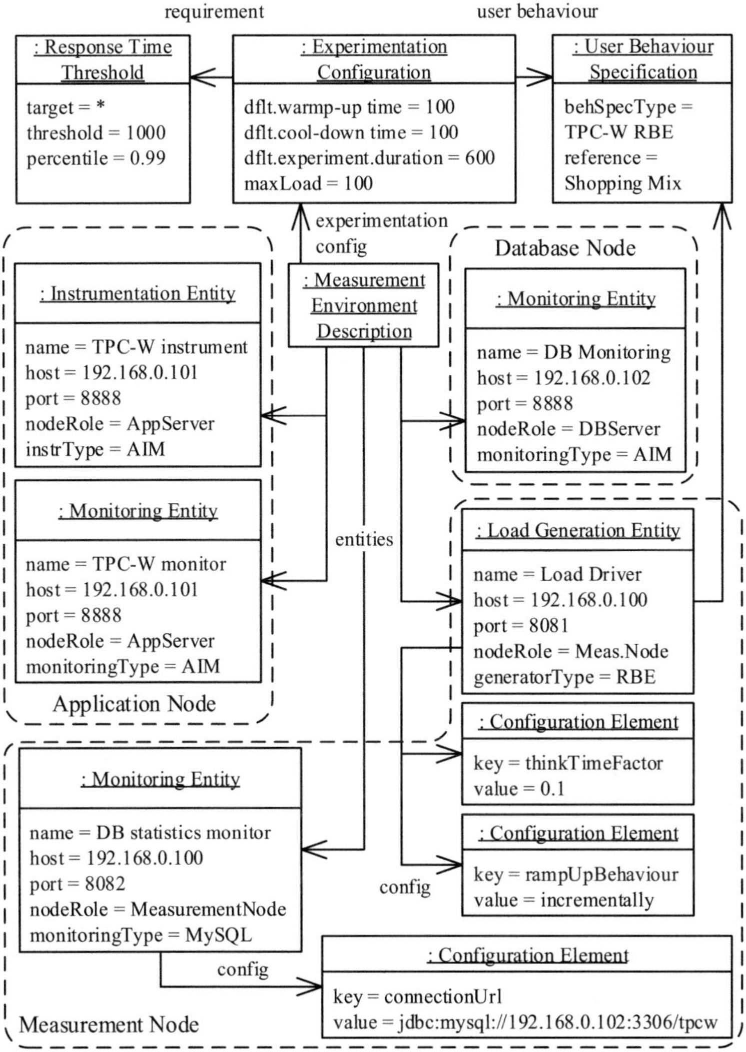

Figure 7.2.: Standard TPC-W: Measurement Environment Description

the database management system by remotely issuing SQL requests to the statistics tables of the database.

In this case study, we configured DynamicSpotter to use the entire PPEP instance as derived in Section 4.4.2. For the nodes of the PPEP instance, DynamicSpotter uses the corresponding detection heuristics comprising the detection strategies that have been selected in Section 6.3 based on the evaluations of the different alternatives. Besides the standard extensions that are bundled with DynamicSpotter, we created an additional DynamicSpotter extension that constitutes an adapter to the RBE workload generator of the TPC-W benchmark.

Overview on Study Execution The investigation in the first part of the case study has been conducted in three iterations. First, we applied DynamicSpotter to the original version of the TPC-W application in the setup described in Section 7.2.2.1.

As shown in Figure 7.3, DynamicSpotter identified a performance problem that has been caused by multiple instances of different manifestations of the One Lane Bridge (OLB) anti-pattern. On the one hand, a long-running database request exhausted the database connection pool so that incoming user requests had to wait for free connections. On the other hand, an unnecessary synchronization block further limited the performance of the application. Hereby, synchronization on Java side has been used to synchronize a select for the maximum id in a table with a subsequent insert using that id. As JDBC and most databases support this scenario by automatically generating ids, the corresponding synchronization block is unnecessary. Overall, these two problems lead to average response times of tens of seconds for the most TPC-W services. We resolved the long-running database request by fixing the corresponding SQL statement and adding an additional index in the accessed database table. Furthermore, we replaced the synchronization block with a built-in solution of JDBC and MySQL that is significantly more efficient than a Java-side synchronization. Thereupon, on the supposedly resolved version of TPC-W, we started a second run of DynamicSpotter. Although the response times of all TCP-W slightly improved , DynamicSpotter, again, reported some performance problems. However, as depicted in Figure 7.3, this time different instances of performance problems emerged compared to the first run of DynamicSpotter. The resolution of the OLB anti-patterns

	Iteration 1	Iteration 2	Iteration 3
Performance Problem	⚑	⚑	✓
├─ Application Hiccups	✓	✓	✗
├─ The Ramp	✓	✓	✗
└─ Continuously Violated Req.	⚑	⚑	✗
└─ Traffic Jam	⚑	⚑	✗
├─ Excessive Messaging	✓	✓	✗
├─ The Blob	✗	✗	✗
└─ Empty Semi Trucks	✗	✗	✗
├─ Database Congestion	✓	⚑	✗
├─ The Stifle	✗	⚑	✗
└─ Expensive DB Call	✗	⚑	✗
└─ One Lane Bridge	⚑	✓	✗
├─ Database OLB	⚑	✗	✗
└─ Dispensable Sync.	⚑	✗	✗

⚑ problem detected ✓ problem not detected ✗ skipped analysis

Figure 7.3.: Standard TPC-W: overview on results

enabled a more frequent emission of another, expensive database request. That database request lead to an overload of the CPU on the database node, thus, has been detected as an Expensive Database call by DynamicSpotter. Furthermore, DynamicSpotter reported a Stifle anti-pattern. However, the corresponding database request has been repeated only twice with the same SQL statement and, thus, did not constitute the root cause for the bad performance behaviour. Based on the second finding by DynamicSpotter, we resolved the Expensive Database Call by rewriting the corresponding SQL statement resulting in a considerably more efficient solution. Finally, we applied DynamicSpotter a third time. As shown in Figure 7.3, the solution of the Expensive Database Call finally resolved all performance problems, the response times of all TPC-W services improved considerably, and DynamicSpotter did not find any performance problems in the resolved TPC-W instance, anymore.

7.2.2.2. Discussion of Results

In the following, we discuss the diagnostics results in more detail for each iteration of the experiment execution.

Experiment Iteration 1 Figure 7.3 shows that, in the first iteration of this part of case study, DynamicSpotter detected the SPAs along the path from the OLB manifestations to the root of the taxonomy. In the following, we discuss the detection results for each individual node in the taxonomy.

By applying the high level Performance Problem heuristic (cf. Section 6.3.1), DynamicSpotter identified a performance problem in the initial state of the TPC-W implementation. According to the experimentation plan of the Performance Problem heuristic, DynamicSpotter applied the maximum load of 100 users. The resulting performance behaviour of the shopping cart interaction of TPC-W is depicted in Figure 7.4, representatively for other services of TPC-W. Figure 7.4a shows the response times over experiment time. The horizontal line shows the response time threshold of one second as defined in the ME Description model in Section 7.2.2.1. We can see, that the response times of the shopping cart interaction exceed the threshold nearly for every request. The cumulative distribution function of the response times is depicted Figure 7.4b. Additionally, the dotted vertical line shows the response time threshold and the dashed horizontal line the target percentile from the performance requirement as defined in the ME Description model. The intersection point of these two lines defines the point, where the CDF curve must have reached a cumulative probability of 99%. However, Figure 7.4b shows that the 0.99 percentile of the response times has a value of about 28 seconds, hence, significantly larger as the prescribed response time threshold. Based on this observation, DynamicSpotter reported an occurrence of a Performance Problem. Other services of TPC-W show a

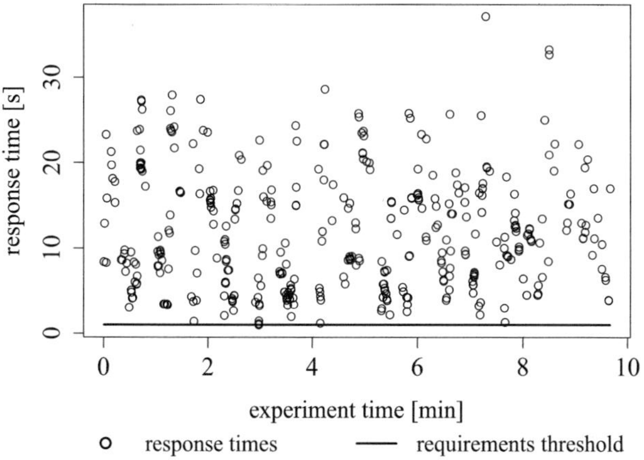

(a) Response times

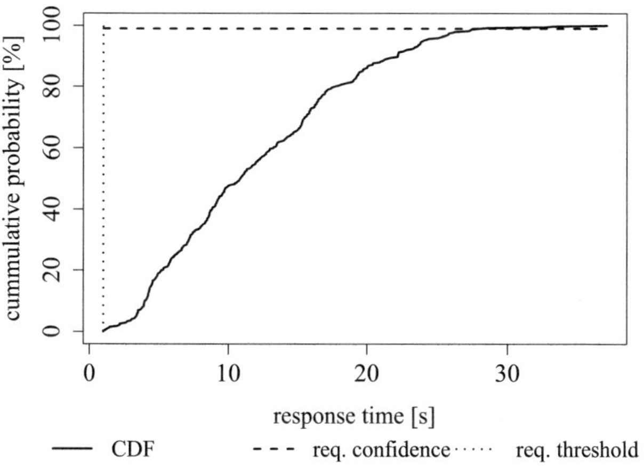

(b) Cumulative distribution function (CDF)

Figure 7.4.: Performance Problem detection: shopping cart interaction (Iteration 1)

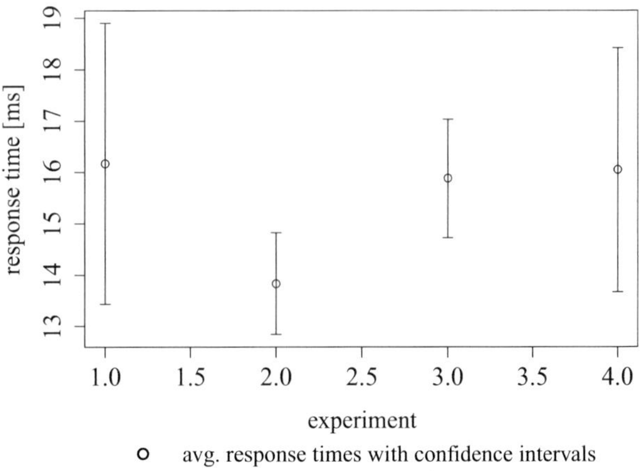

Figure 7.5.: Ramp detection: shopping cart interaction (Iteration 1)

similar performance behaviour, indicating that the root cause of the observed Performance Problem affects multiple services.

According to the performance problem taxonomy, DynamicSpotter resumed its diagnostics with analysing the Application Hiccups, the Ramp and the Continuously Violated Requirements anti-patterns. As we can see in Figure 7.4a, the response times exhibit a continuity over experiment time. In particular, as correctly identified by DynamicSpotter, there are no hiccups in the response times. The same applies for the Ramp anti-pattern. Figure 7.5 shows the detection results of the Ramp heuristic. According to the Time Window strategy of the Ramp heuristic (cf. Section 6.3.3), in Figure 7.5 we see the four experiment executions on the x-axis and the single-user response times of the individual experiments on the y-axis with corresponding confidence intervals. We see that the confidence intervals are overlapping and the average response times do not exhibit an increasing trend. Consequently, the t-test analysis in the Ramp heuristic could neither identify any significant difference in the response time samples nor identify an increase in response times. Hence, DynamicSpotter did not detect a Ramp anti-pattern in TPC-W. By contrast, by applying the Bucket detection strategy as part of the Continuously Violated Requirements heuristic, DynamicSpotter correctly identified the continuity in the response times marking the corresponding anti-patterns in the taxonomy as an existing problem.

As next step, DynamicSpotter conducted an analysis of the Traffic Jam anti-pattern by applying a scaling experiment series (cf. Section 5.3.2.1). The response times for the individual load intensities as well as the confidence intervals for the response times are depicted in Figure 7.6. Under a load intensity of 1 to 60 concurrent users, the response times are very low and have a small variance. However, for a high load intensity the mean response time as well as the variance grow significantly. In Figure 7.6b we can see that, for more than 60 users, the confidence intervals of the response times under different load intensities do not overlap and the mean response times grow with the load intensity. According to this observation, the t-Test strategy of the Traffic Jam heuristic (cf. Section 6.3.5) identified a significant increase in response times, making DynamicSpotter report an occurrence of a Traffic Jam anti-pattern.

Regarding the Excessive Messaging anti-pattern, DynamicSpotter did not identify any messaging activities in the measurement data, hence, marking this anti-pattern as not present in TPC-W. As Excessive Messaging has not been detected, DynamicSpotter skipped the analysis of the Blob and the Empty Semi Trucks anti-patterns because of the Systematic Search Algorithm (cf. Section 4.4.3). The Database Congestion anti-pattern has been detected, neither. Hereby, DynamicSpotter did neither identify an increase in locking times nor a significant utilization of the database. In particular, for all load intensities, the CPU utilization of the database node does not exceed 40% (cf. Figure 7.7a). Consequently, the analysis of the Stifle and the Expensive Database Call (EDC) anti-patterns have been skipped by DynamicSpotter.

As part of the OLB heuristic, DynamicSpotter investigates the CPU utilization on the application and the database server. As depicted in Figure 7.7a, the utilization is relatively low on both nodes. Consequently, the response time threshold that is dynamically calculated by the OLB heuristic based on the CPU utilizations is very low, as shown by the dashed line in Figure 7.7b. For high load intensities (> 60 users), the response time of the shopping cart interaction significantly exceeds the dynamic threshold. Based on this analysis, DynamicSpotter detects an OLB behaviour in 7 services of TPC-W. In

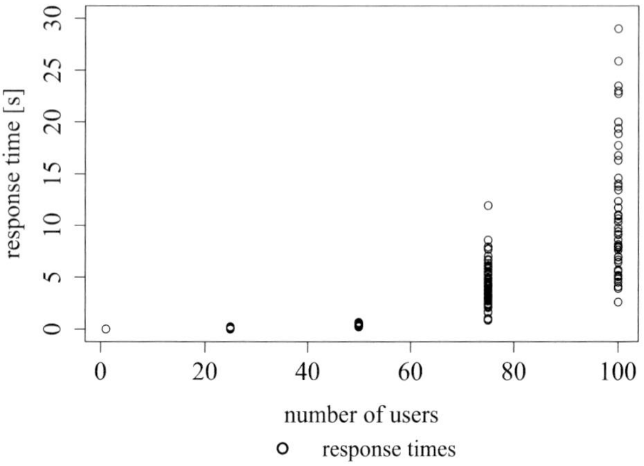

(a) Response times

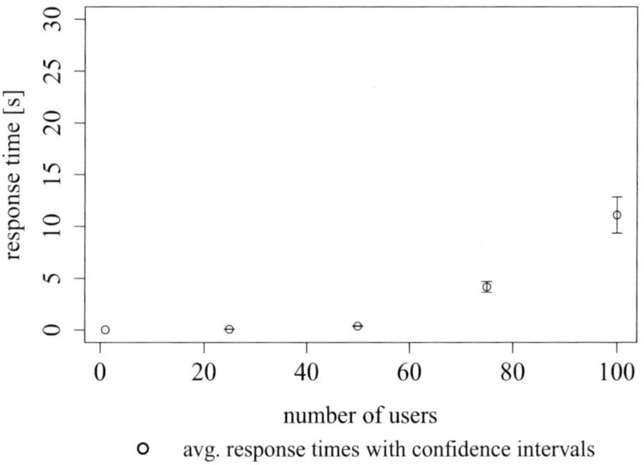

(b) Confidence intervals

Figure 7.6.: Traffic Jam detection: response times and corresponding confidence intervals in dependency on the load for the shopping cart interaction (Iteration 1)

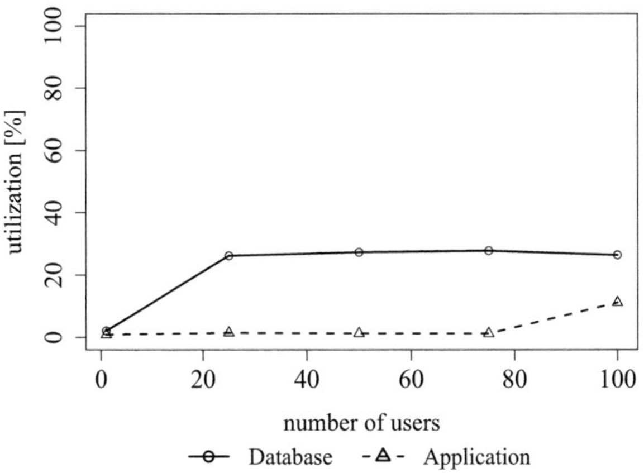

(a) CPU Utilization

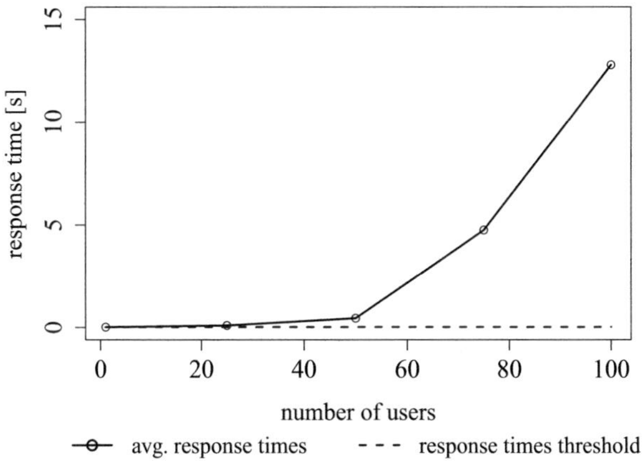

(b) Response times and calculated threshold

Figure 7.7.: OLB detection: shopping cart interaction (Iteration 1) order to locate the root cause of the identified OLB instances, DynamicSpotter applied the OLB heuristic two more times, with the database access scope (i.e. Database OLB) and the synchronization scope (i.e. Dispensable Synchronization anti-pattern). Hereby, DynamicSpotter detected two database queries that constitute an OLB and three synchronized blocks in the Java code of TPC-W that constitute a Dispensable Synchronization anti-pattern. The response times and corresponding calculated thresholds are depicted in Figure 7.8, Figure 7.9, and Figure 7.10.

The queries, identified by DynamicSpotter as Database OLB instances, both serve as a search request. While one of them searches for a book in the database, the other query conducts an author search (cf. Figures 7.8a,7.8b). Both queries contain a *SOUNDEX* expression in the SQL statement that allows to do a similarity search based on the pronunciation of words. However, as *SOUNDEX* is a database function that, in the case of a full table search, is evaluated for each line in the database table, it hinders an efficient usage of existing database indexes. As a result, these database requests become a bottleneck with an increasing load. Interestingly, DynamicSpotter did not detect these queries as Database Congestion anti-patterns as neither the locking times increased nor the database node was significantly utilized. We presume that the detected Dispensable Synchronization anti-pattern instances limit the full effect of the long-running queries to the database utilization. The synchronization scope OLB instances include the *getConnection* method of the database connection pool, as well as two synchronization blocks around multiple database requests. In the latter cases, Java-side synchronization is used to solve the problem of atomically increasing the primary key of a database table while inserting a new line into the same table. Though, with respect to functionality, this is a valid solution, regarding performance, Java-side synchronization over multiple database requests in many cases results in a performance bottleneck. Finally, long waiting times at the *getConnection* method of the database connection pool are rather a side-effect of the remaining problems than a root cause of the observed performance problem. The long-running database queries, as well as the dispensable synchronization blocks quickly exhaust the capacity of the connection pool by holding database connections for a long period of time.

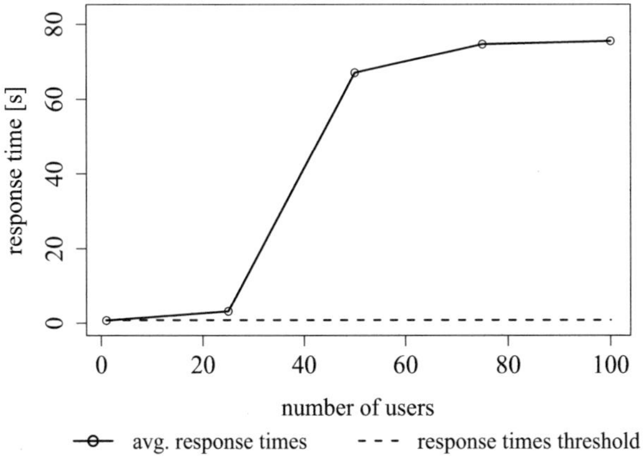

(a) DB request: Book Search

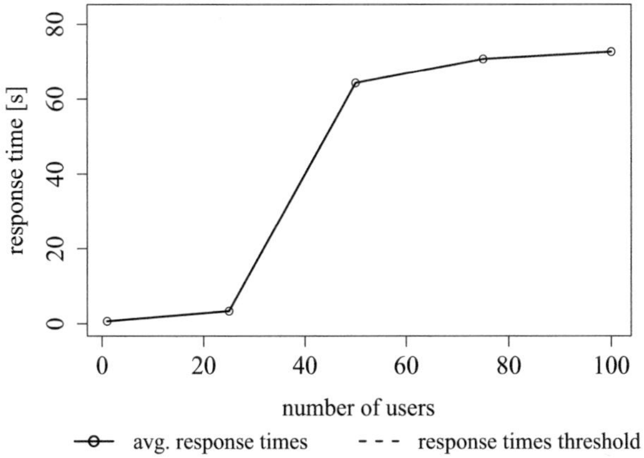

(b) DB request: Author Search

Figure 7.8.: Database OLB detection (Iteration 1)

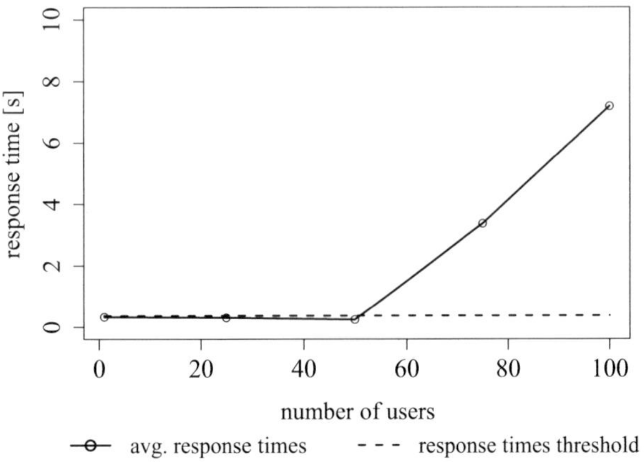

(a) Sync. scope: Insert Address

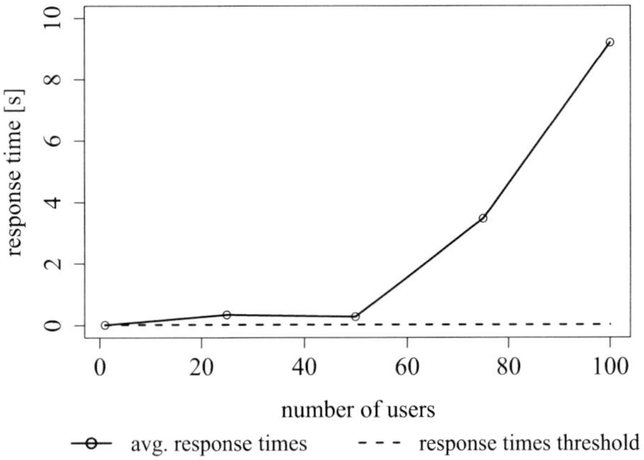

(b) Sync. scope: New Order

Figure 7.9.: Dispensable Synchronization detection 1 (Iteration 1)

To investigate whether the performance problems diagnosed by DynamicSpotter are true positives or false positives, we solved all identified instances of the OLB anti-pattern. In the case of the search requests that use

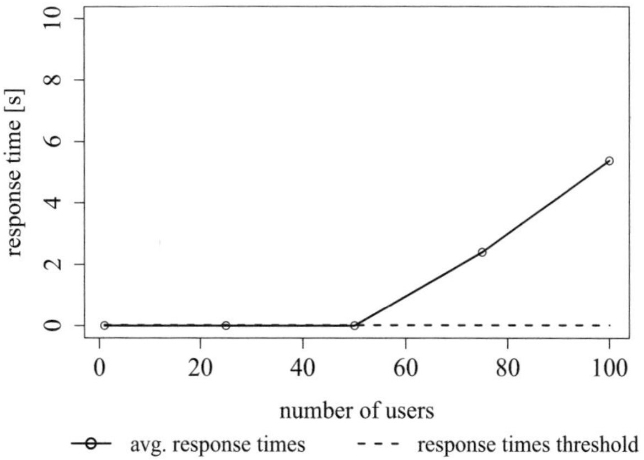

Figure 7.10.: Sync. scope: getConnection

the database function *SOUNDEX*, we resolved the problem by adding an additional column to the corresponding database table. The inserted column contains for each entry in the corresponding table a pre-calculated value of the *SOUNDEX* function applied to the primary key of the corresponding row. Furthermore, we create an additional database index using the newly created column. According to the change in the database schema, we adopted the corresponding SQL queries. For the resolution of the Dispensable Synchronization instances, we used an efficient solution that is a built-in feature in JDBC as well as most database implementations. Thereby, we replaced the synchronization blocks that contained at least a SELECT query for the maximum id of a table and a subsequent INSERT query with the incremented id. Instead, we used the atomic feature of automatically incrementing the primary key when conducting an insert. In this way, we not only eliminated the synchronization block, but also reduced the number of required database queries.

Experiment Iteration 2 In the second iteration of the experiment, we applied DynamicSpotter on the TPC-W implementation that we have resolved at the end of the first iteration. Figure 7.3 gives an overview on the detection results. Although, for most TPC-W services, the performance behaviour improved considerably, the services still violate the specified performance requirements. Figure 7.11 shows the response times over experiment time and the cumulative distribution function of the response times for the shopping cart interaction. Compared to the first iteration where the median response time had a value of 11 seconds, in the second iteration the median has a value of 16 milliseconds. Nevertheless, in Figure 7.11a we can see, that the response times continuously exceed the response time threshold (i.e. performance requirement). Furthermore, Figure 7.11b shows that the response time distribution has a long tail that leads to a violation of performance requirements despite of the low median response time. In particular, the 0.99 percentile has a value of 2.35 seconds which is significantly higher as the required value of 1 second.

While most TPC-W services, similarly to the shopping cart interaction, showed an improvement of the performance behaviour from the first to the second experiment iteration, the performance of the *best sellers* interaction degraded in the second iteration. Figure 7.12 shows the cumulative distribution functions for the response times of the best sellers interaction for both experiment iterations. We can observe that the distribution in the second iteration has a lower standard deviation with a value of 4.72 seconds compared to 5.35 seconds in the first iteration. However, with a value of 17.84 seconds the median is significantly higher than before (11.45 seconds). The best sellers interaction is the only service that shows a degradation in performance compared to the first iteration. This is an indicator for a performance problem in the best sellers service that has not been solved in the first iteration.

Based on the measurement data shown in Figure 7.11 for the shopping cart interaction (representatively for other TPC-W services) and the results for the best sellers service (Figure 7.12), DynamicSpotter identified a Performance Problem that exhibits a Continuous Violation of performance requirements. Hence, DynamicSpotter resumed its diagnostics with the Traffic Jam antipattern. Considering the response times of the best sellers interaction over load intensity in Figure 7.13a, we see that response times are relatively low (i.e. less than 1 second) for load intensities smaller than 80 concurrent users. However, for the maximum load of 100 users, the response times increase considerably to values between 15 and 20 seconds. As depicted in Figure 7.13b, the high CPU utilization of the database node (near to 100%) under a load of 100 users provides an explanation for the significant

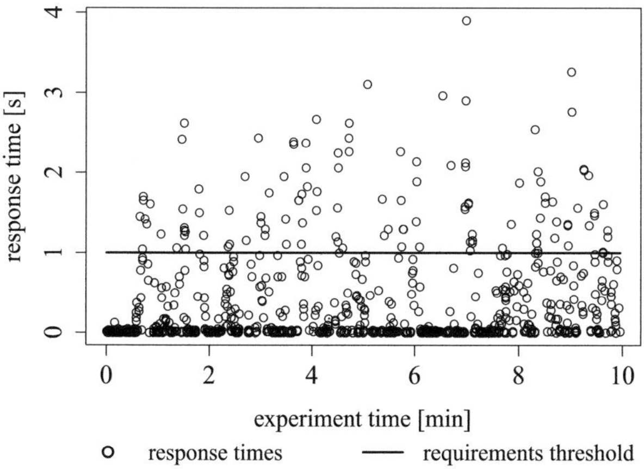

(a) Response times

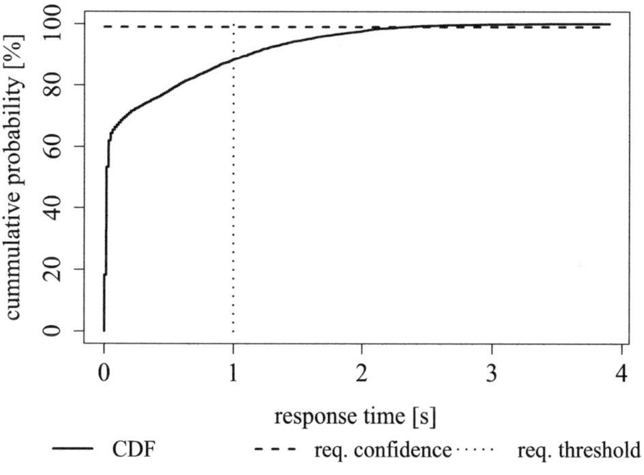

(b) Cumulative distribution function (CDF)

Figure 7.11.: Performance Problem detection: shopping cart interaction (Iteration 2)

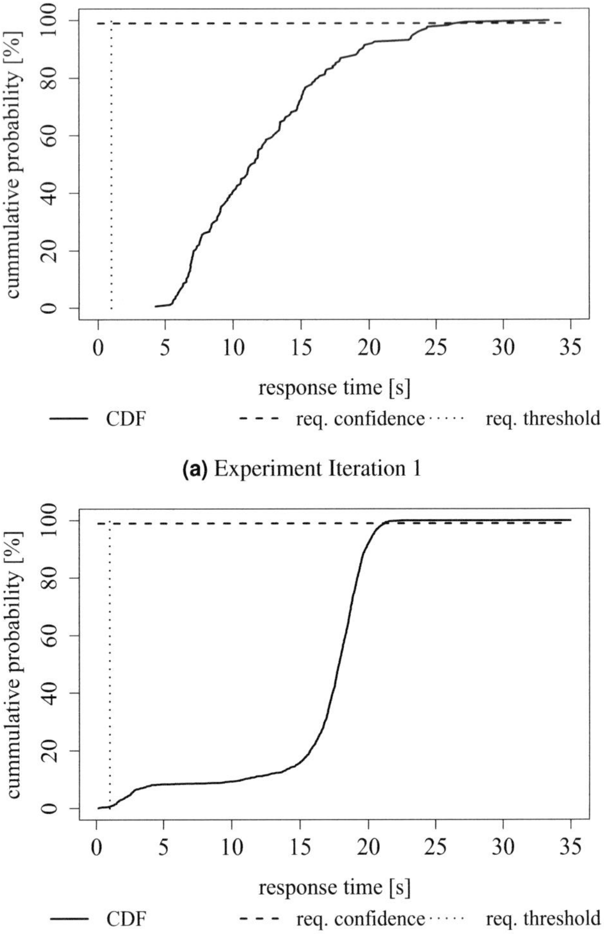

(a) Experiment Iteration 1

(b) Experiment Iteration 2

Figure 7.12.: Comparing cumulative distribution function (CDF) of the best sellers interaction between experiment iteration 1 and 2 increase in the response times. Based on the data shown in Figure 7.13a and the extremely high database utilization, DynamicSpotter identified both a Traffic Jam as well as a Database Congestion anti-pattern. However, in the second iteration no OLB anti-pattern has been detected due to the high CPU utilization on the database node.

Because of the detected Database Congestion anti-pattern, DynamicSpotter conducted an investigation of the EDC and the Stifle anti-pattern. Although both anti-patterns have been identified, in the case of the Stifle anti-pattern DynamicSpotter reports an SQL query that has been repeated only twice. Hence, though a resolution of the Stifle anti-pattern may lead to a small performance improvement, it is not the root cause of the observed performance problem in the best sellers service. Regarding the EDC anti-pattern, DynamicSpotter reports a database query as root cause that is issued by the best sellers service. While the response time ratio of the query and the corresponding best sellers service is very small for a single user experiment ($\approx 1\%$), the ratio increases significantly to 97% for the high load experiment with 100 users. Hence, considering the median response time of the best sellers service (17.84 seconds), 17.3 of 17.84 seconds are spent in the diagnosed database request. Instead of nesting SQL queries for more complex database requests, the developers of the used TPC-W implementation create a temporary database table to store the intermediate results of a sub-query. Subsequently another SQL query is applied on that table, and the temporary table is removed again. This invocation sequence is conducted for each request to the best sellers service leading to an overload of the database node under high load. Interestingly, DynamicSpotter did not diagnose that performance problem in the first iteration of the experiment. Actually, as the OLB anti-patterns from the first iteration have hidden the EDC instance, the EDC problem became visible only after the resolution of the OLB instances. The OLB instances, inter alia, limited the throughput of the best sellers service, hence, alleviating the EDC problem. With their resolution the throughput increased, leading to a much higher load at the database node, caused by the database query that created the temporary table.

Experiment Iteration 3 We resolved the EDC problem detected in the second experiment iteration by replacing the creation of the temporary database table with a nested SQL query. On this third version of the TPC-W imple-

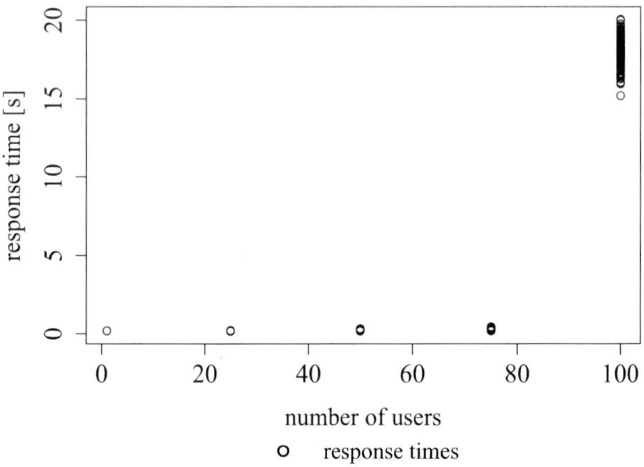

(a) Response times

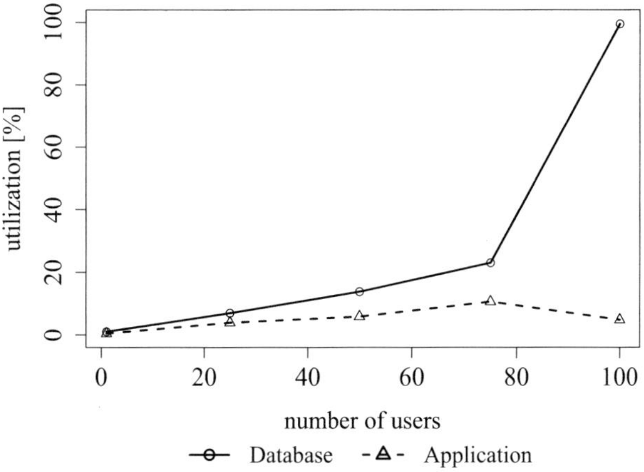

(b) CPU utilization

Figure 7.13.: Response times of best sellers interaction and CPU utilization (Iteration 2) mentation, we again applied DynamicSpotter. This time, DynamicSpotter did not identify any performance problems. As shown in Figure 7.14 for the shopping cart and best sellers interaction (representatively for all services of TPC-W), the response times do not exceed the specified response time threshold anymore. Hence, all performance problems in the used TPC-W implementation have been detected by DynamicSpotter. In this way, we were able to quickly resolve those performance problems yielding a performance improvement of about 3 magnitudes in the response times compared to the initial version of the TPC-W implementation.

7.2.3. Part II - Extended TPC-W

The second part of the TPC-W case study builds upon the final TPC-W implementation from the first study part in which all performance problems have been resolved. The focus of this part of the study lies on the evaluation of the diagnostics of communication-related SPAs, meaning anti-patterns that lead to a performance problem due to an inefficient communication pattern between software components. In particular, this includes the Blob, Empty Semi Trucks (EST) and the Stifle anti-patterns. In contrast to the first part of the case study, in this part we follow the fault injection technique (Hsueh et al., 1997) by consciously injecting different types of performance problems into the purged implementation of TPC-W. Fault injection is the only way to evaluate the diagnostics accuracy of the APPD approach with respect to false negatives. In the following, we introduce the experiment design and discuss the diagnostics results. This part of the case study is part of a supervised Bachelor's Thesis (Oehler, 2014) and has been published in Wert et al., 2014. The following sections contain fragments from that publication.

7.2.3.1. Experiment Design

In this part of the case study, we investigate four different scenarios. While in the first three scenarios the individual anti-patterns (i.e. Blob, EST and Stifle) are evaluated in isolation, the fourth scenario contains a combination of all anti-patterns. The purpose of the fourth scenario is an investigation of the mutual influence of the different anti-patterns. As the experiment setup

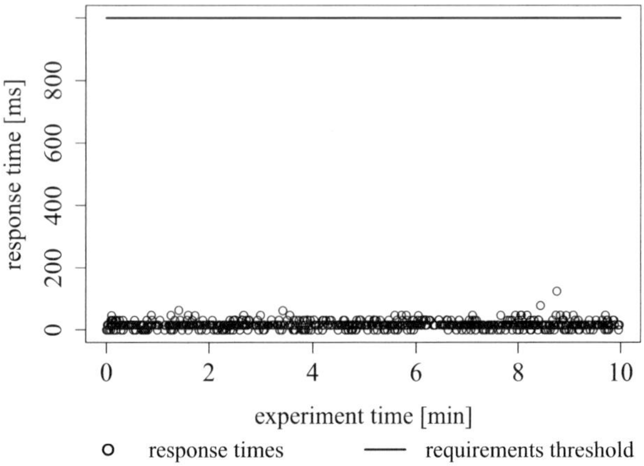

(a) Shopping cart interaction

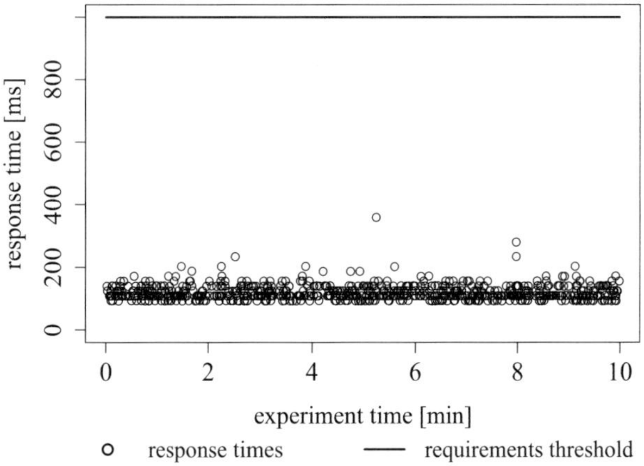

(b) Best sellers interaction

Figure 7.14.: Response times of shopping cart and best sellers interaction (Iteration 3) for the evaluation of the Blob and EST anti-patterns is different compared to the first part of this study, we extend the TPC-W application as described in the following sections.

Experiment Setup The evaluation of diagnosing the Stifle anti-pattern is conducted on a similar measurement environment as already shown in Section 7.2.2.1 for the first part of the case study. The only difference is that, in this part of the study, we use another tool for load generation to investigate how generically the APPD approach can deal with different types of load generation tools. Instead of applying the RBE for load generation, we use HP LoadRunner™ (LoadRunner 2014) that is a load generation tool commonly used in industry. Except for a dedicated Load Driver Node on which HP LoadRunner™ is deployed, the experiment setup for the evaluation of the Stifle anti-pattern is the same as shown in Figure 7.1 for the first part of the case study. By contrast, an evaluation of the Blob and the EST anti-patterns requires a distributed system that allows to investigate the communication behaviour between software components.

Therefore, we extend the standard TPC-W application to a more distributed system as depicted in Figure 7.15. The extended version of TPC-W constitutes a federation of three book shops (*TPC-W instances*). Each TPC-W instance comprises its own application server and its own database instance. The TPC-W instances communicate with each other to enable processing of requests that cannot be served by the individual shops in isolation. The communication is conducted over a *TPC-W Controller* component using Java Message Service (JMS) for message transmission. The TPC-W Controller is deployed on a separate *Controller Node*. As messaging server we use Apache ActiveMQ™ that runs on a dedicated *Messaging Node*. Analogously to the experiment setup in the first part of this case study, on each Application Node and Database Node an AIM agent is deployed for instrumentation and monitoring, respectively. Furthermore, an AIM agent is deployed on the Controller Node to enable instrumentation and monitoring of the TPC-W Controller component, and another AIM component is deployed on the Messaging Node to sample hardware resource statistics on that node.

To guarantee an equal load intensity on all TPC-W instances, we configure LoadRunner™ to equally distribute the user requests to the three TPC-W instances. In contrast to the workload definition of the TPC-W specification,

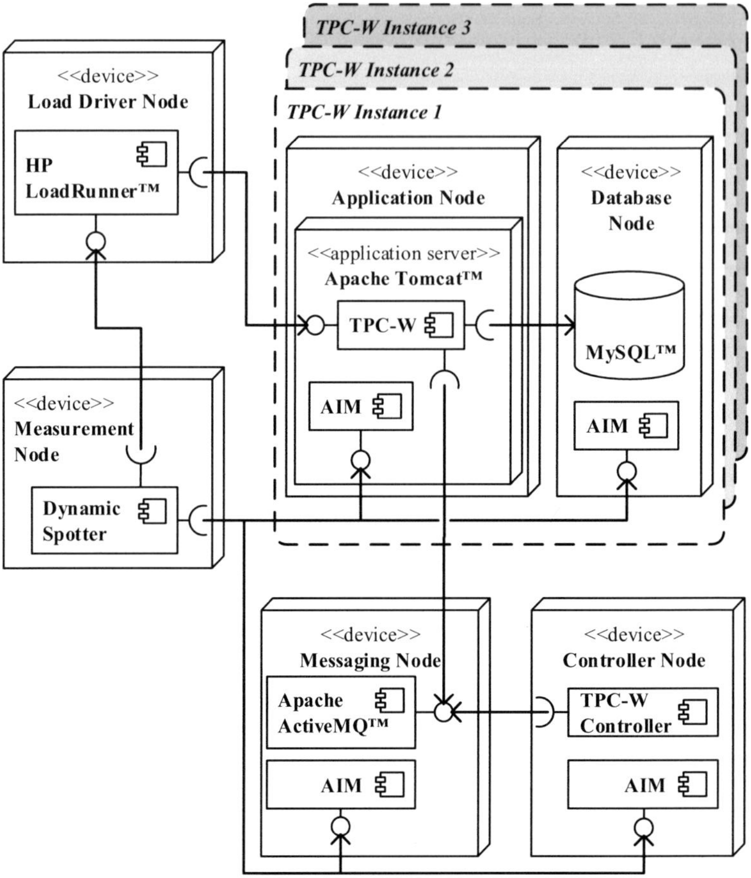

Figure 7.15.: Extended TPC-W: experiment setup

a LoadRunner™ script usually defines a fix sequence of interactions for a virtual user instead of a Markov Model. The script for one iteration of a user in this part of the case study is depicted in Figure 7.16 as a Unified Modeling Language (UML) activity diagram. A user visits the home page of the TPC-W store, browses to a category of books and searches for a specific book. Subsequently, the virtual user conducts a search for a subject yielding

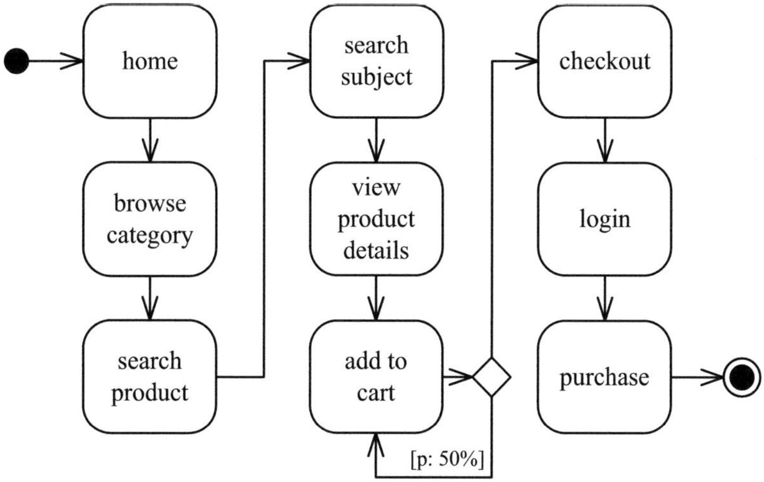

Figure 7.16.: Extended TPC-W: usage script

a list of books which of a book is select to view the product details. Then, the user adds a set of items to the cart, whereby the amount of items is a random number. Finally, the user checks out the cart, conducts a login and finishes the session with purchasing the items in the cart. Between individual user requests we use a randomly distributed think time between 0.5 and 2 seconds. Each experiment conducted by DynamicSpotter has an experiment duration of 10 minutes in the stable phase plus a warm-up and a cool-down phase of approximately 3 minutes. Because of the modification of the experiment setup we adjust the performance requirements to the following specification. The response time of each user request should not exceed the value of 2 seconds in 99% of cases under a maximum load of 180 concurrent users.

Experiment Scenarios To enable an evaluation of the communication-related SPAs, we extend the standard TPC-W as described below, yielding four different experiment scenarios.

Stifle Scenario As already mentioned, the evaluation of the Stifle anti-pattern is based on the experiment setup of the first part of the case study.

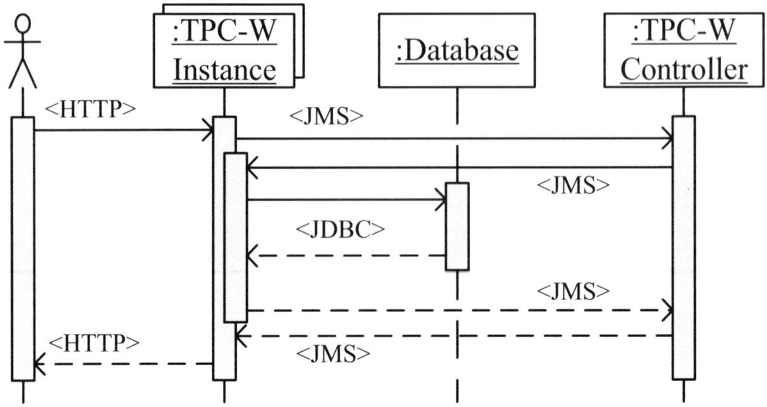

Figure 7.17.: Request processing in the Blob Scenario (Wert et al., 2014)

However, regarding the TPC-W implementation, we injected two instances of the Stifle anti-pattern. First, in the case that a book search request is resolved to a set of books, a database request is issued for each book in that list. Thereby, an initial SQL query retrieves a set of book IDs followed by a loop over the IDs to retrieve product details from the database. The second Stifle instance is injected into the purchase service. A purchase request requires an update of the stock value for each item in the cart. Instead of conducting a batch update on all items, in the Stifle Scenario, each item is updated separately.

Blob Scenario Based on the experiment setup shown in Figure 7.15, we inject a Blob anti-pattern by adapting the architecture of the traditional TPC-W. Assuming that the shopping functionality is equal across all shops within a federation, we move the application logic of all shops to the TPC-W Controller component, while the web servers and the corresponding databases stay with the individual shops. In this way, the TPC-W Controller component constitutes a typical Blob comprising a major part of the processing logic. The result is an unnecessarily high amount of messages that are transmitted for each user request between the TPC-W Controller and all TPC-W Instances. Figure 7.17 illustrates the control flow between the components for a simple user request. First, each user request is delegated to the TPC-W Controller. As soon as the TPC-W Controller requires data, the controller retrieves the data from the corresponding database via the TPC-W Instance. Thus, for each user request at least four messages are transmitted over JMS.

EST Scenario Analogously to the Blob Scenario, the EST Scenario is based on the extended experiment setup. However, the application logic of the shopping system is located with the individual TPC-W Instances such that most requests can be processed by the requested TPC-W Instances without the need to communicate with the TPC-W Controller or other TPC-W instances. However, if a search request for a product yields an empty result, the corresponding TPC-W Instance requests the TPC-W Controller to serve the user request by conducting the search request on another TPC-W Instance. In the case that the search request on the second TPC-W Instance has been successful, each found item is transmitted as an individual JMS message, first to the TPC-W Controller and, finally, to the originally requested TPC-W Instance. As the result of a delegated search request is transmitted as a sequence of small massages instead of an aggregated message, it constitutes a typical EST anti-pattern.

Combined Scenario The Combined Scenario contains all introduced anti-patterns: Stifle, Blob and EST. Based on the extended experiment setup, this scenario combines the characteristics of the other three scenarios. The application logic is centralized in the TPC-W Controller, the results of delegated search requests are transmitted as a series of small messages, and the two Stifle instances cause frequent database requests.

7.2.3.2. Discussion of Results

Applying DynamicSpotter on the individual scenarios we obtained the results as shown in Figure 7.18. On the left, one can see the performance problem taxonomy used for execution of DynamicSpotter. The remaining columns show the detection results for the individual scenarios, whereby the left parts shows the expected detection results and the right parts show the actually

	Stifle Scenario		Blob Scenario		EST Scenario		Comb. Scenario	
	expected	obtained	expected	obtained	expected	obtained	expected	obtained
Performance Problem	⚐	⚐	⚐	⚐	⚐	⚐	⚐	⚐
└ Application Hiccups	✓	✓	✓	✓	✓	✓	✓	✓
└ The Ramp	✓	✓	✓	✓	✓	✓	✓	✓
└ Continuously Violated Req.	⚐	⚐	⚐	⚐	⚐	⚐	⚐	⚐
└ └ Traffic Jam	⚐	⚐	⚐	⚐	⚐	⚐	⚐	⚐
└ └ └ Excessive Messaging	✓	✓	⚐	⚐	⚐	⚐	⚐	⚐
└ └ └ └ The Blob	✗	✗	⚐	⚐	✓	⚐	⚐	⚐
└ └ └ └ Empty Semi Tr.	✗	✗	✓	✓	⚐	⚐	⚐	⚐
└ └ └ Database Congestion	⚐	⚐	✓	✓	✓	✓	⚐	✓
└ └ └ └ The Stifle	⚐	⚐	✗	✗	✗	✗	⚐	✗
└ └ └ └ Expensive DB C.	✓	✓	✗	✗	✗	✗	✗	✗
└ └ └ One Lane Bridge	✓	✓	✓	✓	✓	✓	✓	✓
└ └ └ └ Database OLB	✗	✗	✗	✗	✗	✗	✗	✗
└ └ └ └ Disp. Sync.	✗	✗	✗	✗	✗	✗	✗	✗

⚐ problem detected ✓ problem not detected ✗ skipped analysis

Figure 7.18.: Extended TPC-W: overview on results

obtained results by applying DynamicSpotter. At first glance, DynamicSpotter provides correct results for all cases except for one false positive in the EST Scenario and two false negatives in the Combined Scenario. In the following, we discuss the results for each scenario in more detail.

Results for the Stifle Scenario The response times of the book search interaction are depicted in Figure 7.19 for all investigated scenarios over increasing load intensity (i.e. data from the Traffic Jam heuristic). We see that, in the Stifle Scenario, response times grow with the load intensity and

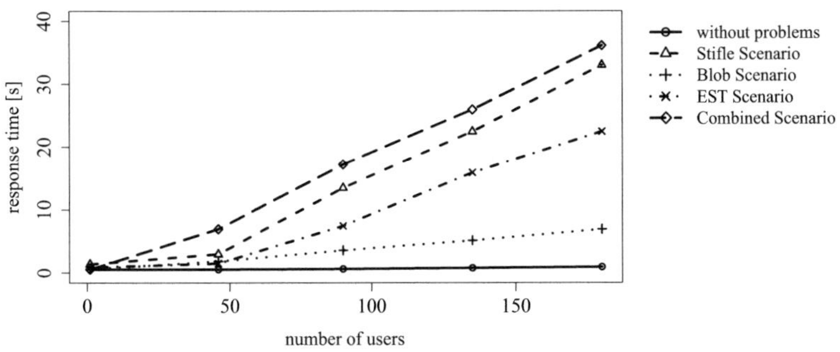

Figure 7.19.: Response times of the book search interaction for the four scenarios (Wert et al., 2014)

exceeded the performance requirement threshold of 2 seconds under the maximum load of 180 users. Based on that information, DynamicSpotter correctly detected the Performance Problem, Continuously Violated Requirements and the Traffic Jam anti-patterns, while the Application Hiccups and the Ramp anti-patterns have not been detected.

As a result of this, DynamicSpotter triggered the investigation of the Excessive Messaging and the Database Congestion anti-patterns (cf. Figure 7.18). DynamicSpotter did not detect the Excessive Messaging anti-pattern in the Stifle Scenario, as in this scenario no messaging has been used by the software components. Although, the CPU utilization of the database node was quite low (smaller than 30%), the locking times increase significantly with the load, from 0 seconds to 22.6 seconds. Consequently, DynamicSpotter detected the Database Congestion anti-pattern and resumed the diagnostics with the Stifle and EDC heuristics. Thereby, no expensive database calls have been found, however, DynamicSpotter identified two Stifle instances. An *update* SQL statement in the purchase service of TPC-W, has been executed between 2 and 4299 times (with different parameters) per transaction, depending on how many and which items have been bought. In the book search service, the Stifle heuristic detected a *select* query that has been executed 6 to 2006 times, depending on the search result. Thus, DynamicSpotter has found both Stifle instances which have been injected in the Stifle-Scenario.

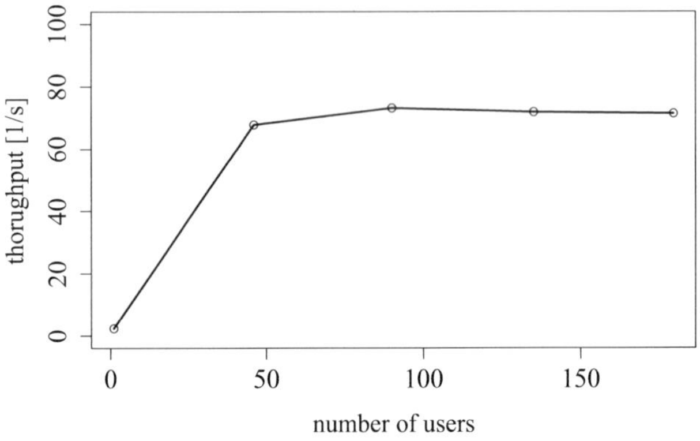

Figure 7.20.: Message throughput over load intensity

Results for the Blob Scenario As indicated by the corresponding curve in Figure 7.19, from a high level perspective the Blob Scenario exhibits a similar behaviour as the Stifle Scenario. Hence again, the Performance Problem, Continuously Violated Requirements and the Traffic Jam anti-patterns have been detected. Further below in the performance problem taxonomy, DynamicSpotter did not identify a Database Congestion anti-pattern as the utilization of all database nodes did not exceed 90% and locking on database tables is negligible.

Figure 7.20 shows the message throughput at the messaging server. The message throughput of the TPC-W Controller does not scale with the number of users, but stagnates with an increasing load intensity. Hence, DynamicSpotter detected an Excessive Messaging problem and resumed its analysis with the Blob and EST anti-patterns. The EST anti-pattern has not been detected in the Blob Scenario as no message transmissions have been found that were executed in a loop. However, DynamicSpotter successfully detected the injected Blob anti-pattern. Table 7.2 shows some details on the detection of the Blob anti-pattern. The first column lists the software components involved in messaging. The second column comprises the messaging times for the individual components. Column three and four show the calculated messaging contributions of the components as well the corresponding thresholds, respectively (cf. Component Exclusion strategy in Section 6.3.11).

component	messaging time [s]	contribution [%]	threshold	result
total	**83 116**	—	—	—
TPC-W 1	24 776	29.8	148.5	No Blob
TPC-W 2	29 943	36.0	150.9	No Blob
TPC-W 3	28 396	34.1	150.4	No Blob
TPC-W Controller	83 116	**100.0**	**41.1**	**Blob**

Table 7.2.: Detailed results on Blob detection in the Blob Scenario (Wert et al., 2014)

Finally, the last column indicates which components have been detected as a Blob. The sum over all message transmission times yields a value of 83116 seconds (including parallel transmission of messages). As all messages pass the TPC-W Controller, its contribution to the total messaging time is 100%. The threshold for the Controller component is 41.1. As the messaging time contribution exceeds the threshold, the Blob heuristic detected the TPC-W Controller as a Blob component. In contrast, the messaging time contributions of the remaining components are below the corresponding thresholds.

Results for the EST Scenario With respect to the anti-patterns on the higher levels of the performance problem taxonomy, for the EST Scenario applies the same as for the Blob Scenario: the response time requirement has been continuously violated, response times increase with the load intensity (cf. Figure 7.19) and the Database Congestion anti-pattern has not been detected because of low database utilizations and negligible database locking times. The heuristic for Excessive Messaging detected a stagnating message throughput under a load of about 90 users. As a consequence, DynamicSpotter applied the Blob and EST heuristics. Thereby, the EST heuristic identified two message dispatching methods that were executed in a loop between 64 to 100 times. The identified methods are responsible for transmitting the result of the book search request from one TPC-W instance via the TPC-W Controller to another TPC-W instance by sending each found item as a single message. The number of loop iterations (64 to 100) corresponds to the number of items found for the search requests. Each message has an average payload of 24 Bytes while exhibiting an additional overhead of 160 Bytes. Thus, 64 messages constitute a network traffic of 11.5 KB. Aggregating these messages to one message yields a saving potential of 9.8 KB (63 times the message overhead of 160 Bytes) which is 85.6% of the network traffic generated by one request. Hence, the EST anti-pattern has been correctly detected. Besides the two EST instances, DynamicSpotter identified the TPC-W Controller as a Blob component in the EST Scenario. At first glance, this detection constitutes a false positive, however, a deeper consideration provides a reasonable explanation for this observation. Actually, the detected EST anti-pattern is at the same time a Blob anti-pattern, as all messages that were transmitted by the EST instances passed through the TPC-W Controller. This messaging behaviour caused a high messaging overhead. Thus, though we preliminary did not expect DynamicSpotter to detect a Blob in the EST Scenario, the detection results are indeed correct.

Results for the Combined Scenario As expected, in the Combined Scenario, DynamicSpotter detected the Excessive Messaging anti-pattern, as well as the Blob and the EST instances as root causes for the Excessive Messaging. The detection details on the Blob and the EST are very similar to the Blob Scenario and the EST Scenario, respectively. However, while the Combined Scenario contains two Stifle instance, the Stifle anti-pattern and the corresponding parent in the performance problem taxonomy (Database Congestion anti-pattern) have not been detected. More precisely, according to the performance problem taxonomy, DynamicSpotter did not investigate the Stifle anti-pattern as the Database Congestion anti-pattern has not been detected (cf. Figure 7.18). Investigating the measurement data shows that all database utilizations are quite low (below 20%) and database locking times do not increase significantly with the load. Thus, the Database Congestion anti-pattern did not become visible in the Combined Scenario. The Excessive Messaging caused by the Blob and the EST instances throttle the performance of the overall system to a degree that no Database Congestion anti-pattern could occur. Hence, the Blob and the EST instances hide the Stifle anti-pattern.

7.2.4. Conclusions on Validation Questions

In this section, we summarize our insights from the TPC-W case study and draw corresponding conclusions on the validation questions described in Section 7.1.1.

In this case study, we have shown for the SPAs covered by the used performance problem taxonomy that they are detectable by measurements (*VQ 1.1*). Solely from the TPC-W case study we cannot draw a comprehensive conclusion on validation question *VQ 1.2*. However, within the two case study parts we have applied the APPD approach on two entirely different experiment setups using different types of load generators. Hence, we can conclude that APPD is generic with respect to the constellation of the SUT's setup as well as used types of load generators. In general, regarding validation question *VQ 1.3*, the TPC-W case study shows that APPD is able to uncover self-injected instances of performance problems (i.e. known in advance by authors of APPD) (second part of case study), as well as performance problem instances that the authors of APPD were not aware of in advance (first part of the case study). Thereby, the study shows that performance problems that occur in isolation in the SUT are detected accurately. In scenarios with multiple instance of performance problems, the circumstances are more complicated. In particular, the most critical performance problem instances (i.e. most narrow performance bottlenecks) may hide other instances of performance problems so that hidden performance problems do not become visible by observable symptoms. Hence, measurement-based diagnostics approaches, like APPD, inherently are not able to detect hidden performance problems. In such cases, the APPD approach detects only the most critical performance problems. In order to overcome this problem, APPD has to be applied iteratively while resolving identified performance problems within each iteration (cf. study execution of part 1, Section 7.2.2.1). In this way, hidden instances of performance problems are gradually uncovered by resolving the problems that have hidden them.

Regarding validation question *VQ 2.1* we can conclude that the performance problem instances observed in the TPC-W case study were reflected by the used performance problem taxonomy. In particular, the identified root causes were observable by the corresponding symptoms as described by the taxonomy. An interesting insight of this case study is that some instance of performance problems are not of an exclusive problem type. More precisely, as shown in the EST Scenario in the seconds part of the study, some instances of performance problems have multiple types at once. So far, our taxonomy does not provide for reflecting performance problem instances of multiple types. However, as shown in the case study, with the current taxonomy schema, this kind of performance problems can be detected as well. Hereby, a correlation of different detected problem instances over their root cause location may be a useful feature to better identify such multi-type performance problems.

With the taxonomy used in this case study, the diagnostics runs took between three and five hours, depending on the existing performance problems. This constitutes reasonable times to be executed as nightly or weekly evaluation tests for performance, for instance, as part of continuous integration of software products. In the third iteration of the first study part, the execution took only 15 minutes. Hence, confirming the qualitative considerations of the time complexity in Section 4.4.3, the diagnostics is faster the less problems the SUT contains.

Similarly to validation question *VQ 1.2*, we cannot draw a comprehensive conclusion on Validation Goal 4 just from the TPC-W case study. Nevertheless, in this study we have applied P^2D^2M to describe the two parts of the case study. The expressiveness of P^2D^2M was sufficient to specify all aspects of the target system for an automatic execution of DynamicSpotter. Furthermore, we were able to apply all detection heuristics of APPD without a need for modification or adoption. This shows that the description languages (i.e. P^2D^2M) used to describe the heuristics in a generic way allow to abstract from the characteristics of concrete scenarios.

A successful (i.e. accurate) diagnostics by DynamicSpotter inherently shows the applicability of the SSE concept, as detailed measurement data has been gathered without significant distortion of the data (cf. *VQ 5.2*). Analogously, validation question *VQ 6.1* is inherently answered by the successful execution of DynamicSpotter. With respect to the efforts required to apply DynamicSpotter on TPC-W (*VQ 6.2*), we summarize which tasks have been necessary. However, we abstain from providing a quantitative analysis of the effort. First of all, for this case study we had to do some tasks that are common for all scenarios where performance testing is applied. This includes the setup of the measurement environment as well as creation of the load generator scripts. In the first part of the case study, we had to create a DynamicSpotter adapter for the RBE load generator of TPC-W. Though this is a very specific case, with that we saved the efforts of creating a load script as the RBE includes the workload specification. The second part of the study rather reflects a scenario that is representative for industrial projects where an established load generation tool (e.g. HP LoadRunner™) is used. However, in this case we had to record a load script for LoadRunner™. The APPD-specific tasks include the deployment of measurement tools (e.g. AIM agents) as well as the description of the scenario using P^2D^2M. The latter task is usually a matter of minutes. The complexity of deploying measurement tools depends on the concrete measurement tools and the existing knowledge or available documentation. Usually this task does not take more than a couple of hours.

7.3. Case Study: nopCommerce

While the TPC-W case study (cf. Section 7.2) has been conducted with a Java-based target application, in this case study, we apply the APPD approach on a .NET application. In this way, we evaluate the generalisability of the APPD approach with respect to the underlying technologies of the SUT.

In the following, we describe the experiment design of this case study including a description of the target application as well as the experiment setup. Subsequently, we discuss the results of this case study. Finally, we summarize the conclusions from this case study to the investigated validation questions.

7.3.1. Experiment Design

In this section, we introduce the application under test, the experiment setup as well as the procedure and execution details of this case study.

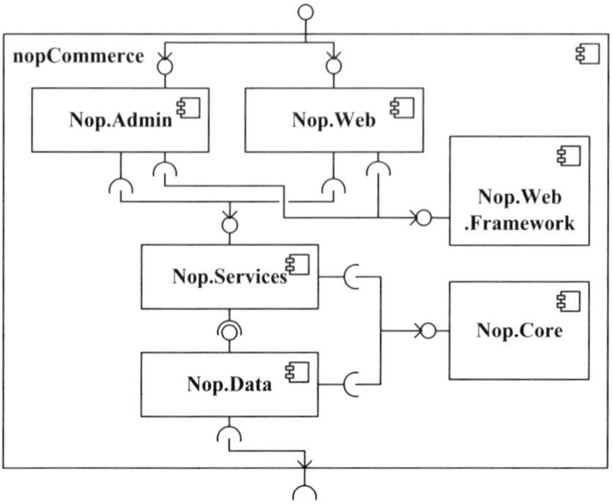

Figure 7.21.: Architecture of the nopCommerce application

7.3.1.1. The Application Under Test: nopCommerce

In this case study, we use nopCommerce (NopCommerce 2015) as the target application of investigation. Similar to the business domain of TPC-W, nopCommerce is an open-source e-commerce solution. Hence, nopCommerce is used to run custom online shops. As nopCommerce is written in the programming language C#, it is intended to be executed on a .NET run-time (Box et al., 2002). As shown in Figure 7.21, the nopCommerce application is structured along a 3-tier architecture.

The application comprises six main components, while four of them realize the Model-View-Controller (MVC) pattern. The application provides two different presentation components depending on the user role: while the *Nop.Admin* component provides views for administrators of the customized online shop, the *Nop.Web* component constitutes the presentation layer for the end-users of the shop. Both presentation components require utility services from the *Nop.Web.Framework* component that provides basic presentation layer functionalities. The presentation layer in nopCommerce builds upon the MVC pattern (Freeman, 2013). Thereby, *Controller* classes constitute the entry point into the backend of nopCommerce, which is important for the instrumentation of the application using the instrumentation description part of P^2D^2M. The presentation components access the *Nop.Services* component that encapsulates the business logic of the online shop and provides corresponding services to the presentation components. Finally, the Nop.Services component retrieves data from the database via the data access layer represented by the *Nop.Data* component. Utility services that are used by the application layer and the data access layer are encapsulated in the *Nop.Core* component.

7.3.1.2. Experiment Setup

The experiment setup of this case study comprises three physical system nodes. As depicted in Figure 7.22, the nopCommerce application runs within a Microsoft Internet Information Services (IIS)™ web server.

As elaborated in this thesis, a realization of the APPD approach requires measurement data from the interior of the target application in order to apply corresponding detection heuristics. As we did not found any free monitoring tools in the area of .NET, we extended the AIM framework (Wert et al., 2015a) with the capability to instrument .NET applications and gather corresponding measurement data. Therefore, we created a light-weight .NET agent for AIM. The *AIM.NET* agent contains measurement probes written in C# that are realized by means of Aspect-oriented Programming (AOP) using the PostSharp™ tool. The *AIM.NET* agent communicates with an AIM-Wrapper Java process that collects the measurement data gathered in the .NET process. Therefore, we us a Java-.Net bridge (JNBridge™) that allows inter-process communication between Java and .NET processes. In contrast to Java, .NET does not provide means to realize dynamically adaptable instrumentation. Hence, in order to enable the SSE concept within APPD, the AIM-Wrapper (cf. Figure 7.22) realizes adaptation of instrumentation by restarting the target application. Thereby, the AIM-Wrapper stops the SUT for each instrumentation request, statically adapts the instrumentation of the application and restarts the SUT again. Though this approach is not as efficient as the dynamically adaptable instrumentation of AIM in Java, it enables automatic execution of DynamicSpotter and, hence, enables a realization of APPD on .NET applications. Finally, the AIM-Wrapper provides instrumentation and measurement services to DynamicSpotter that runs on a dedicated Measurement Node.

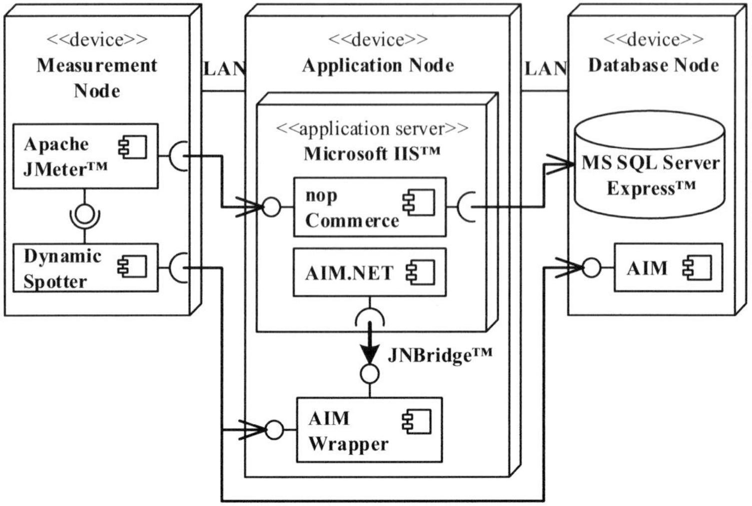

Figure 7.22.: Experiment setup

As the database management system for nopCommerce we use Microsoft SQL Server Express™ that runs on a Database Node. Furthermore, we deploy an AIM component on the Database Node to sample hardware resource statistics during measurements. As load generator we use Apache JMeter™ that is a load generation tool with similar capabilities as HP LoadRunner™. Apache JMeter™ runs on the same node as DynamicSpotter.

Besides the source code of the application, the nopCommerce bundle (NopCommerce 2015) contains test data for a demo shop. In this case study, we use that test data for instantiating the target application.

7.3.1.3. Study Procedure

The goal of this case study is to show the broad applicability of the APPD approach and its ability to abstract from concrete technologies. In particular, in the nopCommerce case study our focus is not on detecting unknown instances of performance problems. As preliminary performance tests showed that nopCommerce did not exhibit performance problems in our experiment setup, we apply fault injection (Hsueh et al., 1997) to investigate whether DynamicSpotter is able to detect the injected performance problem in a .NET environment. Thereto, we inject a synchronized method into the logic of the *ShoppingCartService* of the Nop.Services component (cf. Figure 7.21). The synchronized method contains a Dispensable Synchronization anti-pattern constituting a root cause for an OLB.

Due to license restrictions of the AOP tool PostSharp™, we were not able to realize the whole functionality of AIM for .NET applications. Consequently, the AIM.NET agent supports only a sub-set of model elements from the Instrumentation and Monitoring (IaM) Description model of P^2D^2M (cf. Section 5.3.2.2). In particular, in this case study, instrumentation of database access operations was not possible. Note, as this is not a fundamental restriction of .NET, corresponding measurement and instrumentation tools for .NET that support our IaM Description language can be created by means of an extended licence of PostSharp™. Due to the limitations in the instrumentation capabilities, in this case study, we used only a part of the performance problem taxonomy to apply DynamicSpotter on nopCommerce. The taxonomy used in this case study is shown in the left column of Figure 7.23. Compared to the taxonomy used in the TPC-W case study, we reduced this instance by the messaging-related and database-related SPAs.

Similarly, to the second part of the TPC-W case study, we use a closed workload, whereby each user session is defined by a fix sequence of interactions. The usage script contains four steps in sequence. First, the user visits the home page of the nopCommerce store and browses to the books category in the store. The user then selects a book to view the details and, finally, adds that book to the cart. In between each two user interactions we use a randomly distributed think time between 500 milliseconds and 1 second. The maximum number of users is limited to 100 concurrent users. As performance requirements we prescribe that, in 99% of cases, the response times must not exceed the value of one second. Each experiment is executed for 10 minutes with a preceding warm-up time of 2 minutes and a corresponding cool-down phase.

	expected	obtained
Performance Problem	⚐	⚐
├ Application Hiccups	✓	✓
├ The Ramp	✓	✓
└ Continuously Violated Req.	⚐	⚐
└ Traffic Jam	⚐	⚐
├ Database Congestion	✓	✓
└ One Lane Bridge	⚐	⚐
└ Dispensable Sync.	⚐	⚐

⚐ problem detected ✓ problem not detected

Figure 7.23.: Results overview

7.3.2. Discussion of Results

As described in the previous section, we injected a Dispensable Synchronization anti-pattern into the nopCommerce application. For the performance problem taxonomy used in this case study, Figure 7.23 shows the expected as well as the actual detection results of DynamicSpotter applied on nopCommerce.

As we can see, the diagnostics results of DynamicSpotter coincide with the expectation. As first step, DynamicSpotter detected a performance problem in the shopping cart interaction of the nopCommerce application. The response times of the shopping cart service under a high load intensity of 100 concurrent users are depicted in Figure 7.24a. The response times show a typical, periodic pattern indicating that user requests pile up at a bottleneck. Overall, the response times continuously violate the performance requirements by exceeding the response time threshold. The cumulative distribution function of these response times in Figure 7.24b illustrates the performance requirement violation. In particular, we see that the 99% percentile of the respone times has a value of 7 seconds which is significantly larger then the required threshold of 1 second. Based on this observation and the continuity of the performance requirement violation, DynamicSpotter detected a Performance Problem caused by a Continuously Violated Requirements anti-pattern in the shopping cart service. In the remaining services of nopCommerce, DynamicSpotter did not detect any performance problem.

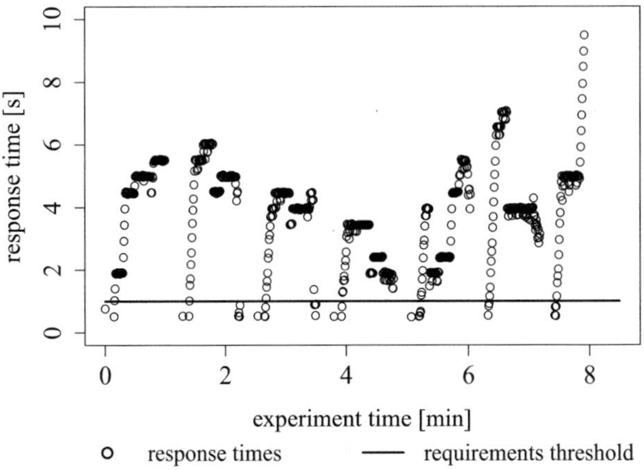

(a) Response times

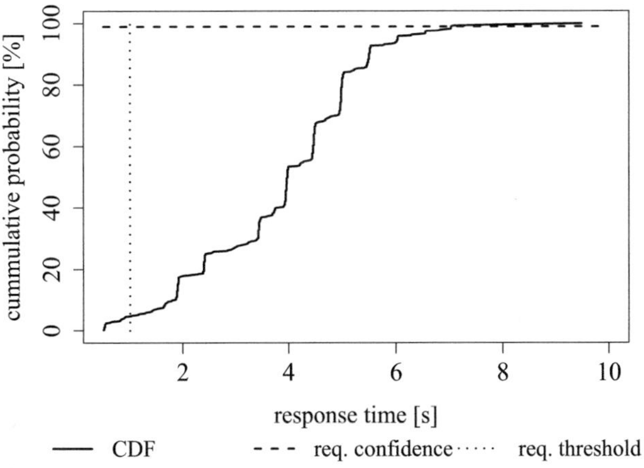

(b) Cumulative distribution function (CDF)

Figure 7.24.: Performance Problem detection: shopping cart interaction

As the response times exceed the threshold in more than 50% of cases, the Application Hiccups detection heuristic did not detect periodic hiccups. Figure 7.25 shows the detection results of the Ramp detection heuristic. The graph shows the mean response times with their confidence intervals for the four single-user experiments conducted by the Time Window detection strategy of the Ramp heuristic. In between the individual single-user experiments the heuristic applied high-load experiments to provoke a potential Ramp anti-pattern. However, as we can see in Figure 7.25, the response times do not increase with the operation time. Consequently, the Ramp anti-pattern has not been detected.

On the next level of the performance problem taxonomy, DynamicSpotter investigated the Traffic Jam anti-pattern. The response times of the shopping cart interaction in dependence on the load intensity are depicted in Figure 7.26a. The mean response times and the corresponding confidence intervals are shown in Figure 7.26b. In both figures, we can observe linear growth in the response times when increasing the load intensity. Furthermore, Figure 7.26b shows that the confidence intervals of the response times are very narrow and do not overlap under different load intensities. This means that the corresponding t-Tests of the Traffic Jam heuristic confirm a statistically significant increase in the response times. Consequently, the Traffic Jam heuristic successfully identified an instance of the Traffic Jam anti-pattern.

With respect to the Database congestion anti-pattern, DynamicSpotter did neither observe a high CPU utilization at the Database Node (cf. Figure 7.27a), nor identified a rise in locking times with increasing load intensity. Hence, DynamicSpotter did not detect a Database Congestion anti-pattern. The CPU utilization of the Application Node (cf. Figure 7.27a) stagnates at approximately 50%. Consequently, the response time threshold that is dynamically caluclated by the OLB detection heuristic is relatively low compared to the significantly increasing response times of the shopping cart interaction (cf. Figure 7.27b). Therefore, the OLB detection heuristic reported an occurrence of the OLB anti-pattern in the shopping cart service. Conducting an OLB analysis on the synchronization scope, DynamicSpotter successfully identified the injected, synchronized method as the root cause of the detected performance problem. In particular, the injected method dominated the response times of the shopping cart service.

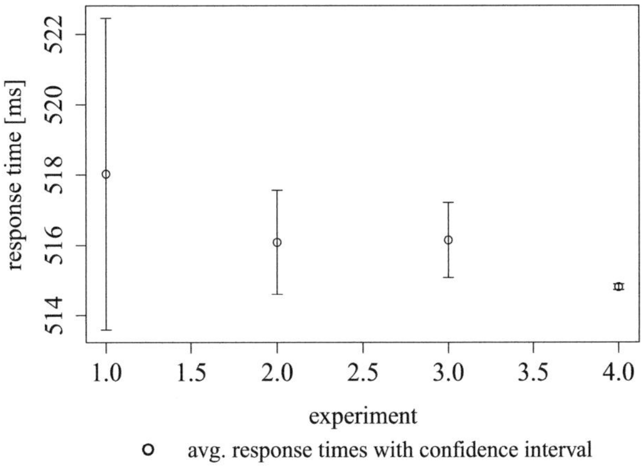

Figure 7.25.: Ramp detection: shopping cart interaction

7.3.3. Conclusions on Validation Questions

In this case study, we analyzed the applicability of the APPD approach on a target system that has been developed for and runs on a run-time environment other than Java.

With respect to validation question *VQ 1.1*, once more, we have shown that the SPAs along the path from the OLB anti-patterns to the root of the performance problem taxonomy are detectable by measurement. This observation analogously applies to validation question *VQ 2.1*, showing that the corresponding path in the performance problem taxonomy is appropriate for performance problems in real applications. Regarding other anti-patterns like messaging-related or database-related SPAs, we cannot draw any conclusions from this case study, as only a Dispensable Synchronization anti-pattern has been injected and analyzed. The main focus of this case study was on the validation of validation question *VQ 1.2* with respect to the aspect whether APPD is able to abstract from specific technologies used by the SUT. From the successful conducting of this case study, we can draw the conclusion that, in general, APPD is generic with respect to the underlying technologies of the SUT. Thereby, APPD was applicable to a .NET application without

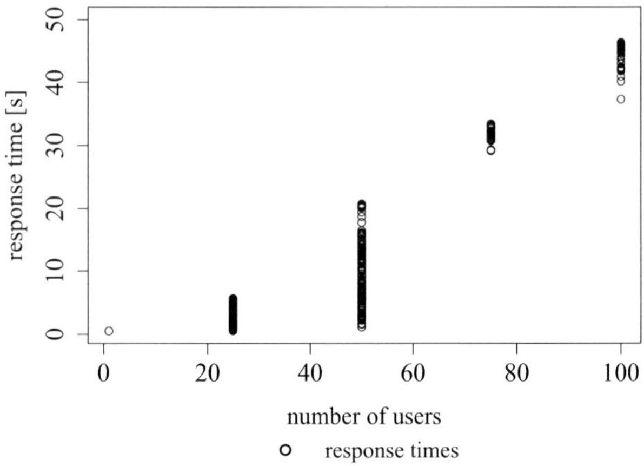

(a) Traffic Jam detection: Response times

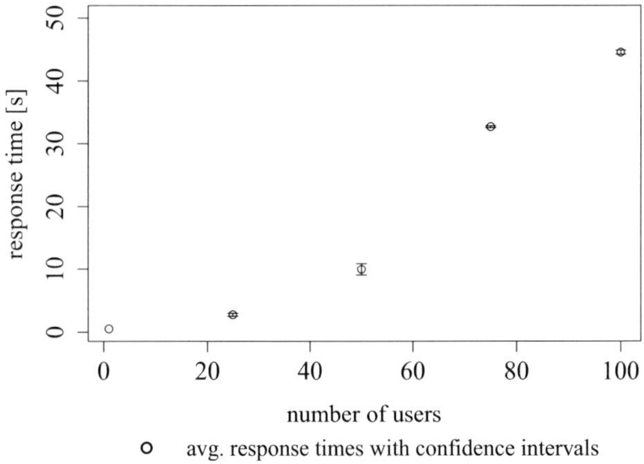

(b) Traffic Jam detection: Confidence intervals

Figure 7.26.: Results on Problem Diagnostics (1)

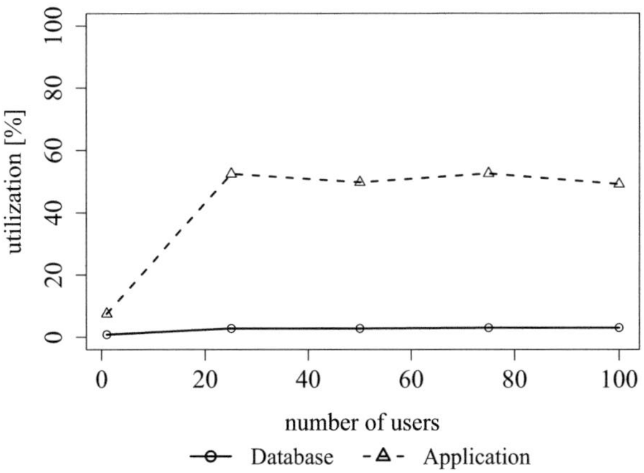

(a) CPU Utilization

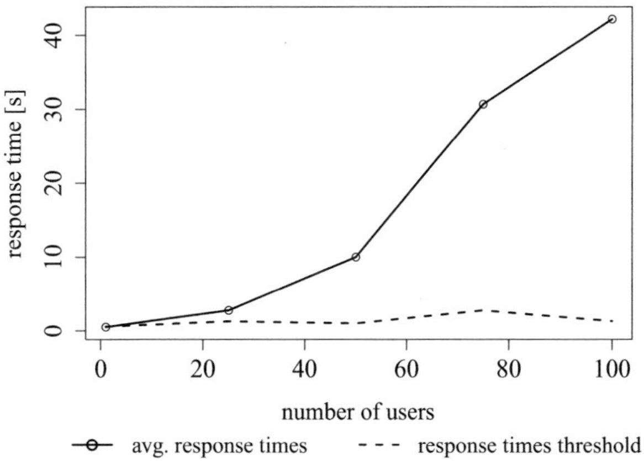

(b) OLB Detection: Response times (shopping cart interaction) and threshold

Figure 7.27.: Results on Problem Diagnostics (2)

any need of adopting the detection heuristics or any other core concepts of APPD. However, this conclusion only applies on systems and common technologies within the domain of enterprise software systems. In particular, we cannot make any statements about the applicability of APPD to software systems beyond that domain.

This case study clearly showed the dependency of APPD on the availability of proper instrumentation and measurement tools. As the .NET community, compared to the Java community, is rather closed and focused on commerce, there are only little or no free instrumentation and measurement tools. The lack of proper (free) instrumentation and measurement tools for .NET was the main challenge in this case study for a successful application of APPD on nopCommerce. Though we found a way to extend our tool AIM for .NET applications, due to license limitations, we were not able to fully support the IaM Description model of P^2D^2M for .NET applications. However, by providing a proof of concept, we can conclude that, in principle with a proper license and enough time for development, an instrumentation and measurement tool for .NET can be built that is similar to corresponding tools in Java (e.g. Kieker (van Hoorn et al., 2012), DiSL (Marek et al., 2012), AIM (Wert et al., 2015a), etc.) and, thus, fully supports the IaM Description part of our P^2D^2M model. In particular, the limitation of instrumentation in this case study was not due to insufficient expressiveness of the IaM Description part of P^2D^2M (*VQ 4.1*). On the contrary, this case study further validated the expressiveness of P^2D^2M. On the one hand, the detection heuristics, which are described with the corresponding sub-models of P^2D^2M, were generically applicable on an entirely different context compared to the TPC-W case study. This shows the expressiveness (*VQ 4.1*) as well as the generalisability (*VQ 4.2*) of the experimentation, IaM and data representation sub-models of P^2D^2M. On the other hand, the ME Description part of P^2D^2M provides a sufficient expressiveness to capture the system-specific information in the .NET scenario (*VQ 4.2*).

Due to limitations of the .NET run-time, in this case study, we were not able to apply dynamically adaptable instrumentation. Instead, we realized the SSE concept by means of restarting the target application for each change in the instrumentation state. Compared to dynamically adaptable instrumentation, restart-based instrumentation is considerably less efficient, which is reflected in the execution time. Although in this case study a smaller performance problem taxonomy has been used as in the TPC-W case study, the diagnostics run of DynamicSpotter took 4 hours and 40 minutes. Hence, with respect to validation question *VQ 3.2*, we can draw the conclusion that a dynamic realization of the SSE concept is more efficient than a restart-based realization with static instrumentation. Nevertheless, this case study shows that the SSE concept can be realized by different means without affecting the quality of the diagnostics process of APPD, except for the diagnostics duration. In this way, we positively validated the automation of APPD (*VQ 6.1*) in scenarios where dynamically adaptable instrumentation is not possible. Thereby, we had to invest a higher up-front effort due to the lack of proper measurement tools. However, our efforts of extending AIM for the .NET environment belongs to the category of one time tasks (cf. Section 3.1). In particular, the resulting measurement tools can be reused in different contexts.

7.4. Case Study: Industrial Large-scale System

In the TPC-W and the nopCommerce case studies (cf. Section 7.2 and Section 7.3) we applied the APPD approach to mid-size enterprise applications (less than 1 million of LOC). Furthermore, both TPC-W and nopCommerce were from the same domain of applications as both applications constitute an e-commerce solution. In this case study, we evaluate the APPD approach on a large-scale application (more than 5 millions of LOC) that is from the domain of enterprise resource management solutions. In particular, we are interested whether APPD, including all its integral parts, is able to handle the high complexity and scale of the target application's code.

Due to reasons of confidentiality, in this case study, we do not provide details on the target application that would provide insights on the vendor or identity of the application. Furthermore, all measurements and performance-related values in this section are normalized by presenting all time values in normalized time units (ntu).

7.4.1. Experiment Design

In the following, we describe the characteristics of the target application that are of interest for this case study. Furthermore, we describe the experiment setup.

7.4.1.1. The Application Under Test: Industrial Large-scale System

The SUT investigated in this case study is an industrially used, Java-based enterprise resource management application. Comprising more than 5 millions of LOC, the ILS application constitutes a large and complex application that meets our requirements for the scalability evaluation of the APPD approach. As ILS has a huge user basis (in the order of millions of users), performance and especially scalability is a crucial extra-functional requirement for ILS. Deployed in a data center, the ILS must be able to serve hundreds of thousands to millions of users simultaneously without considerable, negative effects on performance. Therefore, ILS is an application that is particularly interesting for performance problem diagnostics. As ILS is built upon common Java-technologies like Java Servlets, Enterprise JavaBeans, and SQL over JDBC, the application is representative for other Java-based enterprise applications.

7.4.1.2. Experiment Setup

The measurement environment of this case study comprises four physical nodes. On the Application Node we use JBoss™ as the application server that is the container for the application logic component of the ILS. Analogously to the setup in the TPC-W case study (cf. Section 7.2), besides the target application, an AIM agent runs within the application server to enable instrumentation and measurement of the application under test. The ILS application access a high-performance database that runs on a dedicated Database Node. The AIM component on the Database Node is responsible for sampling hardware resource statistics (e.g. CPU utilization). As load generator we use HP LoadRunner™ that is deployed on a dedicated Load Driver Node. Finally, we use a separate Measurement Node for DynamicSpotter that controls load generation, instrumentation and collection of measurement data.

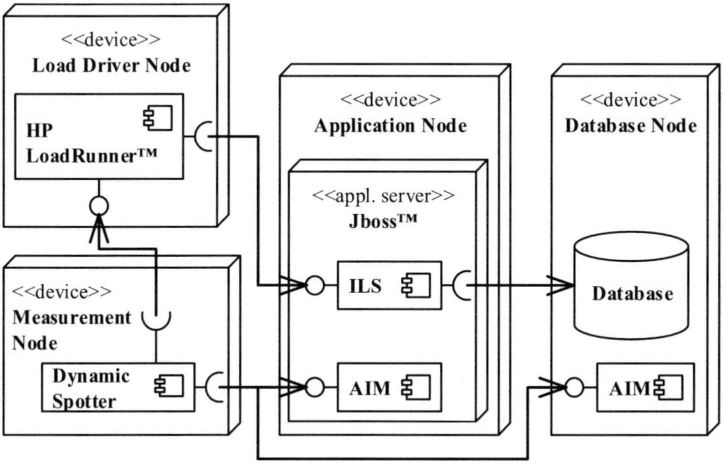

Figure 7.28.: Experiment setup

As the usage behaviour for load generation we use a LoadRunner™ script that has been provided by the performance testing team of the ILS application. The script comprises a fix sequence of six user interactions, each containing a call to a service of the target application. In between the user interactions, the LoadRunner™ script contains a randomly distributed think time between 80% and 120% of a basis value of T_t normalized time units (ntu). Due to reasons of confidentiality, we denote the ILS services as *Service 1 - Service 6*. For the ILS services, we define the performance requirement that in 95% of cases the response times of the services must not exceed a threshold of R_t ntu. In our setup, the performance requirement shell be valid for a load intensity up to 500 concurrent users.

For the configuration of DynamicSpotter, we use the entire performance problem taxonomy covered by the PPEP instance that has been derived in Section 4.4.2. The used taxonomy is depicted in the left column of Figure 7.29. Each experiment that is executed by DynamicSpotter has a duration of E_t ntu with additional warm-up and cool-down phases of a third of E_t.

7.4.2. Discussion of Results

Applying DynamicSpotter on the ILS, we encountered interesting effects and promising diagnostics results. Both are discussed in the following. We first give an outline on the study execution followed by a detailed discussion of the results.

Overview on Study Execution

Similar to the TPC-W case study, the ILS case study has been conducted in three iterations. In the first iteration, we applied DynamicSpotter on the described setup of ILS using the provided load script. As shown in Figure 7.29, DynamicSpotter detected a Performance Problem that is manifested in an Application Hiccups anti-pattern. The applied performance problem taxonomy and the set of detection heuristics created in this thesis do not cover more detailed manifestations of the Application Hiccups anti-pattern. Therefore, based on the DynamicSpotter results in the first iteration, we continued the performance problem diagnostics by manually analyzing the target system as well as the experiment configuration. Thereby, we came to the conclusion that the observed hiccups have been caused by an improperly chosen configuration of the load script. After slightly modifying the configuration of the load generation, we started a second diagnostics run of DynamicSpotter. In this second iteration, DynamicSpotter identified a performance problem that has been caused by a database call manifestation of the OLB anti-pattern limiting the performance of one service of the ILS. Due to the complexity of the ILS application and missing expert knowledge about the specific details of the implementation of ILS, we were not ale to fix the identified instance of the OLB anti-pattern. In order to show that the anti-pattern reported by DynamicSpotter as the root cause for the observed performance problem is a true positive, we removed the corresponding interaction from the load script. With the modified script, we applied DynamicSpotter a third time whereby, this time, no performance problem has been reported by DynamicSpotter.

	Iteration 1	Iteration 2	Iteration 3
Performance Problem	⚑	⚑	✓
— Application Hiccups	⚑	✓	✗
— The Ramp	✓	✓	✗
— Continuously Violated Req.	✓	⚑	✗
—— Traffic Jam	✗	⚑	✗
——— Excessive Messaging	✗	✓	✗
———— The Blob	✗	✗	✗
———— Empty Semi Trucks	✗	✗	✗
——— Database Congestion	✗	✓	✗
———— The Stifle	✗	✗	✗
———— Expensive DB Call	✗	✗	✗
——— One Lane Bridge	✗	⚑	✗
———— Database OLB	✗	⚑	✗
———— Dispensable Sync.	✗	✓	✗

⚑ problem detected ✓ problem not detected ✗ skipped analysis

Figure 7.29.: Overview on results

In the following, we discuss the results of the individual study iterations in more detail.

Iteration 1

In the first iteration of applying DynamicSpotter to ILS, performance problems have been detected in all services provided by the ILS application. Representatively for all services, the response times over experiment time for Service 1 and Service 5 are depicted in Figure 7.30a and Figure 7.30b, respectively. The graphs show that most requests have a low response time

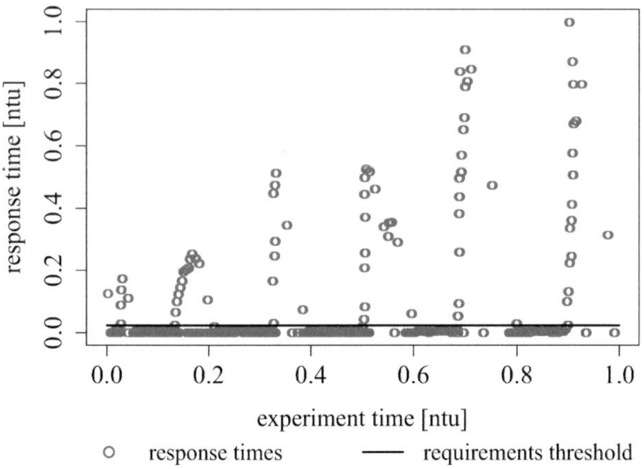

(a) Service 1: response times

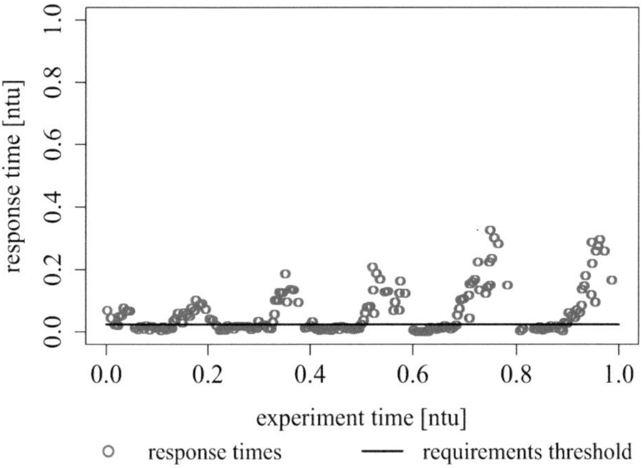

(b) Service 5: response times

Figure 7.30.: Performance Problem detection (1): Service 1 and Service 5 (Iteration 1)

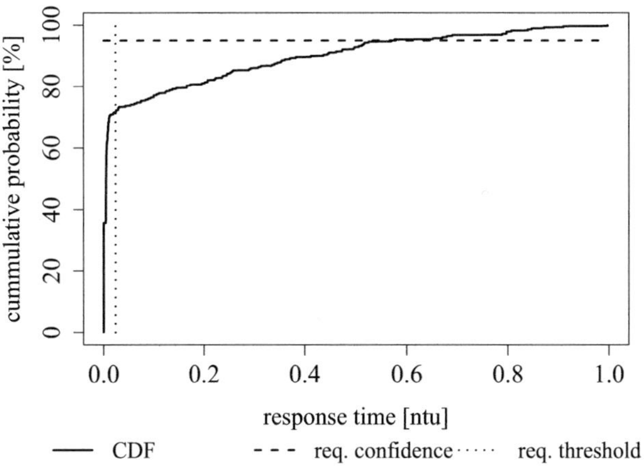

(a) Service 1: cumulative distribution function

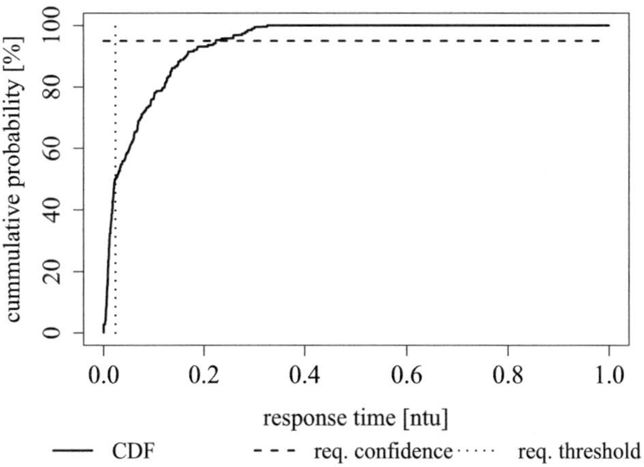

(b) Service 5: cumulative distribution function

Figure 7.31.: Performance Problem detection (2): Service 1 and Service 5 (Iteration 1)

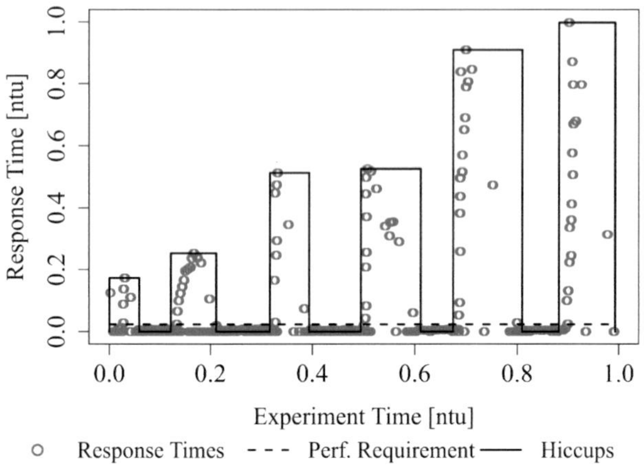

(a) Service 1: hiccups

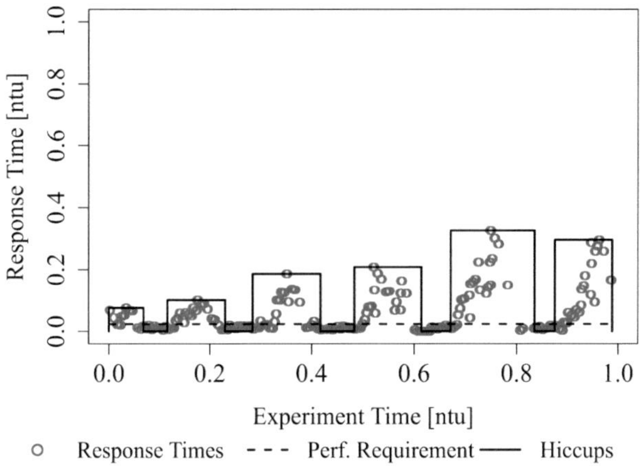

(b) Service 5: hiccups

Figure 7.32.: Performance Problem detection (3): Service 1 and Service 5 (Iteration 1)

that lies under the performance requirement threshold. However, periodically, the response times increase significantly for a short period of time, which in sum leads to a violation of performance requirements. Considering the corresponding cumulative distribution functions (cf. Figure 7.31a and Figure 7.31b), we see that in both cases the median of the response times is slightly below the requirements threshold. However, a long tail in the response times distribution leads to the violation of the performance requirement. While the threshold has a value of 0.03 ntu, the 95% response time percentiles of Service 1 and Service 5 have a value of 0.58 ntu and 0.24 ntu, respectively. Based on this analysis, DynamicSpotter detected a performance problem in each service of ILS.

Continuing the diagnostics run with the Application Hiccups heuristic, DynamicSpotter observed the hiccups behaviour as shown in Figure 7.32a and Figure 7.32b for the two considered services. In both response time series, DynamicSpotter detected six hiccups that map to the previously mentioned periodic increases in response times. Again, this applies to all six analyzed services of ILS, yielding a positive detection of the Application Hiccups anti-pattern. As the response times in between the hiccups are below the response time threshold, the Continuously Violated Requirements anti-pattern has not been detected. Neither has the Ramp anti-pattern been detected. At this point, DynamicSpotter terminated its diagnostics process as no further, detailed heuristics for hiccups-related anti-patterns were available.

We resumed with a manual diagnostics of the root cause for the identified Application Hiccups anti-pattern. Thereto, we manually repeated the load test while additionally measuring the CPU utilization on both nodes, application and database node. The resulting CPU utilization depicted over experiment time (cf. Figure 7.33a) exhibits an interesting pattern. Both curves (application and database CPU utilization) exhibit a wavy pattern, whereby the peaks and troughs of both curves are inverse to each other. Hence, a peak of the database node's CPU utilization is accompanied by a trough of the CPU utilization curve of the application server, and vice versa.

Comparing the response time hiccups in Figure 7.32a and Figure 7.32b with the wave patterns of the CPU utilizations, we see that the frequency of hiccups is the same as the peak frequency in the CPU utilization curves. Hence, it can be assumed that the observed response time hiccups are closely related to the CPU utilizations. As the peaks of the database node's CPU

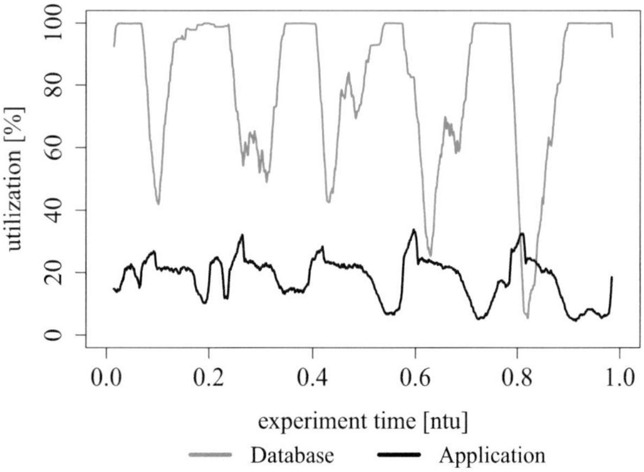

(a) CPU Utilizations: hiccups

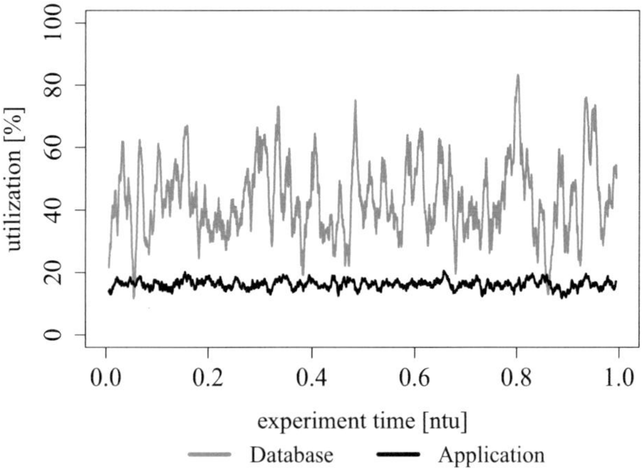

(b) CPU Utilizations: resolved hiccups

Figure 7.33.: Manual analysis: CPU utilizations of database and application server utilization have a value of 100%, the database constitutes the bottleneck in this scenario. However, the periodically high CPU utilization on the database node is rather a symptom than a root cause. If the processing capacity on the database node would be just to small, the corresponding CPU utilization would have been permanently high under a stable load intensity. However, the wave pattern is rather an indicator that the generated virtual users are synchronized which leads to temporary overload situations on the database which, in turn, again leads to reinforced synchronization. Combining this cyclic cause-effect relationship with a closed workload for load generation leads to the observed oscillating behaviour. Assuming that this consideration applies in the investigated scenario, this would mean that load generation is not properly configured for our experiment setup. Manually analyzing the used load script, we observed that the think time distribution and the observed time between the occurrences of two subsequent hiccups is in the same range. This observation strengthens our presumption that the oscillating effect is caused by the load script (or configuration of load generation) rather than by the ILS application. In order to mitigate the oscillating effect, we increased the variance in the think time distribution. Thereto, we configure LoadRunner™ to draw a random value within the range of 50% and 150% of the base value T_t (instead of 80% - 120%). In this way, user requests are more unifomly distributed on the time line, while the mean load intensity stays the same as before. Repeating the load test with the modified load script, we obtained CPU utilizations as depicted in Figure 7.33b. For both servers (application and database server) the major waves in the CPU utilization curves disappeared. The utilization on the application server is very stable at approximately 18% utilization. By contrast, the utilization on the database server varies considerably between 30% and 80%, however, there is no periodic pattern observable. The modified load script constitutes the basis for the second iteration of the case study.

Iteration 2

Using the modified load script, we applied DynamicSpotter a second time on our setup of the ILS. As illustrated in the second column (i.e. Iteration 2) in Figure 7.29, DynamicSpotter again detected a Performance Problem. However, this time, no Application Hiccups anti-pattern has been observed but an instance of the Continuously Violated Requirements anti-pattern.

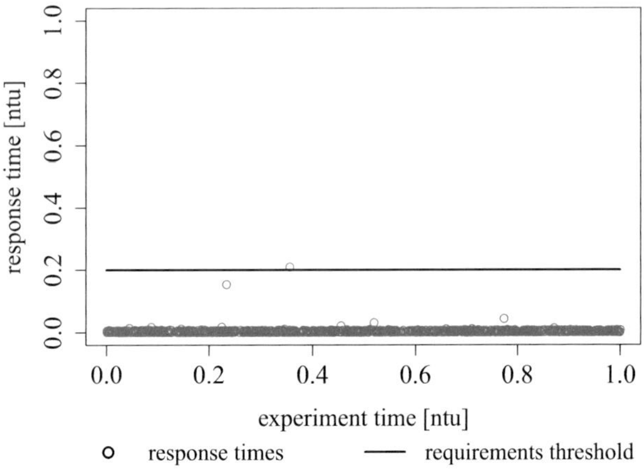

(a) Service 1: response times

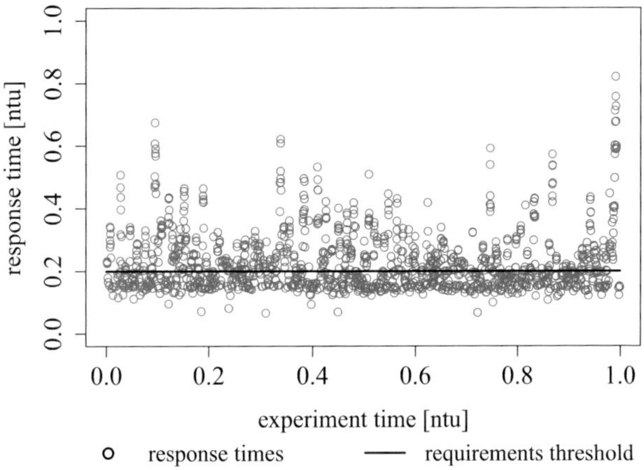

(b) Service 5: response times

Figure 7.34.: Performance Problem detection (1): Service 1 and Service 5 (Iteration 2)

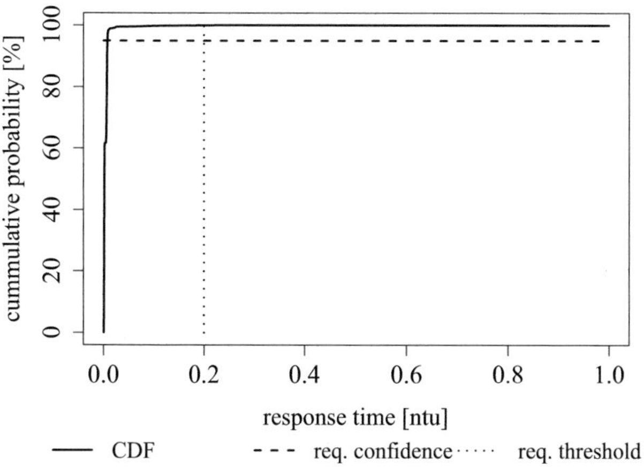

(a) Service 1: cumulative distribution function

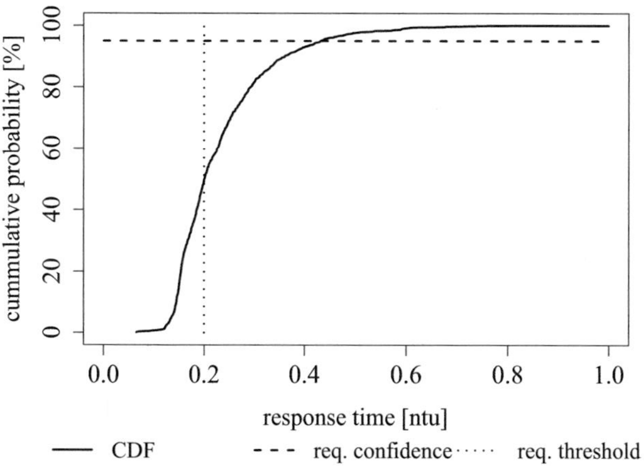

(b) Service 5: cumulative distribution function

Figure 7.35.: Performance Problem detection (2): Service 1 and Service 5 (Iteration 2)

Analogously to the first iteration, Figure 7.34 and Figure 7.35 show the response times over experiment time, as well as the corresponding cumulative distribution functions for Service 1 and Service 5 of the ILS application under a high load of 500 concurrent users.

Although the response times of Service 1 (cf. Figure 7.34a) occasionally exceed the response time threshold, prevailingly, they are below the threshold. Considering Figure 7.35a, we see that the distribution of response times of Service 1 meets the specified performance requirements. In particular, the 95% percentile, with a value cmaller than 0.01 ntu, is considerably smaller than the requirement of 0.2 ntu. Except for Service 5, the remaining services of ILS show a similar behaviour as Service 1, hence, they meet the performance requirements. By contrast, the response times of Service 5 frequently exceed the specified response time threshold (cf. Figure 7.34b). Considering the corresponding cumulative distribution function in Figure 7.35b reveals that in approximately 50% of cases the response times are greater than the threshold. With a value of 0.45 ntu the 95% percentile is more than twice as large as the allowed threshold of 0.2 ntu. Consequently, DynamicSpotter detected a performance problem in Service 5 of the ILS application. As the response times do not exhibit any periodic patterns or any considerable trends, DynamicSpotter neither detected an Application Hiccups anti-pattern nor a Ramp instance. By contrast, a Continuously Violated Requirements anti-pattern has been detected, resulting in an investigation of the Traffic Jam anti-pattern.

The results of the Traffic Jam investigation for Service 5 are depicted in Figure 7.36. The measured response time values over load intensity (cf. Figure 7.36a) show a significant increase in the variance of the response times with increasing load intensity. Though the minimal response times decrease slightly with increasing load intensity, the maximum response times grow considerably. Considering the average response times with corresponding confidence intervals provided by the Traffic Jam heuristic (cf. Figure 7.36b), we observe very narrow confidence intervals with average response times that grow with the load intensity. As the confidence intervals under different load intensities do not overlap, the t-Tests of the Traffic Jam heuristic show a statistically significant increase in the response times. Based on this observation, DynamicSpotter detected a Traffic Jam anti-pattern in Service 5 of the ILS.

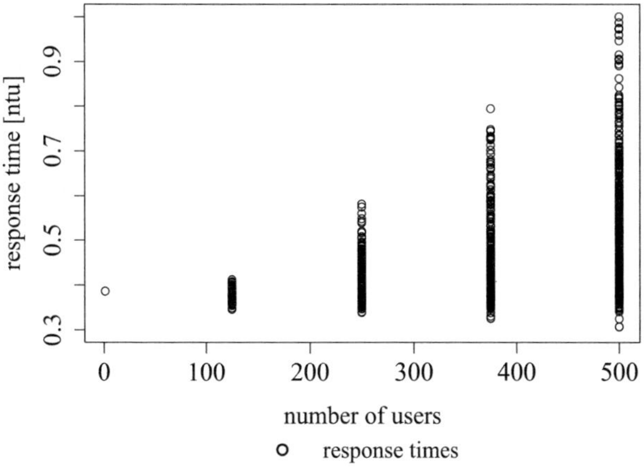

(a) Service 5: response times

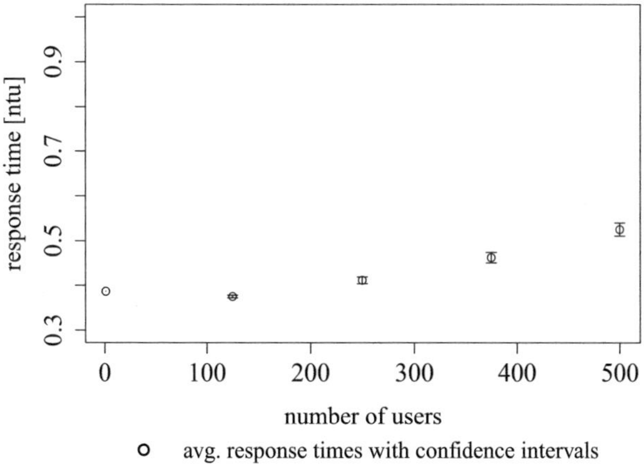

(b) Service 5: confidence interfals

Figure 7.36.: Traffic Jam detection: Service 5

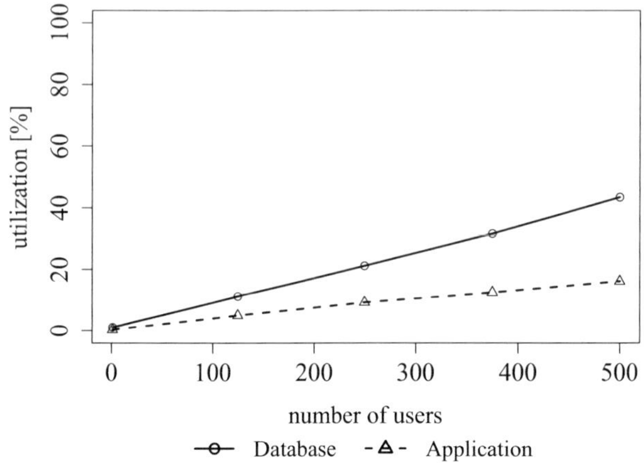

Figure 7.37.: CPU utilization

Consequently, DynamicSpotter resumed its diagnostics with the Excessive Messaging, Database Congestion and OLB heuristics. As the ILS application does not use messaging technologies for inter-component communication, DynamicSpotter did not detect an Excessive Messaging anti-pattern. Neither the Database Congestion anti-pattern has been detected because, in average, the CPU utilization of the database node does not exceed 50% (cf. Figure 7.37) and database locking times do not grow considerably with the load intensity. However, DynamicSpotter detected an OLB instance in Service 5. Figure 7.37 shows that, with respect to CPU utilization, non of the servers is utilized to capacity. Although, the utilizations ,as expected, grow with the load intensity, under the maximum load of 500 concurrent users, the application and database CPU utilizations are still below 20% and 50%, respectively. The dashed line in Figure 7.38a, illustrates the response time threshold that has been calculated by the OLB detection heuristic by means of the described progression of the CPU utilizations using queueing theory (cf. Section 6.3.6). The solid line representing the average response times of Service 5 crosses the threshold curve at a load of 370 users. Hence, for high load intensities the increase in response times cannot be explained by queueing theory anymore. Therefore, DynamicSpotter detected an OLB anti-pattern in Service 5.

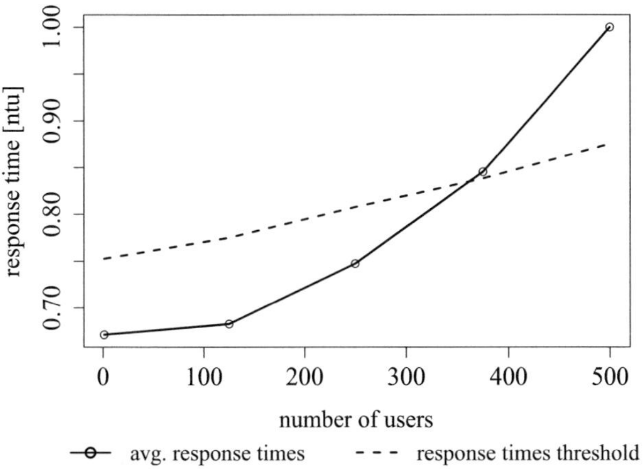

(a) Service 5: response times and threshold

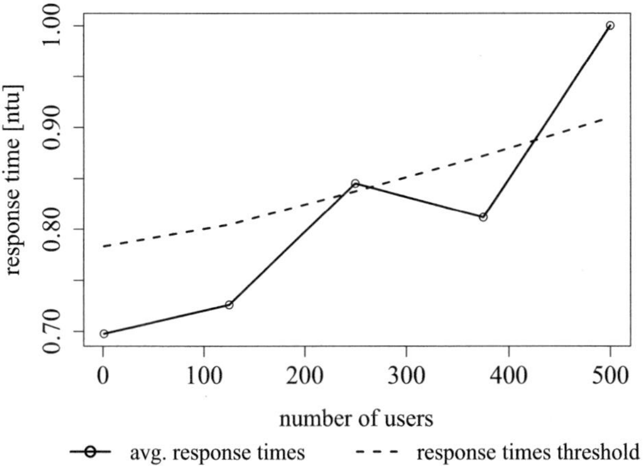

(b) Query operation: response times and threshold

Figure 7.38.: OLB detection

Diagnosing the root cause for the identified OLB instance, DynamicSpotter could not locate any software bottlenecks in the application logic of the ILS. However, applying the OLB heuristic on the database access scope, DynamicSpotter uncovered a database query whose response time behaviour is similar to the response times of Service 5. Figure 7.38b shows the OLB detection results for the *executeQuery* operation executing a specific SQL query. Again, the response times exceed the calculated threshold curve under a high load intensity. Furthermore, the response time of this database query dominates the response time of Service 5, proving that the identified database query constitutes the root cause for the uncovered performance problem.

Iteration 3

In order to show that the OLB instance identified in the second iteration is a true positive, in the third iteration, we tried to solve the problem. However, due to missing expert knowledge in the complex internals of the ILS application, we were not able to solve the problem ourselves without breaking the functionality of the application. Alternatively, we replaced the identified guilty service of ILS to show that the problem identified by DynamicSpotter actually constitutes a performance problem. On the modified ILS, we again applied DynamicSpotter. This time, DynamicSpotter did not report any performance problems. All services met the specified performance requirements. In this way, we have shown that the performance problem observed in Iteration 2 has been caused by the replaced service. This, in turn, shows that the diagnostics result of DynamicSpotter has been correct.

7.4.3. Conclusions on Validation Questions

In this case study, we applied the APPD approach on a large-scale application. On the one hand, the results of this study confirm the findings from the previous case studies (TPC-W, Section 7.2 and nopCommerce, Section 7.3). On the other hand, this case study provides new insights on limitations and assumptions on the applicability of APPD. In this section, we draw conclusions from the results of this case study to the validation questions under investigation (cf. Section 7.1.1).

With respect to validation question *VQ 1.1*, this case study once more showed that the investigated SPAs are detectable by a measurement-based approach. In particular, in this case study, an OLB manifestation as well as an Application Hiccups anti-pattern (though caused by the load script) have been detected. Compared to the previous case studies, in this study we evaluated an additional dimension of generalisability (cf. *VQ 1.2*). The results of this case study show that the APPD approach is able to handle different scales of the target systems, including large, industrial applications. With respect to the diagnostics accuracy of APPD (cf. *VQ 1.3*), this case study revealed an interesting insight. On the one hand, in the second iteration of the ILS case study we have shown that DynamicSpotter accurately detected a performance problem and uncovered its root cause. However, the first iteration of the case study shows that the diagnostics quality of the APPD approach highly depends on the quality and appropriateness of the used load description and configuration. Though according to queueing theory, closed workloads guarantee a stable state of the SUT (i.e. no infinite growth of queues), they can lead to adverse effects that do not represent real situations. In this case study, we have seen that a closed workload may induce an oscillating behaviour. Such a behaviour may result in symptoms that, accordingly to the performance problem taxonomy, do not reflect the actual root cause of the existing performance problem in the SUT. Due to the assumption of APPD that experiments are executed under a stable, non-oscillating load intensity (cf. Section 3.3), in Iteration 1, DynamicSpotter wrongly identified an Application Hiccups anti-pattern in the ILS application. Actually, ILS contained an OLB anti-pattern that leads to continuously violated requirements. However, the oscillating behaviour was induced by the feedback effect of the closed workload. Hence, properly creating and configuring a representative load description is a crucial factor for the accuracy of APPD.

Regarding validation question *VQ 2.1*, this case study allows for a conclusion that is twofold. After having solved the problem with the load description in Iteration 1, the performance problem taxonomy elaborated in this thesis represented the cause-effect-chain (path from root cause to root node of the taxonomy) of the uncovered OLB manifestation very well. However, in this case study we also experienced that other external effects, such as the utilized load script, can affect the actual cause-effect relationship. Hence, root causes of certain performance problems may result in unexpected symptoms. In the concrete example of Iteration 1, the OLB instance caused an Application

Hiccups anti-pattern, which is not covered by the elaborated performance problem taxonomy. Thus, such external effects should be avoided as much as possible when applying APPD. In particular, the challenge of avoiding external effects is an interesting topic for future work.

With respect to Validation Goals 3-6, this case study confirms the conclusions from the previous two case studies. The expressiveness of the P^2D^2M was sufficient to capture the context specific information of the industrial scenario. Furthermore, the experimentation and instrumentation description part of P^2D^2M provided an adequate generalization so that all heuristics were applicable without the need for adaptation. Using AIM as instrumentation framework, the SSE concept within DynamicSpotter was fully automated. The manual efforts for preparing DynamicSpotter for the ILS application are comparable with respect to amount and type of tasks to the the TPC-W case study (cf. Section 7.2).

7.5. Controlled Experiment: Automatic Resource Demand Estimation

The end-to-end case studies for the APPD approach (Sections 7.2-7.4) inherently evaluate the feasibility of the SSE concept in the scope of performance problem diagnostics. Conducting a controlled experiment, in this section, we evaluate the SSE concept in a different experiment-based performance analysis context. In this way, we investigate the benefits of SSE and its scope of applicability.

We utilize the SSE concept to automate measurements for the derivation of resource demands that are used to calibrate an architectural performance model. Thereby, we use a *Palladio Component Model (PCM)* of TPC-W as an architectural performance model to be calibrated (cf. Section 2.2.2). By comparing different combinations of measurement tools and experimentation concepts, we evaluate the accuracy of the resource demands derived with the SSE concept against the alternatives.

In the following, we first introduce the Resource Demand Estimation (RDE) approach applied in this experiment. Subsequently, we describe the experiment design, discuss the results of the experiment and conclude with a discussion of the implications on the investigated Validation Goal 5. This experiment has been conducted as part of the supervised Bachelor's Thesis by Schulz, 2014 and has been published in Wert et al., 2015a. The following sections may contain fragments of this publication.

7.5.1. Resource Demand Estimation Approach

The Resource Demanding Service Effect Specification (RD-SEFF) of the PCM (cf. Section 2.2.2) plays a central role in this experiment, as it captures the performance-relevant behaviour of software components including abstractions of computations that consume hardware resources like CPU, I/O, etc. Hereby, the resource demands of individual computation blocks basically determine the performance behaviour of the modelled system. Hence, the quality of the resource demands that are used to calibrate a PCM model is an essential factor that affects the overall quality of the performance predictions resulting from a (simulative or analytical) solution of the PCM model. Thus, properly conducting resource demand estimation is important to achieve accurate performance prediction results.

In an evolutionary application scenario of PCM, measurement-based derivation of resource demands is a common approach under the assumption that a runnable target system already exists. In a CPU-bound application, the response times of individual methods under a single-user load intensity can be used to calculate a good estimate for the actual CPU demand. Thus, given a method m that calls the methods $m' \in M_C$ as well as the corresponding response times $r(m)$ and $r(m')$, respectively, the exclusive CPU demand $d(m)$ of method m is:

$$d(m) = r(m) - \sum_{m' \in M_C} r(m') \qquad (7.1)$$

Based on this consideration, in this experiment we use the following approach to automatically derive resource demands by measurements. Let us assume that we are interested in the detailed CPU demands along the call path of a single service of the target application. Our resource demand estimation approach comprises four sequential, conceptual steps:

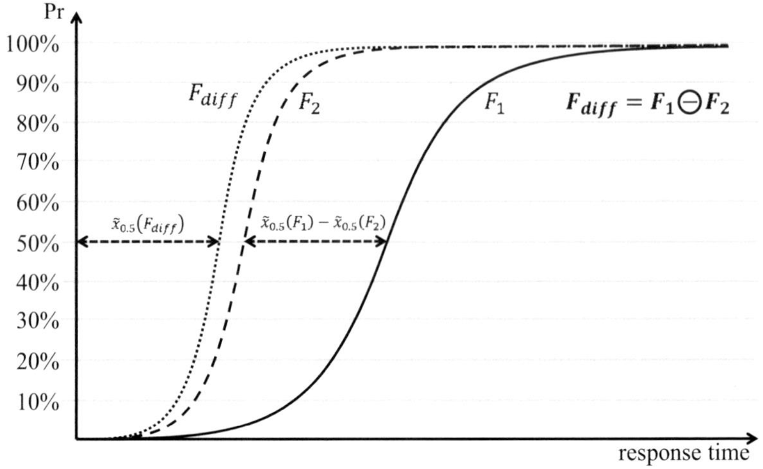

Figure 7.39.: Subtraction of distributions (Schulz, 2014)

1. *Call tree derivation:* In the first step, we derive a call tree for the service of interest. This requires a full instrumentation of the target system to capture all required information for reconstructing the call tree. However, as we do not retrieve performance metrics in this step, the overhead of the excessive instrumentation can be ignored.

2. *Response time measurements:* Based on the call tree derived in the first step, we retrieve a sample of response times for each method along the call tree.

3. *Resource demand calculation:* Finally, we derive the exclusive resource demands for each method in the call tree by using the call tree structure and the measured response times to calculate the difference shown in Equation 7.1.

As the second step provides a sample of response times for each method, in the last step of the approach we need a way to subtract samples. A sample is an empirical representation of a distribution. Hence, in order to enable the subtraction in the third step, we define a subtraction operation $\ominus$ on samples as follows: Let S_1 and S_2 be two samples from the distributions F_1 and F_2.

The difference $F_{diff} = F_1 \ominus F_2$ is defined over the set of p-quantiles $\tilde{x_p}$ of the distribution functions:

$$F_{diff} = F_1 \ominus F_2 : \quad \tilde{x_p}\left(F_{diff}\right) = \tilde{x_p}\left(F_1\right) - \tilde{x_p}\left(F_2\right), \quad p \in (0, 1) \quad (7.2)$$

The difference function $\ominus$ is illustrated in Figure 7.39 by means of cumulative distribution functions. Analogously, the sum function $F_{sum} = F_1 \oplus F_2$ is defined by the following equation:

$$F_{sum} = F_1 \oplus F_2 : \quad \tilde{x_p}\left(F_{sum}\right) = \tilde{x_p}\left(F_1\right) + \tilde{x_p}\left(F_2\right), \quad p \in (0, 1) \quad (7.3)$$

Practically, we calculate a difference sample $S_{diff} = S_1 \ominus S_2$ from the samples S_1 and S_2 by taking a fix set of p-quantiles and applying Equation 7.2. For a method m that calls the methods $m' \in M_C$, let S_m and $S_{m'}$ be the samples of measured response times of m and $m' \in M_C$, respectively. The resource demand distribution is then approximated by the sample D_m:

$$D_m = S_m \ominus \bigoplus_{m' \in M_C} S_{m'} \quad (7.4)$$

This RDE approach constitutes a proof of concept for automatic resource demand estimation. In particular, this approach has some limitations that are subject to future research. First, this approach assumes a deterministic call tree, meaning that for the same input data the the same call tree is executed. Second, because of the definition of the subtraction and addition functions $\ominus$ and $\oplus$, this approach assumes for all methods a unimodal distribution of the response times. Relaxing these assumptions requires further research in this area. However, as RDE is not the main focus of this thesis, we abstain from further evolving the RDE approach. Furthermore, since TPC-W, as the target application in this experiment, meets the mentioned assumptions, the described RDE approach is sufficient to evaluate the scope of applicability of the SSE concept.

7.5.2. Experiment Design

In this controlled experiment, we apply different approaches to derive the resource demands for a PCM model of a target application. Thereby, we compare the resource demand accuracy of the different approaches. Hence, the different approaches constitute the controlled variables of this experiments whose influence on the accuracy is investigated. As target application we use the TPC-W benchmark as already used in Section 7.2. As explained in Section 7.2.1, TPC-W is web-commerce benchmark representing a 3-tier application. As part of the EU funded CloudScale project (Brataas et al., 2013) a PCM model of the TPC-W benchmark has been created. In this experiment, we calibrate that model with resource demands derived from our TPC-W setup using different approaches and compare the quality of the resulting performance model. In the following, we introduce the different investigated RDE scenarios and the execution procedure of the experiment.

7.5.2.1. Scenarios

While the RDE approach introduced in the previous section describes the conceptual steps to be conducted for an automatic, measurement-based RDE, it does not prescribe how to conduct the corresponding measurements. In this experiment, we analyze different experimentation and instrumentation approaches that are applied to realize the described RDE approach. Depending on the instrumentation approach, the monitoring overhead of measurement probes may significantly affect the accuracy of the derived resource demand. There are two different experimentation approaches that can be applied to realize the described RDE approach:

1. We conduct a full instrumentation of the target application while executing one single-user test that covers the first and second step of the RDE approach. This is the standard experimentation approach that does not follow the SSE concept. In particular, this experimentation approach can be conducted with any instrumentation and monitoring tool that allows a full instrumentation of the target application.

2. According to the SSE concept, we automatically execute several experiments using adaptable instrumentation to instrument each method individually in each single experiment. Consequently, this experimentation approach assumes the ability to dynamically adapt the instrumentation state of the target application.

We conduct both experimentation approaches with two different instrumentation and monitoring tools: our AIM framework (Wert et al., 2015a) and the Kieker framework (van Hoorn et al., 2012). Both approaches allow to conduct a full instrumentation of the target application at start-up of the application. Furthermore, AIM allows to dynamically adapt the instrumentation of the target application by dynamic bytecode manipulation and Java class swapping (Dmitriev, 2001). Ehlers et al. (Ehlers et al., 2011) introduce a semi-adaptive instrumentation and monitoring approach for Kieker. Hereby, semi-adaptive means that, initially, the target system is fully instrumented, but, measurement probes can be disabled if not needed. However, for each disabled probe still a minimal overhead remains for checking the state of the measurement probe. The combination of experimentation approaches and measurement tools results in four different RDE scenarios that realize the RDE approach described in the previous section:

Kieker-full: In this scenario, we use Kieker to fully instrument the target application to measure the response times of all call tree methods in one single experiment. Hence, regarding the RDE approach the first two steps are conducted as one experiment.

AIM-full: Analogously to the Kieker-full scenario, in this scenario we use AIM to fully instrument the target application. Again, only one experiment is executed to derive the resource demands.

Kieker-adaptive: In this scenario, we use the adaptive Kieker approach (Ehlers et al., 2011) with switchable measurement probes. Thus, the target application is fully instrumented with probes which can be individually disabled if not required. Utilizing the switchable probes we realize the RDE approach by automatically executing a set of experiments (one for each method of the call tree) while activating during each experiment only the probe for the corresponding method.

AIM-adaptive: In this scenario, we apply the same process as in the *Kieker-adaptive* scenario, however instead of activating and deactivating probes, we utilize AIM's capability of re-instrumenting the target application.

While the first two scenarios constitute the baselines for this experiment, the latter two scenarios follow the SSE concept by applying selective instrumentation combined with systematic experimentation.

7.5.2.2. Study Procedure

For each RDE scenario, we apply the study procedure as shown in Figure 7.40. First, resource demands are automatically derived conducting the RDE approach described in Section 7.5.1 within the corresponding RDE scenarios. In this experiment, the service of interest is the home interaction of the TPC-W application. The result is a set of resource demands for the individual methods of the corresponding call tree. These resource demands are used to calibrate the TPC-W model yielding a calibrated PCM model. Subsequently, the model is simulated with an extrapolated number of user (here: 30 users) to obtain prediction results for the end-to-end response times of the home interaction. Independently from model simulation, we conduct a reference measurement with 30 concurrent users on the corresponding TPC-W setup. Thereby, we measure the end-to-end response times of the investigated TPC-W service. All experiments (RDE derivation and reference measurement) are executed for 10 minutes with an equally distributed think time in the range of 1 to 2 seconds for each user interaction. For the PCM simulation run the PCM usage scenario is configured analogously. Finally, the prediction results are compared to the measurement data of the reference measurement in order to calculate a relative prediction error as a measure of accuracy for the different RDE scenarios. Let P be a set of predicted end-to-end response times with mean μ_P and median $\tilde{x}_{0.5}(P)$. Furthermore, let M be a set with mean μ_M and median $\tilde{x}_{0.5}(M)$ containing the end-to-end response times from the reference measurement. We define two measures for the relative prediction error, the relative mean error e_{mean} and the relative median error e_{med}:

$$e_{mean} = \left| \frac{\mu_P - \mu_M}{\mu_M} \right| \tag{7.5}$$

$$e_{med} = \left| \frac{\tilde{x}_{0.5}(P) - \tilde{x}_{0.5}(M)}{\tilde{x}_{0.5}(M)} \right| \tag{7.6}$$

We use both measures to compare the accuracy of different RDE scenarios. The more accurate an RDE scenario predicts the measured response times, the more eligible is the underlying experimentation approach.

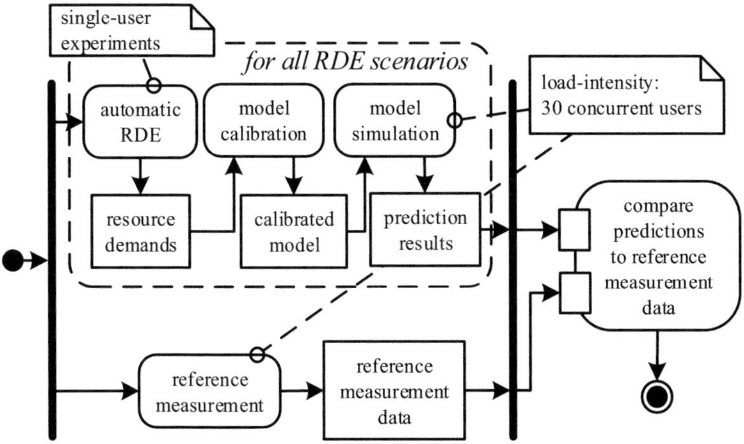

Figure 7.40.: SSE-4-RDE study procedure

7.5.3. Discussion of Results

Simulating four different PCM models that are calibrated with the resource demands from the different RDE scenarios, we obtained diverse results. Figure 7.41 shows the statistics (by means of box-plots) of the predicted response times for the four scenarios (K_f,K_a,A_f,A_a) compared to the response times from the reference measurement (R). The resource demands derived in the Kieker-full scenario yield highly dispersed, simulated response times compared to the remaining scenarios. As the *OperationExecutionProbe* of Kieker is relatively complex, it introduces a high monitoring overhead when conducting full instrumentation. Consequently, the derived resource demands exhibit a corresponding, wide-spread distribution that becomes visible through the PCM simulation results in Figure 7.41. Especially conspicuous is the long tail in the Kieker-full predictions that causes an asymmetry in the corresponding distribution. With respect to the prediction accuracy the Kieker-full scenario provides the most inaccurate resource demands. As shown in Table 7.3, the relative mean error of the predictions in the Kieker-full scenario has a value of 51.2%, and the relative median error of 42.4%, respectively. With a relative mean error of 22.2% and a median error of 25%, the resource demands in the AIM-full scenario lead to more accurate predic-

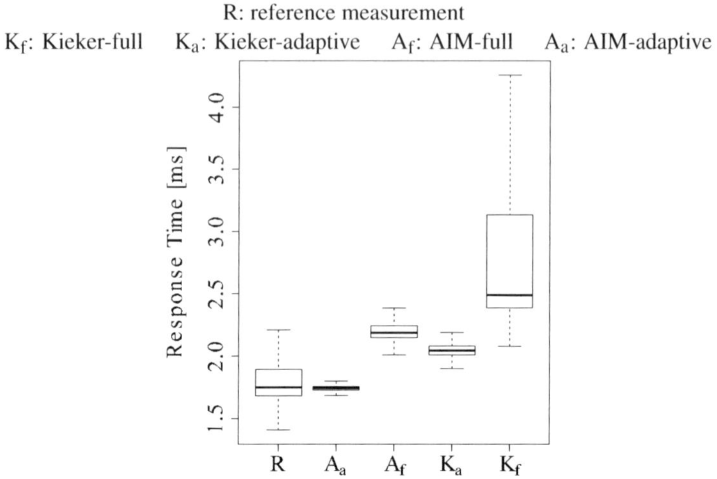

Figure 7.41.: Comparing predictions with measurements (Schulz, 2014)

tion results than with the Kieker-full scenario. This is due to the light-weight implementations of the measurement probes in AIM. In particular, as AIM allows for dynamic adaptation of instrumentation and arbitrary compositions of instrumentation instructions, the probes are kept minimalistic in AIM in order to reduce the monitoring overhead. By contrast, as Kieker's focus is not on dynamically adaptable instrumentation, its probes are packed with multiple aspects to be measured at once which results in a higher monitoring overhead as can be seen in Figure 7.41. The light-weight probes of AIM have also a positive effect on the variance of the derived resource demands, as the corresponding prediction results have a less dispersed distribution.

Following the SSE concept, both adaptive approaches (Kieker-adaptive and AIM-adaptive) perform better than the full instrumentation approaches with one single experiment. With a relative mean error of 13.9% and median error of 16.9% the Kieker-adaptive scenario provides resource demands that lead to an accurate prediction result (error significantly less than 30%, H. Koziolek, 2008). With relative errors less than 4% the AIM-adaptive scenario provides even more accurate results. Thus, we may conclude that the deactivated probes in the Kieker-adaptive scenario still introduce a small monitoring overhead which impairs the accuracy of the derived

			mean value [ms]	mean error [%]	median value [ms]	median error [%]
Reference Measurement		R	**1.80**	—	**1.75**	—
Kieker	full	K_f	2.72	51.2	2.49	42.4
	adaptive	K_a	2.05	13.9	2.04	16.9
AIM	full	A_f	2.20	22.2	2.19	25.0
	adaptive	A_a	1.74	3.1	1.74	0.3

Table 7.3.: Prediction errors (Schulz, 2014)

resource demands. As we can see in Figure 7.41, the distribution of the predicted response times for the AIM-adaptive scenario has a very small variance. In particular, the variance is significantly smaller than in the reference measurement. The narrow distribution is a result of the applied subtraction function $\ominus$ (cf. Section 7.5.1). For instance, in the extreme case that we subtract a distribution F_2 from F_1, whereby F_2 is a translation of F_1, all differences of the p-quantiles have the same value d:

$$\tilde{x_p}\,(F_1) - \tilde{x_p}\,(F_2) = d, \quad p \in (0, 1) \tag{7.7}$$

Consequently, the resulting distribution $F_{diff} = F_2 \ominus F_1$ contains only one single value d and has a variance of zero. Hence, though the AIM-adaptive scenario provides most accurate prediction results with respect to mean and median values, because of the underlying RDE approach, the distribution has a significantly smaller variance than the reference measurements. This effect applies also to the remaining scenarios, however there, the variances caused by the higher monitoring overhead compensate this effect.

7.5.4. Conclusions on Validation Questions

Summarizing the insights gained from the results of this controlled experiment (cf. Section 7.5.3), according to Table 7.1, we draw some conclusions on validation Goal 5 (cf. Section 7.1.1). First of all, with respect to validation question *VQ 5.1* we can draw the following conclusion. In measurement-based performance analysis tasks which are sensitive to monitoring overhead (such as RDE or performance problem diagnostics), an SSE-based approach is considerably advantageous compared to an approach with a single, full-instrumented experiment. Furthermore, a semi-adaptable instrumentation like the adaptive version of Kieker Ehlers et al., 2011 leads to a significantly smaller monitoring overhead than a full instrumentation approach. However, compared to a fully adaptable instrumentation approach as realized by AIM, the disabled probes of a semi-adaptable instrumentation approach still introduce a noticeably high monitoring overhead which may impair the measurement accuracy. Hence, the SSE concept is more effective with fully adaptable than with semi-adaptable instrumentation approaches. Consequently, for the automation of performance analysis tasks, the SSE concept is only applicable with measurement tools that allow to dynamically adapt the instrumentation of the target application. Alternatively, the SSE concept can be applied in performance analysis scenarios where the target application can be automatically restarted to change the instrumentation. Because of the intention of SSE to adapt the instrumentation to the current, focused goal of an experiment, SSE fosters the creation of light-weight measurement probes that reduce the monitoring overhead. An inherent drawback of the SSE concept is the missing dependency on instance level between measurement points from different experiments. By contrast, full instrumentation with a single experiment allows for correlation of measurement values on instance level. For instance, the response time of a called method can be directly subtracted from the measured response time of the parent method. As explained in Section 3.2.1, with the SSE concept correlation of metrics, in most cases, can only be conducted statistically. As shown in this experiment, in some cases, this assumption may lead to some additional challenges (e.g. finding a way to properly subtract distributions) and limitations. Depending on the needs these limitations may be more or less critical. Let us illustrate this on the example of this experiment. On the one hand, if we are interested in the mean and median of the predicted response times, the contraction of the resulting distribution through the subtraction function is less critical as the relative errors are very low. On the other hand, if there is a requirement that simulation results should represent the entire response times distribution, then the advantage of the SSE approach may turn into a drawback as the resulting distribution exhibits a considerably smaller variance. Hence, the application of the SSE concept should always be aligned with the goals of the corresponding performance analysis. As our detection heuristics of the APPD approach mainly utilize statistical values (e.g. means, quantiles, etc.) of measurement data, the limitations of SSE are less relevant for our diagnostics approach.

With respect to validation question *VQ 5.2*, we have shown that, in general, the SSE concept can be applied beyond the context of performance problem diagnostics. The SSE concept is particularly suitable in performance analysis scenarios where detailed monitoring is required and at the same time reducing the overhead of measurement probes plays a crucial role. As mentioned before, prior to applying SSE, the limitations of SSE should be aligned with the goals of the performance analysis activity.

7.6. Empirical Study

While the case studies described so far evaluate the technical applicability, strengths and limitations of APPD (Section 7.2-Section 7.4), they do not capture the perception of external users. In this empirical study, we let users apply parts of the APPD approach on a mid-size target application and gathered their opinion on the APPD approach by means of a questionnaire. The study described in this section has been conducted as part of a supervised Bachelor's Thesis (Merkert, 2014). The content of this section is based on the detailed description in Merkert, 2014. Due to the large extent of the empirical study, in this section, we give only a rough insight into the design and execution of the study and summarize major results and findings. For further details on the conducted empirical study we refer to the Bachelor's Thesis of Merkert, 2014.

7.6.1. Experiment Design

In this section, we describe the main aspects of the design of this study. In particular, we discuss the decision on the type of study, introduce the Goal Question Metric (GQM) plan that were used to structure the study, and describe our design of the execution plan of the study.

7.6.1.1. Type of Empirical Study

Runeson et al. (Runeson et al., 2009) distinguish three major types of studies. (i) A *survey* serves for the "collection of standardized information from a specific population, or some sample from one, usually, but not necessarily by means of a questionnaire or interview" (Robson, 2002). (ii) With a *controlled experiment* the dependencies between controlled and observed variables are analyzed (Robson, 2002; Wohlin et al., 2001). (iii) Finally, *action research* (close to *case studies*) aims at conducting a change in the topic of research, while the purpose of a *case study* is pure observation (Robson, 2002; Runeson et al., 2009).

The primary goal of our empirical study is to grasp the user perception of the APPD approach. In order to capture that perception, the subjects (i.e. the participants) of the empirical study first have to form an own opinion about APPD. To this end, they have to apply the implementation of APPD (i.e. DynamicSpotter) for the diagnostics of performance problems on a representative scenario. Due to this requirement, a pure survey is not applicable for our validation goal, as a survey would only capture the existing opinion of the subjects (Robson, 2002) who, potentially, have never heard of the APPD approach before. For a controlled experiment (Runeson et al., 2009) we would have to divide our set of subjects into a treatment group using DynamicSpotter and a control group that do not use DynamicSpotter. Due to the expectation during the design of the study that our set of subjects will be relatively small, we discarded the option of conducting a controlled experiment. Finally, a pure case study (as described in Sections 7.2 – 7.4) does not capture the perception of users. Based on these considerations, we decided to conduct a study of a mixed type, which is an established approach in empirical software engineering (Runeson et al., 2009). We combine a case study, in which the subjects apply DynamicSpotter, with a survey to capture their formed opinion. Due to the extent of information that the subjects require to fully understand the context in our study, we conduct the study as a face-to-face experiment (Seale, 2011, pp. 181), meaning that subjects are treated individually. In this way, subjects can clarify facts that are unclear through interaction with the experimenter during the execution of the experiment without affecting other subjects. For the survey part, we conduct an interview that is guided by a questionnaire. A questionnaire allows for a standardized conduction (e.g. same wording, same process, etc.)

	Goal 1	Goal 2	Goal 3
Analyze		DynamicSpotter	
for the purpose of	grasping the complexity	grasping the understandability	outlining the general applicability
with respect to	the setup effort	the results	the user's opinion
from the viewpoint		of a potential user of DynamicSpotter (e.g. developer, performance engineer, ...)	
with respect to		DynamicSpotter's usage cycle	

Table 7.4.: GQM goals (Merkert, 2014)

of the experiment iterations for the individual treatments of the subjects. For the case study part, we prepare the open-source, Java-based e-commerce system broadleaf (Broadleaf 2015) as the system under test. Using the fault injection technique (Hsueh et al., 1997), we insert performance problems into broadleaf that shell be analyzed by the subjects using DynamicSpotter.

7.6.1.2. Goal-Question-Metric Plan

In order to systematically answer the validation questions associated with the empirical study (cf. Section 7.1.3), we use the GQM approach (Basili, 1992). With the GQM approach, Basili et al. (Basili, 1992) propose to structure the measurement plan for answering certain research questions along three levels: Goals, Questions and Metrics. Goals describe the purpose of the investigation while capturing the context, issue, object and viewpoint of the investigation. A question is a means to achieve the goal by measurement. Finally, a metric allows to quantitatively answer a question.

Based on the validation questions *VQ 7.1* and *VQ 7.2* (cf. Section 7.1.3), we defined three GQM goals that are depicted in Table 7.4 (Merkert, 2014). In all three goals, the object of investigation is DynamicSpotter representing the APPD approach. Furthermore, the viewpoints of and the contexts in the goals are the same. In particular, the goals are investigated from the viewpoint of potential users of DynamicSpotter in the context of its usage cycle. According to validation question *VQ 7.1*, Goal 1 aims at grasping the complexity of setting up DynamicSpotter for a specific context. Goal 2 aims at grasping the understandability of the results provided by DynamicSpotter. Finally, Goal 3 captures the general opinion of the subjects with respect to DynamicSpotter.

The GQM goals are broken down into 14 questions that are investigated in the empirical study. Adopted from Merkert, 2014, the questions are shown in Table 7.5. Questions Q_1-Q_6 evaluate on different levels of complexity the ability of the subjects to correctly configure DynamicSpotter for a successful, automatic execution. As Goal 2 aims at grasping how good the subjects understand the results of DynamicSpotter, we divided corresponding GQM questions into four cognitive levels. Bloom et al. (Bloom et al., 1984) introduce a taxonomy for distinguishing different levels of knowledge. Using four of the six cognitive levels, we are able to distinguish at which level the subjects understand the results provided by DynamicSpotter. In particular, we distinguish between *Comprehension*, *Interpretation*, *Application* and *Evaluation*. Comprehension means that subjects are able to correctly reproduce the obtained knowledge. While the Interpretation level covers the ability to transfer the obtained knowledge to a modified context, the Application level requires a successful application of that knowledge. Finally, the Evaluation level aims at the ability to reason beyond the obtained knowledge. Question Q_7 evaluates whether the subjects understand the concepts behind the anti-patterns detected by DynamicSpotter (*Comprehension*). Question Q_9 investigates whether subjects are able to interpret the results (e.g. charts) provided by DynamicSpotter. Questions Q_{10} and Q_{11} aim at evaluating the ability of subjects to pinpoint the root cause of performance problems by means of the results provided by DynamicSpotter. And finally, Q_8 and Q_{12} investigate whether subject are able to propose solutions for the detected performance problems. The questions for Goal 3 directly capture the opinion of the subjects about DynamicSpotter and the APPD approach. The GQM questions constitute the basis for deriving corresponding questions for the questionnaire. In this thesis, we abstain from describing corresponding metrics and the questionnaire design and refer to Merkert, 2014 for further details.

№	Question
	Goal 1
Q_1	Did probands understand the configuration requirements of DynamicSpotter?
Q_2	Are probands able to configure a complete DynamicSpotter project with every aspect of an analysis?
Q_3	How long does the configuration task take?
Q_4	How complex is DynamicSpotter regarding the analysis of the SUT?
Q_5	Are study participants able to correctly configure measurement adapters in an existing DynamicSpotter project?
Q_6	How difficult is the selection of a specific measurement adapter type?
	Goal 2
Comprehension	
Q_7	Did the probands understand the presented performance problems?
Interpretation	
Q_9	Did the probands understand the charts of a specific performance problem?
Application	
Q_{10}	Were probands able to detect the source code responsible for the performance problem?
Q_{11}	Are the results adequate to located the root causes of the performance problems?
Evaluation	
Q_8	Is the output of DynamicSpotter results exhaustive?
Q_{12}	Were the probands able to determine correct solutions for a Stifle anti-pattern with a pre-defined set of possible adjustments?
	Goal 3
Q_{11}	Are the results adequate to located the root causes of the performance problems?
Q_{13}	Would the probands reuse DynamicSpotter for their projects?
Q_{14}	Does DynamicSpotter hide the complexity of the SUT?

Table 7.5.: GQM questions (Merkert, 2014)

7.6.1.3. Execution Design

The design of the study execution highly depends on some boundary conditions coming from the limits of feasibility of the empirical experiment as well as the inherent characteristics of the APPD approach. As already discussed in the case studies (Section 7.2-Section 7.4), an automatic run of DynamicSpotter is not a matter of minutes, but rather a matter of hours. Hence, a live execution of DynamicSpotter within the empirical experiment would mean that subjects have to wait several hours for the termination of DynamicSpotter. However, the willingness of potential subjects to attend an empirical experiment decreases if the experiment takes too long. According to Sjoberg et al. (Sjoberg et al., 2007), one hour is a good orientation for the duration of an empirical experiment. Hence, we need to find a way to evaluate DynamicSpotter by the subjects without significantly exceeding the proposed experiment duration of one hour. To this end, we split the empirical experiment into two parts while extracting the execution of DynamicSpotter from the execution of the empirical experiment. The process in Figure 7.42 shows the main steps of each iteration of the empirical experiment.

At the beginning of each individual treatment of a subject, the experimenter gives an introduction into the context, the APPD approach, as well as a short tutorial on the usage of DynamicSpotter. Subsequently, the experimenter guides the subject through the first part of the experiment by reading out the task descriptions as well as corresponding questions from the questionnaire. Thereby the subject is asked to fully configure DynamicSpotter for an automatic execution. However, this includes only those tasks that are specific to the APPD approach. In particular, all tasks that are common in all measurement-based performance analysis approaches are conducted by the experimenter in advance to the empirical experiment. For instance, setting up the measurement environment (including the SUT, load generator and measurement tools) as well as creating load scripts, are tasks that need to be conducted for any measurement-based performance analysis approach. Including these tasks into the empirical experiment would bias the subject's perception of the complexity of applying the APPD approach. In the first part of the experiment, we cover the first goal of the GQM plan, evaluating the subject's perception of the configuration part of DynamicSpotter. In this part of the experiment, the subjects use the Eclipse-based (Eclipse 2015) user interface of DynamicSpotter to create the corresponding configuration.

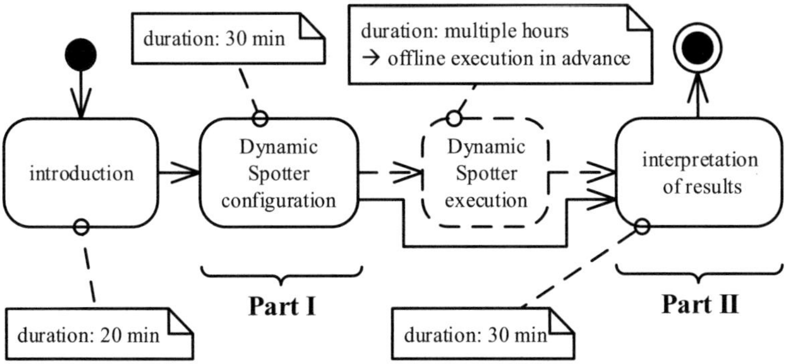

Figure 7.42.: Experiment execution plan

After the subject has created a complete configuration, ideally, DynamicSpotter would be executed to diagnose performance problems. However, due to the reasons discussed before, we skip that step in the empirical experiment. Instead, we execute DynamicSpotter with a correct configuration offline, in advance to conducting the empirical experiment. In that offline execution, DynamicSpotter has been applied to the same experiment setup of the target application (*broadleaf*) as the subjects are confronted with in Part I of the empirical experiment. DynamicSpotter detects all previously injected performance problems including three instances of the OLB anti-pattern (cf. Table 2.1(e), Chapter 2.4) and two instances of the Stifle (cf. Table 2.1(k), Chapter 2.4). The injected performance problems exhibit differently high complexity in their root causes in order to evaluate the interpretability of DynamicSpotter results on different levels.

Directly after the DynamicSpotter configuration part, the empirical experiment is continued with Part II. Thereby, the subjects are asked to interpret the results provided by DynamicSpotter from the offline execution. Part II of the experiment aims at investigating Goal 2 of the GQM plan. Hereby, we evaluate the ability of the subject to interpret the results of DynamicSpotter on different levels of complexity regarding the diagnosed performance problems. The empirical experiment is finalized with the part of the questionnaire that covers the evaluation of GQM Goal 3.

7.6.2. Discussion of Results

From the invited potential test persons, 24 persons agreed to participate in the empirical experiment. Due to a *mortality* number of 2 (Carver et al., 2003), 22 persons remained as subjects for our experiment. In this section, we present the result of the empirical study with respect to the three GQM goals that have been introduced above.

The results presented in the following are a summary of the detailed discussion of results by Merkert, 2014. For details beyond the presented summary we refer to the corresponding Bachelor's Thesis (Merkert, 2014).

Goal 1 – Configuration Complexity

The fact that the subjects correctly understand the requirements for applying DynamicSpotter is a precondition for evaluating the actual intention of GQM Goal 1. Thereto, question Q_1 tests the level of comprehension of the subjects. The study results significantly show a positive answer to question Q_1. Hence, as the subjects entirely understood the requirements for DynamicSpotter, we can exclude distortion of further results due to lack of understanding. For the evaluation of GQM question Q_3, we took the time for subjects configuring a DynamicSpotter project. We terminated the configuration task after 15 minutes, if the subjects have not finished the configuration, yet. With Q_3 we investigate whether pressure of time is a possible root cause for potentially biased results of the remaining questions. With an average duration of 11 minutes and only some few outliers (4 of 22) who did not finish within 15 minutes, we evaluate the available time as adequate. Hence in the following, we can exclude pressure of time as potential cause for biased results.

Question Q_4 directly captures the subjects' perception of the complexity of configuring DynamicSpotter for the analysis of a SUT. The collected answers to corresponding questions from the questionnaire show a significant result: 81% of the subjects perceive the difficulty of setting up DynamicSpotter as low. However, though most subjects rated the difficulty of configuring DynamicSpotter as low, the results for question Q_2 show that most subjects did some mistakes in the configuration of DynamicSpotter. Hereby, the most frequent source of failure was an incorrect selection of measurement adapters in the DynamicSpotter configuration for the measurement tools that were deployed with the measurement environment of the SUT. Question Q_6 confirms that observation, as subjects significantly rate the selection of measurement adapters as the most difficult part of the configuration task. Nevertheless, according to Q_4, the subjects rated the overall complexity of setting up DynamicSpotter as low. A possible explanation for the discrepant results of the questions Q_2, Q_4, and Q_6 is the following. The mistakes that have been made by the subjects during the configuration are perceived as minor mistakes that could have been avoided by better documentation of the measurement adapters. Therefore, the mistakes and the perception regarding question Q_6 (difficulty of selecting measurement adapter) did not significantly influence the subjects' overall perception of the complexity of configuring DynamicSpotter. Evaluating whether subjects are able to extend an existing DynamicSpotter configuration project (Q_5), from the results for question Q_5, we conclude that subjects who, in the first place, managed to successfully configure a DynamicSpotter project are also able to extend those projects.

Summing up the results for GQM Goal 1, we can conclude that, in general, the subjects of the experiment perceived the complexity of setting up DynamicSpotter for the analysis of a SUT as low. Because of insufficient documentation of measurement adapters and (at this point in time) preliminary user interface, many subjects provided an erroneous configuration for DynamicSpotter. All in all, the subjects correctly understood the main concepts behind APPD and, based on that understanding, rated the complexity of configuring DynamicSpotter as low.

Goal 2 – Result Interpretability

The second goal of the GQM plan is evaluated along the taxonomy on cognitive levels adopted from Bloom's Taxonomy (Bloom et al., 1984). In this way we can more precisely evaluate the interpretability of the results provided by DynamicSpotter. As explained above, we distinguish four cognitive levels. Furthermore, we injected two Stifle instances and three OLB instances into the investigated broadleaf application. In this part of the experiment, DynamicSpotter presents the diagnostics results to the subjects for the injected problems. An important fact is that the injected problems are on a different level of complexity with respect to their root cause. For instance, an obvious OLB instance is a synchronized method that contains a sleep for a delay of the corresponding execution thread. By contrast, in a more complex OLB instance the root cause for the delay is hidden in the call hierarchy within a synchronized block.

Question Q_7 evaluates the ability of the subjects to understand the concepts behind the considered SPAs. According to the experiment results for question Q_7, the subjects understood the concepts behind the OLB and Stifle anti-patterns. Hence, the subjects positively achieved the first cognitive level with respect to the interpretability of the DynamicSpotter results.

With respect to the Interpretation level, question Q_9 investigates the ability of the subjects to transfer their knowledge on the anti-pattern concepts (for OLB and Stifle) to the concrete occurrences of these anti-patterns as reported by DynamicSpotter. Thereby, the participants are asked to interpret the charts provided by DynamicSpotter for the individual occurrences of anti-pattern instances. Though most subjects correctly understood the graphs for the OLB instances, only a slight majority of the subjects was able to correctly transfer their knowledge about the Stifle anti-pattern to the Stifle graphs. From that result, we conclude that the representation of diagnostics results by DynamicSpotter for the Stifle anti-pattern may be misleading. Hence, with respect to the user interface, the representation of the Stifle anti-pattern exhibits potential for improvement.

For the third cognitive level (Application) the levels of complexity of the injected performance problems plays a crucial role. GQM question Q_{10} aims at evaluating the ability of the subjects to pinpoint the root causes of the performance problems in the source code of broadleaf, based on the results provided by DynamicSpotter. For the Stifle anti-pattern, a clear majority (64%) of the subjects pinpointed to the correct location in the source code. The remaining subjects, also selected that location, however, they identified other, wrong locations as the root cause for the Stifle anti-pattern, as well. Hence, we can conclude that, regarding the Stifle anti-pattern, a majority of the subjects reached the Application cognitive level with the help of the diagnostics results from DynamicSpotter. The fact that, with respect to the Stifle anti-pattern, more subjects reached the Application level than the Interpretation level confirms our presumption that the Stifle charts provided by DynamicSpotter have potential for improvement. Regarding the OLB anti-pattern, the subjects were only able to pinpoint the root cause up to the medium complexity of the injected OLB instances. The lack of knowledge about the details of broadleaf is an explanation for the inability to pinpoint the root cause for the complex OLB instance. Nevertheless, asking the subjects for their opinion about the usefulness of the DynamicSpotter results for locating root causes of performance problems, we obtained positive results. Question Q_{11} shows that a clear majority of subjects agree that the diagnostics results provided by DynamicSpotter are useful to identify the root cause of a performance problem.

Going a step beyond the scope of APPD, with question Q_{12} we investigated whether the subjects are able to select correct solutions to the identified performance problems from a predefined set of options. The results for Q_{12} show that most subjects were not able to select correct solutions.

Overall, with respect to GQM Goal 2, we can conclude that subjects of the experiment perceive the results provided by DynamicSpotter as useful for locating root causes of performance problems. However, due to the lack of knowledge about the internals of the SUT, in some cases the subjects were not able to correctly describe the root cause of diagnosed performance problems based on the available diagnostics results.

Goal 3 – Opinion on Applicability

Goal 3 solely aims at capturing the opinion of the subjects about the applicability of the APPD approach. As already discussed before, the results of Q_{11} show that subjects perceive the results provided by DynamicSpotter as useful and adequate to locate root causes of performance problems. Considering the results of question Q_{11} for GQM Goal 3 is essential, as the main focus of the APPD approach lies on supporting the localization of root causes (i.e. diagnostics) of performance problems. Furthermore, evaluating the results of question Q_{14} we come to the conclusion that the APPD approach hides the complexity of the SUT. In particular, it is remarkable that subjects who did not knew the target application at all were able to partly pinpoint root causes of performance problems by means of the diagnostics results provided by DynamicSpotter. This means, that subjects did not need to understand the internals of broadleaf to be able to analyze the performance problems. As part of GQM question Q_{13}, we asked the subjects whether they would use DynamicSpotter for diagnosing performance problems in their own software projects. A clear majority (87%) of the subjects agreed with the statement that they would reuse DynamicSpotter. Hence, we can conclude that, all in all, the subjects perceived the APPD approach as a useful support in diagnosing performance problems.

7.6.3. Conclusions on Validation Questions

The main goal of the empirical study was the evaluation of the validation questions *VQ 6.2*, *VQ 7.1* and *VQ 7.2*. Summarizing the results for the thee GQM goals, we draw the following conclusions on the validation questions.

The answer to validation questions *VQ 6.2* and *VQ 7.1* is twofold. Apart from the tasks that need to be done for any measurement-based performance analysis approach, the evaluation of GQM Goal 1 shows that external users of the APPD approach perceive the up-front complexity and the associated effort as low. However, the empirical study also shows that the complexity and effort highly depends on the documentation of the tooling for APPD (i.e. DynamicSpotter) and the functional scope of the corresponding user interface. This is especially important because APPD constitutes an approach that automates a complex task. Hence, the remaining manual effort highly depends on the usability of the tool that realizes APPD.

The second GQM goal only partly shows that external users are able to fully interpret the results provided by the APPD approach. However, due to the circumstances in the empirical study, the results of Goal 2 and Goal 3 constitute a positive answer to validation question *VQ 7.2*. First, according to the opinion of the experiment subjects, the diagnostics results of the APPD approach are adequate to locate the root cause of a performance problem. Second, more than 90% of the subjects didn't knew the target application before. This is very likely the reason why subjects partly failed to pinpoint the root cause of some performance problems in the experiment. However, this circumstances are not representative for real application scenarios of the APPD approach. In real application scenarios, the users of APPD are usually developers of the target application. Hence, the results provided by APPD may be of greater help for them than for users that are not familiar with the SUT. Though, subjects are partly able to pinpoint the root causes by means of the APPD results, they are not able to select proper solutions to those problems. Hence, according to its main focus, the APPD approach is useful to diagnose performance problems, but does not provide sufficient support in finding adequate solutions. In particular, resolution of performance problems is a topic on its own that is addressed by Heger, 2015.

7.7. Discussion

In this chapter, we conducted a validation of the APPD approach with regards to different aspects. Therefore, we conducted five studies that provide interesting insights on the investigated validation goals. This includes confirmation of hypotheses as well as unexpected aspects that affect the applicability of the APPD approach. In this section, we summarize the conclusions from the individual studies. Furthermore, we discuss the threats to validity of our validation.

7.7.1. Conclusion

Summarizing and aggregating the insights from the conducted studies, we discuss the conclusions for the seven validation goals outlined in the beginning of this chapter.

Validation Goal 1 – Functionality of APPD

In the three case studies with TPC-W, nopCommerce and the ILS, different types of SPAs have been investigated. In particular, each SPA from the investigated performance problem taxonomy has been correctly diagnosed in at least one of the case studies (except for the Ramp anti-pattern). Hence, with respect to validation question *VQ 1.1* we can conclude that the set of considered SPAs is detectable by systematic experimentation.

Furthermore, the case studies covered technical variability with respect to different dimensions which shows the generalisability of the APPD approach. The following dimensions of variability have been investigated:

- *programming languages:* While the TPC-W benchmark and the ILS are Java-based applications, with the nopCommerce case study we investigated the applicability of APPD in the area of .NET. The case studies have shown that the generic concepts of APPD, in particular the instrumentation description part of P^2D^2M are not restricted to a particular programming language or run-time environment. Though, in the nopCommerce case study, we were restricted with respect to the instrumentation capabilities due to license issues, in general, there are no major restrictions that would limit the applicability of the APPD approach to target applications that are not Java-based.
- *server technologies:* Within the case studies different products have been used as application server (Apache Tomcat™ for TPC-W, JBoss™ for ILS, IIS™ for nopCommerce) and database server (MySQL™ for TPC-W, MS SQL Server Express™ for nopCommerce, high-performance database for ILS). In this way, we have shown that instrumentation and collection of measurement data can be applied on different underlying technologies, while the resulting measurement data have a common representation for APPD. Hence, we can conclude that APPD is independent of the underlying server technology.
- *load generators:* In the case studies we used three different load generators (Apache JMeter™, HP LoadRUnner™, and TPC-W RBE) demonstrating that APPD and ,especially, the ME Description language of P^2D^2M reasonably abstract from concrete measurement and load generation tools.
- *system characteristics:* Finally, the case studies cover applications and experiments setups with different characteristics. This includes different experiment setups (3 versus 7 system nodes in the TPC-W case study), different business domains of the applications (e-commerce versus enterprise resource management), and different scales and complexity of the applications (middle-size versus large-scale systems). The studies confirm that the applicability and functionality of APPD are independent of all these characteristics.

Hence, with respect to validation question *VQ 1.2* we can conclude that APPD is generically applicable on systems with different characteristics, environment setups and technologies. Regarding validation question *VQ 1.3*, all three case studies show that, in general, APPD provides accurate and precise diagnostics results if all assumptions for APPD are met. Besides these confirming results, the case studies revealed two unexpected insights on the accuracy of APPD under specific conditions. First, both parts of the TPC-W case study have shown that multiple instances of performance problems can hide each other. In such cases, APPD is only able to detect the most critical problem. From that observation, we have to conclude that the application process of APPD must be iterative. Hence, if the APPD approach detects a performance problem, the problem needs to be resolved before APPD can be applied again to uncover the next performance problem instance. The second unexpected insight emphasizes the importance of the workload configuration and description for a successful diagnostics by APPD. In the industrial case study we experienced that an improperly configured load generation can induce symptoms that indicate wrong occurrences of performance problems. Therefore, it is important that workload descriptions used for APPD are representative for real usage scenarios and are configured properly for the underlying setup of the measurement environment. Thereto, approaches for deriving effective load models can be applied (Barber, 2004; Krishnamurthy et al., 2006; van Hoorn et al., 2014).

Validation Goal 2 – Appropriateness of the Performance Problem Taxonomy

Under the assumption that all assumptions for APPD are met, in all conducted case studies, the applied performance problem taxonomy reasonably represented the cause-effect chains of the occurred instances of performance problems. This applies for both injected as well as previously unknown instances of SPAs. However, the ILS case study has shown that the appropriateness of the performance problem taxonomy can be impaired, if the assumption on stable load intensities is not met. In such cases, root causes of performance problems may exhibit other symptoms than described by the performance problem taxonomy. Hence, for Validation Goal 2 we can conclude that the taxonomy appropriately represents the cause-effect relationship of performance problems in real scenarios, if the assumption on stable load intensities during corresponding measurement experiments is met.

Validation Goal 3 – Efficiency of APPD

In Section 4.4.3.2, we discussed the theoretical complexity of the Systematic Search Algorithm and, hence, of a diagnostics run of the APPD approach. These considerations, with respect to efficiency, clearly illustrate the benefit of the Systematic Search Algorithm compared to an alternative, naive approach. In particular, the theoretical complexity considerations prove that in a specific application context, the absolute execution time of APPD would be smaller than of a naive diagnostics approach with comparable configurations of the experiments. However, besides the theoretical considerations, the absolute execution time of APPD highly depends on the configuration of the concrete application scenario. From the case studies we can conclude as a rule of thumb that the execution time of APPD is the longer the more complex the SUT is. This is due to the fact that more complex system are usually tested with higher load intensities and, thus, require longer warm-up phases for stabilization of measurements and longer experiment durations to obtain significant measurement data. In general, we have shown that APPD can be executed in a couple of hours. Thus, APPD can be embedded into regular, automated processes (e.g. daily, weekly, monthly, etc.), for instance as part of continuous integration.

Validation Goal 4 – Appropriateness of P^2D^2M

Using the Measurement Environment (ME) Description part of the P^2D^2M, in all case studies we were able to capture all scenario-specific aspects that are required to bridge the gap between the generic core of APPD and the concrete application contexts. Hence, with respect to the investigated contexts, the expressiveness of the Measurement Environment (ME) Description model is sufficient for real application scenarios. As already discussed above (for Validation Goal 1), the investigated scenarios cover a broad range of different techniques, tools and environment. A successful, uniform description of these diverse scenarios shows that the corresponding language is appropriately generic. With respect to the generic sub-models of P^2D^2M (i.e. Experimentation Description, IaM Description and Data Representation sub-models) we can draw the same conclusion. In Chapter 6, we used these meta-models to describe detection heuristics in a generic way. Successfully applying the generically defined heuristics to diverse, concrete scenarios shows the appropriateness of the corresponding languages. In particular, the diversity in the case studies shows that the corresponding modelling languages are neither too specific, as they abstract from context-specific details, nor the languages are too abstract, as they provide the required expressiveness to define detection heuristics for different types of SPAs. All in all, with respect to the three end-to-end case studies conducted in this chapter, we can draw the conclusion that P^2D^2M is appropriate for the purpose of performance problem diagnostics.

Validation Goal 5 – Necessity of SSE

Besides the end-to-end case studies, we have applied the SSE concept for automated resource demand estimation in the SSE-4-RDE experiment (cf. Section 7.5). Hence, SSE is not only an enabler for the automation of performance problem diagnostics, but can be applied to further experiment-based performance evaluation scenarios (e.g. resource demand estimation). With respect to validation question *VQ 5.2*, the case studies in this chapter indicate a broader scope of applicability for the SSE concept. Furthermore, comparing an automated SSE-based approach for resource demand estimation against a simple, single-experiment approach, in the SSE-4-RDE experiment, we showed the benefit of SSE with respect to the trade-off between resulting monitoring overhead and detail of measurement data. While SSE allows to achieve both requirements (i.e. low monitoring overhead and detailed measurement data), alternative approaches sacrifice one of the requirements in favor for the other requirement.

Validation Goal 6 – Automation of APPD

In all case studies, the execution of the APPD approach was fully automated using DynamicSpotter, an implementation of APPD. By means of dynamically adaptable instrumentation with AIM (Wert et al., 2015a), for Java-based applications, the SSE concept has been realized very efficiently. In particular, adaptation of instrumentation is possible without restart of the target application. However, as experienced in the nopCommerce case study (cf. Section 7.3), dynamically adaptable instrumentation cannot be realized in all contexts. As an alternative, the SSE concept and, thus, the

APPD approach can be realized by automating the restart of the application under test to enable adaptation of instrumentation. APPD cannot be applied in contexts where neither dynamically adaptable instrumentation is possible nor an automated restart of the target application.

With respect to the up-front effort to prepare a concrete application context for the application of APPD, in general, the experiences in the case studies were comparable. In all case studies we had to set up the measurement environment and create corresponding usage profiles (or load scripts). These two task constitute the major part of the up-front effort to run APPD. However, these tasks are not specific to APPD, but need to be executed for any measurement-based approach for performance evaluation. Furthermore, we had to deploy measurement tools and calibrate the ME Description for DynamicSpotter. Assuming that the created adapters for different measurement tools and load generators are reusable for future scenarios, the remaining tasks have been conducted in a couple of hours. Hence, from our subjective point of view, the manual effort to set up APPD for a new specific application context is negligible compared to manual diagnostics of performance problems.

To get a more objective opinion on that validation question, we evaluated the perception of external users of the APPD approach in the empirical study (cf. Section 7.6). Though a comprehensive documentation is required for DynamicSpotter and all available measurement adapters to increase its usability, the empirical study showed that external users perceive the manual effort for setting up DynamicSpotter as low.

Validation Goal 7 – Practicability of APPD

Validation Goal 7 has been evaluated with the empirical study in Section 7.6. As already mentioned before, the empirical study shows that external users prevailingly perceive the complexity of applying the APPD approach as low. However, the study also shows that the manual effort of using the APPD approach highly depends on the usability of the corresponding implementation and user interface. In particular, many tasks for configuring DynamicSpotter can be facilitated by an advanced user interface. For instance, a graphical modelling interface for the creation of the measurement environment description would reduce the overhead compared to textual syntax. However, as the usability of DynamicSpotter is not the focus of the validation in this chapter, we conclude that, overall, the complexity of applying the APPD is perceived as low.

With respect to validation question *VQ 7.2*, the empirical study provides two major insights. On the one hand, it shows that external users perceive the diagnostics results provided by the APPD approach as useful for uncovering performance problems and locating their root causes. On the other hand, in the empirical study we gained the following insight: users of the APPD approach should be experts with respect to the SUT in order to be able to reasonably interpret the diagnostics results of APPD. Hence, developers of the target application constitute the ideal target group for interpreting the reports that are provided by the APPD approach.

Due to feasibility reasons, we are not able to conduct a Type 3 validation of the APPD approach. Therefore, we cannot make any statements on the economic efficiency of APPD (*VQ 7.3*).

7.7.2. Threats to Validity

In this section, we discuss the threats to construct and external validity of the conclusions derived from the conducted studies. Threats to construct validity aim at ensuring that the right issue (the one that was intended to be evaluated) has been evaluated (Sjoberg et al., 2007). In particular, threats to construct validity arise if some unintended aspects in the design or setup of the corresponding experiment affect the observed results that are used to draw conclusions. External validity is about the ability to project the conclusions from the investigated set of subjects or objects to the general class of that subjects or objects, respectively.

7.7.2.1. Construct Validity

Analogously to Heisenberg's uncertainty principle (Busch et al., 2007) in physics, in measurement-based software performance evaluation a common threat to construct validity is the distortion of measurements through the injection of measurement probes. In particular, the higher the monitoring overhead the more the measurement data are distorted. With the SSE concept in the APPD approach we inherently avoid high monitoring overheads. When detection heuristics of APPD apply experiments to measure performance metrics (e.g. response times, throughput, etc.), they apply selective, minimal-invasive instrumentation to keep monitoring overhead small. Expensive instrumentation is only applied when structural data is retrieved (e.g. call trees). However, in this cases the monitoring overhead is irrelevant as no performance metrics are measured.

In the second part of the TPC-W case study and in the nopCommerce case study, we applied the fault injection technique (Hsueh et al., 1997) for the evaluation of APPD. Fault injection is not suited to derive any conclusions on the ability of APPD to diagnose performance problem instances that were unknown to the authors of APPD. While diagnostics of unknown performance problems has been investigated in the first part of the TPC-W case study and the ILS case study, fault injection is an established approach (Hsueh et al., 1997) and has its rationale in the remaining case studies. In the nopCommerce case study our goal was to show the ability of APPD to abstract from implementation details and, thus, to deal with a wide range of technologies (e.g. .NET area). Hereby, the source of investigated performance problems is subordinate. Despite fault injection, we obtained interesting and unexpected insights on the applicability of APPD from the corresponding case studies.

In the second part of the TPC-W case study we extended the TPC-W application ourselves for the investigation of communication-related SPAs. Though this may constitute a threat to construct validity, we strove to preserve the complexity of the TPC-W as well as its core functionality.

In the SSE-4-RDE experiment we introduced an automated RDE approach. We acknowledge that this approach constitutes only a proof of concept for resource demand estimation. In particular, the described approach builds on some assumptions and limitations, such as CPU-bound applications under test, deterministic behaviour of system services and uni-modal distributions of response times. However, as all assumptions were met by the target application, we assume that the effect of this threat to construct validity is minimal.

The major threat to construct validity in the empirical study is the difficulty of evaluating the APPD approach without the influence of the usability of DynamicSpotter. On the one hand, we required an adequate user interface to reasonably be able to conduct the study. On the other hand, a user interface has the disadvantage that it may bias the opinion of the experiment participants. For instance, the participants may get a negative impression of the overall APPD approach, if the user interface exhibits an insufficient usability. Unfortunately, we did not find a way to reasonably avoid that threat to construct validity. With respect to the threats of construct validity of the questionnaire, we reduced the threats by piloting the questionnaire with some pretests. Thereby, we were able to identify some issues (e.g. too many tasks, wording issues, etc.) that we fixed before conducting the actual experiments. Furthermore, as already mentioned in Section 7.7.1, the fact that the subjects of the empirical study where unfamiliar with the SUT lead to some negatively biased results.

7.7.2.2. External Validity

In our studies we did not practically investigate other SPAs of the created taxonomy in Figure 4.2 (cf. Section 4.3) than the anti-patterns that are included in the used PPEP instance (e.g. GC Hiccups anti-pattern, Dormant References, Unbalanced Processing, etc.). However, as the set of investigated SPAs comprises conceptually different types of performance problems, we presume that our evaluation results are representative for the remaining anti-patterns of the taxonomy. An in depth investigation of the remaining SPAs is a task for future work.

Primarily, all conclusions stated in Section 7.7.1 only apply to the conducted case studies. However, the case studies cover a broad range of technologies and application domains. Furthermore, the investigated applications (at least nopCommerce and ILS) constitute real, industrially used software products that are representative for other enterprise software systems. Hence, we have reason to assume that our findings in the case studies are representative for other software systems in the domain of server-based, enterprise software systems.

In our case studies, we investigated the software systems on a static infrastructure. In particular, we did not conduct any evaluation of the APPD approach on applications that run on elastic cloud platforms. Consequently, we cannot provide any statements about the applicability of APPD on cloud-based applications. Moreover, we presume that some of the assumptions of APPD would not hold with a typical cloud application running on an elastic infrastructure (e.g. assumption on stable load intensity) posing a risk for the diagnostics accuracy of APPD.

Regarding SSE, in this thesis, we applied the concept on two entirely different performance evaluation contexts (i.e. RDE and performance problem diagnostics). In both contexts the SSE concept constituted an enabler for reasonable automation of the corresponding performance evaluation tasks. Whether SSE can be applied in further performance evaluation areas is a research question for future work. However, due to the entirely different nature of the both investigated contexts, we presume, that the SSE concept can be applied in a similar way in further experiment-based scenarios where reducing monitoring overhead plays an important role.

The participants of the empirical study prevailingly were from a scientific domain (students and scientists). Hence, in general, we cannot project the findings of the conducted empirical study to the class of software engineers including developers from industry. However, evaluating APPD in an industrial context falls into the same category as the Type 3 validation that has been omitted due to reasons of feasibility.

7.8. Summary

In this chapter, we validated our APPD approach with respect to the research hypotheses defined in Section 3.4. From the hypotheses, we derived more fine-grained validation questions that have been investigated in this chapter. Overall, we conducted five studies that cover all validation questions except for the investigation of the economical cost-benefit ratio of the APPD approach. We conducted three case studies to evaluate the end-to-end functionality and applicability of APPD. The case studies have been conducted on a Java implementation of the e-commerce benchmark TPC-W, an open-source .NET e-commerce solution, and a large-scale, industrial Java application for enterprise resource management. In the different case studies, we used different tools for load generation. Despite the high variety in the case studies, APPD has been successfully applied in all case studies and, in general, was able to accurately diagnose performance problems. By means of a controlled experiment we investigated the benefits and limitations of the SSE concept. In the controlled experiment, we applied the SSE concept for automatic measurements of resource demands used for the calibration of performance models. The experiment shows that, apart from some limitations, SSE is a promising concept to overcome the trade-off between measurement accuracy and precision. Finally, we conducted an empirical study in which external participants applied the APPD approach. The external users evaluated APPD as a useful support in diagnosing performance problems.

8. Related Work

In this chapter, we provide a survey on research work that is related to our approach as well as its integral parts. As elaborated in this thesis, we provide contributions in different research areas. Figure 8.1 gives an overview on the main concepts and artifacts of the Automatic Performance Problem Diagnostics (APPD) approach (solid-border boxes) as well as the research areas (dashed-border boxes) they are related to.

With the taxonomy on performance problems described in Chapter 4, we contribute to the research field of *Definition and Classification of Performance Problems*. In the area of *Experiment-based Performance Evaluation* we introduced the Systematic Selective Experimentation (SSE) concept (cf. Chapter 3.2.1) to mitigate the trade-off between precision and accuracy of measurement data. Performance Problem Diagnostics Description Model (P^2D^2M) as a tailored specification language for performance problem diagnostics (cf. Chapter 5) constitutes a contribution in the field of *Models*

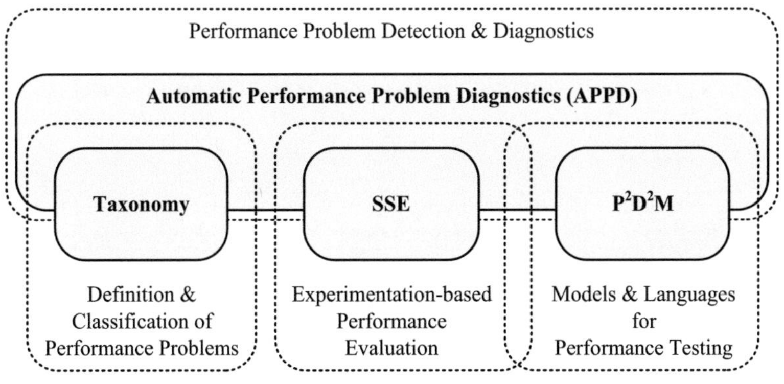

Figure 8.1.: Areas of Related Work

and Languages for Performance Testing. The latter two research areas are closely interrelated as most experiment-based approaches utilize models to describe the experimentation plans. The performance problem taxonomy, SSE and P^2D^2M constitute the main building blocks for the overall APPD approach. Therefore, with APPD the main contribution of this thesis is in the field of *Performance Problem Detection and Diagnostics*. In the following, we discuss related work in the four research areas shown in Figure 8.1, with a strong focus on the field of Performance Problem Detection and Diagnostics. This chapter is structured as follows. In Section 8.1, we discuss research work that address definition and classification of performance problems. Due to the close interrelation, in Section 8.2, we consider related work in the research areas of experimentation and models in measurement-based performance evaluation. Finally, we discuss performance problem detection and diagnostics approaches along different sub-categories in Section 8.3.

8.1. Description and Classification of Performance Problems

Generically describing and classifying knowledge about performance problems is a prerequisite for an engineering approach in detecting and diagnosing performance problems. This especially applies to automation of such engineering approaches. In his early work on performance analysis, Jain introduces a systematic approach on performance analysis of computer systems (Jain, 1991). Thereby, the author describes common mistakes, techniques and best practices in conducting performance measurements, selecting proper metrics and workloads, and reasonably interpreting performance data. The work of Jain is based on the following assumption:

> "Most performance problems are unique. The metrics, workload, and evaluation techniques used for one problem generally cannot be used for the next problem. Nevertheless, there are steps common to all performance evaluation projects that help you avoid the common mistakes [...]" (Jain, 1991)

In that context, the term *performance problem* has a general meaning that covers any concern related to performance evaluation (e.g. capacity management, performance tuning, performance model calibration, etc.). While Jain's assumption is true for the field of performance evaluation in general, in the field of analyzing software performance problems, subsequent work on *software performance anti-patterns* by Smith et al. (Smith et al., 2002b; Smith et al., 2002a; Smith et al., 2003) and research work based thereon (Trubiani et al., 2011; Parsons, 2007) have shown that many performance problems are recurrent. Prior to the notion of software performance anti-patterns, performance problems were simply referred to as *performance bottlenecks*. Jain defines a performance bottleneck as "the resource with the highest utilization"(Jain, 1991). While this definition is limited to hardware resources, Neilson et al. provide a definition of a *software bottleneck* as a "[...] task [that] exhibits a high utilization which is also high relative to the utilizations of each of its servers, either direct or indirect" (Neilson et al., 1995). Franks et al. extend that definition for the context of layered services, whereby services depend on other services including their waiting times (Franks et al., 2006).

Performance bottlenecks constitute a rather general notion of performance problems that is applicable in abstract models of computer systems such as queueing networks or layered queueing networks (Franks et al., 1996). However, the notion of performance bottlenecks does not cover the diversity of different aspects and manifestations of recurrent performance problems in real enterprise software systems. By contrast, the notion of software performance anti-patterns allows to describe different types of recurrent performance problems with their characteristic aspects. The notion of software performance anti-patterns is derived from the idea on software anti-patterns (Brown et al., 1998), design patterns (Gamma et al., 1994) and architectural patterns (Buschmann et al., 2007). Software performance anti-patterns have been introduced by Smith et al. (Smith et al., 2002b; Smith et al., 2002a; Smith et al., 2003; Smith et al., 2000) whereby each anti-pattern is specified by a name, a description of the problem, and a set of possible solutions. Besides the work from Smith et al., anti-patterns (partly) with a software performance impact have been defined by others as well. While the anti-patterns described by Smith et al. are technology independent, Tate (Tate, 2002; Tate et al., 2003) and Dudney et al. (Dudney et al., 2003) introduce anti-patterns that are specific for Java and Java Enterprise applications. Chis et al. introduce memory patterns that result in an inefficient use of the Java Heap and, thus, may result in poor performance, e.g. due to increased garbage collection (Chis et al., 2011). Hallal et al. introduce anti-patterns in the domain of multi-threaded software (Hallal et al., 2004). As multi-threading is closely related to performance, many of the anti-patterns defined by the authors have a negative impact on the performance. Smaalders reports on a set of performance anti-patterns that have been experienced at Sun Microsystems during refactoring of the Solaris operating system (Smaalders, 2006). The individual anti-patterns that are relevant for enterprise software systems from research work as well as industrial collections have been described in Chapter 2.4 of this thesis. These anti-patterns constitute the basis for our taxonomy on performance problems.

While the notion of anti-patterns lays the basis for classifying different kind of performance problems, considering the relationship between individual anti-patterns and identifying categories on anti-patterns is another important step towards understanding the nature of performance problems and improving performance problem diagnostics.

Based on the notions of bottlenecks, software bottlenecks and layered bottlenecks, Meszaros, 1996 and Petriu et al., 1997 introduce a pattern language for the analysis of contention in layered reactive systems. Similar to our performance problem taxonomy, the pattern language in (Petriu et al., 1997) constitutes a hierarchical structure on bottlenecks and solutions. While the top layers of the hierarchy describe different types of bottlenecks like Memory Capacity, Intermediate Server Bottleneck or Processing Capacity, the lower levels constitute different solution strategies for the individual bottlenecks. For instance, Petriu et al., 1997 propose to apply the Server Multi-threading pattern to alleviate the Intermediate Server Bottleneck. Thereby, Thread Pooling, Thread per Request and Thread per Session constitute different solution strategies. Unlike our taxonomy, the pattern language in (Meszaros, 1996) and (Petriu et al., 1997) is limited to bottlenecks. Furthermore, the purpose of the pattern language is to document common solutions to different types of bottlenecks. By contrast, our performance problem taxonomy aims at capturing the cause-effect relationships between individual performance anti-patterns.

Moha et al. propose a taxonomy and classification scheme for software architectural defects (Moha et al., 2005). In their taxonomy, the authors differentiate between anti-patterns as "bad solutions to recurring design problems", design defects as "bad use of design patterns", and code smells that "refer to symptoms or problems at the code level". Besides the taxonomy, the authors propose a scheme that comprises two dimensions for the classification of software architectural defects. In the first dimension, the authors distinguish between intra-classes, inter-classes and behavioural defects. That dimension is similar to our classification dimensions *Type of Pattern* and *Level of Abstraction* in Chapter 4.2.1. In the second dimension, Moha et al. distinguish between anti-patterns, design defects and distorted anti-patterns. Though Moha et al. consider defects that are not specifically related to performance, the general purpose of their classification is similar to ours. In particular, the authors emphasize the need for formalizing software architectural defects and corresponding processes and techniques to uncover them. With our classification of performance anti-patterns, the derived Performance Problem Evaluation Plan (PPEP) (cf. Chapter 4.2.1) and the detection heuristics (cf. Chapter 6.3) we address the same goal in the domain of performance anti-patterns.

Based on years of experience in fixing code defects, Reimer et al. report on a categorization of critical problems that typically occur in large-scale Java (J2EE) systems (Reimer et al., 2004). Thereby, Reimer et al. partition critical problems into the following five categories: Resource Management, Concurrency, Server-side Java, Persistent Data Management, and Implementation Contract Violation. With respect to their static analysis tool SABER, the authors further classify code defects in Java into six classes. Thereby, the classification is based on the underlying artifacts that are analyzed and rules applied to detect the defects. Though Reimer et al. do not consider performance-related problems, their classification scheme shows a similarity to one aspect of our classification. Similarly to (Reimer et al., 2004), with our classification template, inter alia, we categorize performance anti-patterns along the dimension *Detection Method* (cf. Chapter 4.2.1).

Hallal et al. introduce a classification scheme for anti-patterns that are related to multi-threading (Hallal et al., 2004). The authors consider 38 anti-pattern that they partition into two main categories: (i) *correctness problems* that lead to wrong or no results of computation and (ii) *efficiency and quality problems* that provide a correct result, however, at the expense of performance and other quality attributes. Due to their impact on performance, the latter category of anti-patterns is closely related to the anti-patterns considered in this thesis. On a more detailed level, Hallal et al. further refine the categories into six detailed categories of multi-threading anti-patterns: Deadlocks, Livelocks, Race Conditions, Efficiency Problems, Quality and Style Problems, and problems leading to Unpredictable Consequences. Using this classification scheme the authors introduce a description template for archiving anti-patterns in the field of multi-threading. Compared to the anti-pattern description by Smith et al., 2000, Hallal et al. include a categorization aspect into their template for describing multi-threading anti-patterns. However, neither Smith et al., 2000 nor Hallal et al., 2004 explicitly consider the aspect of causal relationships between anti-patterns. By contrast, we provide a causal taxonomy on performance problems by including explicit consideration of cause-effect relationships in our categorization template.

Analyzing the work of Brown et al., 1998, Smith et al., 2000 and Tate (Tate, 2002; Tate et al., 2003), Parsons derives a hierarchy for the classification of anti-patterns, whereby the hierarchy comprises four levels of categorization (Parsons, 2007). Starting with anti-patterns in general (root of the hierarchy), Parsons distinguishes between performance anti-patterns and anti-patterns that are related to other quality attributes. Performance anti-patterns are further partitioned along a technological dimension (Java (EJB), .NET, etc.). Finally, on the fourth level, Parsons distinguished between *deployment*, *design* and *programming* anti-patterns. While deployment anti-patterns describe common mistakes in distributing software components or configuring deployment, design anti-patterns represent recurrent design decisions that lead to poor performance. Finally, programming anti-patterns are errors that are unconsciously introduced by developers during the implementation phase. By means of the categorization hierarchy, Parsons highlight the categories of anti-patterns that are detectable by the Performance Anti-pattern Detection (PAD) tool described in (Parsons, 2007). Unlike our classification and taxonomy on performance problems, the hierarchy in (Parsons, 2007) is on a more abstract level and does not consider characteristics and interrelationships of individual anti-patterns.

To sum up, the related work in describing and classifying performance problems provides essential explicit knowledge about recurrent types of performance problems. Various anti-patterns have been defined and classified in different domains. Definitions of software performance anti-patterns cover generic, technology-independent as well as technology-specific anti-patterns. Though multiple classification schemes exist for anti-patterns, none of the discussed research works explicitly considers causal effects between individual types of anti-patterns. By contrast, in this, thesis we provide a causal taxonomy on performance problems that increases the systematology of diagnosing performance problems.

8.2. Experimentation and Models in Measurement-based Performance Evaluation

Common methods, techniques and considerations in experiment-based performance evaluation have been introduces in (Jain, 1991) and (Menascé et al., 2001). General performance testing approaches are described in (Weyuker et al., 2000) and (Avritzer et al., 1996). In this section we focus on approaches that apply systematic experimentation to achieve a certain goal. Furthermore, we consider research work that provides models for specification and management of performance tests. The discussed approaches are compared to P^2D^2M as well as our SSE concept.

Westermann introduces the Software Performance Cockpit (SoPeCo) approach for measurement-based, experimental derivation of performance models (D. J. Westermann, 2014). In that context, performance models are regression functions that describe a functional dependency between a set of independent variables and a set of dependent variables of a measurement-based evaluation context. Westermann proposes a systematic execution of measurement experiments to capture such functional dependencies. For a systematic derivation of performance models, the SoPeCo approach provides a language for the specification of the evaluation context, experiments to be executed in that context, as well as execution strategies for the experiments (D. Westermann et al., 2013). The SoPeCo approach comprises four steps: *context definition*, *understanding performance behaviour*, *derivation of performance model*, and *validation of performance model*. The first step encapsulates all tasks required to set up and describe the evaluation context by means of the corresponding specification language. In the second step, assumptions on influences between independent and dependent variables of the evaluation context are tested and improved. During performance model derivation, a set of experiments is executed and different regression strategies are applied to derive a regression function. Finally, the prediction accuracy of the derived regression function is validated. The SoPeCo framework fully automates the execution of experiments and the subsequent analysis tasks. Due to its focus on deriving regression functions, the SoPeCo specification language is more abstract than the P^2D^2M introduced in this thesis (Chapter 5). In particular, in (D. J. Westermann, 2014), the measurement environment is simply described by a set of parameters whose semantics come from extensions for the SoPeCo framework that need to be provided by the users of SoPeCo. Complex hierarchical situations, such as comprehensive instrumentation descriptions, cannot be described easily by a plain set of parameter values. By contrast, P^2D^2M provides a language that is tailored for performance problem diagnostics and, thus, allows to intuitively describe experiments for that purpose. Similar to the SSE concept, SoPeCo applies systematic experimentation. However, as SoPeCo entirely abstracts from the internals of individual experiments, it does not explicitly cover instrumentation aspects. By contrast, in addition to systematic experimentation, the selective, goal-oriented instrumentation in each experiment is a core part of the SSE concept.

With the same goal of deriving measurement-based performance models, Thakkar et al., 2008 propose a framework that is similar to the SoPeCo framework by D. J. Westermann, 2014. The framework in (Thakkar et al., 2008) supports the performance engineer throughput the entire experimentation cycle by automating the tasks from test specification over test execution to data analysis and model building. Analogously to the work of Westermann, Thakkar et al. apply statistical methods for test case selection and reduction, as well as for model building. Similarly to the implementation of our APPD approach (i.e. DynamicSpotter), the framework of Thakkar et al. allows for connecting different load generation tools, such as HP LoadRunner™. In contrast to our work,Thakkar et al., 2008 do not explicitly introduce a language for specifying experiments. Furthermore, though Thakkar et al. apply systematic experimentation for the derivation of performance models, in contrast to our SSE concept, they do not consider selective instrumentation.

Woodside et al. (Woodside et al., 2001) propose a workbench for automated derivation of resource functions. In that context, resource functions describe parametric dependencies between some influencing parameters an resource demands (such as CPU demand) of software components or entire target systems. In general, they pursue the same goal as already described for

D. J. Westermann, 2014 and Thakkar et al., 2008. The workbench provided by Woodside et al. automatically executes a set of experiments for the parameter space spanned by the influencing parameters. Their experiment specification language is limited to the description of parameter variations and is way to abstract for the purpose of diagnosing performance problems by measurement. Overall, the difference of the work in (Woodside et al., 2001) to our SSE concept and our P^2D^2M is analogous to the work by D. J. Westermann, 2014 and Thakkar et al., 2008: no consideration of selective instrumentation and experiment specification languages that are on an abstract level with respect to the purpose of diagnosing performance problems.

For the derivation of performance-relevant properties of infrastructures Hauck et al. introduce the GINPEX approach (Hauck et al., 2011). Using a custom load driver, GINPEX applies multiple experiments with different load profiles to analyze the performance-relevant parameters of the infrastructure under test. Hauck et al. propose the following process for the application of the GINPEX approach: (i) In the first step a load driver that is shipped with GINPEX needs to be deployed on all machines that belong to the infrastructure under test. (ii) The load drivers are then used to conduct diverse experiments, while gathering different measurements. (iii) In the third step, the measurements are analyzed to derive performance-relevant properties of the infrastructure. (iv) Finally, the results are integrated in a performance model, for instance, in order to derive software performance predictions. For the specification of experiments, Hauck et al. provide a tailored meta-model. A model instance comprises a description of the target environment, a set of sensors to be measured, as well as a structure on tasks to be executed. The are different types of tasks including control flow tasks and machine tasks. While the control flow tasks allow to build complex task structures, machine tasks constitute different load components, such as CPU load, network load, etc. In this way, experiments can be specified with different load constellations and progression. With respect to systematic experimentation, the difference between the work in (Hauck et al., 2011) and our SSE is the same as it was the case for the work of D. J. Westermann, 2014. Though Hauck et al. apply systematic experimentation, they do not consider the aspect of selective instrumentation. Regarding the experiment specification language of Hauck et al., there are similarities to P^2D^2M with respect to the intention of the individual model parts, including specification of the measurement environment, metrics and experiment series. However, as the focus in (Hauck et al., 2011) is on performance analysis of infrastructure properties, their model is tailored for that specific purpose and, thus, aims at modelling other aspects than the P^2D^2M.

Bertolino et al. propose a model-driven approach for monitoring (Bertolino et al., 2011). The proposed approach comprises two major parts: a generic, yet domain-specific meta-model and a generic monitoring infrastructure. The former part is called Property Meta-Model (PMM) and allows to generically specify observable properties of the target system. The model allows to describe prescriptive and descriptive, as well as qualitative and quantitative properties. For quantitative properties, PMM provides means to specify metrics. The properties can be assigned to different categories of software quality that are evaluated, including performance, security, trust and dependability. The second part of the approach is a monitoring infrastructure called GLIMPSE. The purpose of glimpse is to interpret PMM instances, apply them on the target systems, and to conduct data interpretation, transmission and aggregation. Similar to the Instrumentation and Monitoring (IaM) Description part of P^2D^2M described in this thesis, PMM allows to describe monitoring instructions. However, the focus of the languages is a different. While, PMM has a strong focus on specifying properties and their metrics, the IaM meta-model in P^2D^2M encapsulates domain-specific knowledge in instrumentation and monitoring for performance evaluation. In particular, the IaM meta-model contains concrete elements on typical, partly complex, instrumentation scopes and probes. In this way, the IaM description language allows to describe complex instrumentation instruction in a compositional, yet intuitive way.

Bošković et al., 2009 introduce an approach for Model Driven Performance Measurement and Assessment with Relational Traces (MoDePeMART). Under the assumption of a model-driven development process, MoDePeMART provides means to declaratively specify performance metrics in a domain specific language. Thereby, the model elements of the MoDePeMART language directly refer to elements of the target system model. Similar to Bertolino et al., 2011, the modelling approach proposed by Bošković et al., 2009 for measurement specification depends on the availability of a system model. Furthermore, a MoDePeMART model instances is specific to one concrete system model. In contrast, instances of our IaM Description language can be created in a generic way so that they can be applied to a broad range of target systems.

The Object Management Group introduces the Structured Metrics Meta-Model (SMM) standard for the specification of model-based measurements (Object Management Group, 2015a). The central element in SMM is a *measure* that, in a generic way, allows to describes calculations of certain properties of a software system. In this way, a measure can be used to describe metrics of different kinds including quality attributes like response times, system size, failure rates, etc. The scope of a measure can be limited by using OCL expressions or a dedicated scope meta-model element. Besides simple measures, SMM provides the notion of *collective measures* to describe aggregated measures such as average, minimum or maximum. *Measurements* capture the results for individual measures. Based on the SMM standard, Van Hoorn introduces the MAMBA approach that, basically, extends SMM and facilitates its usage (van Hoorn, 2014). In particular, MAMBA provides additional aggregate functions, collective measures, as well as the support for describing periodic measures and querying measurement data. Furthermore, MAMBA provides tool support for model execution and integration of raw measurement data. Hence, both SMM and MAMBA provide comprehensive and expressive means to describe measurement data. Therefore, these modeling languages are closely related to the data representation part of our P^2D^2M. In particular, within P^2D^2M we could theoretically use SMM or MAMBA. However, in the APPD approach, auxiliary functions like measurement aggregation or ranking are integrated into the individual heuristics and are tailored for the individual needs of the heuristics. SMM and MAMBA are way to complex for the needs of the APPD approach. Therefore, the data representation part of P^2D^2M is a light-weight meta-model compared to SMM and MAMBA.

Apart from MAMBA, Van Hoorn proposes a model-driven instrumentation as part of the SLAstic approach (van Hoorn, 2014). SLAstic is an approach for model-driven, online capacity management and is discussed in Section 8.3.2. In the context of the SLAstic approach, all aspects of the target system are represented in a system model, including software architecture, behaviour and performance characteristics. For model-driven instrumentation, van Hoorn proposes to specify instrumentation directives as annotations, for instance on operations or software components, in the corresponding system model. Assuming that a model-driven software engineering

(MDSE) development process is applied, model-to-model and model-to-text transformations are used to derive implementation skeletons from the system model. This also applies for the instrumentation directives. For example, instrumentation annotations in the system model may be transformed to configuration files for corresponding Aspect-oriented Programming (AOP) tools that weave instrumentation instructions into the source code of the target application. Similar to our IaM Description part of P^2D^2M, the instrumentation approach proposed by Van Hoorn uses modeling to describe instrumentation. However, they differ in one essential aspect. In (van Hoorn, 2014), instrumentation instructions are modeled as annotations that decorate elements from a comprehensive system model. Hence, unlike IaM in P^2D^2M, the instrumentation instructions of the SLAstic approach are not first-class model entities but depend on the availability of a comprehensive system model. By contrast, APPD and P^2D^2M do not require a system model.

Bernardino et al., 2014 discuss the requirements and design decisions for a domain-specific language for specifying performance tests. The authors propose that a corresponding language should cover three aspects: (i) A monitoring specification describes where and what should be measured in the target system. This part also includes the description of the measurement environment. (ii) A scenario specification should allow to describe user and workload profiles, including configurations like warm-up and cool-down phases, as well as constellations of different workload classes. (iii) Finally, the behaviour of each workload class needs to be specified by means of a user script. The description of requirements in (Bernardino et al., 2014) perfectly maps to P^2D^2M in this thesis. However, while we provide concrete meta-models in this thesis (cf. Chapter 5), Bernardino et al. discuss only the requirements and design decisions without showing concrete realizations of their considerations.

8.3. Performance Problem Detection and Diagnostics

There is a large body of literature in the field of detecting software problems in general. Approaches for the detection of functional errors are often based on statical code analysis (Reimer et al., 2004; Evans, 1996; Detlefs,

1996). In contrast to functional aspects, performance is a software quality attribute that is inherently dynamic. Hence, in order to detect performance problems the dynamic aspects of a software system need to be analyzed. This can be either accomplished by analyzing performance models and system models that are annotated with performance characteristics, or by conducting measurements on an implemented system. Accordingly, the related work in the field of performance problem detection and diagnostics can be roughly divided into purely model-based and measurement-based approaches. In the latter case, the approaches may also use system models for detection of performance problems, however, the models are either directly derived from measurements or are used to support measurement-based detection.

8.3.1. Model-based Detection

The major benefit of model-based performance evaluation approaches is their applicability in early development phases. In this way, design-level performance problems can be uncovered and resolved before they reach the implementation or even operations phase. In this sub-section, we describe related work in the field of model-based detection and diagnostics of performance problems. Table 8.1 gives an overview on the research work discussed in this section and provides a classification along five aspects. The first two columns give a reference to the corresponding work and a short description, respectively. The third column (*Model*) shows the modeling languages that the different approaches are applied to. The *Detection* and *Diagnostics* columns indicate whether the approaches solely discover the existence of a performance problem, or whether they also conduct a diagnostics, hence, provide insights on the location and nature of the problem's root cause. The *Anti-patterns* column denotes approaches that are based on the notion of performance anti-patterns (Smith et al., 2000). Finally, the last column indicates whether the approaches are fully automated or not. In the following, we discuss the individual approaches in more detail and their relation to our APPD approach.

Based on Layered Queueing Network (LQN) models, Franks et al. provide a framework for identifying bottlenecks in the corresponding models and providing solutions for their mitigation (Franks et al., 2006). The work in

(Franks et al., 2006) is limited to one single type of problems (i.e. bottlenecks). Furthermore, due to the big semantic gap between LQN models and the actual target systems, the feedback provided by the proposed approach entails extensive interpretation effort by the software engineers.

Williams et al. introduce the PASA (Performance Assessment of Software Architectures) method describing a systematic process for performance evaluation (Williams et al., 2002). Similar to the methods SAAM (Software Architecture Analysis Method, Kazman et al., 1996) and ATAM (Architecture Tradeoff Analysis Method, Kazman et al., 1998), the PASA method is based on scenarios that describe different usage patterns of the target system. The PASA process comprises nine steps which of one is *architectural analysis*. This step includes identification of architectural styles, identification of performance anti-patterns, as well as performance modeling and analysis. Hence, as part of the PASA method, Williams et al. propose to identify and refactor performance anti-patterns based on available architectural models to improve the performance of a system under design. However, Williams et al. do not propose any tool support or automation for the detection of performance anti-patterns.

Xu describes the Performance Booster (PB) approach for automatic diagnosis of performance problems at design time (Xu, 2012). PB is a rule-based approach that operates on performance models (i.e. Layered Queueing Network models). Xu proposes to derive performance models from specifications of the target system. Thereby, the target system needs to be modeled using Unified Modeling Language (UML) and the UML MARTE (Modeling and Analysis of Real-Time and Embedded Systems, Object Management Group, 2015b) profile. The MARTE profile allows to annotate a UML model with performance characteristics. Based on this information, a performance model can be automatically derived. The performance model is then solved to obtain performance measures. Xu defines a set of diagnostics and change rules that describe performance problem localization and model improvement strategies. Building on the bottleneck definition in (Franks et al., 2006), Xu considers two types of performance problems: *bottlenecks* as causes for low throughput and *long paths* as cause for high response times. Furthermore, Xu shows the causal relationship between the two performance problem types. Bottlenecks and long paths are detected by applying corresponding diagnostics rules on the performance measures obtained from performance model solving. By automatically applying change rules on the LQN model,

Literature	Description	Model	Detection	Diagnostics	Anti-patterns	Automated
Franks et al., 2006	Framework for detection and mitigation of layered bottlenecks	LQN	✓	—	—	✓
Williams et al., 2002	PASA – Performance Assessment of Software Architectures method	any	✓	✓	✓	—
Xu, 2012	Performance Booster – automatic diagnosis of performance problems	UML & LQN	✓	✓	—	✓
Benoit, 2005	Diagnostics of performance problems in database management systems	custom	✓	✓	—	✓
Cortellessa et al., 2007	Framework for automated performance feedback generation	LQN	✓	✓	✓	(✓)
Cortellessa et al., 2010a, Cortellessa et al., 2014	Rule-based detection of performance anti-patterns	custom XML	✓	✓	✓	✓
Cortellessa et al., 2010b	Detection of performance anti-patterns in UML models	UML	✓	✓	✓	✓
Trubiani et al., 2011	Automatic detection and resolution of performance anti-patterns	PCM	✓	✓	✓	✓

Table 8.1.: Overview on model-based performance problem detection approaches

PB mitigates the detected performance problems. In order to provide meaningful design feedback, Xu propose to manually transform the changes on the LQN model to the design model (i.e. UML). Due to the focus on LQN models and the notion of performance problems as defined in (Franks et al., 2006), the PB approach is limited to the detection of bottlenecks and long paths. Hence, in contrast to anti-pattern-based approaches, PB is not able to provide insights on the nature of the detected problems. Moreover, the interpretation step from the changes on the LQN model to corresponding activities on the design model has to be conducted manually.

Benoit introduces an automatic diagnostics approach for performance problems in database management systems (Benoit, 2005). In this context, Benoit define the process of diagnosing a problems as "[...] determining which resource(s) is responsible for the performance problem" (Benoit, 2005). Benoit uses a decision tree to guide the diagnostics process. The inner nodes of the tree evaluate different performance metrics of the database management system. The leaf nodes represent resources that constitute the root cause of a performance problem. Hence, the systematic search in (Benoit, 2005) follows a similar idea as our APPD approach with the performance problem taxonomy. However, while our taxonomy organizes different performance anti-patterns, the decision tree in (Benoit, 2005) is limited to specific performance questions in the domain of database management systems.

The research group around Cortellessa have conducted some research work in detecting and solving performance anti-patterns based on different system model representations. In their early work, Cortellessa et al. describe a framework for automated generation of architecture-level feedback when conducting analyses on performance models (Cortellessa et al., 2007). The authors propose a multi-level approach for performance evaluation of a model. Starting with an abstract system-level model, the proposed approach conducts an analysis of the corresponding derived performance model (e.g. Layered Queueing Networks). The obtained performance metrics are used to automatically generate feedback on further actions by means of so called *interpretation matrices*. Considering different performance metrics and corresponding performance requirements, the interpretation matrices describe different potential scenarios and corresponding actions for further analysis. If in a system-level model a violation of requirements has been detected, the corresponding interpretation matrix proposes to refine the model and to search for anti-patterns on the sub-system level of the model. As soon as the model has been changed due to a proposed solution alternative, the process starts from beginning to evaluate the change. Though in (Cortellessa et al., 2007), the feedback is generated automatically by means of the interpretation matrices, the whole process is not fully automated. In particular, performance engineers have to further interpret and apply the actions suggested by the matrices. Furthermore, as the proposed approach works on low level performance models, the gap between the generated feedback and the actual system is still big.

In (Cortellessa et al., 2010a; Cortellessa et al., 2014), the authors use first-order logic predicates to formalize descriptions of performance anti-patterns. This work assumes that a system model is available in a custom XML format. The XML model captures three view types of the target system. (i) The static view captures all relevant elements of the system as well as their relationships. (ii) The dynamic view describes interactions between individual elements. (iii) Finally, the deployment view captures the allocation of the software elements to hardware resources. Based on the system model representations, Cortellessa et al. provide system-independent specifications of performance anti-patterns in form of first-order logic rules. The rules contain supporting functions as well as fix thresholds that are used to evaluate certain metrics. The threshold values need to be set by software architects based on some heuristics. Finally, a rule engine applies the anti-pattern rules to the system model and, as the result, provides a list of detected anti-patterns.

In (Cortellessa et al., 2010b), the authors apply the same concepts to detect and solve performance anti-patterns in systems that are modeled using UML. Thereby, the static, dynamic, and deployment aspects of the target system are modeled using UML notation. Furthermore, the UML model is annotated with performance characteristics using the UML MARTE profile. Analogously to the first-order logic predicates in (Cortellessa et al., 2010a), in (Cortellessa et al., 2010b), the authors formalize performance anti-patterns as Object Constraint Language (OCL) rules and a set of actions to resolve the anti-patterns on the UML model. An OCL rule engine is employed for evaluation of the corresponding rules on the UML model to detect performance anti-patterns. While the detection of anti-patterns is fully automated, the resolution remains a manual task in (Cortellessa et al., 2010b).

By contrast, in (Trubiani et al., 2011), the authors provide a fully automatic approach for detecting and solving performance anti-pattern in software systems that are modeled with the Palladio Component Model (PCM). Analogously to the research work in (Cortellessa et al., 2010a) and (Cortellessa et al., 2010b), Trubiani et al. provide a formalization of the performance anti-patterns by means of rules based on PCM meta-model elements, as well as corresponding actions to solve identified anti-patterns in a PCM instance. As the target system may contain multiple anti-patterns and each anti-pattern may have several solution alternatives, Trubiani et al. propose an iterative process of detecting and solving performance-antipatterns to find the best fitting solution.

As the detection of performance anti-patterns in (Cortellessa et al., 2010a; Cortellessa et al., 2010b) and (Trubiani et al., 2011) is based on heuristics that may produce false positives, Cortellessa et al. propose a process to extract "guilty" anti-patterns that actually lead to a performance requirement violation. First, performance requirements and a system model are evaluated by means of analytical methods or through simulation. The result is a system model annotated with performance characteristics and a set of violated performance requirements. Using one of the described approaches (Cortellessa et al., 2010a; Cortellessa et al., 2010b; Trubiani et al., 2011) the annotated system model is evaluated against a set of performance anti-pattern rules, yielding a set of detected anti-patterns. The set of identified anti-patterns is then compared to the set of violated requirements to extract only those anti-patterns that actually lead to a performance requirement violation. Finally, anti-patterns are ranked by means of calculated guiltiness scores.

The work conducted by the research group of Cortellessa shares some similarities with our approach. Analogously to those work we utilize the notion of performance anti-patterns to provide meaningful feedback as the result of performance problem diagnostics. Furthermore, all described approaches by Cortellessa et al. and Trubiani et al. share the common core of formalizing performance anti-patterns by means of rules that are based on corresponding meta-model elements. For the APPD approach we encapsulated the formalization of anti-patterns in from of detection heuristics. The notion of detection strategies of our heuristics expressed as algorithms come closest to the rules specified by Cortellessa et al. In addition to the detection strategies, our detection heuristics encapsulate experimentation rules that describe how to detect corresponding performance anti-patterns by experimentation. A detailed, yet essential, difference to our detection heuristics is the explicit and intentional usage of fix thresholds in the anti-pattern rules. In (Trubiani et al., 2011), the authors say: "The binding of thresholds is a critical point of the whole approach." Furthermore, in this thesis we have shown that fix thresholds hinder generic applicability of the heuristics to different target systems (cf. Chapter 6). The same applies for the anti-pattern rules specified by Cortellessa et al., as the authors assign the responsibility of determining reasonable threshold values to software architects or domain experts.

To sum up, apart from typical benefits of model-based performance problem detection approaches, such as the possibility of design time evaluation, these approaches inherently entail some drawbacks. Firstly, model-based approaches assume the availability of a system model (e.g. modeled in UML, PCM, etc.) which is an assumption that often does not apply in practise and industrial development projects. Secondly, as design time models exhibit a high abstraction level, they inherently are not able to cover performance problems that are manifested in the implementation details of a target system. Finally, due to the abstraction level, models usually exhibit deviations in their performance predictions compared to the actual implemented system. These inaccuracies may also impact the diagnostics approaches that are based on the modeled performance characteristics. In order to take advantages from both model-based and measurement-based approaches, we propose to apply approaches such as described in (Trubiani et al., 2011) during the design phase of a development process, and approaches as described in this thesis during the implementation and testing phase.

8.3.2. Measurement-based Detection

While model-based performance problem detection approaches can be applied during design time, measurement-based approaches require a runnable implementation of fragments or the entire target system for their execution. Hence, measurement-based detection approaches can either be applied during development (e.g. as part of continuous integration and testing phases) or during operation. Approaches that can be applied during development detect performance problems before they appear in operation. By contrast, operation-phase approaches have a rather reactive nature, as they report performance problems that have already been experienced by the users of the target system.

	Literature	Description	Phase	Detection	Diagnostics	Mult. Types	Anti-patterns	Impl. Level	Tech.-indep.
Multiple Problem Types	Miller et al., 1995	Paradyn – systematic search for performance bottlenecks	O	✓	✓	✓	—	✓	✓
	Parsons, 2007 Parsons et al., 2008	PAD – rule-based performance anti-pattern detection in JEE applications	O	✓	✓	✓	✓	—	—
	Peiris et al., 2014	NiPAD – non-intrusive detection of performance anti-patterns	T, O	✓	—	✓	—	—	—
	Grechanik et al., 2012	FOREPOST – feedback-directed learning to select input data for performance tests	T	✓	—	✓	—	✓	✓
	Marwede et al., 2009	RanCorr – correlation of anomaly score for problem localization	O	✓	—	✓	—	—	✓
	Ehlers et al., 2011	Localization of performance anomalies by self-adaptive monitoring	O	✓	(✓)	✓	—	✓	✓
	Di Marco et al., 2014	Model-driven approach for measurementbased detection of perf. anti-patterns	D, T	✓	✓	✓	✓	—	✓

Table 8.2.: Overview on measurement-based performance problem detection approaches: Multiple Problem Types

	Literature	Description	Phase	Detection	Diagnostics	Mult. Types	Anti-patterns	Impl. Level	Tech.-indep.
Specific Problem Types	Nistor et al., 2013	Toddler – inefficiencies in loops	T	✓	✓	—	—	✓	✓
	Espinosa et al., 1998	Automatic evaluation of performance problems in parallel programs	T	✓	✓	—	—	✓	—
	Vetter, 2000	Automatic localization of communication performance problems in MPI applications	T	✓	✓	—	—	✓	—
	Yan et al., 2012	Detecting run-time bloat by analyzing the reference propagation graph	T	✓	✓	—	—	✓	—
	Chen et al., 2014	CauseInfer – inference of performance problem causes in distributed applications	T, O	✓	(✓)	—	—	—	✓

Table 8.3.: Overview on measurement-based performance problem detection approaches: Specific Problem Types

	Literature	Description	Phase	Detection	Diagnostics	Mult. Types	Anti-patterns	Impl. Level	Tech.-indep.
Detection of Performance Regressions	Bulej et al., 2005	Performance regression benchmarking on middleware software	T	✓	—	✓	—	✓	—
	Foo et al., 2010	Detection of performance regressions by mining regression testing repositories	T	✓	—	✓	—	✓	✓
	Heger et al., 2013	PRCA – performance regression root cause analysis by unit testing	T	✓	(✓)	✓	—	✓	✓
	Nguyen et al., 2012	Control charts for automated detection of performance regressions	T	✓	—	✓	—	✓	✓
	Pradel et al., 2014	SpeedGun – automatic detection of performance regressions in concurrent classes	T	✓	—	—	—	✓	✓
	Ghaith et al., 2015	Workload-independent detection of performance regressions	T	✓	—	✓	—	✓	✓
	Waller et al., 2015	Regression benchmarking in continuous integration	T	✓	—	✓	—	✓	✓
Online P&C Management	Kounev et al., 2010 Brosig et al., 2011	Descartes – self-aware computing systems for managing efficiency and dependability	O	✓	—	✓	—	—	✓
	van Hoorn, 2014 van Hoorn et al., 2009	SLAstic – model-driven online capacity management	O	✓	—	✓	—	—	✓
	Automatic Performance Problem Diagnostics (APPD)		T	✓	✓	✓	✓	✓	✓

Table 8.4.: Overview on measurement-based performance problem detection approaches: Regression & Online P.&C. Management

In this sub-section, we consider the related work in the field of measurement-based detection and diagnostics of performance problems. The Tables 8.2, 8.3, 8.4 show the different approaches that are discussed in the following and provides a classification of the related work in this area. Analogously to Table 8.1, the second and the third columns provide references and short descriptions for the individual approaches. Considering the variety of measurement-based approaches for performance problem detection, we identified four main categories. The first category comprises generic approaches that are able to detect multiple, different types of performance problems. By contrast, the approaches in the second category focus on the detection of specific types of performance problems. The third category comprises approaches that apply performance regression testing to detect degradations in performance. Finally, approaches that realize online performance and capacity management are related to performance problem detection, too. In particular, the self-adaptation aspect of these approaches is triggered by detected inefficiencies and problems in performance. Besides the four main categories, we further categorize the measurement-based approaches along another seven aspects. The *Phase* column indicates in which development phase an approach is applicable. Hereby *D*, *T* and *O* stand for *Design Phase*, *Testing Phase* and *Operations Phase*, respectively. Furthermore, we distinguish between approaches that only do a pure detection and those that conduct a diagnostics of performance problems. In this context, diagnostics covers two aspects. (i) Root causes of performance problems must be localized (as precise as possible). (ii) Information on the nature and type of performance problems and their root causes must be provided. The *Mult. Types* column explicitly reflects the difference between the first two main categories for all approaches. The *Anti-patterns* column indicates whether the corresponding approaches use the notion of anti-patterns (Smith et al., 2000) for their detection or diagnostics. Approaches that have a checkmark in the *Impl.-Level* column are able to detect performance problems that are manifested in the implementation details of a target system rather than in the design or deployment. Finally, the last column indicates whether the approaches are independent of specific technologies of the target system. The last row in Table 8.4 shows the classification of the APPD approach into this scheme.

In the following we discuss the approaches shown in Table Tables 8.2, 8.3, 8.4 in more detail and explain in which aspects the APPD approach differs from existing approaches.

Detection of Multiple Performance Problem Types

The work that is closest related to our APPD approach is the Paradyn tool introduced by Miller et al., 1995. Actually, the work in this thesis has been inspired by the Paradyn approach. Paradyn is a tool for automatic detection of performance bottlenecks in large-scale parallel programs. Paradyn combines dynamic instrumentation with systematic search to localise specific locations of performance bottlenecks. In (Miller et al., 1995), dynamic instrumentation is realized by dynamic modification of the binary program conducted by platform-specific Paradyn daemons. Thereby, an instrumentation instruction is defined by an instrumentation point (i.e. location), a primitive (i.e. the instrumentation code to be injected) and predicates that check conditions for instrumentation primitives to be executed. Guided by the systematic search process as well as other influencing factors (such as monitoring overhead) Paradyn's Performance Consultant decides where and which instrumentation instructions shell be placed. The data collected by the instrumentation instructions is aligned along an abstract data structure. The data structure is a matrix (*metric-focus grid*) of metrics (such as CPU times, blocking times, etc.) and locations (system nodes, software objects, software blocks, etc.). Furthermore, the data is captured in from of time histograms, to capture the relation to the execution time of the program. The systematic bottleneck diagnostics is guided by the W^3 model that spans a three dimensional space of search aspects: (i) *Why* does a performance bottleneck occur? (ii) *Where* is the location of the bottleneck? (iii) *When* did the bottleneck occur? Along the *Why-axis* different hypotheses about typical manifestations of performance bottlenecks are tested. Furthermore, these hypotheses can be refined, which results in a hierarchical structure that is similar to our performance problem taxonomy. The *Why-axis* enables a systematic search from abstract symptoms to concrete manifestations of a bottleneck. The *When-axis* is used to narrow down the location of a bottlenecks. Hereby, system elements (e.g. system nodes, components, code blocks, hardware resources, etc.) are structured in an hierarchical way to enable a systematic search for the location. Finally, the *When-axis* allows to identify the time frame when a performance problem occurred. The APPD approach has been inspired by the Paradyn approach with respect to two aspects: (i) The idea of dynamically adapting the instrumentation of the target system is the basis for the SSE concept. In addition to (Miller et al., 1995), the SSE concept combines dynamic instrumentation with systematic experimentation. In this way, the analysis of the target system can be conducted in a more goal-oriented and effective way. In particular, experimentation allows to analyse the target system under different load intensities, according to the performance problem under investigation. (ii) Systematically searching for performance problems from generic symptoms to concrete root causes is the core idea in both approaches, Paradyn and APPD. While the understanding of performance problems in (Miller et al., 1995) has a rather generic nature (i.e. notion of bottlenecks), in this thesis, we utilize the notion of performance anti-patterns. As already discussed in Section 8.1, anti-patterns encapsulate more semantics about the nature of corresponding performance problems. In particular, the anti-patterns encapsulate domain knowledge (e.g. messaging related problems, database related problems, etc.) as well as typical manifestations and root causes. By contrast, Miller et al. refer to a root cause of a performance problem abstractly as "parts of the program that contribute significant time to its execution" (Miller et al., 1995). On top of Paradyn,Karavanic et al., 1999 include knowledge from historical data from previous runs of Paradyn to increase the efficiency of Paradyn in finding bottlenecks.

Parsons et al. describe an approach for automatic detection of performance anti-patterns in the domain of component-based enterprise applications that are written in Java using Java EE technologies (Parsons et al., 2004; Parsons, 2007; Parsons et al., 2008). The authors introduce the Performance Antipattern Detection (PAD) tool that is based on the principles of a knowledge base and a rule engine. The PAD approach comprises three main parts: monitoring, analysis and detection. The monitoring part is responsible for collecting measurement data throughout the entire target system. This includes identification of software components, their interaction and communication patterns, objects that are transferred across components, and utilization of hardware resources. Monitoring is conducted on component level, hence, internals of the components are not monitored. The monitoring data is used to reconstruct a run-time design of the system in the analysis part. A run-time design captures structural as well as behavioural aspects of the system under execution. Structural aspects cover the identification of software components and their relationships. Run-time paths, tracked objects and communication patterns are core behavioural concepts in PAD. Basically, the run-time design constitutes a model that reflects the system under execution. The run-time design is permanently analyzed by a rule engine for potential anti-patterns. Thereby, each performance anti-pattern is formulated as a set of rules using the Java rule engine (Friedman-Hill, 2013). If any of the anti-pattern rules fires, an occurrence of the corresponding anti-pattern is reported. Though Parsons et al., similarly to our approach, utilize the notion of anti-patterns for measurement-based detection of performance problems, the PAD approach differs from the APPD approach with respect to some aspects. The PAD approach is a knowledge-based approach instead of an experiment-based approach as it is the case with APPD. To gather enough data for a representative run-time design, the approach by Parsons et al. needs to be executed for a longer period of time. Hence, PAD is rather intended to be used at operation time. By contrast, the APPD approach is explicitly designed for the testing phase of a software development process. In this way APPD allows to diagnose and fix of performance problems before they reach the operations phase. Furthermore, Parsons et al. focus on Java EE anti-patterns within the categories of design and deployment anti-patterns. In particular, the authors explicitly exclude anti-patterns that are related to implementation details. By contrast, in this thesis, we have shown that the APPD is able to deal with different target technologies as well as different types of anti-patterns (design and implementation anti-patterns).

Peiris et al. propose a non-intrusive performance anti-pattern detection (NiPAD) approach (Peiris et al., 2014). Instead of instrumenting the target application, the NiPAD approach solely requires system-level metrics that can be monitored without instrumentation of the application's code (e.g. CPU utilization, network utilization, etc.). Based on the values of the system-level metrics the NiPAD approach applies classification techniques to distinguish systems that contain a performance anti-pattern from those that do not contain an anti-pattern. Given two applications which of one contains a performance anti-pattern, the assumption is that a discriminant function exists that separates the values of the system-level metrics of the applications. The metric values are obtained by executing performance tests. The discriminant function is derived by applying different machine learning approaches whereby labeled scenarios are used for learning the scenarios that contain performance anti-patterns. In (Peiris et al., 2014) the authors demonstrate a proof of concept for the non-intrusive detection approach by means of the One Lane Bridge (OLB) anti-pattern. Due to the high level observation of the target system, apart from detecting that an anti-pattern exists, the NiPAD approach inherently lacks the ability of diagnosing the root causes of performance problems. Moreover, from the work in (Peiris et al., 2014) it does not become clear whether the NiPAD approach is applicable to other anti-patterns than the OLB.

Grechanik et al. propose another approach that applies machine learning techniques for identification of performance bottlenecks (Grechanik et al., 2012). Thereby the authors utilize performance testing based on the idea of feedback-directed learning. The work in (Grechanik et al., 2012) is based on the assumption that occurrences of performance problems depend on input data of performance tests. With their approach FOREPOST, Grechanik et al. focus on efficiently finding proper input data that triggers a performance problem without the need to fully explore the parameter space of input data. Starting with a small set of performance tests with random allocations of input variables, FOREPOST extracts execution traces that are used to derive rules for data input. The rules describe dependencies between input values and corresponding performance behaviour or computational load, respectively. Hence, the rules constitute discriminant functions that separate input data for "good" and "bad test cases", whereby the "good test cases" uncover bad performance behaviour. The rules are used in a feedback loop to partition the input data (in good and bad data) for further test cases from which, again, rules are extracted. This cycle is repeated until the set of rules does not change anymore. Bottleneck methods are uncovered by identifying expensive methods in the traces that occur in good test cases but not in the set of bad test cases. The identification of proper input data for performance and load tests is an essential topic for measurement-based diagnostics of performance problems. Hence, this aspect of the work in (Grechanik et al., 2012) is complementary to our APPD approach, as we have shown that APPD depends on proper load scripts (cf. Section 7.7). The problem detection part of the FOREPOST approach is limited to the localization of expensive methods. In particular, the FOREPOST approach does not provide information on the nature of performance problems. By contrast, by utilizing the notion of anti-pattern our approach provides more semantics in the results of the diagnostics.

Marwede et al., 2009 introduce the anomaly correlation approach RanCorr for the localization of causes of anomalies. RanCorr is based on the working assumption that anomaly scores (e.g. response time deviations from a base-line) for individual software components are available. Based on these anomaly scores, Marwede et al. utilize the calling behaviour of components to localize components that are responsible for an anomaly. Using monitoring data, a calling dependency graph is derived. The nodes of the calling dependency graph constitute operations that call other operations. The graph captures the dynamic aspects of a request trace as well as correspondences to architectural elements (i.e. software components and deployment contexts) the operations belong to. Utilizing the fact that anomalies propagate through all parent nodes of the calling dependency graph, Marwede et al. conduct an analysis of the backward propagation of anomaly scores to uncover the guilty software components. While our approach is explicitly designed for the testing phase of a development process, the RanCorr approach is intended to support operators of a software application. Furthermore, though RanCorr is able to locate a performance problem, it does not provide insights on the type of the problem. By contrast, the results of the APPD approach provide information on the location and type of a problem's root cause.

Ehlers et al. propose a self-adaptive monitoring approach for localization of performance anomalies at operation time of a target system (Ehlers et al., 2011). Using the Kieker monitoring framework (van Hoorn et al., 2012), Ehlers et al. fully instrument the target application with measurement probes that can be enabled and disabled when needed. Guided by some evaluation goals, performance engineers define rules that describe the on-demand activation and deactivation of measurement probes. For the localization of performance anomalies, Ehlers et al. propose to refine instrumentation in the corresponding location whenever the calculated anomaly score for an operation exceeds a threshold. The monitoring rules are continuously evaluated based on the calculated anomaly scores. For the calculation of anomaly scores, the authors use forecasting techniques that allow to predict future values in a time series. Observed measurement values (i.e. response times) are compared to the forecasted values to detect anomalies. Anomaly scores for each operation are derived from the rates of observed anomalies. With their approach, Ehlers et al. are able to detect performance anomalies and precisely localize the their source. The systematic analysis of the source of a problem by refining instrumentation on demand is an approach that is very similar to the systematic search in our APPD approach. However, in contrast to APPD, the approach in (Ehlers et al., 2011) is intended to be used during operation of a software system. Furthermore, through the proposed approach is able to precisely localize the source of a performance anomaly, it does not provide insights on the type of the localized performance problem.

Di Marco et al. propose a model-driven approach for measurement-based detection of performance anti-patterns (Di Marco et al., 2014). Assuming that an architectural model exists for the target system, Di Marco et al. utilize the information available in the model to narrow the scope for measurement-based anti-pattern detection. In their previous work (Cortellessa et al., 2014) (cf. Section 8.3.1), Di Marco et al. introduced an anti-pattern formalization approach. Thereby, performance anti-patterns are described by means of first-order logic rules (predicates) along four view types: static (e.g. components and interfaces), dynamic (e.g. messages and operation calls), deployment (i.e. component allocation), and performance view (e.g. response times). In (Di Marco et al., 2014), the authors exploit the information in the system model to pre-calculate predicates from the static, dynamic and deployment views. In this, way the set of anti-patterns is filtered prior to execution of the target system. During execution only a sub-set of all anti-patterns needs to be analyzed with respect to the performance view. Gathering monitoring data, the proposed approach dynamically evaluates the performance view predicates to identify actual performance anti-patterns in the target system. Though the approach in (Di Marco et al., 2014) is a measurement-based approach, it assumes the availability of a fully specified, architectural system model. However, in many cases, this assumption cannot be met in practice. Furthermore, the analysis of anti-patterns in (Di Marco et al., 2014) is conducted on the component level and, thus, does not cover anti-patterns that are manifested in the implementation details of the target system.

Detection of Specific Performance Problem Types

Toddler is an approach for performance problem detection by analysing memory access patterns (Nistor et al., 2013). Nistor et al. focus on the detection of one particular type of performance problems: inefficient nested loops. The authors categorize loop-related performance problems along two dimensions resulting in four categories of loop-related problems. Thereby

Nistor et al. differentiate between problems that are caused by inner or outer loops and whether the problem is caused by redundant computations or inefficient computations. All these cases provide potential for performance improvement by reducing redundancy. The performance problems from the four categories described in (Nistor et al., 2013) exhibit the common characteristic that the memory access patterns are repeated between individual loop iterations in an equal or similar way. The authors exploit that fact by detecting this kind of performance problems by analyzing the memory access patterns of loops during execution of performance tests or even unit tests. Though Toddler very effectively detects inefficient nested loops, the scope of applicability is limited to one single type of performance problem. In particular load and scalability related performance problems are not covered by this approach.

Espinosa et al introduce an approach for automatic evaluation of performance problems in parallel programs (Espinosa et al., 1998). The authors focus on identifying inefficient intervals in the execution traces. Inefficient intervals are time periods in which the full potential of parallelization could not be used. Based on a classification of performance problems that constitute inefficient parallelization intervals, Espinosa et al. define a set of rules that represent the individual root causes of the specific performance problems. The rules constitute a knowledge base that is used to evaluate traces that are retrieved through monitoring the application. A inefficient interval problem is reported if at least one of the rules matches to the monitored traces. In contrast to our approach, the focus in the work by Espinosa et al., 1998 lies on detecting problems that only occur in the domain of parallel programs.

An approach for automatically localizing communication performance problems is presented by Vetter, 2000. The author proposes an approach for Message Passing Interface (MPI) applications that uses a decision tree for classifying communication-related performance problems in an execution of the application. The approach comprises three phases in order to be applied on a target system: modeling phase, classification phase and source code mapping phase. The modeling phase encapsulates the learning process of a decision tree. Thereto, different micro-benchmarks are executed containing scenarios with and without communication performance problems. During execution of the benchmark, MPI events are monitored that are used for calibration of the decision tree. The decision tree is then used in the classification phase for the identification of inefficiencies in MPI communication. In the final phase, the identified inefficiencies are mapped to the source code of the application. With respect to the goal, the work of Vetter is similar to the communication-related detection heuristics of the APPD approach. However, in contrast to the heuristics of APPD, the approach in (Vetter, 2000) requires learning of the decision tree for each individual target system the approach is applied on. Furthermore, the performance problems that can be detected by the approach in (Vetter, 2000) are specific to the technology MPI.

Yan et al. introduce a profiling approach for detecting run-time bloat (Yan et al., 2012). Thereby, run-time bloat denotes excessive memory usage that leads to performance degradation due to the overhead caused by according memory management activities (e.g. garbage collection). The reference propagation graph constitutes the central concept in (Yan et al., 2012), capturing the life cycles of Java objects. The graph comprises three different types of nodes, for object creation, assignment of objects, and object usage. In order to derive the reference propagation graph, Yan et al. fully instrument the target application using the special virtual machine RVM (Research Virtual Machine). By analyzing the paths in the reference propagation graph, the proposed approach is able to automatically identify inefficiencies in memory usage. Typical inefficiencies that can be detected by this approach are shortly living objects and created objects that are never used. Both cases lead to an unnecessarily increased garbage collection activity. Furthermore, by means of the propagation graph the approach in (Yan et al., 2012) is able to pinpoint to the code locations where the corresponding objects are unnecessarily created. Besides the fact that the approach proposed by Yan et al. focuses on the detection of one specific type of performance problem, the analysis approach completely differs from the APPD approach. Firstly, Yan et al. apply full instrumentation of the target application leading to performance overheads in the range of 3000% - 5000% (Yan et al., 2012). Secondly, the proposed approach analyzes the memory usage behaviour without considering the actual performance effect of the detected memory inefficiencies. In particular, the approach may report code places that potentially can be improved with respect to the memory usage behaviour, that in fact, however, do not impair the performance behaviour.

Chen et al. introduce the CauseInfer approach for performance diagnosis of distributed, cloud-centric applications (Chen et al., 2014). In a distributed environment of services, CauseInfer non-intrusively (without instrumentation of the application) detects violations of Service Level Objectives (SLO) and localizes the causes for the observed violations. Thereby, Chen et al. focus on root causes of performance problems that are manifested in improper utilization of physical and logical resources. CauseInfer comprises two main concepts: causality graphs and cause inference. Based on collected monitoring data (TCP traces, resource utilizations, etc.) CauseInfer creates a two-layered hierarchical causality graph including causality between sub-services and causality between collected metrics on each service node. If CauseInfer detects a violation of an SLO, it starts inferring the root cause by traversing the causality graph. Thereby, a root cause is typically a metric that caused the SLO violation. A close similarity to our APPD approach is the idea of conducting systematic search for the root cause by utilizing a causality-based hierarchical structure. However, the notion of causality is different in our APPD approach. In (Chen et al., 2014) the causality graph is dynamically built for each target system describing the dependency between services and metrics. By contrast, the performance problem taxonomy of the APPD approach is a generic, system-independent structure. Furthermore, though CauseInfer comprises a diagnostics of performance problems (i.e. cause inference), the level of detail of the diagnostics results differs from the APPD approach. In particular, Chen et al. do not analyze the internals of the application, hence, are not able to diagnose the actual application-internal root causes that lead to increased utilization of physical or logical resources.

Detection of Performance Regressions

Regression testing is a common approach in identifying functional problems in software (Leung et al., 1989). Unit testing is a well-known and established means to realize regression testing (Onoma et al., 1998). In recent decades the idea of regression testing has been applied to the field of performance evaluation. A performance regression is a degradation in performance compared to a baseline or some historic measurement data. In this context, detection of performance regressions is a sub-discipline of detecting performance problems. In the following, we consider different approaches that apply performance regression testing for identification of performance problems.

Bulej et al. introduce the regression benchmark approach as a combination of regression testing with benchmarking concepts (Bulej et al., 2005). While regression testing traditionally aims at uncovering functional regressions in an application, performance benchmarking is used to evaluate and compare the performance aspects of software systems. In order to identify performance regressions in middleware software, Bulej et al. propose to utilize established performance benchmarks. As existing middleware performance benchmarks are tailored for revealing performance issues in the tested middleware solutions, they constitute a promising means to conduct performance regression testing. Thereto, the benchmarks need to be highly automated to be executed repeatedly and tightly coupled to the development process and continuous integration. In this way performance problems can be detected early in the development phase. The shortcoming of regression benchmarking is the limited general applicability of the benchmarks to other types of software applications. In (Bulej et al., 2005), the authors do not explain whether and how regression benchmarking can be applied to diagnose the root causes of observed performance regressions.

Foo et al. propose a performance regression detection approach that utilizes regression test repositories (Foo et al., 2010). For each executed regression test (i.e. load test), the approach by Foo et al. gathers a large set of metrics including workload-specific metrics (e.g. arrival rates) as well as performance metrics (e.g. CPU utilization, response times, etc.). Based on the gathered metrics, the proposed approach calculates performance signatures. Therefore, correlations are identified on the metrics using concepts from the domain of data mining. Once a performance signature is calculated, the approach compares it to a corresponding, historical signature from a regression testing repository. If the new signature significantly deviates from the historical signature, the approach by Foo et al. signals a potential performance regression. Thereby, the approach reports a set of metrics that violate the correlation. Further interpretation of the results as well as root cause analysis have to be conducted manually by the performance engineer. In contrast to APPD, the approach in (Foo et al., 2010) is limited to detection of performance regression, abstaining from analysing the root cause.

Heger et al. introduce an approach for Performance regression Root Cause Analysis (PRCA) (Heger et al., 2013). The PRCA approach utilizes unit tests and the commit history of the target application's source code to identify performance regressions and isolating their root causes. Analogously to functional regression testing, Heger et al. utilize unit tests to test the performance of individual operations. Employing the revision history of the source code, the PRCA approach compares measured response times to older revisions. Statistical techniques (e.g. ANOVA) are applied to identify performance regressions (i.e. significant increase in response times). In case that a regression has been identified, PRCA conducts a binary search on the revision graph to isolate the commit that introduced the performance regression. For that commit, PRCA measures the response times for all operations along the call tree of the unit test operations. The response times are compared to corresponding measurements for previous revisions. In this way, PRCA is able to identify the methods that are responsible for the observed performance regression. Apart from regression detection, the PRCA approach conducts a root cause diagnostics. However, in contrast to our APPD approach, PRCA solely points to the location of a root cause without providing information on the type of problem. Furthermore, as in (Heger et al., 2013) unit tests are used for executing the performance tests, the operations of interest are tested with a single-user load. Performance problems that are sensitive to load cannot be detected under a low load of one single thread.

A performance regression detection approach that is based on control charts is introduced in (Nguyen et al., 2012). When comparing two sets of measurements, control charts allow to differentiate the causes for deviations in some target metrics. In particular, control charts indicate whether deviations are caused by some changes in the input data or due to some defects. Nguyen et al. propose to use control charts for automatic detection of performance regressions when a large amount of performance metrics are collected during regression test execution. Control charts entail two essential assumptions that, in general, cannot be met in the domain of performance testing: non-varying load within a single performance test and uni-modal normal distribution of the target performance metrics. In (Nguyen et al., 2012), the authors propose solutions to mitigate these assumptions for the application of control charts for performance regression testing. Applying the approach on two case studies, Nguyen et al. show that control charts constitute a promising means for automatically detecting performance regressions. However, the work in (Nguyen et al., 2012) is limited to regression detection and does not cover diagnostics of root causes.

Pradel et al. introduce the SpeedGun regression testing approach for automatic detection of performance degradations in thread-safe classes (Pradel et al., 2014). SpeedGun comprises two main components: a generator for concurrent performance tests and a regression analysis component. Given two different versions of a class (e.g. Java class), the test generator creates a performance test with multiple concurrent threads that test the classes under different conditions. Furthermore, the authors propose an algorithm that automatically determines a reasonable length for the execution of the concurrent performance tests. Given the generated tests, SpeedGun executes the tests on both versions of the classes under test and compares the measurement results. SpeedGun reports a performance regression if the results for the newer version of the class exhibit a degradation in performance. The SpeedGun approach is able to detect potential for performance optimization in thread-safe classes. As SpeedGun works on a very detailed level of granularity (i.e. implementation level of classes), the corresponding detection of performance regressions is tightly coupled to the actual root causes for the regressions. However, the approach by Pradel et al. is limited to concurrency problems and does not diagnose the nature (i.e. the specific problem types) of the detected performance regressions.

A performance regression detection approach that is independent of the applied workload during performance testing is introduced in (Ghaith et al., 2015). Ghaith et al. address the problem that, in the context of performance regression testing, workloads vary from one regression test to the next. Instead of comparing response times, the authors propose to use transaction profiles that are workload-independent. Transaction profiles encapsulate the sum of all service demands of a user request, excluding waiting times for resources. In order to automatically derive a transaction profile, the approach in (Ghaith et al., 2015) derives a queueing network model of the target system by means of the measurement data collected during the regression tests. Applying concepts from queueing theory and reversely solving the queueing network model, the proposed approach automatically derives the resource demands for the transaction profile. Finally, transaction profiles of different system versions are compared to identify regressions in performance and the affected resources (e.g. CPU, network, etc.). Apart from pinpointing the affected resources, the approach in (Ghaith et al., 2015) does not analyze the root causes of observed performance regressions.

Waller et al., 2015 show an example of incorporating performance regression benchmarking into continuous integration (Duvall et al., 2007). During the development of the monitoring framework *Kieker* (van Hoorn et al., 2012), the authors applied the micro-benchmark MooBench (Waller et al., 2013) as part of continuous integration to regularly and promptly evaluate the progression of the monitoring overhead of the Kieker framework. Waller et al. report that no performance regressions occurred in the released versions of Kieker anymore since MooBench has been incorporated into continuous integration of the Kieker framework. In contrast, applying MooBench on a series of earlier revisions of Kieker reveals some performance regressions. Based on these observations, the authors suggest to apply regression benchmarking from the very beginning of the implementation phase.

To sum up, regression testing is an excellent means to identify problems in an early stage of implementation. In particular, regression testing is tightly incorporated into the continuous integration method (Duvall et al., 2007). However, as we have shown, except for Heger et al., 2013 none of the approaches provides means for diagnostics of performance problems. Integrating our APPD approach into continuous integration overcomes this problem and, yet, allows to regularly scan the target system for performance problems.

Online Performance and Capacity Management

Cloud computing and virtualization techniques promise some benefits for the operation of software applications. This includes lower resource consumption and, therewith, lower operation costs while at the same time providing the flexibility to achieve quality of service requirements. These technologies constitute an enabler for self-adaptive software systems, that depending on the circumstances (e.g. load situation, available resources, etc.) are able to adopt their architecture and resource allocation in order to meet Quality of Service (QoS) requirements or to save operation costs. Cheng et al., 2009 provide a survey on challenges and state-of-the-art approaches in the field of self-adaptive systems. Approaches for realizing self-adaptive software systems, such as (Garlan et al., 2004; Kramer et al., 2007; Oreizy et al., 1999; Diaconescu et al., 2005; Huber et al., 2011; Kounev et al., 2010; van Hoorn, 2014), have one goal in common that is related to the field of performance problem detection: the approaches try to anticipate, predict or detect performance problems at run-time in order to proactively or reactively resolve the problems by adapting the architecture or resource allocation of the target system.

Focusing on virtualized environments, the Descartes research group (Kounev et al., 2010; Huber et al., 2011; Huber et al., 2014; Brosig et al., 2011) develops a model-based approach for self-adaptive software systems. The Descartes approach utilizes run-time system models that describe architectural aspects, the run-time environment as well as performance-related aspects of the target system. Using workload forecasting, the approach evaluates the effects of different system adaptation alternatives that could be applied to meet the quality of service requirements in the near future. Thereby, the Descartes approach utilizes the run-time models to conduct what-if analyses by means of performance prediction techniques. The analysis step provides the necessary information to decide which adaptation alternatives to execute. Finally, the adaptation of the target system is applied by re-allocating software components, removing or adding further resources, etc.

Van Hoorn et al. introduce the SLAstic approach (van Hoorn et al., 2009; van Hoorn, 2014) that pursues a similar goal as the Descartes approach. Combining the SLAstic approach with the Kieker monitoring framework (van Hoorn et al., 2012), van Hoorn, 2014 provide a framework for online capacity management of software systems that are built using component technologies. While Kieker is responsible for continuous monitoring and analysis of the target system, SLAstic is a technology- and implementation-independent approach for online capacity management. Similar to the Descartes approach, Van Hoorn utilizes run-time system models for analysis of adaptation alternatives. The system models include structural and behavioural aspects of the target architecture. Measurements gathered by Kieker are expressed using the MAMBA modeling language and are attached to the architectural models. As a joint work with the Descartes group, Van Hoorn uses the S/T/A (strategies/tactics/actions) modeling language (Huber et al., 2014) for describing adaptation plans.

During the analysis step, the described approaches implicitly evaluate the run-time models for potential performance problems. Hence, this part is conceptually similar to model-based performance problem detection approaches (cf. Section 8.3.1). Diagnosing root causes of performance problems is not of primary relevance for the self-adaptation of software systems. Therefore, the Descartes and SLAstic approaches only evaluate whether individual adaptation alternatives lead to insufficient performance or not, without further investigation of the root causes.

9. Conclusion

In this section, we conclude the work at hand by providing a summary on the main contributions, insights and validation results (Section 9.1). Furthermore, we discuss the benefits, assumptions and limitations of the presented approach in Section 9.2. Finally, in Section 9.3 we give an outlook on research ideas and directions for future work.

9.1. Summary

In this work, we presented an automatic approach for measurement-based diagnostics of performance problems. Conducting a systematic, experiment-based search for performance problems and their root causes, the presented Automatic Performance Problem Diagnostics (APPD) approach imitates the process that is, otherwise, executed manually by performance experts. The full automation of the APPD approach allows it to be incorporated into regular testing, for instance as part of continuous integration. To automate the diagnostics process the APPD approach combines multiple concepts. Firstly, APPD is based on the notion of Software Performance Anti-patterns (SPAs), i.e. recurrent performance problem types. Using a taxonomy on recurrent performance problem types, the APPD approach executes a set of systematic experiments to search for root causes of performance problems. Within the domain of enterprise software systems, the APPD approach is fully generic (i.e. technology- and context independent). This is realized by a set of generic description languages that allow to describe experimentation plans as well as instrumentation and monitoring instructions in a generic way. By this means, the detection heuristics for individual performance problem types can be specified in a context-independent manner. Overall, in this thesis we made the following contributions:

Taxonomy on Performance Problems In this thesis, we introduced the notion of a *performance problem taxonomy*. The proposed taxonomy captures the knowledge about individual performance problem types (i.e. SPAs) and reflects the causality relationships between individual symptoms and causes of performance problems. We introduced a generic method to derive a taxonomy on performance problems from a set of performance problem descriptions. Thereby, we developed a categorization scheme covering multiple aspects of SPAs. Based on the categorization of SPAs, a static taxonomy on performance problems can be derived. Finally, the taxonomy is augmented with additional information on diagnostics activities. Applying the method on 27 SPAs from literature, in this thesis, we created a taxonomy on common performance problem types occurring in practice. The APPD approach uses the taxonomy as a decision tree for a systematic search for root causes of performance problems.

Systematic Experimentation and Diagnostics Approach We introduced the Systematic Selective Experimentation (SSE) concept for experiment-based performance evaluation scenarios. The SSE concept addresses the problem of the contradicting nature of performance measurement data with respect to accuracy and precision. Because of the monitoring overhead introduced by any measurement probe, in general, it is not possible to obtain accurate (i.e. low deviation from reality) and precise (i.e. highly detailed) performance measurement data, at once. The SSE concept overcomes this trade-off by a set of independent, light-weight experiments. For each experiment, the target application is selectively instrumented with a minimal monitoring overhead. Correlating measurement data across experiments allows to derive precise and accurate performance data. The APPD approach utilizes the SSE concept to systematically iterate the performance problem taxonomy while conducting specific experiments for individual types of performance problems.

Problem Diagnostics Specification Languages In order to decouple the generic processes and algorithms for performance problem diagnostics from specific application contexts (including technologies, tools, etc.) in which they are applied, we developed a set of abstraction languages. An experimentation description language allows to specify different experiments for performance problem diagnostics. A generic instrumentation and monitoring description language provides means to specify instrumentation instructions in an abstract way, without the need of knowing the target system in advance. Measurement data that is gathered during experimentation is captured in a common, context-independent format. Finally, a description language for the specification of concrete measurement environments bridges the gap between generic diagnostics algorithms and specific application contexts.

Detection Heuristics Within the APPD approach, detection heuristics encapsulate the generic knowledge about the evaluation of individual performance problem types. This includes strategies on experiment executions as well as analysis algorithms. In this thesis, we introduce a process for developing accurate and generic detection heuristics. For a selected, versatile set of SPAs from the previously mentioned performance problem taxonomy, we created multiple detection strategies and evaluated them by means of the proposed process. The result is a set of 12 detection heuristics covering the diagnostics of 12 diverse performance problems, symptoms and root causes.

We evaluated the APPD approach along seven research hypotheses addressing different aspects of the individual contributions of this thesis as well as the overall approach. The validation goals included the appropriateness of the performance problem taxonomy and the description languages, the necessity of the SSE concept, as well as the functionality, efficiency, automation and practicability of the overall APPD approach. Thereto, we conducted three end-to-end case studies covering most validation aspects, one controlled experiment to evaluate the benefits of the SSE concept, and an empirical study to capture the external users' perception of the APPD approach.

The case studies showed that the taxonomy reasonably represents the cause-effect relationships of real performance problems as long as the assumptions for APPD are met. Hence, the taxonomy correctly guided the diagnostics process until the root causes of the performance problems have been found. Furthermore, with the specification languages we were able to describe the diverse scenarios of the case studies, showing the expressiveness and generalisability of the proposed languages. By applying the SSE concept on a performance evaluation scenario beyond performance problem diagnostics, we demonstrated the scope of its applicability and evaluated its promise to overcome the trade-off between accuracy and precision of measurement data. With respect to the overall APPD approach, the case studies as well as the empirical study yielded promising results. First of all, APPD is generically applicable on diverse contexts with different technologies, scales and application domains (within enterprise software systems). If all assumptions for the application of APPD are met (cf. next section), APPD provides accurate diagnostics results that pinpoint root causes of detected performance problems. As part of the empirical study, external users applied the APPD approach on an unfamiliar target system. Prevailingly, the users were able to diagnose the performance problems in the target system with the support of the diagnostics results of APPD. Most study participants evaluated APPD as a useful approach for automatic performance problem diagnostics.

9.2. Benefits, Assumptions and Limitations

In this section, we summarize the benefits of the APPD approach as well as its assumptions and limitations.

9.2.1. Benefits

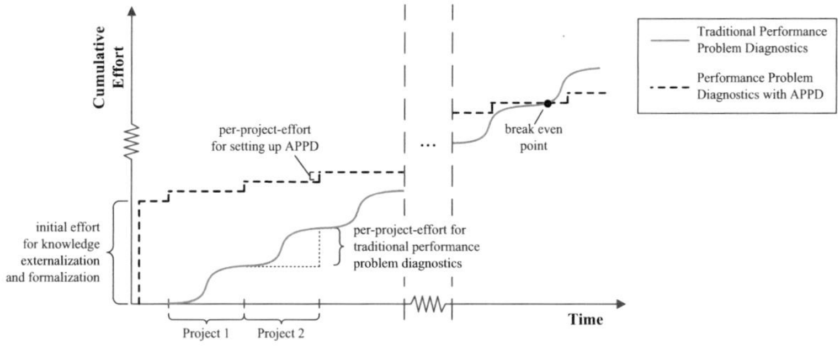

Figure 9.1.: Comparing the cumulative manual effort of using APPD and traditional diagnostics of performance problems

The main goal of APPD is to reduce the manual effort per project (i.e. concrete application context) required to conduct performance problem diagnostics, by automating tasks which are often repeated manually in practice. Figure 9.1 qualitatively illustrates the cumulative effort over time (i.e. number of projects) comparing traditional diagnostics of performance problems with APPD.

The cumulative effort of the traditional diagnostics approach is proportional to the number of projects. Upfront, there is no initial effort required, however, with the traditional diagnostics approach the per-project-effort (i.e. the slope of the curve) is relatively high due to the tedious, manual tasks (e.g. execution of performance tests, analyzing measurement data, etc.) which are recurrent among separate projects. At the beginning of each project, the effort is low as performance evaluation is often omitted until serious performance problems emerge, for instance in the operations phase. However, as soon as a performance problem is observed in operation, a lot of effort and resources are spent to quickly diagnose and resolve the performance problems. By contrast, APPD requires an initial investment of manual effort in order to externalize and formalize expert knowledge including creation and extension of the performance problem taxonomy and the detection heuristics. As formalization of knowledge is a conceptually and practically complex task, presumably, the initial effort associated with that task is significantly higher than the per-project-effort of the traditional diagnostics approach. Furthermore, for each project, APPD needs to be configured and the measurement environment needs to be set up entailing additional per-project-effort when using APPD. However, assuming that the effort to set up APPD is significantly smaller than the per-project-effort of the traditional diagnostics approach, there is a number of projects determining the *break even point* where the initial effort of APPD starts to pay off. Thus, in the long term, APPD is more efficient in terms of effort than the traditional diagnostics approach. As APPD is intended to be executed fully automatically, once set up, the manual effort to conduct an APPD run is close to zero. Hence, APPD allows to conduct performance problem diagnostics on a regular basis while avoiding high effort and costs for manual investigation.

Automatically executing APPD as part of integration testing (Jorgensen et al., 1994) and continuous integration (Duvall et al., 2007) makes continuous diagnostics of performance problems feasible with respect to effort and costs and, thus, allows to detect performance problems early in the development process. Moreover, our approach allows the involved stakeholders to focus more on the core tasks associated with their roles. For instance, relieving performance engineers from repeatedly detecting similar performance problems in different contexts, our approach provides performance engineers more time to externalize and formalize their knowledge on detection of performance problems. In turn, this knowledge can be used to improve APPD.

The precise and implementation-related diagnostics results provided by APPD enable non-performance experts to understand performance problems and their root causes. Hence, with the feedback provided by APPD developers and system operators (who are the actual experts of a concrete target system) can be directly involved into the problem resolution process, instead of employing external performance experts who need lead time to get familiar with the target system.

9.2.2. Assumptions and Limitations

The main assumptions for the applicability of the APPD approach are discussed in Section 3.3. The focus of the APPD approach is on diagnosing performance problems in the application logic of user-based enterprise software systems. Consequently, APPD assumes that the programming languages used to build the target applications support common concepts in the field of enterprise software development (e.g. database access, messaging, etc.). APPD is an experiment-based approach, hence, requiring the availability of a testing environment including corresponding measurement tools as well as load scripts and load generators. Finally, as occurrences of performance problems are relative to the performance requirements, APPD assumes performance requirements to be available at the service level. For further details on the summarized assumptions, we refer to Section 3.3.

Apart from the assumptions described in Section 3.3, there are further assumptions and limitations regarding the APPD approach and its constituent parts.

Validity of the Performance Problem Taxonomy When using the performance problem taxonomy (Chapter 4) in the scope of APPD or elsewhere as a guidance in performance problem diagnostics, it is important to keep in mind the original intention of the taxonomy. The categorization scheme, taxonomy design and Performance Problem Evaluation Plan (PPEP) presented in Chapter 4 aim at supporting a diagnostics process as conducted by the APPD approach. The causal relations between individual nodes in the taxonomy are based on observations that are obtained from performance experiments. Thereby, the stability of the load intensity during individual experiments is an important assumption. If this assumption is not met, the taxonomy may not correctly reflect the causal relations between symptoms and causes of performance problems observed in the corresponding software system. In the industrial case study (Section 7.4) we observed this effect leading to an incorrect performance problem detection. Thereby, an oscillating load intensity lead to periodic peaks in the response times making APPD detect another performance problem type in the target system than the system actually contained.

Coverage of Performance Problem Types The APPD approach is based on explicit knowledge that is encoded into the performance problem taxonomy (Chapter 4) and the detection heuristics (Chapter 6). Therefore, the APPD approach can only analyze those performance problems that are included in the performance problem taxonomy in place, and for which corresponding detection heuristics exist. As both the taxonomy and the detection heuristics can be easily extended, APPD's coverage of performance problem types grows with the knowledge that is externalized and formalized over time.

Importance of Load Scripts APPD is an approach that builds on existing artifacts and tools, including measurement tools and load generators as well as corresponding load scripts. Load scripts significantly affect the diagnostics results of the APPD approach. In particular, the applied load scripts determine which parts of the target system are investigated by APPD. Furthermore, APPD is only able to detect performance problems that emerge under the applied load intensity and workload mix. Existing performance problems that are not covered by the load scripts will not be detected by APPD. Similarly, performance problems that only occur after several weeks or month of operation of the target system (e.g. the Ramp anti-pattern,

Table 2.1(b), Chapter 2.4) cannot be detected with performance test durations in the range of minutes. Thus, the diagnostics quality of APPD highly depends on the available load scripts. Therefore, it is essential to derive representative and effective load scripts.

Iterative Application of APPD The case studies conducted in this thesis (Chapter 7) revealed an important insight regarding the application of the APPD approach. In the case of multiple simultaneous performance problems, often only one performance problem dominates the performance of the software system while hiding other problems. As APPD diagnoses performance problems by means of performance observations, in such cases it would detect only the most severe performance problem and neglect the remaining, hidden performance problems. Therefore, it is important to apply APPD iteratively. If APPD diagnoses a performance problem, the problem must be resolved before APPD can be applied again to reveal further potential problems.

Applicability of SSE The SSE concept (Section 3.2.1) allows to gather precise and accurate performance data by conducting independent experiments with selective instrumentation and monitoring. Depending on the goals of a performance evaluation scenario, the independence of experiments may constitute a drawback. As individual measurement values come from different experiments, they cannot be correlated individually. Instead, measurements are set into relation by means of statistical measures like average, median, etc. In general, with the SSE concept, important correlation information may get lost in the statistical aggregations. Therefore, before adopting the SSE for performance evaluation scenarios other than considered in this thesis (i.e. performance problem diagnostics and resource demand measurements) the applicability of the SSE concept needs to be evaluated with respect to the described concern.

9.3. Future Work

In this section, we discuss potential enhancements of the APPD approach that can be addressed by future work (Section 9.3.1) as well as long-term research directions related to the field of performance problem diagnostics (Section 9.3.2).

9.3.1. Enhancing Automatic Performance Problem Diagnostics

Explicit Knowledge on Performance Problems The taxonomy described in this thesis covers some of the most frequent performance problem types in practice. However, the presented performance problem taxonomy is not exhaustive. There are further recurrent performance problem types that are not included in the presented taxonomy. Many performance problems are explicitly described in numerous Internet blogs, technical reports and scientific literature, or constitute implicit knowledge of performance experts. Conducting a comprehensive survey on recurrent performance problem types is an essential task for future work to increase the scope of the APPD approach. A survey would include a thorough literature review as well as interviews with performance engineers and performance consultants who experience many different performance problems in different contexts. The method introduced in this thesis (Chapter 4) can then be applied on the information gathered in the survey to derive a comprehensive taxonomy on recurrent performance problem types.

Instrumentation Description Language In this thesis, we introduced an Instrumentation and Monitoring (IaM) description language that is tailored for performance evaluation. The language encapsulates domain knowledge about typical instrumentation scopes in the field of enterprise software systems as well as typical performance measures (i.e. probes) of interest. Besides the scopes and probes defined in this thesis there may be further instrumentation places and measures that are required for performance evaluation. With respect to the IaM description language there are two potential tasks for future work. Firstly, a mechanism is required that allows to extend the IaM language in a non-intrusive way regarding the instrumentation tools and tool adapters that interpret corresponding model instances. Secondly, further generic scopes and probes need to be defined as well as their mapping to different technology specific elements.

Repository for Tool Adapters A big advantage of the APPD approach is, that it superimposes existing measurement and load generation tools instead of replacing them. However, as most existing tools use proprietary configuration languages, they do not support the generic languages introduced in this thesis. In this work we proposed to provide light-weight adapters for the tools to enable APPD to use corresponding tools. The existence of a comprehensive repository of adapters for common measurement tools would significantly lower the hurdle for using APPD in a new application context. Creating such a repository and developing adapters for instrumentation, monitoring and load generation tools that are often used for performance testing is an important part for future work.

Improving Diagnostics Efficiency The APPD approach is intended to be incorporated into continuous testing, for instance, as part of nightly tests or weekend tests. On the one hand, the execution time of APPD should be in a reasonable range of time to be integrated into continuous testing. On the other hand, the diagnostics duration increases with a larger taxonomy on performance problems. Therefore, improving the efficiency of the APPD approach is another aspect of improving the acceptance and applicability of the approach. This can be accomplished by means of three directions. Firstly, the duration of experiments can be optimized. Up to now, a domain expert defines a fix duration for individual performance experiments. This can be optimized by means of statistics. For instance, experiments can be terminated if a certain level of confidence in the measurement data is reached. Secondly, so far, there is no prevention of executing duplicate experiments (e.g. for different problems under investigation). Hence, a more sophisticated management of gathered measurement data would allow to more effectively reuse existing measurement data instead of repeating lengthy performance tests. Finally, analysis of measurement data can be optimized with respect to performance by realizing pipelining and parallelization of the corresponding algorithms.

9.3.2. Long-term Research Directions

Evaluation of Costs and Benefits In this thesis, we evaluated the feasibility, applicability and practicability of the APPD approach. In order to evaluate the economic benefits of APPD, the approach needs to be integrated into real software development projects and has to be examined over a long period of time. Thereby, two aspects need to be evaluated. Firstly, does APPD reduce the amount of performance problems that emerge during operations? And secondly, how big are the ongoing costs to maintain and apply the APPD approach throughout the lifecycle of a software product. Conducting a comprehensive, empirical study, preferably in multiple contexts, would provide important insights on the economic benefits of the APPD approach.

Making Use of DevOps Principles In recent years, DevOps principles emerged in the field of software engineering, leading to a paradigm shift that brings software development and operations closer together. DevOps aims at improving the information flow between development and operations. Up-to-date and detailed information from the opposing party creates benefits in both areas, development and operations. In the field of performance problem diagnostics, DevOps principles can be applied to improve the efficiency and accuracy of diagnostics. As discussed before, the accuracy of APPD highly depends on the load scripts used for testing. DevOps principles may help to derive more representative and effective load scripts. Applying approaches for automatic workload derivation during operation (Vögele et al., 2015; van Hoorn et al., 2008; van Hoorn et al., 2014) to derive up-to-date, representative load scripts for APPD provides for more accurate diagnostics results. Furthermore, high-level monitoring during operations may provide initial hypotheses that may more efficiently guide performance problem diagnostics in the testing phase. For instance, problematic software services can already be identified or certain types of performance problems can be already excluded before applying in-depth diagnostics by APPD. In this way, the diagnostics efficiency of APPD can be significantly increased.

Machine Learning for Performance Problem Diagnostics Detection of performance problems is basically a binary classification problem. Therefore, performance problem diagnostics is an interesting application case for the research field of machine learning. Machine learning techniques have the advantage to be more generically applicable on different kind of problem types than explicitly defining detection rules and algorithms for individual performance problem types. Primary research results in utilizing machine learning for the detection of performance anti-patterns have been presented by Peiris et al., 2014. However, Peiris et al. focused on non-intrusive detection by means of high level metrics and analyzed only one type of performance problems. Hence, many research question and challenges are still open with respect to this field of research:

- *Are other performance anti-patterns than considered by Peiris et al., 2014 also detectable by means of machine learning techniques?*
- *Are root causes of performance problems detectable by means of detailed performance metrics when using machine learning techniques?*
- *What is an effective way of learning performance problems and where to get the huge amount of required training data from?*

Assuming that machine learning techniques can be effectively applied to detect different types of performance anti-patterns, integrating the APPD approach with corresponding techniques is an interesting research direction for future work. Detection heuristics that, up to now, need to be explicitly designed and evaluated by performance experts could be, for instance, replaced by self-learning algorithms.

Transfer to Other Domains In this thesis, our focus was on the performance of enterprise software systems. Though we applied the APPD approach solely for performance problem diagnostics within the scope of enterprise software, evaluating its applicability to other domains is an interesting direction for future research. The core concepts of the APPD approach, such as the causal problem taxonomy, systematic search and systematic, selective experimentation, are per se generic. The scope of these concepts can be evaluated along two dimensions. Firstly, it is an interesting question which aspects of APPD need to be adopted to apply it on a different domain of applications (e.g. desktop applications, embedded systems, etc.). Presumably, other application domains have other types of performance problems and anti-patterns. Hence, the taxonomy on performance problems and corresponding detection heuristics needs to be adopted to corresponding domains. Furthermore, in other domains, the notion of load differs to the domain of enterprise software, impacting the way of conducting performance experiments. All in all, interesting research questions arise when transferring the APPD approach to other domains of software. Furthermore, investigating whether the concepts of APPD can be used to diagnose problems regarding other quality of service dimensions (e.g. reliability or security) is an interesting direction for future work.

Performance Problem Resolution Performance problem resolution is a complementary discipline to diagnostics of performance problems. Though sometimes solutions to performance problems are trivial, in most cases, performance problem resolution is a highly complex task. Often it is not clear which solution alternatives exist and whether certain alternatives actually resolve detected problems. Hence, supporting developers in resolving performance problems is an interesting research field that is closely related to problem diagnostics. Heger, 2015 introduces Vergil, a systematic approach for guiding developers in resolving performance problems. Vergil is a semi-automated approach that evaluates the impact of different solution alternatives and provides a ranking of solutions. An open question is, whether sophisticating solutions to performance problems can be found in a fully automatic way. Automatic, pattern-based application and evaluation of solutions (e.g. by means of code manipulation) is an interesting direction for future work.

A. Appendix

A.1. Algorithms for Detection Heuristics

A.1.1. Performance Problem Heuristic

Algorithm 2 Detection Strategy for a Performance Problem

```
Input:
𝒟   // Dataset of Dataset Type, containing the measurement data
ρ   // response time requirements threshold (from Measurement Environment (ME) Description model)
π   // percentile for ρ (from ME Description model)
Output:
ℒ   // set of system services violating the requirements
Init:
ℒ ← ∅
Algorithm:
𝒪 ← query('SELECT DISTINCT Location FROM 𝒟')
for all ω ∈ 𝒪 do
    𝒱 ← query('SELECT Response Time FROM 𝒟 WHERE Location=ω')
    υ_π ← percentile(𝒱 , π)
    if υ_π > ρ then
        ℒ ← ℒ ∪ {ω}
    end if
end for

return ℒ
```

A.1.2. Application Hiccups Heuristic

A.1.2.1. Core Strategy

Algorithm 3 Application Hiccups Core Detection Strategy

`Input:`
$\mathcal{D}$ *// Dataset of Dataset Type, containing the measurement data*
ρ *// response time requirements threshold (from ME Description model)*
π *// cumulative probability for ρ (from ME Description model)*
ϕ *// maximum allowed time proportion of hiccups*
`Output:`
$\mathcal{L}$ *// set of system services that exhibit a hiccup behaviour*
`Init:`
$\mathcal{L} \leftarrow \emptyset$
`Algorithm:`
$\mathcal{O} \leftarrow$ query(`'SELECT DISTINCT Location FROM` $\mathcal{D}$`'`)
for all $\omega \in \mathcal{O}$ **do**
  $\mathcal{P} \leftarrow$ query(`'SELECT Timestamp, Response Time FROM` $\mathcal{D}$ `WHERE Location=`ω `ORDER BY Timestamp'`)
  $\mathcal{H} \leftarrow$ **findHiccups(**$\mathcal{P}, \rho, \pi$**)**
  $\delta \leftarrow$ experimentDuration($\mathcal{P}$)
  $\beta \leftarrow$ cumulativeHiccupDuration($\mathcal{H}$)
  if $\mathcal{H} \neq \emptyset$ AND $\beta < \delta\phi$ **then**
    $\mathcal{L} \leftarrow \mathcal{L} \cup \{\omega\}$
  end if
end for

return $\mathcal{L}$

A.1.2.2. Moving Percentile Strategy

Algorithm 4 findHiccups: Moving Percentile Strategy

`Input:`
$\mathcal{P}$ *// response time series*
ρ *// response time req. threshold (from ME Description)*
π *// cumulative probability for ρ (from ME Description model)*
χ *// window size for moving window*
`Output:`
$\mathcal{H}$ *// set of detected hiccups*
`Init:`
$\mathcal{H} \leftarrow \emptyset$
$\theta \leftarrow NULL$ *// current hiccup*
`Algorithm:`
$\mathcal{M} \leftarrow$ calculateMovingPercentileTimeSeries($\mathcal{P}$, χ, π)
for all $\mu \in \mathcal{M}$ **do**
  if μ[`'Response Time'`] $> \rho$ AND $\theta = NULL$ **then** *// start of new hiccup*
    $\theta \leftarrow$ new hiccup
    set μ[`'Timestamp'`] as start of θ
  else if (μ[query(`'Response Time'`)] $\leq \rho$ OR μ is last element) AND $\theta \neq NULL$ **then** *// end of hiccup*
    set μ[`'Timestamp'`] as end of θ
    $\mathcal{H} \leftarrow \mathcal{H} \cup \{\theta\}$
    $\theta \leftarrow NULL$
  end if
end for

return $\mathcal{H}$

A.1.2.3. Buckets Strategy

Algorithm 5 findHiccups: Bucket Strategy

`Input:`
$\mathcal{P}$ *// response time series*
ρ *// response time req. threshold (from ME Description)*
π *// cumulative probability for ρ (from ME Description model)*
`Output:`
$\mathcal{H}$ *// set of detected hiccups*
`Init:`
$\mathcal{H} \leftarrow \emptyset$
$\theta \leftarrow NULL$ *// current hiccup*
`Algorithm:`
$\tau \leftarrow$ meanInterRequestTime($\mathcal{P}$)
$\xi \leftarrow min(50 * \tau, 5sec)$ *// bucket width*
$\mathcal{B} \leftarrow$ divideIntoBuckets($\mathcal{P}$, ξ)
for all bucket $\beta \in \mathcal{B}$ **do**
    if β violates requirements (ρ, π) AND $\theta = NULL$ **then** *// start of new hiccup*
        $\theta \leftarrow$ new hiccup
        set start of θ to the left border of β
    else if (β meets requirements (ρ, π) OR β is last bucket) AND $\theta \neq NULL$ **then** *// end of hiccup*
        set end of θ to the right border of β
        $\mathcal{H} \leftarrow \mathcal{H} \cup \{\theta\}$
        $\theta \leftarrow NULL$
    end if
end for
return $\mathcal{H}$

A.1.3. The Ramp Heuristic

A.1.3.1. Linear Regression Strategy

Algorithm 6 The Ramp: Linear Regression Strategy

`Input:`
$\mathcal{D}$ *// Dataset of defined Dataset Type, containing the measurement data*
τ *// threshold for the linear regression slope*

`Output:`
$\mathcal{L}$ *// set of system services exhibiting a ramp behaviour*

`Init:`
$\mathcal{L} \leftarrow \emptyset$

`Algorithm:`
$\mathcal{O} \leftarrow$ query(`'SELECT DISTINCT Location FROM` $\mathcal{D}$`)'`)
for all $\omega \in \mathcal{O}$ **do**
  $\mathcal{P} \leftarrow$ query(`'SELECT Timestamp, Response Time FROM` $\mathcal{D}$ `WHERE Location=`ω`'`)
  $\kappa \leftarrow$ linearRegressionSlope($\mathcal{P}$)
  if $\kappa > \tau$ **then**
    $\mathcal{L} \leftarrow \mathcal{L} \cup \{\omega\}$
  end if
end for

return $\mathcal{L}$

A.1.3.2. Direct Growth Strategy

Algorithm 7 The Ramp: Direct Growth Strategy

`Input:`
$\mathcal{D}$ *// Dataset of defined Dataset Type, containing the measurement data*
α *// significance level for t-test*

`Output:`
$\mathcal{L}$ *// set of system services exhibiting a ramp behaviour*

`Init:`
$\mathcal{L} \leftarrow \emptyset$

`Algorithm:`
$\mathcal{O} \leftarrow$ query(`'SELECT DISTINCT Location FROM` $\mathcal{D}$`'`)
for all $\omega \in \mathcal{O}$ **do**
  $\mathcal{P} \leftarrow$ query(`'SELECT Timestamp, Response Time FROM` $\mathcal{D}$ `WHERE Location=`ω`'`)
  $\mathcal{R}_1 \leftarrow$ first half of response times from $\mathcal{P}$
  $\mathcal{R}_2 \leftarrow$ second half of response times from $\mathcal{P}$
  $\mu_1 \leftarrow$ mean($\mathcal{R}_1$) , $\mu_2 \leftarrow$ mean($\mathcal{R}_2$)
  $\mathcal{B}_1 \leftarrow$ bootstrap($\mathcal{R}_1$) , $\mathcal{B}_2 \leftarrow$ bootstrap($\mathcal{R}_2$)
  $p \leftarrow$ t-test($\mathcal{B}_1, \mathcal{B}_2$)
  if $p < \alpha$ AND $\mu_1 < \mu_2$ **then**
    $\mathcal{L} \leftarrow \mathcal{L} \cup \{\omega\}$
  end if
end for

return $\mathcal{L}$

A.1.3.3. Time Window Strategy

Algorithm 8 The Ramp: Time Window Strategy

`Input:`
$\mathcal{D}$ *// Dataset of Dataset Type, containing the measurement data*
α *// significance level for t-test*
`Output:` $\mathcal{L}$ *// set of system services exhibiting a ramp*
`Init:` $\mathcal{L} \leftarrow \emptyset$
`Algorithm:`
$\mathcal{O} \leftarrow$ query(`'SELECT DISTINCT Location FROM` $\mathcal{D}$`'`)
$\mathcal{S} \leftarrow$ query(`'SELECT DISTINCT Step FROM` $\mathcal{D}$ `ORDER BY Step'`)
for all $\omega \in \mathcal{O}$ **do**
  $\nu \leftarrow 0$
  for all $\eta \in \mathcal{S}$ **do**
    $\mathcal{R}_\eta \leftarrow$ query(`'SELECT Response Time FROM` $\mathcal{D}$ `WHERE Location=`ω `AND Step=`η`'`)
    if not first iteration **then**
      $\mu_\eta \leftarrow \text{mean}(\mathcal{R}_\eta)$, $\mu_{\eta-1} \leftarrow \text{mean}(\mathcal{R}_{\eta-1})$
      $\mathcal{B}_\eta \leftarrow \text{bootstrap}(\mathcal{R}_\eta)$, $\mathcal{B}_{\eta-1} \leftarrow \text{bootstrap}(\mathcal{R}_{\eta-1})$
      $p \leftarrow \text{t-test}(\mathcal{B}_\eta, \mathcal{B}_{\eta-1})$
      if $p < \alpha$ AND $\mu_{\eta-1} < \mu_\eta$ **then** $\nu \leftarrow \nu + 1$
      end if
    end if
    $\mathcal{R}_{\eta-1} \leftarrow \mathcal{R}_\eta$
  end for
  if $\nu = 3$ **then** $\mathcal{L} \leftarrow \mathcal{L} \cup \{\omega\}$
  end if
end for
return $\mathcal{L}$

A.1.4. Continuously Violated Requirements Heuristic

A.1.4.1. Core Strategy

Algorithm 9 Continuously Violated Requirements Core Detection Strategy

`Input:`
$\mathcal{D}$ *// Dataset of defined Dataset Type, containing the measurement data*
ρ *// response time requirements threshold (from ME Description model)*
π *// cumulative probability for ρ (from ME Description model)*

`Output:`
$\mathcal{L}$ *// set of system services that continuously violate requirements*

`Init:`
$\mathcal{L} \leftarrow \emptyset$

`Algorithm:`
$\mathcal{O} \leftarrow$ query(`'SELECT DISTINCT Location FROM` $\mathcal{D}$`'`)
for all $\omega \in \mathcal{O}$ **do**
  $\mathcal{P} \leftarrow$ query(`'SELECT Timestamp, Response Time FROM` $\mathcal{D}$ `WHERE Location=`ω `ORDER BY Timestamp'`)
  $\delta \leftarrow$ **evaluateContinuousViolation(**$\mathcal{P}, \rho, \pi$**)**
  if δ **then**
    $\mathcal{L} \leftarrow \mathcal{L} \cup \{\omega\}$
  end if
end for

return $\mathcal{L}$

A.1.4.2. Moving Percentile Strategy

Algorithm 10 evaluateContinuousViolation: Moving Percentile Strategy

```
Input:
𝒫   // response time series
ρ   // response time requirements threshold (from ME Description model)
π   // cumulative probability for ρ (from ME Description model)
χ   // window size for moving window

Output:
boolean value indicating whether the passed response time series
continuously violates the performance requirements

Algorithm:
ℳ ← calculateMovingPercentileTimeSeries(𝒫, χ, π)
for all μ ∈ ℳ do
  if μ['Response Time'] < ρ then
    return false
  end if
end for

return true
```

A.1.4.3. Buckets Strategy

Algorithm 11 evaluateContinuousViolation: Bucket Strategy

`Input:`
$\mathcal{P}$ *// response time series*
ρ *// response time requirements threshold (from ME Description model)*
π *// cumulative probability for ρ (from ME Description model)*
ϕ *// minimum proportion of buckets that violate performance requirements*

`Output:`
boolean value indicating whether the passed response time series continuously violates the performance requirements

`Algorithm:`
$\iota \leftarrow$ meanInterRequestTime($\mathcal{P}$)
$\xi \leftarrow 50 * iota$ *// bucket width*
$\mathcal{B} \leftarrow$ divideIntoBuckets($\mathcal{P}$, ξ)
$\eta \leftarrow 0$
for all bucket $\beta \in \mathcal{B}$ **do**
  if β violates requirements (ρ, π) **then**
    $\eta \leftarrow \eta + 1$
  end if
end for
if $\eta > \phi * sizeOf(\mathcal{B})$ **then**
  return true
else
  return false
end if

A.1.5. The Traffic Jam Heuristic

A.1.5.1. Linear Regression Strategy

Algorithm 12 Traffic Jam: Linear Regression Detection Strategy

`Input:`
$\mathcal{D}$ *// Dataset of defined Dataset Type, containing the measurement data*
τ *// threshold for the linear regression slope*

`Output:`
$\mathcal{L}$ *// set of system services containing a Traffic Jam*

`Init:`
$\mathcal{L} \leftarrow \emptyset$

`Algorithm:`
$\mathcal{O} \leftarrow$ query(`'SELECT DISTINCT Location FROM` $\mathcal{D}$`'`)
for all $\omega \in \mathcal{O}$ **do**
  $\mathcal{P}_u \leftarrow$ query(`'SELECT #Users, Response Time FROM` $\mathcal{D}$ `WHERE Location=`ω`'`)
  $\kappa \leftarrow$ linearRegressionSlope($\mathcal{P}_u$)
  if $\kappa > \tau$ **then**
    $\mathcal{L} \leftarrow \mathcal{L} \cup \{\omega\}$
  end if
end for

return $\mathcal{L}$

A.1.5.2. t-Test Strategy

Algorithm 13 Traffic Jam: t-Test Detection Strategy

`Input:`
$\mathcal{D}$ *// Dataset of Dataset Type, containing the measurement data*
α *// significance level for t-test* , (ρ, π) *// perf. req.*
`Output:`
$\mathcal{L}$ *// set of system services exhibiting a Traffic Jam behaviour*
$\mathcal{I}$ *// load under which performance requirements are violated*
`Init:` $\mathcal{L} \leftarrow \emptyset$ $\mathcal{I} \leftarrow \emptyset$
`Algorithm:`
$\mathcal{O} \leftarrow$ query(`'SELECT DISTINCT Location FROM` $\mathcal{D}$`'`)
$\mathcal{U} \leftarrow$ query(`'SELECT DISTINCT Number of Users FROM` $\mathcal{D}$`'`)
for all $\omega \in \mathcal{O}$ **do** $\vartheta \leftarrow 0$, $\nu \leftarrow 0$, $\eta \leftarrow 1$
  for all $\upsilon \in \mathcal{U}$ **do**
    $\mathcal{R}_\eta \leftarrow$ query(`'SELECT Response Time FROM` $\mathcal{D}$ `WHERE Location=`ω `AND #Users=`υ`'`)
    if $\mathcal{R}_\eta$ violates requirements (ρ, π) **then**
      $\vartheta \leftarrow \vartheta + 1$, $\mathcal{I} \leftarrow \mathcal{I} \cup \{\upsilon\}$
    end if
    if not first iteration **then**
      $\mu_\eta \leftarrow$ mean($\mathcal{R}_\eta$), $\mu_{\eta-1} \leftarrow$ mean($\mathcal{R}_{\eta-1}$),$p \leftarrow$ t-test($\mathcal{B}_\eta$, $\mathcal{B}_{\eta-1}$)
      $\mathcal{B}_\eta \leftarrow$ bootstrap($\mathcal{R}_\eta$) , $\mathcal{B}_{\eta-1} \leftarrow$ bootstrap($\mathcal{R}_{\eta-1}$)
      if $p < \alpha$ AND $\mu_{\eta-1} < \mu_\eta$ **then** $\nu \leftarrow \nu + 1$ **else** $\nu \leftarrow 0$ **end if**
    end if
    $\mathcal{R}_{\eta-1} \leftarrow \mathcal{R}_\eta$, $\eta \leftarrow \eta + 1$
  end for
  if $\nu = \vartheta$ **then** $\mathcal{L} \leftarrow \mathcal{L} \cup \{\omega\}$ **end if**
end for
return $\mathcal{L}, \mathcal{I}$

A.1.6. One Lane Bridge Heuristic

A.1.6.1. CPU Threshold Strategy

Algorithm 14 One Lane Bridge: CPU Threshold Detection Strategy

`Input:`
$\mathcal{D}_{CPU}$ *// CPU utilization dataset*
θ *// CPU utilization threshold*
`Output:`
β *// boolean value indicating whether the Traffic Jam services are One Lane Bridges*
`Init:`
$\beta \leftarrow$ **true**
`Algorithm:`
$C \leftarrow$ query(`'SELECT DISTINCT Node FROM` $\mathcal{D}_{CPU}$`'`)
$\mathcal{U} \leftarrow$ query(`'SELECT DISTINCT Number of Users FROM` $\mathcal{D}_R$`'`)
for all $\zeta \in C$ **do**
  for all $\upsilon \in \mathcal{U}$ **do**
    $\mathcal{T} \leftarrow$ query(`'SELECT Utilization FROM` $\mathcal{D}_{CPU}$ `WHERE Node=`ζ `AND #Users=`υ`'`)
    $U \leftarrow$ mean($\mathcal{T}$)
    if $U > \theta$ **then**
      $\beta \leftarrow$ **false**
    end if
  end for
end for
return β

A.1.6.2. Queueing Theory Strategy

Algorithm 15 One Lane Bridge: Queueing Theory Detection Strategy

Input: $\mathcal{D}_R$ *// response time dataset* , $\mathcal{D}_{CPU}$ *// CPU util. dataset*
Output: $\mathcal{L}$ *// set of locations exhibiting a OLB*
Init: $\mathcal{L} \leftarrow \emptyset$
Algorithm:
$\mathcal{O} \leftarrow$ query(`'SELECT DISTINCT Location FROM` $\mathcal{D}_R$`'`)
$\mathcal{U} \leftarrow$ query(`'SELECT DISTINCT Number of Users FROM` $\mathcal{D}_R$`'`)
$C \leftarrow$ query(`'SELECT DISTINCT Node FROM` $\mathcal{D}_{CPU}$`'`)
$\nu \leftarrow$ query(`'COUNT(SELECT DISTINCT Node FROM` $\mathcal{D}_{CPU}$`)'`)
for all $\omega \in \mathcal{O}$ **do** $\varrho_s \leftarrow 0, \quad \beta \leftarrow$ false
  for all $\upsilon \in \mathcal{U}$ **do**
    $\mathcal{R} \leftarrow$ query(`'SELECT Response Time FROM` $\mathcal{D}_R$ `WHERE Location=`ω `AND #Users=`υ`'`)
    if $\upsilon = 1$ **then** $\varrho_s \leftarrow \max(\text{ mean}(\mathcal{R}) , 15)$
    else
      $\varrho_m \leftarrow \text{mean}(\mathcal{R})$
      for all $\zeta \in C$ **do**
        $\mathcal{T} \leftarrow$ query(`'SELECT Utilization FROM` $\mathcal{D}_{CPU}$ `WHERE Node=`ζ `AND #Users=`υ`'`)
        $U \leftarrow \text{mean}(\mathcal{T}),\ c_E \leftarrow \text{erlangC}(\nu,U)$
        $\tau_{\omega,\upsilon,\zeta} = 1.1 * \frac{\varrho_s}{n_C} \frac{1}{1-U} c_E + \varrho_s$
        if $\varrho_m > \tau_{\omega,\upsilon,\zeta}$ **then** $\beta \leftarrow$ true **end if**
      end for
    end if
  end for
  if β = true **then** $\mathcal{L} \leftarrow \mathcal{L} \cup \{\omega\}$ **end if**
end for
return $\mathcal{L}$

A.1.7. Database Congestion Heuristic

A.1.7.1. Fix Threshold Strategy

Algorithm 16 Database Congestion: Fix Threshold Strategy

Input: $\mathcal{D}_{CPU}$ *// CPU dataset* , $\mathcal{D}_{DB}$ *// DB dataset*
$\mathcal{I}$ *// load under which perf. requirements are violated*
α *// significance for t-test* t_{CPU} *// CPU util. threshold*
Output: β *// boolean indicating a DB congestion*
Init: $\beta \leftarrow$ **false**
Algorithm:
$C \leftarrow$ query('SELECT DIST. Node FROM $\mathcal{D}_{CPU}$')
$\mathcal{U} \leftarrow$ query('SELECT DIST. #Users FROM $\mathcal{D}_{CPU} ORDERBY\#Users$')
for all $\zeta \in C$ **do**
  $v_p \leftarrow NULL, \quad s \leftarrow 0$
  for all $v \in \mathcal{U}$ **do**
    $\mathcal{T} \leftarrow$ query('SELECT Utilization FROM $\mathcal{D}_{CPU}$ WHERE Node=ζ AND #Users=v')
    $U \leftarrow$ mean($\mathcal{T}$)
    if $U > t_{CPU}$ **then** $\beta \leftarrow$ **true end if**
    if $v_p \neq NULL$ AND $v \in \mathcal{I}$ **then**
      $[\mathcal{W}, \mathcal{W}_p] \leftarrow$ query('SELECT #Lock Waits FROM $\mathcal{D}_{DB}$ WHERE Node=ζ AND #Users=$[v, v_p]$')
      $[Q, Q_p] \leftarrow$ query('SELECT Waiting Time FROM $\mathcal{D}_{DB}$ WHERE Node=ζ AND #Users=$[v, v_p]$')
      $Q' \leftarrow$ pairwiseDifferences(Q) / pairwiseDifferences($\mathcal{W}$)
      $Q'_p \leftarrow$ pairwiseDifferences(Q_p) / pairwiseDifferences($\mathcal{W}_p$)
      $\mathcal{B} \leftarrow$ bootstrap(Q'), $\mathcal{B}_p \leftarrow$ bootstrap(Q'_p), $m \leftarrow$ mean($\mathcal{B}$), $m_p \leftarrow$ mean($\mathcal{B}_p$), $p \leftarrow$ t-test($\mathcal{B}$,$\mathcal{B}_p$)
      if $p < \alpha$ AND $m_p < m$ **then** $s \leftarrow s + 1$ **end if**
    end if
    $v_p \leftarrow v$
  end for
  if $s = |\mathcal{I}|$ **then** $\beta \leftarrow$ **true end if**
end for
return β

A.1.7.2. Queueing Theory Strategy

Algorithm 17 Database Congestion: Queueing Theory Strategy

Input: $\mathcal{D}_{CPU}$ *// CPU dataset* , $\mathcal{D}_{DB}$ *// DB dataset*
$\mathcal{I}$ *// load under which perf. requirements are violated*
f_R *// rel. RT increase factor* , α *// significance for t-test*
Output: β *// boolean indicating whether a DB congestion exists*
Init: $\beta \leftarrow$ **false**
Algorithm:
$C \leftarrow$ query('SELECT DIST. Node FROM $\mathcal{D}_{CPU}$')
$\mathcal{U} \leftarrow$ query('SELECT DIST. #Users FROM $\mathcal{D}_{CPU} ORDERBY \#Users$')
for all $\zeta \in C$ **do**
  $n_C \leftarrow$ numCores($\mathcal{D}_{CPU}, \zeta$) , $\upsilon_p \leftarrow NULL$, $s \leftarrow 0$
  for all $\upsilon \in \mathcal{U}$ **do**
    $\mathcal{T} \leftarrow$ query('SELECT Utilization FROM $\mathcal{D}_{CPU}$ WHERE Node=ζ AND #Users=υ')
    $m_U \leftarrow$ mean($\mathcal{T}$) , $t^{qt}_{CPU} \leftarrow$ utilizationForRTFactor(f_R, n_C)
    if $m_U > t^{qt}_{CPU}$ **then** $\beta \leftarrow$ **true end if**
    if $\upsilon_p \neq NULL$ AND $\upsilon \in \mathcal{I}$ **then**
      $[\mathcal{W}, \mathcal{W}_p] \leftarrow$ query('SELECT #Lock Waits FROM $\mathcal{D}_{DB}$ WHERE Node=ζ AND #Users=$[\upsilon, \upsilon_p]$')
      $[Q, Q_p] \leftarrow$ query('SELECT Waiting Time FROM $\mathcal{D}_{DB}$ WHERE Node=ζ AND #Users=$[\upsilon, \upsilon_p]$')
      $Q' \leftarrow$ pairwiseDifferences(Q) / pairwiseDifferences($\mathcal{W}$)
      $Q'_p \leftarrow$ pairwiseDifferences(Q_p) / pairwiseDifferences($\mathcal{W}_p$)
      $\mathcal{B} \leftarrow$ bootstrap(Q'), $\mathcal{B}_p \leftarrow$ bootstrap(Q'_p), $m \leftarrow$ mean($\mathcal{B}$), $m_p \leftarrow$ mean($\mathcal{B}_p$), $p \leftarrow$ t-test($\mathcal{B}$,$\mathcal{B}_p$)
      if $p < \alpha$ AND $m_p < m$ **then** $s \leftarrow s + 1$ **end if**
    end if
    $\upsilon_p \leftarrow \upsilon$
  end for
  if $s = |\mathcal{I}|$ **then** $\beta \leftarrow$ **true end if**
end for
return β

A.1.8. The Stifle Heuristic

Algorithm 18 Stifle Detection Strategy

`Input:`
$\mathcal{D}_R$ *// Response time dataset*
$\mathcal{D}_{SQL}$ *// SQL queries dataset*
`Output:`
$\mathcal{S}$ *// set of system services and corresponding SQL queries constituting a Stifle anti-pattern*
`Init:`
$\mathcal{S} \leftarrow \emptyset$
`Algorithm:`
$\mathcal{D}_C \leftarrow$ correlate($\mathcal{D}_R$,$\mathcal{D}_{SQL}$)
$\mathcal{O} \leftarrow$ query(`'SELECT DISTINCT Location FROM` $\mathcal{D}_C$`'`)
for all $\omega \in \mathcal{O}$ **do**
  $\mathcal{Q} \leftarrow$ query(`'SELECT Query FROM` $\mathcal{D}_C$ `WHERE Location=`ω`'`)
  $\mathcal{Q}' \leftarrow$ clusterQueries($\mathcal{Q}$)
  for all $\zeta \in \mathcal{Q}'$ **do**
    if $|\zeta| > 1$ **then**
      $\mathcal{S} \leftarrow (\omega, \zeta)$
    end if
  end for
end for

return $\mathcal{S}$

A.1.9. Expensive Database Call Heuristic

Algorithm 19 Expensive Database Call Detection Strategy

`Input:`
$\mathcal{D}_R$ *// RT dataset* , $\mathcal{D}_Q$ *// DB dataset* , $\mathcal{D}_T$ *// tracing dataset*
$\mathcal{V} = \{(\varsigma_i, \varrho_i, \varphi_i)\}_i$ *// set of service name (ς_i), single-user response time (ϱ_i), and high load response times (φ_i) tuples for all system services that have been detected as a Traffic Jam*
τ *// threshold for the query response time proportion compared to the corresponding system service time*
`Output:`
$\mathcal{S}$ *// set of system services and corresponding SQL queries constituting an Expensive Database Call anti-pattern*
`Init:` $\mathcal{S} \leftarrow \emptyset$
`Algorithm:`
$C \leftarrow$ correlateServicesAndQueries($\mathcal{D}_R$,$\mathcal{D}_Q$,$\mathcal{D}_T$)
for all $(\varsigma, \varrho, \varphi) \in \mathcal{V}$ **do**
  $Q \leftarrow$ query(`'SELECT DISTINCT Query FROM` C `WHERE` $\mathcal{D}_R$`.Location=`ς`'`)
  for all $\eta \in Q$ **do**
    $\nu_s \leftarrow$ query(`'SELECT mean(Response Time) FROM` C `WHERE` $\mathcal{D}_Q$`.Query=`η `AND #Users=1'`)
    $\nu_h \leftarrow$ query(`'SELECT mean(Response Time) FROM` C `WHERE` $\mathcal{D}_Q$`.Query=`η `AND #Users=maxLoad'`)
    if $\frac{\nu_h}{\varphi} \geq \tau$ AND $\frac{\nu_s}{\varrho} < \frac{\nu_h}{\varphi}$ **then**
      $\mathcal{S} \leftarrow \mathcal{S} \cup \{(\varsigma, \eta)\}$
    end if
  end for
end for
return $\mathcal{S}$

A.1.10. Excessive Messaging Heuristic

A.1.10.1. Network Utilization Threshold Strategy

Algorithm 20 Excessive Messaging: Network Utilization Threshold Strategy

Input:
$\mathcal{D}_{NW}$ *// Network I/O dataset* , $\mathcal{D}_{MS}$ *// Messaging dataset*
$\mathcal{I}$ *// load under which performance requirements are violated*
α *// significance level for t-test*
Output: β *// boolean indicating whether Excessive Messaging exists*
Init: $\pi \leftarrow 1452$ *// TCP packet size* , $\beta \leftarrow$ **false**
Algorithm:
$\mathcal{U} \leftarrow$ query('SELECT DISTINCT #Users FROM $\mathcal{D}_{NW}$ ORDER BY #Users')
$\mathcal{N} \leftarrow$ query('SELECT DISTINCT Node, Interface Name FROM $\mathcal{D}_{NW}$')
$\mu \leftarrow$ mean(query('SELECT Avg. Message Size FROM $\mathcal{D}_{MS}$'))
for all $\nu \in \mathcal{N}$ **do**
  $\chi \leftarrow$ query('SELECT DISTINCT Speed FROM $\mathcal{D}_{NW}$ WHERE Node=ν[Node] AND Interface Name=ν[Interface Name]')
  $\rho \leftarrow \frac{\chi}{\pi}$ *// TCP packet rate*
  if $\mu < \pi$ **then** $\tau \leftarrow 0.9\rho\left(\lfloor\frac{\pi}{\mu}\rfloor + 1\right)\frac{\mu}{2}$ *// max TCP throughput*
  else $\tau \leftarrow 0.9B_w$
  end if
  for all $\upsilon \in \mathcal{U}$ **do** $\mathcal{T} \leftarrow$ query('SELECT BytesReceived, BytesTransferred, Timestamp FROM $\mathcal{D}_{NW}$ WHERE Node=ν[Node] AND Interface Name=ν[Interface Name] AND #Users=υ')
    $\theta_r \leftarrow \frac{max(\mathcal{T}[\text{BytesReceived}])-min(\mathcal{T}[\text{BytesReceived}])}{max(\mathcal{T}[\text{Timestamp}])-min(\mathcal{T}[\text{Timestamp}])}$
    $\theta_t \leftarrow \frac{max(\mathcal{T}[\text{BytesTransferred}])-min(\mathcal{T}[\text{BytesTransferred}])}{max(\mathcal{T}[\text{Timestamp}])-min(\mathcal{T}[\text{Timestamp}])}$
    $\theta \leftarrow max(\theta_r, \theta_t)$
    if $\theta > \tau$ **then** $\beta \leftarrow$ **true end if**
  end for
end for
return β AND queSizeAnalysis($\mathcal{D}_{MS}$,$\mathcal{I}$,α) *// cf. Algorithm 21*

Algorithm 21 Excessive Messaging: queue size analysis

`Input:`
$\mathcal{D}_{MS}$ *// Messaging statistics dataset*
$\mathcal{I}$ *// load intensities under which performance requirements are violated*
α *// significance level for t-test*
`Output:`
β *// boolean value indicating whether Excessive Messaging is present*
`Init:`
$\beta \leftarrow$ **false**
for all $\chi \in \mathcal{Q}$ **do**
  $\upsilon_p \leftarrow NULL$, $\sigma \leftarrow 0$
  for all $\upsilon \in \mathcal{U}$ **do**
    if $\upsilon_p \neq NULL$ AND $\upsilon \in \mathcal{I}$ **then**
      $\mathcal{S} \leftarrow$ query(`'SELECT Queue Size FROM` $\mathcal{D}_{MS}$ `WHERE Queue Name=`χ `AND #Users=`υ`'`)
      $\mathcal{S}_p \leftarrow$ query(`'SELECT Queue Size FROM` $\mathcal{D}_{MS}$ `WHERE Queue Name=`χ `AND #Users=`υ_p`'`)
      $\mathcal{B} \leftarrow$ bootstrap($\mathcal{S}$), $\mathcal{B}_p \leftarrow$ bootstrap($\mathcal{S}_p$), $m \leftarrow$ mean($\mathcal{B}$), $m_p \leftarrow$ mean($\mathcal{B}_p$)
      $p \leftarrow$ t-test($\mathcal{B}$,$\mathcal{B}_p$)
      if $p < \alpha$ AND $m_p < m$ **then**
        $\sigma \leftarrow \sigma + 1$
      end if
    end if
    $\upsilon_p \leftarrow \upsilon$
  end for
  if $\sigma = |\mathcal{I}|$ **then**
    $\beta \leftarrow$ **true**
  end if
end for
return β

A.1.10.2. Network Utilization Stagnation Strategy

Algorithm 22 Excessive Messaging: Network Utilization Stagnation Strategy

`Input:`
$\mathcal{D}_{NW}$ *// Network I/O dataset* , $\mathcal{D}_{MS}$ *// Messaging dataset*
$\mathcal{I}$ *// load under which performance requirements are violated*
α *// significance for t-test* , ϵ *// increase in the utilization*
`Output:` β *// boolean indicating whether Excessive Messaging exists*
`Init:` $\pi \leftarrow 1452$ *// TCP packet size* , $\beta \leftarrow$ **false**
`Algorithm:`
$\mathcal{U} \leftarrow$ query(`'SELECT DIST. #Users FROM` $\mathcal{D}_{NW}$ `ORDER BY #Users'`)
$\mathcal{N} \leftarrow$ query(`'SELECT DIST. Node, Interface Name FROM` $\mathcal{D}_{NW}$`'`)
$\mu \leftarrow$ mean(query(`'SELECT Avg. Message Size FROM` $\mathcal{D}_{MS}$`'`))
for all $\nu \in \mathcal{N}$ **do**
  $\sigma \leftarrow 0, \quad \theta_p \leftarrow NULL$
  for all $\upsilon \in \mathcal{U}$ **do**
    $\mathcal{T} \leftarrow$ query(`'SELECT BytesReceived, BytesTransferred, Timestamp FROM` $\mathcal{D}_{NW}$ `WHERE Node=`ν`[Node] AND Interface Name=`ν`[Interface Name] AND #Users=`υ`'`)
    $\theta_r \leftarrow \frac{max(\mathcal{T}[\text{BytesReceived}])-min(\mathcal{T}[\text{BytesReceived}])}{max(\mathcal{T}[\text{Timestamp}])-min(\mathcal{T}[\text{Timestamp}])}$
    $\theta_t \leftarrow \frac{max(\mathcal{T}[\text{BytesTransferred}])-min(\mathcal{T}[\text{BytesTransferred}])}{max(\mathcal{T}[\text{Timestamp}])-min(\mathcal{T}[\text{Timestamp}])}$
    $\theta \leftarrow max(\theta_r, \theta_t)$
    if $\theta_p \neq NULL$ **then**
      if $\theta > \theta_p + \epsilon$ **then** $\sigma \leftarrow \sigma + 1$ **end if**
    end if
    $\theta_p \leftarrow \theta$
  end for
  $B_w \leftarrow$ query(`'SELECT DISTINCT Speed FROM` $\mathcal{D}_{NW}$ `WHERE Node=`ν`[Node] AND Interface Name=`ν`[Interface Name]'`)
  if $\sigma = |\mathcal{I}|$ AND $\theta > \frac{1}{2}B_w$ **then** $\beta \leftarrow$ **true end if**
end for
return β AND queSizeAnalysis($\mathcal{D}_{MS}$,$\mathcal{I}$,α) *// cf. Algorithm 21*

A.1.10.3. Message Throughput Strategy

Algorithm 23 Excessive Messaging: Message Throughput Detection Strat.

`Input:`
$\mathcal{D}_{NW}$ *// Network I/O dataset*
$\mathcal{D}_{MS}$ *// Messaging statistics dataset*
$\mathcal{I}$ *// load intensities under which performance requirements are violated*
α *// significance level for t-test*
`Output:`
β *// boolean indicating whether Excessive Messaging exists*
`Init:` $\beta \leftarrow$ **false**, $\mu_p \leftarrow NULL$
`Algorithm:`
$\mathcal{U} \leftarrow$ query(`'SELECT DISTINCT #Users FROM` $\mathcal{D}_{MS}$ `ORDER BY #Users'`)
for all $v \in \mathcal{U}$ **do**
  $\mathcal{M} \leftarrow$ query(`'SELECT Message Count, Timestamp FROM` $\mathcal{D}_{MS}$`'`)
  $\mu_{min} \leftarrow$ min($\mathcal{M}$[Message Count]), $\mu_{max} \leftarrow$ max($\mathcal{M}$[Message Count])
  $\sigma \leftarrow 0$
  $\mathcal{M} \leftarrow$ query(`'SELECT Message Count, Timestamp FROM` $\mathcal{D}_{MS}$`'`)
  $\tau_{min} \leftarrow$ min($\mathcal{M}$[Timestamp]), $\tau_{max} \leftarrow$ max($\mathcal{M}$[Timestamp])
  $\mu \leftarrow \frac{\mu_{max} - \mu_{min}}{\tau_{max} - \tau_{min}}$
  if $\mu_p \neq NULL$ **then**
    if $\mu > \mu_p + \epsilon$ **then**
      $\sigma \leftarrow \sigma + 1$
    end if
  end if
  $\mu_p \leftarrow \mu$
end for
if $\sigma = |\mathcal{I}|$ **then**
  $\beta \leftarrow$ **true**
end if
return β AND queSizeAnalysis($\mathcal{D}_{MS}$,$\mathcal{I}$,α) *// cf. Algorithm 21*

A.1.11. The Blob Heuristic

A.1.11.1. Mean Analysis Strategy

Algorithm 24 The Blob: Mean Analysis Strategy

`Input:`
$\mathcal{D}_M$ *// Messaging dataset*
`Output:`
$\mathcal{B}$ *// set of components that are detected as Blob components*
`Init:`
$\mathcal{B} \leftarrow \emptyset$
`Algorithm:`
$C \leftarrow$ query(`'SELECT DISTINCT Component ID FROM` $\mathcal{D}_M$`'`)
$\mathcal{M} = \{v_\zeta\}_{\zeta \in C} \leftarrow$ correlateMessageTimes($\mathcal{D}_M$) *// assigns message transmission times to the involved components*
$\mu \leftarrow$ mean($\mathcal{M}$)
$\sigma \leftarrow$ standardDeviation($\mathcal{M}$)
$\tau \leftarrow \mu + 3\sigma$
for all $\zeta \in C$ **do**
  $v \leftarrow \mathcal{M}(\zeta)$
  if $v > \tau$ **then**
    $\mathcal{B} \leftarrow \mathcal{B} \cup \{\zeta\}$
  end if
end for

return $\mathcal{B}$

A.1.11.2. Component Exclusion Analysis Strategy

Algorithm 25 The Blob: Component Exclusion Analysis Strategy

`Input:`
$\mathcal{D}_M$ *// Messaging dataset*
`Output:`
$\mathcal{B}$ *// set of components that are detected as Blob components*
`Init:` $\mathcal{B} \leftarrow \emptyset, \mathcal{P} \leftarrow \emptyset$
`Algorithm:`
$C \leftarrow$ query(`'SELECT DISTINCT Component ID FROM` $\mathcal{D}_M$`'`)
$\mathcal{M} = \leftarrow$ correlateMessageTimes($\mathcal{D}_M$) *// assigns message transmission times to the involved components*
$\omega \leftarrow \sum_{\nu \in \mathcal{M}} (\nu)$
for all $\zeta \in C$ **do**
  $\mathcal{M}_\zeta \leftarrow \bigcup_{c \in C \setminus \{\zeta\}} (\mathcal{M}(c))$
  $\omega_\zeta \leftarrow \sum_{\nu \in \mathcal{M}_\zeta} (\nu)$
  $\pi_\zeta \leftarrow 1 - \frac{\omega_\zeta}{\omega}$ *// messaging contribution of component* ζ
  $\mathcal{P} \leftarrow \mathcal{P} \cup (\zeta, \pi)$
end for
for all $(\zeta, \pi) \in \mathcal{P}$ **do**
  $\mathcal{P}_\zeta \leftarrow \mathcal{P} \setminus \{(\zeta, \pi)\}$
  $\mu_\zeta \leftarrow$ mean($\mathcal{P}_\zeta$)
  $\sigma_\zeta \leftarrow$ standardDeviation($\mathcal{P}_\zeta$)
  $\tau_\zeta \leftarrow \mu_\zeta + 3\sigma_\zeta$
  if $\pi > \tau_\zeta$ **then**
    $\mathcal{B} \leftarrow \mathcal{B} \cup \{\zeta\}$
  end if
end for
return $\mathcal{B}$

A.1.12. Empty Semi Trucks Heuristic

Algorithm 26 Empty Semi Trucks Detection Strategy

Input:
$\mathcal{D}_T$ *// tracing dataset*
$\mathcal{D}_{MS}$ *// message size dataset*
Output:
$\mathcal{E}$ *// set of traces pointing to repeated message transmission, indicating saving potential in data transmission overhead*
Init:
$\mathcal{E} \leftarrow \emptyset$
Algorithm:
$\mathcal{T} \leftarrow$ extractTraceInstances($\mathcal{D}_T$)
$\mathcal{T} \leftarrow$ addMessagingInformation($\mathcal{T}$,$\mathcal{D}_{MS}$) *// annotates each message dispatch operation call with the size of the transmitted message*
$\mathcal{T} \leftarrow$ identifyAndAggregateLoops($\mathcal{T}$)
$C \leftarrow$ clusterTraces($\mathcal{T}$)
for all $\zeta \in C$ **do**
  if ζ contain message dispatch method in a loop **then**
    $\nu \leftarrow$ numMessagesSent(ζ)
    $\sigma \leftarrow$ avgMessageSize(ζ)
    $\beta \leftarrow$ avgMessagePayloadSize(ζ)
    $\pi \leftarrow (\nu - 1)(\sigma - \beta)$ *// saving potential*
    $\mathcal{E} \leftarrow \mathcal{E} \cup \{(\zeta, \pi)\}$
  end if
end for

sort $\mathcal{E}$ descending by saving potential π
return $\mathcal{E}$

A.2. Additional Information on Validation

A.2.1. Case Study: TPC-W

	CPU	Memory (RAM)	Operating System	Relevant Applications	Network Interface
Measurement Node	Intel® Core™ i7 2640M, 2.8Ghz 4 virtual cores	8GB	Windows 7 64bit	Java 7.0.45 RBE for TPC-W DynamicSpotter	Ethernet 100Mbit
Application Node	Intel® Core™ i3 M370, 2.4Ghz 4 virtual cores	4GB	Windows 7 64bit	Java 7.0.45 Apache Tomcat 6.0.43 AIM	Ethernet 100Mbit
Database Node	Intel® Core™ i7 4712MQ, 2.3Ghz 8 virtual cores	8GB	Windows 8 64bit	Java 7.0.45 MySQL 5.6.23, InnoDB AIM	Ethernet 100Mbit

Table A.1.: TPC-W case study Part I: details on measurement environment

	CPU	Memory (RAM)	Operating System	Relevant Applications	Network Interface
Measurement Node	Intel® Core™ i7 2640M, 2.8Ghz 4 virtual cores	8GB	Windows 7 64bit	Java 7.0.45 RBE for TPC-W DynamicSpotter	Ethernet 100Mbit
Application Nodes 1-3	Intel® Core™ 2 Duo E8400, 3.0Ghz 2 virtual cores	4GB	Ubuntu 12.04.3	Java 7.0.45 Apache Tomcat 7.0.30 AIM	Ethernet 100Mbit
Database Nodes 1-3	Intel® Xeon™ L5630, 2.13Ghz 16 virtual cores	16GB	Linux Enterprise Server 11 SP2 64bit	Java 7.0.45 MySQL 5.6.23, InnoDB AIM	Ethernet 100Mbit
Load Driver Node	Intel® Core™ i7 2600, 3.4Ghz 8 virtual cores	16GB	Windows 7 64bit	Java 7.0.45 HP LoadRunner™ 11.52	Ethernet 100Mbit
Messaging Node	Intel® Xeon™ L5630, 2.13Ghz 16 virtual cores	16GB	Linux Enterprise Server 11 SP2 64bit	Java 7.0.45 Apache ActiveMQ 5.9 AIM	Ethernet 100Mbit
Controller Node	Intel® Core™ i7 2600, 3.4Ghz 8 virtual cores	16GB	Ubuntu 12.04.3	Java 7.0.45 Apache Tomcat 7.0.30 AIM	Ethernet 100Mbit

Table A.2.: TPC-W case study Part II: details on measurement environment

A.2.2. Case Study: NopCommerce

	CPU	Memory (RAM)	Operating System	Relevant Applications	Network Interface
Measurement Node	Intel® Core™ i7 2640M,2.8Ghz 4 virtual cores	8GB	Windows 7 64bit	Java 7.0.45 Apache JMeter 2.9 DynamicSpotter	Ethernet 100Mbit
Application Node	Intel® Core™ i3 M370,2.4Ghz 4 virtual cores	4GB	Windows 7 64bit	.NET Framework 4.0 PostSharp 4.1 JNBridge 7.2 IIS 8 Java 7.0.45 AIM	Ethernet 100Mbit
Database Node	Intel® Core™ i7 4712MQ,2.3Ghz 8 virtual cores	8GB	Windows 8 64bit	Java 7.0.45 MS SQL Server Express 2014 AIM	Ethernet 100Mbit

Table A.3.: nopCommerce case study: details on measurement environment

Bibliography

Publications

Wert, A. (2013). "Performance Problem Diagnostics by Systematic Experimentation". In: *Proceedings of the 18th International Doctoral Symposium on Components and Architecture*. WCOP '13. Vancouver, British Columbia, Canada: ACM, pp. 1–6.

– (2015). "DynamicSpotter: Automatic, Experiment-based Diagnostics of Performance Problems (Invited Demonstration Paper)". In: *Proceedings of the 6th ACM/SPEC International Conference on Performance Engineering*. ICPE '15. Austin, Texas, USA: ACM, pp. 105–106.

Wert, A., J. Happe, and L. Happe (2013). "Supporting Swift Reaction: Automatically Uncovering Performance Problems by Systematic Experiments". In: *Proceedings of the 2013 International Conference on Software Engineering*. ICSE '13. San Francisco, CA, USA: IEEE Press, pp. 552–561.

Wert, A., J. Happe, and D. Westermann (2012). "Integrating Software Performance Curves with the Palladio Component Model". In: *Proceedings of the 3rd ACM/SPEC International Conference on Performance Engineering*. ICPE '12. Boston, Massachusetts, USA: ACM, pp. 283–286.

Wert, A., M. Oehler, C. Heger, and R. Farahbod (2014). "Automatic Detection of Performance Anti-patterns in Inter-component Communications". In: *Proceedings of the 10th International ACM Sigsoft Conference on Quality of Software Architectures*. QoSA '14. Marcq-en-Bareul, France: ACM, pp. 3–12.

Wert, A., H. Schulz, and C. Heger (2015a). "AIM: Adaptable Instrumentation and Monitoring for Automated Software Performance Analysis". In: *Proceedings of the 10th International Workshop on Automation of Software Test*. AST 2015. Florence, Italy: ACM.

Wert, A., H. Schulz, C. Heger, and R. Farahbod (2015b). "Generic Instrumentation and Monitoring Description for Software Performance Evaluation". In: *Proceedings of the 6th ACM/SPEC International Conference on Performance Engineering*. ICPE '15. Austin, Texas, USA: ACM, pp. 203–206.

Happe, J., W. Theilmann, and A. Wert (2011). "Service Construction Meta-Model". English. In: *Service Level Agreements for Cloud Computing*. Ed. by P. Wieder, J. M. Butler, W. Theilmann, and R. Yahyapour. Springer New York, pp. 69–78.

Heger, C., A. Wert, and R. Farahbod (2014). "Vergil: Guiding Developers Through Performance and Scalability Inferno". English. In: *The Ninth International Conference on Software Engineering Advances (ICSEA)*. Ed. by H. Mannaert, L. Lavazza, R. Oberhauser, M. Kajko-Mattsson, and M. Gebhart. IARIA, pp. 598–608.

Krebs, R., A. Wert, and S. Kounev (2013). "Multi-tenancy Performance Benchmark for Web Application Platforms". English. In: *Web Engineering*. Ed. by F. Daniel, P. Dolog, and Q. Li. Vol. 7977. Lecture Notes in Computer Science. Springer Berlin Heidelberg, pp. 424–438.

Supervised Theses

Dogan, Y. (2013). "Detection of Relevant Variation Points in Software Workload Monitoring Data for Performance Antipattern Detection with Regression Analysis Techniques". Master's Thesis. Karlsruhe Institute of Technology.

Erdogan, I. (2012). "Simulationsbasierte Erkennung von Performance Anti-Pattern in Palladio-Modellen". Master's Thesis. Karlsruhe Institute of Technology.

Kohlhaas, S. (2014). "Systematic Investigation of Performance Anti-Patterns in In-Memory Database Queries". Bachelor's Thesis. Karlsruhe Institute of Technology.

Löwen, O. (2014). "Analyse der Speicherverwaltungskonfiguration in Java zur Lösung von Performance-Problemen". MA thesis. Karlsruhe Institute of Technology.

Merkert, P. (2014). "An Empirical Study for the Evaluation of a Performance Problem Detection Approach". Bachelor's Thesis. Karlsruhe Institute of Technology.

Oehler, M. (2014). "Automatic Diagnosis of Software Performance Problems by Analysis of Profiling Data". Bachelor's Thesis. Stuttgart Media University.

Schulz, H. (2014). "Adaptive Instrumentation of Java-Applications for Experiment-Based Performance Analysis". Bachelor's Thesis. Karlsruhe Institute of Technology.

Tran, L.-H. S. (2013). "Measurement-Based Diagnosis of Performance Problems in Cloud Applications". Master's Thesis. Karlsruhe Institute of Technology.

References

Filman, R. E. and K. Havelund (2002). *Source-code instrumentation and quantification of events*. Tech. rep. NASA Ames Research Center (cit. on p. 39).

Stecklein, J. M., J. Dabney, B. Dick, B. Haskins, R. Lovell, and G. Moroney (2004). *Error cost escalation through the project life cycle*. Tech. rep. JSC-CN-8435. NASA Johnson Space Center (cit. on p. 2).

Alexander, C. (1982). *A pattern language : towns, buildings, construction*. Oxford University Press (cit. on p. 40).

Allspaw, J. and J. Robbins (2010). *Web Operations: Keeping the Data On Time*. O'Reilly Media (cit. on p. 37).

Angel, D., J. Kumorek, F. Morshed, and D. Seidel (2001). *Byte code instrumentation*. US Patent 6,314,558 (cit. on p. 39).

Atkinson, C., B. Kennel, and B. Goß (2011). "The Level-Agnostic Modeling Language". English. In: *Software Language Engineering*. Ed. by B. Malloy, S. Staab, and M. van den Brand. Vol. 6563. Lecture Notes in Computer Science. Springer Berlin Heidelberg, pp. 266–275 (cit. on pp. 151, 153).

Atkinson, C. and T. Kühne (2001). "The Essence of Multilevel Metamodeling". English. In: *«UML» 2001 — The Unified Modeling Language. Modeling Languages, Concepts, and Tools*. Ed. by M. Gogolla and C.

Kobryn. Vol. 2185. Lecture Notes in Computer Science. Springer Berlin Heidelberg, pp. 19–33 (cit. on p. 151).

Avritzer, A. and E. J. Weyuker (1996). "Deriving Workloads for Performance Testing". In: *Software: Practice and Experience* 26.6, pp. 613–633 (cit. on p. 347).

Ayewah, N., D. Hovemeyer, J. Morgenthaler, J. Penix, and W. Pugh (2008). "Using Static Analysis to Find Bugs". In: *Software, IEEE* 25.5, pp. 22–29 (cit. on p. 5).

Barber, S. (2004). "Creating effective load models for performance testing with incomplete empirical data". In: *Telecommunications Energy Conference, 2004. INTELEC 2004. 26th Annual International*, pp. 51–59 (cit. on p. 331).

Basili, V. R. (1992). *Software modeling and measurement: the Goal/Question/Metric paradigm*. Tech. rep. Techreport UMIACS TR-92-96, University of Maryland at College Park, College Park, MD, USA (cit. on p. 319).

Bause, F. (1993). "Queueing Petri Nets-A formalism for the combined qualitative and quantitative analysis of systems". In: *Petri Nets and Performance Models, 1993. Proceedings., 5th International Workshop on*, pp. 14–23 (cit. on p. 24).

Becker, S., H. Koziolek, and R. Reussner (2009). "The Palladio component model for model-driven performance prediction". In: *Journal of Systems and Software* 82.1. Special Issue: Software Performance - Modeling and Analysis, pp. 3–22 (cit. on pp. 24, 30–32).

Benoit, D. (2005). "Automatic Diagnosis of Performance Problems in Database Management Systems". In: *Autonomic Computing, 2005. ICAC 2005. Proceedings. Second International Conference on*, pp. 326–327 (cit. on pp. 355, 356).

Bernardino, M., A. F. Zorzo, E. Rodrigues, F. de Oliveira, and R. Saad (2014). "A Domain-Specific Language for Modeling Performance Testing: Requirements Analysis and Design Decisions". English. In: *The Ninth International Conference on Software Engineering Advances (ICSEA)*. Ed. by H. Mannaert, L. Lavazza, R. Oberhauser, M. Kajko-Mattsson, and M. Gebhart. IARIA, pp. 609–614 (cit. on p. 352).

Bertolino, A., A. Calabrò, F. Lonetti, A. Di Marco, and A. Sabetta (2011). "Towards a Model-Driven Infrastructure for Runtime Monitoring". English. In: *Software Engineering for Resilient Systems*. Ed. by E. Troubitsyna.

Vol. 6968. Lecture Notes in Computer Science. Springer Berlin Heidelberg, pp. 130–144 (cit. on p. 350).

Bloom, B. S. and D. R. Krathwohl (1984). *Taxonomy of educational objectives book 1: Cognitive domain.* Addison Wesley Publishing Company (cit. on pp. 320, 325).

Boehm, B. (1981). *Software Engineering Economics.* Prentice-Hall advances in computing science and technology series. Prentice-Hall (cit. on p. 2).

Böhme, R. and R. Reussner (2008). "Validation of Predictions with Measurements". English. In: *Dependability Metrics.* Ed. by I. Eusgeld, F. Freiling, and R. Reussner. Vol. 4909. Lecture Notes in Computer Science. Springer Berlin Heidelberg, pp. 14–18 (cit. on pp. 224, 232, 233).

Bolch, G., S. Greiner, H. de Meer, and K. Trivedi (2006). *Queueing Networks and Markov Chains: Modeling and Performance Evaluation with Computer Science Applications.* Wiley (cit. on p. 24).

Boroday, S., A. Petrenko, J. Singh, and H. Hallal (2005). "Dynamic Analysis of Java Applications for Multithreaded Antipatterns". In: *SIGSOFT Softw. Eng. Notes* 30.4, pp. 1–7 (cit. on p. 49).

Bošković, M. and W. Hasselbring (2009). "Model Driven Performance Measurement and Assessment with MoDePeMART". English. In: *Model Driven Engineering Languages and Systems.* Ed. by A. Schürr and B. Selic. Vol. 5795. Lecture Notes in Computer Science. Springer Berlin Heidelberg, pp. 62–76 (cit. on p. 350).

Box, D. and T. Pattison (2002). *Essential .NET: The common language runtime.* Addison-Wesley Longman Publishing Co., Inc. (cit. on pp. 67, 142, 276).

Brataas, G., E. Stav, S. Lehrig, S. Becker, G. Kopčak, and D. Huljenic (2013). "CloudScale: Scalability Management for Cloud Systems". In: *Proceedings of the 4th ACM/SPEC International Conference on Performance Engineering.* ICPE '13. Prague, Czech Republic: ACM, pp. 335–338 (cit. on p. 310).

Brosig, F., N. Huber, and S. Kounev (2011). "Automated extraction of architecture-level performance models of distributed component-based systems". In: *Automated Software Engineering (ASE), 2011 26th IEEE/ACM International Conference on*, pp. 183–192 (cit. on pp. 362, 377).

Brown, W. J., R. C. Malveau, H. W. McCormick III, and T. J. Mowbray (1998). *AntiPatterns: Refactoring Software, Architectures, and Projects in*

Crisis. New York, NY, USA: John Wiley & Sons, Inc. (cit. on pp. 41, 343, 346).

Bulej, L., T. Kalibera, and P. Tma (2005). "Repeated Results Analysis for Middleware Regression Benchmarking". In: *Perform. Eval.* 60.1-4, pp. 345–358 (cit. on pp. 35, 362, 373).

Burke, B. (2009). *RESTful Java with JAX-RS*. O'Reilly Media (cit. on p. 142).

Busch, P., T. Heinonen, and P. Lahti (2007). "Heisenberg's uncertainty principle". In: *Physics Reports* 452.6, pp. 155–176 (cit. on pp. 38, 335).

Buschmann, F., K. Henney, and D. Schmidt (2007). *Pattern-Oriented Software Architecture, On Patterns and Pattern Languages*. Pattern-Oriented Software Architecture. Wiley (cit. on pp. 40, 343).

Calvert, C. and D. Kulkarni (2009). *Essential LINQ*. Microsoft Windows Development Series. Pearson Education (cit. on p. 143).

Carver, J., L. Jaccheri, S. Morasca, and F. Shull (2003). "Using Empirical Studies during Software Courses". English. In: *Empirical Methods and Studies in Software Engineering*. Ed. by R. Conradi and A. Wang. Vol. 2765. Lecture Notes in Computer Science. Springer Berlin Heidelberg, pp. 81–103 (cit. on p. 324).

Chen, P., Y. Qi, P. Zheng, and D. Hou (2014). "CauseInfer: Automatic and distributed performance diagnosis with hierarchical causality graph in large distributed systems". In: *INFOCOM, 2014 Proceedings IEEE*, pp. 1887–1895 (cit. on pp. 11, 361, 371, 372).

Cheng, B., R. de Lemos, H. Giese, P. Inverardi, J. Magee, J. Andersson, B. Becker, N. Bencomo, Y. Brun, B. Cukic, G. Di Marzo Serugendo, S. Dustdar, A. Finkelstein, C. Gacek, K. Geihs, V. Grassi, G. Karsai, H. Kienle, J. Kramer, M. Litoiu, S. Malek, R. Mirandola, H. A. Müller, S. Park, M. Shaw, M. Tichy, M. Tivoli, D. Weyns, and J. Whittle (2009). "Software Engineering for Self-Adaptive Systems: A Research Roadmap". English. In: *Software Engineering for Self-Adaptive Systems*. Ed. by B. Cheng, R. de Lemos, H. Giese, P. Inverardi, and J. Magee. Vol. 5525. Lecture Notes in Computer Science. Springer Berlin Heidelberg, pp. 1–26 (cit. on pp. 60, 376).

Chis, A. E., N. Mitchell, E. Schonberg, G. Sevitsky, P. O'Sullivan, T. Parsons, and J. Murphy (2011). "Patterns of Memory Inefficiency". English. In: *ECOOP 2011 — Object-Oriented Programming*. Ed. by M. Mezini. Vol. 6813. Lecture Notes in Computer Science. Springer Berlin Heidelberg, pp. 383–407 (cit. on p. 344).

Chou, Y. and B. Bauer (1975). *Statistical Analysis with Business and Economic Applications: Instructor's Manual with Solutions*. Holt, Rinehart and Winston (cit. on p. 178).

Cortellessa, V., A. Di Marco, and C. Trubiani (2010a). "Performance Antipatterns as Logical Predicates". In: *Engineering of Complex Computer Systems (ICECCS), 2010 15th IEEE International Conference on*, pp. 146–156 (cit. on pp. 355, 357, 358).

Cortellessa, V., A. Di Marco, R. Eramo, A. Pierantonio, and C. Trubiani (2010b). "Digging into UML Models to Remove Performance Antipatterns". In: *Proceedings of the 2010 ICSE Workshop on Quantitative Stochastic Models in the Verification and Design of Software Systems*. QUOVADIS '10. Cape Town, South Africa: ACM, pp. 9–16 (cit. on pp. 355, 357, 358).

Cortellessa, V., A. Di Marco, and C. Trubiani (2014). "An approach for modeling and detecting software performance antipatterns based on first-order logics". English. In: *Software & Systems Modeling* 13.1, pp. 391–432 (cit. on pp. 10, 355, 357, 369).

Cortellessa, V. and L. Frittella (2007). "A Framework for Automated Generation of Architectural Feedback from Software Performance Analysis". English. In: *Formal Methods and Stochastic Models for Performance Evaluation*. Ed. by K. Wolter. Vol. 4748. Lecture Notes in Computer Science. Springer Berlin Heidelberg, pp. 171–185 (cit. on pp. 355–357).

Dahm, M. (1999). "Byte Code Engineering". English. In: *JIT'99*. Ed. by C. Cap. Informatik aktuell. Springer Berlin Heidelberg, pp. 267–277 (cit. on p. 139).

Detlefs, D. L. (1996). "An overview of the Extended Static Checking system". In: *Proceedings of the First Workshop on Formal Methods in Software Practice*. Citeseer, pp. 1–9 (cit. on p. 352).

Di Marco, A. and C. Trubiani (2014). "A model-driven approach to broaden the detection of software performance antipatterns at runtime". In: *Proceedings 11th International Workshop on Formal Engineering approaches to Software Components and Architectures*. (Grenoble, France). Ed. by B. Bühnová, L. Happe, and J. Kofroň. Vol. 147. Electronic Proceedings in Theoretical Computer Science. Open Publishing Association, pp. 77–92 (cit. on pp. 360, 369).

Diaconescu, A. and J. Murphy (2005). "Automating the Performance Management of Component-based Enterprise Systems Through the Use of Redundancy". In: *Proceedings of the 20th IEEE/ACM International Con-*

ference on Automated Software Engineering. ASE '05. Long Beach, CA, USA: ACM, pp. 44–53 (cit. on p. 376).

Dmitriev, M. (2001). *Safe Class and Data Evolution in Large and Long-Lived Java[Tm] Applications*. Tech. rep. Mountain View, CA, USA: Sun Microsystems, Inc. (cit. on p. 311).

Downing, D. and J. Clark (2003). *Business Statistics*. Barron's Business Review Series. Barron's (cit. on pp. 182, 184, 191, 201, 211).

Dudney, B., S. Asbury, J. K. Krozak, and K. Wittkopf (2003). *J2EE antipatterns*. John Wiley & Sons (cit. on pp. 46, 50, 343).

Dugan Jr., R. F., E. P. Glinert, and A. Shokoufandeh (2002). "The Sisyphus Database Retrieval Software Performance Antipattern". In: *Proceedings of the 3rd International Workshop on Software and Performance*. WOSP '02. Rome, Italy: ACM, pp. 10–16 (cit. on p. 48).

Durdik, Z. (2014). "Architectural Design Decision Documentation with Reuse of Design Patterns". PhD thesis. Karlsruhe Institute of Technology (cit. on p. 233).

Duvall, P., S. Matyas, and A. Glover (2007). *Continuous Integration: Improving Software Quality and Reducing Risk*. Addison-Wesley Signature Series. Pearson Education (cit. on pp. 5, 6, 376, 383).

Ehlers, J., A. van Hoorn, J. Waller, and W. Hasselbring (2011). "Self-adaptive Software System Monitoring for Performance Anomaly Localization". In: *Proceedings of the 8th ACM International Conference on Autonomic Computing*. ICAC '11. Karlsruhe, Germany: ACM, pp. 197–200 (cit. on pp. 11, 311, 316, 360, 368, 369).

Espinosa, A., T. Margalef, and E. Luque (1998). "Automatic performance evaluation of parallel programs". In: *Parallel and Distributed Processing, 1998. PDP '98. Proceedings of the Sixth Euromicro Workshop on*, pp. 43–49 (cit. on pp. 361, 370).

Evans, D. (1996). "Static Detection of Dynamic Memory Errors". In: *Proceedings of the ACM SIGPLAN 1996 Conference on Programming Language Design and Implementation*. PLDI '96. Philadelphia, Pennsylvania, USA: ACM, pp. 44–53 (cit. on p. 352).

Fink, A. (2003). *The Survey Handbook*. Survey Kit Second Edition 1 1. SAGE Publications (cit. on p. 16).

Flanagan, D. and Y. Matsumoto (2008). *The Ruby Programming Language*. O'Reilly Media (cit. on p. 68).

Foo, K., Z. M. Jiang, B. Adams, A. Hassan, Y. Zou, and P. Flora (2010). "Mining Performance Regression Testing Repositories for Automated Performance Analysis". In: *Quality Software (QSIC), 2010 10th International Conference on*, pp. 32–41 (cit. on pp. 362, 373).

Fowler, M., K. Beck, J. Brant, W. Opdyke, and D. Roberts (2012). *Refactoring: Improving the Design of Existing Code*. Addison-Wesley Object Technology Series. Pearson Education (cit. on p. 45).

Fowler, M. (2002). *Patterns of Enterprise Application Architecture*. Boston, MA, USA: Addison-Wesley Longman Publishing Co., Inc. (cit. on pp. 21, 22).

Franks, G., D. Petriu, M. Woodside, J. Xu, and P. Tregunno (2006). "Layered Bottlenecks and Their Mitigation". In: *Quantitative Evaluation of Systems, 2006. QEST 2006. Third International Conference on*, pp. 103–114 (cit. on pp. 10, 343, 353–356).

Franks, G., S. Majumdar, J. Neilson, D. Petriu, J. Rolia, and M. Woodside (1996). "Performance analysis of distributed server systems". In: *Proceedings of the 6th International Conference on Software Quality*, pp. 15–26 (cit. on p. 343).

Freeman, A. (2013). *Pro ASP.NET MVC 5*. Expert's Voice in ASP.Net. Apress (cit. on p. 276).

Frølund, S. and J. Koisten (1998). *QML: A Language for Quality of Service Specification*. Tech. rep. Technical Report HPL-98-10. Hewlett-Packard Laboratories (cit. on p. 133).

Gamma, E., R. Helm, R. Johnson, and J. Vlissides (1994). *Design Patterns: Elements of Reusable Object-Oriented Software*. Pearson Education (cit. on pp. 40, 343).

Garlan, D., S.-W. Cheng, A.-C. Huang, B. Schmerl, and P. Steenkiste (2004). "Rainbow: architecture-based self-adaptation with reusable infrastructure". In: *Computer* 37.10, pp. 46–54 (cit. on p. 376).

Ghaith, S., M. Wang, P. Perry, Z. M. Jiang, P. O'Sullivan, and J. Murphy (2015). "Anomaly detection in performance regression testing by transaction profile estimation". In: *Software Testing, Verification and Reliability*, n/a–n/a (cit. on pp. 362, 375).

Grechanik, M., C. Fu, and Q. Xie (2012). "Automatically finding performance problems with feedback-directed learning software testing". In: *Software Engineering (ICSE), 2012 34th International Conference on*, pp. 156–166 (cit. on pp. 234, 360, 367).

Gross, D., J. Shortle, J. Thompson, and C. Harris (2011). *Fundamentals of Queueing Theory*. Wiley Series in Probability and Statistics. Wiley (cit. on p. 25).

Grosso, W. (2002). *Java RMI*. Designing and building distributed applications. O'Reilly Media, Incorporated (cit. on p. 142).

Gupta, S. (2005). *Pro Apache Log4j*. Expert's voice in Java. Apress (cit. on p. 143).

Hallal, H., E. Alikacem, W. Tunney, S. Boroday, and A. Petrenko (2004). "Antipattern-based detection of deficiencies in Java multithreaded software". In: *Quality Software, 2004. QSIC 2004. Proceedings. Fourth International Conference on*, pp. 258–267 (cit. on pp. 344–346).

Hauck, M., M. Kuperberg, N. Huber, and R. Reussner (2011). "Ginpex: Deriving Performance-relevant Infrastructure Properties Through Goal-oriented Experiments". In: *Proceedings of the Joint ACM SIGSOFT Conference – QoSA and ACM SIGSOFT Symposium – ISARCS on Quality of Software Architectures – QoSA and Architecting Critical Systems – ISARCS*. QoSA-ISARCS '11. Boulder, Colorado, USA: ACM, pp. 53–62 (cit. on pp. 349, 350).

Heger, C. (2015). "An Approach for Guiding Developers to Performance and Scalability Solutions". PhD thesis. Karlsruhe Institute of Technology (cit. on pp. 4, 329, 391).

Heger, C., J. Happe, and R. Farahbod (2013). "Automated Root Cause Isolation of Performance Regressions During Software Development". In: *Proceedings of the 4th ACM/SPEC International Conference on Performance Engineering*. ICPE '13. Prague, Czech Republic: ACM, pp. 27–38 (cit. on pp. 35, 362, 373, 374, 376).

Heinrich, R. and B. Paech (2014). *Aligning Business Processes and Information Systems: New Approaches to Continuous Quality Engineering*. Springer (cit. on p. 233).

Hitt, L. M. and X. Z. DJ Wu (2002). "Investment in enterprise resource planning: Business impact and productivity measures". In: *Journal of Management Information Systems* 19.1, pp. 71–98 (cit. on p. 1).

Holzner, S., R. Howell, and B. Howell (2003). *Ado.NET Programming in Visual Basic .NET*. Prentice Hall PTR (cit. on pp. 142, 143).

Hsueh, M.-C., T. Tsai, and R. Iyer (1997). "Fault injection techniques and tools". In: *Computer* 30.4, pp. 75–82 (cit. on pp. 261, 279, 319, 336).

Huber, N., F. Brosig, and S. Kounev (2011). "Model-based Self-adaptive Resource Allocation in Virtualized Environments". In: *Proceedings of the 6th International Symposium on Software Engineering for Adaptive and Self-Managing Systems*. SEAMS '11. Waikiki, Honolulu, HI, USA: ACM, pp. 90–99 (cit. on pp. 376, 377).

Huber, N., A. van Hoorn, A. Koziolek, F. Brosig, and S. Kounev (2014). "Modeling run-time adaptation at the system architecture level in dynamic service-oriented environments". In: *Service Oriented Computing and Applications* 8.1, pp. 73–89 (cit. on p. 377).

Hunter, J. and W. Crawford (2001). *Java Servlet Programming*. Java Series. O'Reilly Media (cit. on pp. 142, 240).

ISO/IEC/IEEE (2010). "Systems and software engineering – Vocabulary". In: *International Standard ISO/IEC/IEEE 24765:2010(E)*, pp. 1–418 (cit. on p. 38).

Jain, R. (1991). *The Art of Computer Systems Performance Analysis: Techniques for Experimental Design, Measurement, Simulation, and Modeling*. Wiley professional computing. Wiley (cit. on pp. 3, 37, 133, 342, 343, 347).

Johnson, S. C. (1977). *Lint, a C program checker*. Citeseer (cit. on p. 5).

Jorgensen, P. C. and C. Erickson (1994). "Object-oriented Integration Testing". In: *Commun. ACM* 37.9, pp. 30–38 (cit. on p. 383).

Karavanic, K. and B. Miller (1999). "Improving Online Performance Diagnosis by the Use of Historical Performance Data". In: *Supercomputing, ACM/IEEE 1999 Conference*, pp. 42–42 (cit. on p. 365).

Karwin, B. (2010). *SQL Antipatterns: Avoiding the Pitfalls of Database Programming*. 1st. Pragmatic Bookshelf (cit. on p. 48).

Kazman, R., G. Abowd, L. Bass, and P. Clements (1996). "Scenario-based analysis of software architecture". In: *Software, IEEE* 13.6, pp. 47–55 (cit. on p. 354).

Kazman, R., M. Klein, M. Barbacci, T. Longstaff, H. Lipson, and J. Carriere (1998). "The architecture tradeoff analysis method". In: *Engineering of Complex Computer Systems, 1998. ICECCS '98. Proceedings. Fourth IEEE International Conference on*, pp. 68–78 (cit. on p. 354).

Keith, M. and M. Schincariol (2006). *Pro EJB 3: Java Persistence API*. Expert's voice in Java. Apress (cit. on p. 143).

Keller, A. and H. Ludwig (2003). "The WSLA Framework: Specifying and Monitoring Service Level Agreements for Web Services". English. In: *Journal of Network and Systems Management* 11.1, pp. 57–81 (cit. on p. 133).

Kephart, J. and D. Chess (2003). "The vision of autonomic computing". In: *Computer* 36.1, pp. 41–50 (cit. on p. 60).

Kiczales, G., J. Lamping, A. Mendhekar, C. Maeda, C. Lopes, J.-M. Loingtier, and J. Irwin (1997). "Aspect-oriented programming". English. In:

ECOOP'97 — Object-Oriented Programming. Ed. by M. Aksit and S. Matsuoka. Vol. 1241. Lecture Notes in Computer Science. Springer Berlin Heidelberg, pp. 220–242 (cit. on p. 39).

Koenig, A. (1998). "Patterns and Antipatterns". In: *The Patterns Handbooks*. Ed. by L. Rising. New York, NY, USA: Cambridge University Press, pp. 383–389 (cit. on p. 41).

Kohavi, R. and R. Longbotham (2007). "Online Experiments: Lessons Learned". In: *Computer* 40.9, pp. 103–105 (cit. on pp. 1, 23).

Kounev, S. (2006). "Performance Modeling and Evaluation of Distributed Component-Based Systems Using Queueing Petri Nets". In: *Software Engineering, IEEE Transactions on* 32.7, pp. 486–502 (cit. on p. 24).

Kounev, S., F. Brosig, N. Huber, and R. Reussner (2010). "Towards Self-Aware Performance and Resource Management in Modern Service-Oriented Systems". In: *Services Computing (SCC), 2010 IEEE International Conference on*, pp. 621–624 (cit. on pp. 11, 362, 376, 377).

Koziolek, A. (2014). *Automated improvement of software architecture models for performance and other quality attributes*. Vol. 7. KIT Scientific Publishing (cit. on p. 233).

Koziolek, H. (2008). "Parameter dependencies for reusable performance specifications of software components". PhD thesis. Universität Oldenburg (cit. on pp. 224, 232–234, 314).

– (2010). "Performance evaluation of component-based software systems: A survey". In: *Performance Evaluation* 67.8. Special Issue on Software and Performance, pp. 634–658 (cit. on p. 3).

Kramer, J. and J. Magee (2007). "Self-Managed Systems: an Architectural Challenge". In: *Future of Software Engineering, 2007. FOSE '07*, pp. 259–268 (cit. on p. 376).

Krishnamurthy, D., J. Rolia, and S. Majumdar (2006). "A Synthetic Workload Generation Technique for Stress Testing Session-Based Systems". In: *Software Engineering, IEEE Transactions on* 32.11, pp. 868–882 (cit. on p. 331).

Lamanna, D. D., J. Skene, and W. Emmerich (2003). "SLAng: A Language for Defining Service Level Agreements". In: *Proceedings of the The Ninth IEEE Workshop on Future Trends of Distributed Computing Systems*. FTDCS '03. Washington, DC, USA: IEEE Computer Society, pp. 100– (cit. on p. 133).

Leue, S. (1995). "Specifying real-time requirements for SDL specifications-a temporal logic-based approach". In: *Proceedings of the Fifteenth IFIP*

WG6. 1 International Symposium on Protocol Specification, Testing and Verification XV. Chapman & Hall, Ltd., pp. 19–34 (cit. on p. 133).

Leung, H. and L. White (1989). "Insights into regression testing [software testing]". In: *Software Maintenance, 1989., Proceedings., Conference on*, pp. 60–69 (cit. on p. 372).

Liu, H. (2011). *Software Performance and Scalability: A Quantitative Approach*. Quantitative Software Engineering Series. Wiley (cit. on pp. 34, 36).

Lowy, J. (2010). *Programming WCF Services: Mastering WCF and the Azure AppFabric Service Bus*. O'Reilly Media (cit. on pp. 142, 143).

Marek, L., A. Villazón, Y. Zheng, D. Ansaloni, W. Binder, and Z. Qi (2012). "DiSL: A Domain-specific Language for Bytecode Instrumentation". In: *Proceedings of the 11th Annual International Conference on Aspect-oriented Software Development*. AOSD '12. Potsdam, Germany: ACM, pp. 239–250 (cit. on pp. 39, 131, 286).

Marsan, M. A., G. Balbo, G. Conte, S. Donatelli, and G. Franceschinis (1994). *Modelling with Generalized Stochastic Petri Nets*. 1st. New York, NY, USA: John Wiley & Sons, Inc. (cit. on p. 24).

Martens, A., S. Becker, H. Koziolek, and R. Reussner (2008). "An Empirical Investigation of the Effort of Creating Reusable, Component-Based Models for Performance Prediction". English. In: *Component-Based Software Engineering*. Ed. by M. Chaudron, C. Szyperski, and R. Reussner. Vol. 5282. Lecture Notes in Computer Science. Springer Berlin Heidelberg, pp. 16–31 (cit. on p. 234).

Martens, A., H. Koziolek, L. Prechelt, and R. Reussner (2011). "From monolithic to component-based performance evaluation of software architectures". English. In: *Empirical Software Engineering* 16.5, pp. 587–622 (cit. on p. 235).

Marwede, N., M. Rohr, A. Van Hoorn, and W. Hasselbring (2009). "Automatic Failure Diagnosis Support in Distributed Large-Scale Software Systems Based on Timing Behavior Anomaly Correlation". In: *Software Maintenance and Reengineering, 2009. CSMR '09. 13th European Conference on*, pp. 47–58 (cit. on pp. 360, 368).

McAffer, J., P. VanderLei, and S. Archer (2010). *OSGi and Equinox: Creating Highly Modular Java Systems*. Eclipse Series. Pearson Education (cit. on p. 143).

Menascé, D. A. (2002). "TPC-W: A benchmark for e-commerce". In: *Internet Computing, IEEE* 6.3, pp. 83–87 (cit. on pp. 229, 240).

Menascé, D. A., V. Almeida, L. Dowdy, and L. Dowdy (2004). *Performance by Design: Computer Capacity Planning by Example*. Prentice Hall PTR (cit. on pp. 25, 27, 29, 195, 201).

Menascé, D. A. and V. Almeida (2001). *Capacity Planning for Web Services: Metrics, Models, and Methods*. 1st. Upper Saddle River, NJ, USA: Prentice Hall PTR (cit. on pp. 34, 35, 347).

Meszaros, G. (1996). "A Pattern Language for Improving the Capacity of Reactive Systems". In: *Pattern Languages of Program Design 2*. Ed. by J. M. Vlissides, J. O. Coplien, and N. L. Kerth. Boston, MA, USA: Addison-Wesley Longman Publishing Co., Inc., pp. 575–591 (cit. on p. 344).

Mielke, A. (2006). "Elements for response-time statistics in {ERP} transaction systems". In: *Performance Evaluation* 63.7, pp. 635–653 (cit. on p. 62).

Miller, B., M. Callaghan, J. Cargille, J. Hollingsworth, R. Irvin, K. Karavanic, K. Kunchithapadam, and T. Newhall (1995). "The Paradyn parallel performance measurement tool". In: *Computer* 28.11, pp. 37–46 (cit. on pp. 11, 360, 364, 365).

Minshall, G., Y. Saito, J. C. Mogul, and B. Verghese (2000). "Application Performance Pitfalls and TCP's Nagle Algorithm". In: *SIGMETRICS Perform. Eval. Rev.* 27.4, pp. 36–44 (cit. on p. 211).

Moha, N. and Y.-g. Guéhéneuc (2005). "On the Automatic Detection and Correction of Software Architectural Defects in Object-Oriented Designs". In: *In Proceedings of the 6 th ECOOP Workshop on Object-Oriented Reengineering. Universities of Glasgow and Strathclyde* (cit. on p. 344).

Monson-Haefel, R. (2004). *Enterprise JavaBeans*. Java Series. O'Reilly (cit. on p. 143).

Neilson, J., C. Woodside, D. Petriu, and S. Majumdar (1995). "Software bottlenecking in client-server systems and rendezvous networks". In: *Software Engineering, IEEE Transactions on* 21.9, pp. 776–782 (cit. on p. 343).

Nguyen, T. H., B. Adams, Z. M. Jiang, A. E. Hassan, M. Nasser, and P. Flora (2012). "Automated Detection of Performance Regressions Using Statistical Process Control Techniques". In: *Proceedings of the 3rd ACM/SPEC International Conference on Performance Engineering*. ICPE '12. Boston, Massachusetts, USA: ACM, pp. 299–310 (cit. on pp. 362, 374).

Nistor, A., L. Song, D. Marinov, and S. Lu (2013). "Toddler: Detecting Performance Problems via Similar Memory-access Patterns". In: *Proceedings of the 2013 International Conference on Software Engineering*. ICSE '13.

San Francisco, CA, USA: IEEE Press, pp. 562–571 (cit. on pp. 11, 234, 361, 369, 370).

Onoma, A. K., W.-T. Tsai, M. Poonawala, and H. Suganuma (1998). "Regression Testing in an Industrial Environment". In: *Commun. ACM* 41.5, pp. 81–86 (cit. on p. 372).

Oreizy, P., M. M. Gorlick, R. N. Taylor, D. Heimbigner, G. Johnson, N. Medvidovic, A. Quilici, D. S. Rosenblum, and A. L. Wolf (1999). "An architecture-based approach to self-adaptive software". In: *IEEE Intelligent systems* 14.3, pp. 54–62 (cit. on p. 376).

Palma, F., M. Nayrolles, N. Moha, Y.-G. Gueheneuc, B. Baudry, and J.-M. Jézéquel (2013). "SOA Antipatterns: an Approach for their Specification and Detection". In: *International Journal of Cooperative Information Systems* 22.04 (cit. on pp. 44, 45, 50, 51).

Parsons, T. (2007). "Automatic Detection of Performance Design and Deployment Antipatterns in Component Based Enterprise Systems". PhD thesis. University College Dublin (cit. on pp. 234, 343, 346, 360, 365).

Parsons, T. and J. Murphy (2004). "A Framework for Automatically Detecting and Assessing Performance Antipatterns in Component Based Systems Using Run-Time Analysis". In: *The 9th International Workshop on Component Oriented Programming, part of ECOOP* (cit. on p. 365).

– (2008). "Detecting Performance Antipatterns in Component Based Enterprise Systems". In: *Journal of Object Technology* 7.3, pp. 55–90 (cit. on pp. 11, 40, 41, 360, 365).

Peiris, M. and J. H. Hill (2014). "Towards Detecting Software Performance Anti-patterns Using Classification Techniques". In: *SIGSOFT Softw. Eng. Notes* 39.1, pp. 1–4 (cit. on pp. 360, 366, 367, 390).

Petriu, D. and G. Somadder (1997). "A pattern language for improving the capacity of layered client/server systems with multi-threaded servers". In: *Proceedings of EuroPLoP'97* (cit. on p. 344).

Podelko, A. (2005). "Workload Generation: Does One Approach Fit All?" In: *CMG-CONFERENCE-*. Vol. 1. Computer Measurement Group; 1997, p. 301 (cit. on p. 37).

Pradel, M., M. Huggler, and T. R. Gross (2014). "Performance Regression Testing of Concurrent Classes". In: *Proceedings of the 2014 International Symposium on Software Testing and Analysis*. ISSTA 2014. San Jose, CA, USA: ACM, pp. 13–25 (cit. on pp. 362, 375).

Pukelsheim, F. (1994). "The three sigma rule". In: *The American Statistician* 48.2, pp. 88–91 (cit. on p. 215).

Rayside, D. and L. Mendel (2007). "Object Ownership Profiling: A Technique for Finding and Fixing Memory Leaks". In: *Proceedings of the Twenty-second IEEE/ACM International Conference on Automated Software Engineering*. ASE '07. Atlanta, Georgia, USA: ACM, pp. 194–203 (cit. on p. 47).

Redkar, A., K. Rabold, R. Costall, S. Boyd, and C. Walzer (2004). *Pro MSMQ: Microsoft Message Queue Programming*. Apresspod Series. Apress (cit. on p. 142).

Reese, G. (2000). *Database Programming with JDBC and Java*. Java (o'Reilly) Series. O'Reilly (cit. on pp. 142, 240).

Reimer, D., E. Schonberg, K. Srinivas, H. Srinivasan, B. Alpern, R. D. Johnson, A. Kershenbaum, and L. Koved (2004). "SABER: Smart Analysis Based Error Reduction". In: *Proceedings of the 2004 ACM SIGSOFT International Symposium on Software Testing and Analysis*. ISSTA '04. Boston, Massachusetts, USA: ACM, pp. 243–251 (cit. on pp. 345, 352).

Ren, S., N. Venkatasubramanian, and G. Agha (1997). "Formalising multimedia QoS constraints using actors". In: *2 nd IFIP Workshop on Formal Methods for Open Object-based Distributed Systems*. Citeseer, pp. 139–153 (cit. on p. 133).

Rettig, C. (2007). "The trouble with enterprise software". In: *MIT Sloan Management Review* 49 (cit. on p. 23).

Richards, M., R. Monson-Haefel, and D. Chappell (2009). *Java Message Service*. O'Reilly Media (cit. on p. 142).

Robson, C. (2002). *Real world research*. Vol. 2. Blackwell publishers Oxford (cit. on p. 318).

Rohr, M., A. van Hoorn, S. Giesecke, J. Matevska, W. Hasselbring, and S. Alekseev (2008). "Trace-Context Sensitive Performance Profiling for Enterprise Software Applications". English. In: *Performance Evaluation: Metrics, Models and Benchmarks*. Ed. by S. Kounev, I. Gorton, and K. Sachs. Vol. 5119. Lecture Notes in Computer Science. Springer Berlin Heidelberg, pp. 283–302 (cit. on p. 62).

Rokach, L. and O. Maimon (2008). *Data Mining with Decision Trees: Theory and Applications*. Vol. 69. Series in machine perception and artificial intelligence. World Scientific Publishing Company, Incorporated (cit. on pp. 58, 65, 105, 107).

Rotem-Gal-Oz, A., E. Bruno, and U. Dahan (2012). *SOA patterns*. Manning (cit. on p. 51).

Runeson, P. and M. Höst (2009). "Guidelines for conducting and reporting case study research in software engineering". English. In: *Empirical Software Engineering* 14.2, pp. 131–164 (cit. on pp. 16, 318).

Seale, C. (2011). *Researching Society and Culture*. SAGE Publications (cit. on p. 318).

Shams, M., D. Krishnamurthy, and B. Far (2006). "A Model-based Approach for Testing the Performance of Web Applications". In: *Proceedings of the 3rd International Workshop on Software Quality Assurance*. SOQUA '06. Portland, Oregon: ACM, pp. 54–61 (cit. on p. 131).

Sjoberg, D. I. K., T. Dyba, and M. Jorgensen (2007). "The Future of Empirical Methods in Software Engineering Research". In: *2007 Future of Software Engineering*. FOSE '07. Washington, DC, USA: IEEE Computer Society, pp. 358–378 (cit. on pp. 322, 335).

Smaalders, B. (2006). "Performance Anti-Patterns". In: *Queue* 4.1, pp. 44–50 (cit. on p. 344).

Smith, C. U. (1993). "Software performance engineering". English. In: *Performance Evaluation of Computer and Communication Systems*. Ed. by L. Donatiello and R. Nelson. Vol. 729. Lecture Notes in Computer Science. Springer Berlin Heidelberg, pp. 509–536 (cit. on pp. 2, 3, 24, 33).

Smith, C. U. and L. G. Williams (2000). "Software Performance Antipatterns". In: *Proceedings of the 2nd International Workshop on Software and Performance*. WOSP '00. Ottawa, Ontario, Canada: ACM, pp. 127–136 (cit. on pp. 4, 12, 41, 43–46, 78, 343, 346, 353, 363).

– (2002a). "New software performance antipatterns: More ways to shoot yourself in the foot". In: *Int. CMG Conference*, pp. 667–674 (cit. on pp. 42, 48, 50, 78, 343).

– (2002b). "Software Performance AntiPatterns; Common Performance Problems and their Solutions". In: *CMG-CONFERENCE-*. Vol. 2. Citeseer, pp. 797–806 (cit. on pp. 42, 343).

– (2003). "More New Software Antipatterns: Even More Ways to Shoot Yourself in the Foot". In: *Int. CMG Conference*, pp. 717–725 (cit. on pp. 43, 45, 343).

Sommerville, I. (2007). *Software Engineering*. International computer science series. Addison-Wesley (cit. on pp. 68, 69).

Sriganesh, R., G. Brose, and M. Silverman (2006). *Mastering Enterprise JavaBeans 3.0*. Wiley (cit. on p. 143).

Stärk, R., J. Schmid, and E. Börger (2001). *Java and the Java Virtual Machine*. Vol. 24. Springer-Verlag (cit. on pp. 67, 142).

Swets, J. (1988). "Measuring the accuracy of diagnostic systems". In: *Science* 240.4857, pp. 1285–1293 (cit. on pp. 164, 165).

Szpuszta, M. and I. Rammer (2005). *Advanced .NET Remoting*. ITPro collection. Apress (cit. on p. 142).

Tabor, R. (2001). *Microsoft.NET XML Web Services*. Sams White Book Series. Sams (cit. on p. 142).

Tate, B. (2002). *Bitter Java*. Bitter Java. Manning (cit. on pp. 343, 346).

Tate, B., M. Clark, and B. Lee (2003). *Bitter EJB*. Manning Pubs Co Series. Manning (cit. on pp. 41, 343, 346).

Thakkar, D., A. E. Hassan, G. Hamann, and P. Flora (2008). "A Framework for Measurement Based Performance Modeling". In: *Proceedings of the 7th International Workshop on Software and Performance*. WOSP '08. Princeton, NJ, USA: ACM, pp. 55–66 (cit. on pp. 348, 349).

Trubiani, C. and A. Koziolek (2011). "Detection and Solution of Software Performance Antipatterns in Palladio Architectural Models". In: *Proceedings of the 2Nd ACM/SPEC International Conference on Performance Engineering*. ICPE '11. Karlsruhe, Germany: ACM, pp. 19–30 (cit. on pp. 10, 234, 343, 355, 357–359).

van Hoorn, A. (2014). *Model-Driven Online Capacity Management for Component-Based Software Systems*. Books on Demand (cit. on pp. 11, 351, 352, 362, 376, 377).

van Hoorn, A., M. Rohr, A. Gul, and W. Hasselbring (2009). "An Adaptation Framework Enabling Resource-efficient Operation of Software Systems". In: *Proceedings of the Warm Up Workshop for ACM/IEEE ICSE 2010*. WUP '09. Cape Town, South Africa: ACM, pp. 41–44 (cit. on pp. 362, 377).

van Hoorn, A., M. Rohr, and W. Hasselbring (2008). "Generating Probabilistic and Intensity-Varying Workload for Web-Based Software Systems". English. In: *Performance Evaluation: Metrics, Models and Benchmarks*. Ed. by S. Kounev, I. Gorton, and K. Sachs. Vol. 5119. Lecture Notes in Computer Science. Springer Berlin Heidelberg, pp. 124–143 (cit. on pp. 37, 69, 131, 132, 389).

van Hoorn, A., C. Vögele, E. Schulz, W. Hasselbring, and H. Krcmar (2014). "Automatic Extraction of Probabilistic Workload Specifications for Load Testing Session-Based Application Systems". In: *Proceedings of the 8th International Conference on Performance Evaluation Methodologies and Tools (ValueTools 2014)* (cit. on pp. 37, 69, 331, 389).

van Hoorn, A., J. Waller, and W. Hasselbring (2012). "Kieker: A Framework for Application Performance Monitoring and Dynamic Software Analysis". In: *Proceedings of the 3rd ACM/SPEC International Conference on Performance Engineering*. ICPE '12. Boston, Massachusetts, USA: ACM, pp. 247–248 (cit. on pp. 131, 286, 311, 368, 376, 377).

Vetter, J. (2000). "Performance Analysis of Distributed Applications Using Automatic Classification of Communication Inefficiencies". In: *Proceedings of the 14th International Conference on Supercomputing*. ICS '00. Santa Fe, New Mexico, USA: ACM, pp. 245–254 (cit. on pp. 361, 370, 371).

Vögele, C., A. van Hoorn, and H. Krcmar (2015). "Automatic Extraction of Session-Based Workload Specifications for Architecture-Level Performance Models". In: *Proceedings of the 4th International Workshop on Large-Scale Testing*. LT '15. Austin, Texas, USA: ACM, pp. 5–8 (cit. on p. 389).

Vohra, D. (2012). *Java 7 Jax-Ws Web Services*. Professional expertise distilled. Packt Publishing, Limited (cit. on p. 142).

Waller, J., N. C. Ehmke, and W. Hasselbring (2015). "Including Performance Benchmarks into Continuous Integration to Enable DevOps". In: *SIGSOFT Softw. Eng. Notes* 40.2, pp. 1–4 (cit. on pp. 362, 376).

Waller, J. and W. Hasselbring (2013). "A Benchmark Engineering Methodology to Measure the Overhead of Application-Level Monitoring". In: *Proceedings of the Symposium on Software Performance: Joint Kieker/Palladio Days 2013*. CEUR Workshop Proceedings, pp. 59–68 (cit. on p. 376).

Wert, A. (2012). "Uncovering Performance Antipatterns by Systematic Experiments". Master's Thesis. Karlsruhe Institute of Technology (cit. on pp. 53, 76, 157).

Westermann, D. J. (2014). "Deriving Goal-oriented Performance Models by Systematic Experimentation". PhD thesis. Karlsruhe Institute of Technology (cit. on pp. 22, 35, 153, 163, 347–349).

Westermann, D., J. Happe, and R. Farahbod (2013). "An Experiment Specification Language for Goal-driven, Automated Performance Evaluations". In: *Proceedings of the 28th Annual ACM Symposium on Applied Computing*. SAC '13. Coimbra, Portugal: ACM, pp. 1043–1048 (cit. on pp. 129, 347).

Weyuker, E. J. and F. I. Vokolos (2000). "Experience with Performance Testing of Software Systems: Issues, an Approach, and Case Study". In:

IEEE Transactions on Software Engineering 26.12, pp. 1147–1156 (cit. on p. 347).

Williams, L. G. and C. U. Smith (2002). "PASASM: A Method for the Performance Assessment of Software Architectures". In: *Proceedings of the 3rd International Workshop on Software and Performance*. WOSP '02. Rome, Italy: ACM, pp. 179–189 (cit. on pp. 354, 355).

Wohlin, C., P. Runeson, M. Höst, M. Ohlsson, B. Regnell, and A. Wesslén (2012). *Experimentation in Software Engineering*. Computer Science. Springer (cit. on pp. 16, 17).

Wohlin, C. and M. Höst (2001). "Special section: Controlled Experiments in Software Engineering". In: *Information and Software Technology* 43.15, pp. 921–924 (cit. on p. 318).

Woodside, M., G. Franks, and D. Petriu (2007). "The Future of Software Performance Engineering". In: *Future of Software Engineering, 2007. FOSE '07*, pp. 171–187 (cit. on pp. 3, 6, 8, 33).

Woodside, M., V. Vetland, M. Courtois, and S. Bayarov (2001). "Resource Function Capture for Performance Aspects of Software Components and Sub-systems". English. In: *Performance Engineering*. Ed. by R. Dumke, C. Rautenstrauch, A. Scholz, and A. Schmietendorf. Vol. 2047. Lecture Notes in Computer Science. Springer Berlin Heidelberg, pp. 239–256 (cit. on pp. 348, 349).

Xu, J. (2012). "Rule-based automatic software performance diagnosis and improvement". In: *Performance Evaluation* 69.11, pp. 525–550 (cit. on pp. 10, 354, 355).

Yan, D., G. Xu, and A. Rountev (2012). "Uncovering Performance Problems in Java Applications with Reference Propagation Profiling". In: *Proceedings of the 34th International Conference on Software Engineering*. ICSE '12. Zurich, Switzerland: IEEE Press, pp. 134–144 (cit. on pp. 11, 361, 371).

Zhu, H., P. A. V. Hall, and J. H. R. May (1997). "Software Unit Test Coverage and Adequacy". In: *ACM Comput. Surv.* 29.4, pp. 366–427 (cit. on p. 5).

Online References

Commons Logging (2014). *Apache Commons Logging: The Logging Component*. URL: http://commons.apache.org/proper/commons-logging/ (visited on 01/05/2015) (cit. on p. 143).

JMeter (2014). *Apache JMeter™*. URL: http://jmeter.apache.org/ (visited on 01/02/2015) (cit. on pp. 125, 131).

AppDynamics (2015). *AppDynamics*. URL: http://www.appdynamics.com/ (visited on 04/02/2015) (cit. on p. 11).

Compuware (2015). *Application Performance Management Survey*. URL: http://www.cnetdirect%20intl.com/direct/compuware/Ovum_APM/APM_Survey_Report.pdf (visited on 04/02/2015) (cit. on pp. 2, 23).

Broadleaf (2015). *broadleaf*. URL: http://www.broadleafcommerce.org/ (visited on 04/05/2015) (cit. on p. 319).

CSL (2015). *Checkstyle*. URL: http://checkstyle.sourceforge.net/ (visited on 04/02/2015) (cit. on p. 5).

Dynatrace (2015). *Dynatrace*. URL: www.dynatrace.com/dynaTrace (visited on 04/02/2015) (cit. on p. 11).

Eclipse (2015). *Eclipse*. URL: https://eclipse.org/ (visited on 04/05/2015) (cit. on p. 322).

Enterprise Library (2015). *Enterprise Library*. URL: http://msdn.microsoft.com/en-us/library/cc467894.aspx (visited on 01/05/2015) (cit. on p. 143).

Friedman-Hill, E. (2013). *Jess*. URL: http://www.jessrules.com/jess/index.shtml (visited on 04/05/2015) (cit. on p. 366).

Grabner, A. (2010). *Top 10 Performance Problems taken from Zappos, Monster, Thomson and Co*. URL: http://apmblog.compuware.com/2010/06/15/top-10-performance-problems-taken-from-zappos-monster-and-co/ (visited on 12/08/2014) (cit. on pp. 44, 49, 67, 108).

Huang, J. (2003). *Understanding Gigabit Ethernet Performance on Sun Fire Systems*. URL: http://www.sun.com/blueprints (visited on 01/02/2015) (cit. on p. 211).

Java Logging (2014). *Java Logging Technology*. URL: http://docs.oracle.com/javase/8/docs/technotes/guides/logging/index.html (visited on 01/02/2015) (cit. on p. 143).

Kopp, M. (2011). *The Top Java Memory Problems*. URL: http://apmblog.compuware.com/2011/12/15/the-top-java-memory-problems-part-2 (visited on 12/08/2014) (cit. on p. 47).

LoadRunner (2014). *LoadRunner™*. URL: http://www8.hp.com/us/en/software-solutions/loadrunner-load-testing/ (visited on 01/02/2015) (cit. on pp. 125, 131, 263).

Log4Net (2013). *log4net™*. URL: http://logging.apache.org/log4net/ (visited on 01/05/2015) (cit. on p. 143).

NLog (2014). *NLog: Flexible and free open-source logging for .NET*. URL: http://nlog-project.org/ (visited on 01/12/2015) (cit. on p. 143).

NopCommerce (2015). *nopCommerce web site*. URL: http://www.nopcommerce.com/ (visited on 04/03/2015) (cit. on pp. 230, 276, 278).

Object Management Group (2015a). *Architecture-Driven Modernization (ADM): Structured Metrics Meta-Model (SMM)*. URL: http://www.omg.org/spec/SMM/1.0/ (visited on 04/05/2015) (cit. on p. 351).

– (2015b). *The UML Profile for MARTE: Modeling and Analysis of Real-Time and Embedded Systems*. URL: http://www.omgmarte.org/ (visited on 04/12/2015) (cit. on pp. 24, 354).

Reitbauer, M. N. A. (2010). *Flush and Clear: O/R Mapping Anti-Patterns*. URL: http://www.developerfusion.com/article/84945/flush-and-clear-or-mapping-antipatterns (visited on 12/08/2014) (cit. on p. 49).

SLF4J (2014). *Simple Logging Facade for Java*. URL: http://www.slf4j.org/ (visited on 01/02/2015) (cit. on p. 143).

SmartInspect (2014). *SmartInspect*. URL: http://www.gurock.com/smartinspect/ (visited on 01/12/2015) (cit. on p. 143).

Smith, C. U. (2015). *The Top 10 Ways to Kill an SPE Initiative*. URL: http://www.perfeng.com/top10.htm (visited on 04/02/2015) (cit. on p. 3).

SPEC (2015). *Standard Performance Evaluation Corporation*. URL: www.spec.org (visited on 04/02/2015) (cit. on p. 34).

Still, A. (2013). *Category Archives: Performance Anti-Patterns*. URL: http://performance-patterns.com/category/performance-anti-patterns/ (visited on 12/08/2014) (cit. on p. 46).

Tene, G. (2014). *Understanding Application Hiccups: An Introduction to the Open Source jHiccup Tool*. URL: http://www.azulsystems.com/webinar/understanding-application-hiccups-on-demand (visited on 12/08/2014) (cit. on pp. 42, 43).

TPC-W (2015). *TPC Benchmark W (web e-Commerce) Specification v.1.8*, URL: http://www.tpc.org (visited on 03/05/2015) (cit. on pp. 239, 242).

TPC-W Java (2015). *TPC-W Benchmark Java implementation*. URL: http://jmob.ow2.org/tpcw.html (visited on 04/03/2015) (cit. on pp. 229, 238, 240).

TPC (2015). *Transaction Performance Processing Council.* URL: http://www.tpc.org (visited on 03/05/2015) (cit. on pp. 34, 238).

The Karlsruhe Series on Software Design and Quality

Edited by Prof. Dr. Ralf Reussner // ISSN 1867-0067

Band 1 **Steffen Becker**
Coupled Model Transformations for QoS Enabled Component-Based Software Design.
ISBN 978-3-86644-271-9

Band 2 **Heiko Koziolek**
Parameter Dependencies for Reusable Performance Specifications of Software Components.
ISBN 978-3-86644-272-6

Band 3 **Jens Happe**
Predicting Software Performance in Symmetric Multi-core and Multiprocessor Environments.
ISBN 978-3-86644-381-5

Band 4 **Klaus Krogmann**
Reconstruction of Software Component Architectures and Behaviour Models using Static and Dynamic Analysis.
ISBN 978-3-86644-804-9

Band 5 **Michael Kuperberg**
Quantifying and Predicting the Influence of Execution Platform on Software Component Performance.
ISBN 978-3-86644-741-7

Band 6 **Thomas Goldschmidt**
View-Based Textual Modelling.
ISBN 978-3-86644-642-7

Band 7 **Anne Koziolek**
Automated Improvement of Software Architecture Models for Performance and Other Quality Attributes.
ISBN 978-3-86644-973-2

Die Bände sind unter www.ksp.kit.edu als PDF frei verfügbar oder als Druckausgabe bestellbar.

Band 8 **Lucia Happe**
Configurable Software Performance Completions through Higher-Order Model Transformations.
ISBN 978-3-86644-990-9

Band 9 **Franz Brosch**
Integrated Software Architecture-Based Reliability Prediction for IT Systems.
ISBN 978-3-86644-859-9

Band 10 **Christoph Rathfelder**
Modelling Event-Based Interactions in Component-Based Architectures for Quantitative System Evaluation.
ISBN 978-3-86644-969-5

Band 11 **Henning Groenda**
Certifying Software Component Performance Specifications.
ISBN 978-3-7315-0080-3

Band 12 **Dennis Westermann**
Deriving Goal-oriented Performance Models by Systematic Experimentation.
ISBN 978-3-7315-0165-7

Band 13 **Michael Hauck**
Automated Experiments for Deriving Performance-relevant Properties of Software Execution Environments.
ISBN 978-3-7315-0138-1

Band 14 **Zoya Durdik**
Architectural Design Decision Documentation through Reuse of Design Patterns.
ISBN 978-3-7315-0292-0

Band 15 **Erik Burger**
Flexible Views for View-based Model-driven Development.
ISBN 978-3-7315-0276-0

Band 16 **Benjamin Klatt**
Consolidation of Customized Product Copies into Software Product Lines.
ISBN 978-3-7315-0368-2

Band 17 **Andreas Rentschler**
Model Transformation Languages with Modular Information Hiding.
ISBN 978-3-7315-0346-0

Band 18 **Omar-Qais Noorshams**
Modeling and Prediction of I/O Performance in Virtualized Environments.
ISBN 978-3-7315-0359-0

Band 19 **Johannes Josef Stammel**
Architekturbasierte Bewertung und Planung von Änderungsanfragen.
ISBN 978-3-7315-0524-2

Band 20 **Alexander Wert**
Performance Problem Diagnostics by Systematic Experimentation.
ISBN 978-3-7315-0677-5